THE SUNDAY TIMES

1000 DAYS OUT

in Great Britain and Ireland

MACDONALD
MACDONALD FUTURA PUBLISHERS
LONDON

First published in 1981 in Great Britain
by Macdonald Futura · London and Sydney
Revised and expanded from material first
published in Great Britain in 1980 in
The Sunday Times Book of the Countryside.

Macdonald Futura Publishers Limited
Paulton House
8 Shepherdess Walk
London N1 7LW

ISBN 0 354 04679 9 (cased)
       0 7088 2026 3 (limp)

Filmset in Monophoto Baskerville by
Servis Filmsetting Ltd, Manchester

Printed in Great Britain by
Hazell, Watson & Viney Ltd
Aylesbury, Bucks.

CONTENTS

Editors
Philip Clarke
Brian Jackman
Derrik Mercer
Art Director
Clive Crook

Contributors
Rosemary Atkins

Alec Clifton-Taylor

A.W. Coysh

Barry Dennis, editor, *Angling Times*

Jane Evans

Mark Girouard, formerly Slade Professor of Art, University of Oxford

Anthony Greenbank

Francesca Greenoak

Arthur Hellyer, formerly editor of *Gardening Illustrated* and *Amateur Gardening*

Roy Milward, reader in geography, University of Leicester

Dr Adrian Robinson, reader in geography, University of Leicester

Dr John Whittow, senior lecturer in geography, University of Reading

Illustrations by Kathleen Lindsley
Location maps prepared by David Worth, Line and Line
Map section: Cartographic Services (Cirencester) Ltd
Additional researchers and consultants are named in the acknowledgments, page 285

INTRODUCTION

A day out in the countryside is Britain's most popular form of recreation.* A close second is a day out at the seaside. Both experiences feature in this book and within each of these two broad categories the variety seems at times infinite. This diversity reflects the distinctive splendour of the British Isles as much as the individual preferences of their 59 million inhabitants. In few other countries are areas of natural beauty so easily accessible; in no others of comparable size are the contrasts so dramatic.

The popularity of the countryside has scarcely faltered since, ironically, people left the land to seek a new life in the towns of Victorian England. Before then the countryside as a place for mass recreation did not exist; it was, as it remains for farmers and foresters, simply the place where most people worked and lived. The advent of the railways first turned the countryside into an urban playground, but the motor car, increased affluence and more time for leisure have transformed rural pleasures into a growth industry.

Think back 10 or 15 years, if you can, let alone 30. There were no designated Country Parks, no farm museums or farm trails, few waymarked forest or nature trails. Even the Pennine Way, the first long-distance footpath, was not officially established until 1965 and the growth of visitor or information centres within national parks is largely a phenomenon of the 1970s.

In some places the explosion of interest has proved a dubious blessing. Who of the pioneers who staked out the route of the Pennine Way – often risking arrest or abuse from outraged landowners – would have imagined that it would become so popular that rubber matting would have to be laid to protect the soil from erosion? Hilltops as diverse as Box Hill, in Surrey, and Snowdon, in North Wales, are also being worn away by the tramp of visitors' feet. Traffic jams clog country lanes at summer and holiday weekends – driving around to admire the view or have a picnic emerged from the survey referred to earlier as the most popular 'day out' of all.

But problems are only one side of the coin. Of course, it is regrettable that litter or garish caravan sites should mar beauty spots. Of course it is worrying if crowds shatter the tranquillity – and, worse, displace the wildlife – that draws so many to the countryside. However there are other manifestations of public interest which will help to conserve and even enhance the countryside. Amenity and wildlife societies have all grown to record numbers; the Royal Society for the Protection of Birds

*National Opinion Polls survey of more than 5000 people aged 16–70 in England and Wales commissioned by the Countryside Commission in 1977.

1

and the National Trust, for instance, each now have more members than any political party in Britain. Geography (often rechristened 'environmental studies') has become one of the most popular subjects in schools and colleges. And who would guess correctly the second most popular form of day out after a country drive? A visit to a stately home? or a safari park? No, it is walking, hiking or rambling.

What makes a good day out will reflect not only varied interests but also different circumstances: age, family commitments and geographical base can all restrict choice. Yet the scope is still immense. We have suggested 1000 Days Out covering all parts of the British Isles. Nobody is normally more than an hour's drive from at least one such 'day out'; most people are considerably closer to more.

These 1000 Days Out have their origins in *The Sunday Times Book of the Countryside* (also published by Macdonald Futura). They are a fundamental part of that book because we believe its readers will wish to see and enjoy for themselves aspects of the countryside which it describes. Now, however, we have expanded and developed the 1000 Days Out to stand by themselves. A few entries are entirely new but all have been re-checked for accuracy of details such as opening times, location and telephone numbers. Most entries have been expanded to provide more information which should enhance enjoyment; more than 70 are now accompanied by individual maps.

The section of the book which follows this introduction – 'How to use this book' – describes the 'Days Out' concept in more detail. However one dilemma remained constant for both books. Are we making the problems of overcrowding worse by suggesting some places at all? Are we destroying the peace and charm of less well known places? These questions, over which we had agonised ourselves, were raised by many reviewers and interviewers. They deserve answers.

To some extent compilers of books such as this cannot win. Include a 'tourist honeypot' such as Castle Combe in Wiltshire and you risk spoiling further an already crowded village. Omit it and you risk accusations of ignorance but, more serious, you may deny genuine pleasure to readers from more far-flung corners of the British Isles (let alone overseas) who may be unaware of its existence. But at least Britain – especially England – is so richly endowed with villages that showpieces such as Castle Combe can be mentioned only in passing. Other dilemmas are not resolved so readily. Sissinghurst Castle and Hidcote Manor, for instance, are the two most notable 20th-century gardens in the country. A characteristic of such gardens is a smallness of scale that renders them particularly vulnerable to overcrowding. Yet could we really exclude the two prime examples of 20th-century gardens? No – but both appear with warnings about crowds at peak weekends.

What we have attempted to achieve therefore is a sense of balance. Some of the suggestions will appear well known, especially if you live in the area. For this reason we have not always described in detail such cornerstones of the tourist industry as Warwick Castle or Stonehenge, Harewood House or Longleat. We have preferred to concentrate on additional locations or, as in places such as the Lake District, to suggest where crowds might be avoided, even on a Bank Holiday weekend in the height of summer.

The Days Out include less familiar, indeed virtually un-discovered, territory. Sometimes this is because places such as nature trails, farm museums or forest drives have only recently opened. However it is often because it has taken the eyes of our experts to appreciate the attraction or importance of what otherwise might be neglected. Little-known valleys in Snow-donia and Northumberland, for instance; the sites of deserted villages and failed medieval towns; and walks or drives along old drovers' roads.

Generally towns have been included only where they remain rooted in the countryside or where they possess a building of particular importance. Villages are included where they, too, possess a feature of outstanding or unusual interest; mere 'prettiness' was not enough, if only because it would have resulted in more than 1000 Days Out suggestions for villages alone. Readers of this book may well find, possibly with some relief, that their 'favourite' village has thus been omitted.

This could also be a consequence of ensuring that each of the ten regions into which this section is divided has a comprehensive range of suggested Days Out. It cannot always be totally comprehensive: geology and history have not shaped the countryside that way. However we have tried to present the broadest possible range of suggestions for each region, even at the cost of excluding places from regions which are particularly rich in certain fields.

Take just one example of this – churches. Those which are suggested here in detail as churches worth visiting are not necessarily our nomination as the best churches in the British Isles nor even the best country churches. Areas such as Suffolk and the Cotswolds are so rich in churches that some have been excluded in order to accommodate interesting churches from other regions. We have also tried to select a variety of *types* of church. Much the same applies to categories as diverse as nature reserves and country inns, beaches and country houses.

3

This book comes onto the market with one distinct advantage over its parent volume: the overwhelming majority of entries have been exposed to the observations of the 200,000 people who have bought *The Sunday Times Book of the Countryside*. We gladly acknowledge our debt to the researchers, university geography academics and tourist boards who checked and re-checked the original entries of that book's 1000 Days Out section. Much the same process of checking has been repeated for this book but we entered 1981 amid greater uncertainty than we did 1980. For the countryside is immune to neither recession nor reduced public expenditure.

When we were researching this book these were among the replies which we encountered:

☐ 'There is a leaflet available, but it's out of print and we don't know whether or not we'll have the money to reprint.' – a Forestry Commission official when asked about explanatory leaflets for a forest trail.

☐ 'We don't know yet about the opening times of the visitor centres. We may have to close some mobile centres altogether since that saves more money than simply shortening the opening season.' – a National Park officer.

☐ 'In cash terms our budget is static. If this continues it will affect recreational facilities from the provision of picnic tables to clearing huge sites for country parks.' – a spokesman for the Countryside Commission.

Such uncertainty makes life difficult for us – see following section – but, far more important, diminishes public enjoyment of their favourite recreation at a time when more people than ever might be expected to seek solace in the countryside as an antidote to the general gloom. The unavailability of some leaflets and the closed sign on the doors of visitor centres does not mean that the countryside cannot be enjoyed; many, perhaps most, day-trippers use neither. But the development of such services over the last decade has greatly enhanced understanding of the countryside. And as knowledge increases, so does the capacity for appreciation. Who can doubt, too, that informative trails and visitor centres have led to a greater respect for wildlife and aided the cause of conservation within the countryside?

At a time when so many bemoan increased violence and anti-social behaviour, is it not bizarre to erode one of the more constructive forms of recreation which families, in particular, can enjoy together? This is not to equate the losses of leaflets and visitor centres with the more serious deprivations of a recession such as lost jobs. But it is to question whether society in general is aware of the ways in which the countryside of 1981 will be less satisfying than it was 12 months earlier – and all because of savings inflicted upon bodies such as National Parks and the Forestry Commission which are utterly miniscule to the Exchequer as a whole.

Many naturalists will say that such losses are the least of our worries. They will point to the hastening piecemeal destruction of Britain's wildlife habitats as woods are cut down, marshes drained, hedgerows torn up, motorways built and moors ploughed. And, of course, they are right. But money is also at the root of this conservation crisis (described in detail in *The Sunday Times Book of the Countryside*) and the naturalists' cause will be strengthened – perhaps conclusively – by public support. Such support is most likely to stem from exposure to the kind of sophisticated information which is the hallmark of the best nature trails and visitor centres.

However, concern should not obliterate pleasure. The countryside remains a source of inspiration and enjoyment to millions of people whether they be naturalists or those to whom 'habitat' means furniture rather than wildlife. That, surely, is the magic of the British countryside: it can be so many things to so many people. We hope that these 1000 Days Out will be the starting point for many journeys of discovery – that its readers will not be deterred by the unfamiliar. To quote novelist and nature-lover John Fowles:

Of course some names and explanations are necessary for the hard knowledge that must underlie genuine feeling and affection, as opposed to mere sentiment. But never be brainwashed into thinking that the countryside is like some fiendish identification test, which you fail if you cannot name everything you meet. Seeing and feeling are just as important, and too many names act like blinkers: they narrow vision. Truly knowing any form of life – or way of life – is always as much an art as a science. In this we are all amateurs, and start equal.

HOW TO USE THIS BOOK

How the Days Out are organised

The diversity which is a hallmark of the British countryside is reflected in these Days Out. Some are very detailed, with enough information for several days out. Some are broad descriptions of large areas, such as national parks or areas of outstanding natural beauty. Others are more limited in scale, possibly no more than a focal point of a day's drive.

One reason for such variety is the diversity of interests which can be pursued in the British countryside. Thus, for example, the naturalist will be able to use this book to devise the Days Out most likely to appeal to him while the garden-lover can compile a completely separate itinerary. A few of the larger entries are more catholic in their appeal.

The 1000 suggested Days Out are divided into 10 sections – six regions of England plus Wales, Scotland, Northern Ireland and the Republic of Ireland. Within each section the Days Out appear under their country heading, with both counties and the Days Out themselves presented in alphabetical order. Each county also begins with a short summary which includes the names of well known attractions not described in detail as a Day Out plus information about the relevant regional or national tourist offices.

The only exceptions to this county-by-county presentation are national parks and 'areas of outstanding natural beauty'. These appear at the start of each regional section. Where such areas are so large that they extend into two regions, the main description will appear in the regional section where most of the area falls. Many features within national parks and areas of outstanding natural beauty are also described in more detail as separate Day Out entries. A few panels of general interest also appear alongside the Days Out.

How to use the maps

Each Day Out is numbered and these numbers appear on the maps of the British Isles at the end of the book. They are described in chronological sequence on the pages which now follow. If you are starting from the Days Out text itself, you will find a map reference at the end of each Day Out entry. This will direct you to the page and the appropriate part of the relevant map to locate any particular Day Out.

Day Out numbers which appear on the map in boxes either cover large areas such as national parks or are locations where the suggested Day Out is particularly detailed or varied. It is therefore always worth looking at such boxed numbers even if they appear to be some distance away from where you happen to be.

What about opening times?

The standard opening hours for historic or ancient monuments run by the Department of the Environment (DoE) are given below. But the opening hours of many privately run attractions, such as country houses, gardens and museums, frequently vary from month to month. In some cases even the months when places would be open were uncertain when this book went to press. We also discovered that a few places had closed to the public during the course of 1980. All these places have been removed from the 1000 Days Out and every entry that remains has been re-checked for accuracy of opening times, location, access and telephone number. However because opening times do vary – and also because of the uncertain finances of some public bodies, referred to in the introduction – readers are strongly advised to check times for themselves. This can usually be done using the telephone numbers given as part of the Days Out information. However a few such numbers are for offices which are manned only on weekdays. National Trust regions, for instance, have varying policies; some give numbers of individual properties while others prefer to give details of regional offices. Other sources of information about opening times are tourist information offices (see the appendix) and some of the publications mentioned below under Further Information. A particular problem which occasionally arises is entry to churches. If a church is closed, ask nicely for a key at the vicarage.

Standard DoE hours
The Department of the Environment is the body responsible for historic monuments. In Wales and Scotland the Secretaries of State take over these responsibilities. The term 'standard DoE hours' is used in the 1000 Days Out for historic monuments where access is possible only at certain times and sometimes at a charge. These hours are detailed in the table below. Many historic monuments are also open Sunday mornings from the beginning of April until the end of September; a few of the larger monuments are also open on Sunday mornings during the winter. To be absolutely certain of opening hours check first with tourist offices. When monuments are open on Sunday mornings they open at 9.30 am. Information about historic monuments in Northern Ireland and the Republic of Ireland can be obtained from tourist offices.

What the abbreviations mean
AM. Ancient Monument. This is often used to denote an ancient or historic monument which is open at any reasonable time rather than at the standard DoE hours described above.
AONB. Area of Outstanding Natural Beauty (see *How the Days Out are organised*, above).
Grid ref. The precise grid reference on an Ordnance Survey map, although in practice only the 1:50,000 or still larger scale maps can be used satisfactorily or precisely to identify particular grid references. See overleaf.
Km. Kilometres.
Map ref. Map reference in order to locate a Day Out on the maps.
NT. National Trust.
NTS. National Trust for Scotland.
OS map. Unless otherwise stated an OS map number refers to a map in the Ordnance Survey 1:50,000 series.
RSPB. Royal Society for the Protection of Birds.
Tel no. Telephone numbers are given with the exchange but not the STD code.
□ The symbol is used at the end of each Day Out to denote the details required, in terms of distances and roads etc, in order to find any particular Day Out location.

Further information
The tourist boards indicated for each county within the Days Out and the national tourist boards detailed in the appendix are invaluable sources of information. In the summer there are also many smaller tourist information offices throughout the country. Useful reference works include:
Historic Houses, Castles and Gardens: an annual publication from ABC Historic Publications.
Properties Open: an annual publication by the National Trust.
Historic Monuments: a booklet published for the DoE by HMSO.

Road classification
The classification of roads in the Republic of Ireland is in the course of being changed. Where necessary the old and new classification are given.

Standard Department of Environment opening hours

England and Wales	Weekdays	Sundays
Mid-Mar to mid-Oct	9.30am-6pm	2-6.30pm
Mid-Oct to mid-Mar	9.30am-4pm	2-4pm
Scotland		
Apr to Sept	9.30am-7pm	2-7pm
Oct to Mar	9.30am-4pm	2-4pm

HOW TO READ A MAP

Scale. This tells you how to relate the area shown on a map to the area it represents on the ground. It takes only a little practice to judge distances simply by looking at a map. Most maps are now produced on a metric scale. The most popular Ordnance Survey (OS) series are those with a scale of 1:50,000. This means that one centimetre on the map represents 50,000 centimetres (or half a kilometre) on the ground. For many people, though, it may be easier to think in terms of inches and miles. In the case of the 1:50,000 maps approximately 1¼ inches on the map represents one mile on the ground. Although these maps show all footpaths many walkers prefer the extra clarity and detail of the 1:25,000 maps. Because they have this larger scale they normally show a smaller area but the OS is developing a useful series of 1:25,000 'Outdoor Leisure' maps for popular tourist areas such as national parks.

The key explains all the symbols used on OS maps. It is not necessary to memorise these details (although this is often easily done) since all OS maps have a clearly laid out key and some maps will incorporate features which others lack. Use the key to pick out points that interest you.

The National Grid is explained on the keys of most small-scale OS maps although the detail provided varies. The grid is a framework of artificial lines spaced at one or 10 kilometre intervals, according to the scale of the map. These not only enable distance to be judged more easily (remembering that one kilometre is roughly equal to 0.6 miles) but, more important, by this means places can be located with complete precision by stating their coordinates or numbers on the national grid. This is how to do it.

First study the key. Look for the two grid letters which cover the part of the map for which you want to give a reference. For the 1:25,000 series it is simply the two letters in the map's overall code number. For smaller-scale maps there may be several sets of letters, each covering part of the map, so use the key to find out where these sets begin and end.

Second, take the west edge of the kilometre square in which the point lies and read the large figures printed against this line on north or south margins, then estimate the position of the point in tenths eastwards.

Third, take the south edge of the kilometre square in which the point lies and read the large figures opposite line on the east or west margins. Then estimate in tenths the position of the point northwards of this line.

This gives a full reference number which is accurate to within 100 metres. No other place within Britain has this reference – *if* the grid letters are included. If the letters are omitted, the numbers will recur at intervals of 100 kilometres. Obviously the grid is seen most clearly and used most easily on the larger scale maps where the key is also invariably fuller.

Contours show places of equal height above sea level (in feet or the metric equivalent according to the key). If in doubt a good rule of thumb is to divide metres by three to get the measurement in feet. Closely spaced contours indicate steep slopes while a lack of contours indicates a plain, river valley or hilltop plateau. A good eye for contour patterns will reveal promising viewpoints: where closely spaced contours give way to few contours, for instance, or where closely spaced contours jut out into a valley and thus allow panoramic views. (Somewhat confusingly the 1:50,000 OS maps show contour values to the nearest metre but the vertical interval between contour lines remains at 50 *feet*.)

Special features are included in all but the smaller scale route-planning OS maps, so that the locations of, say, battlegrounds, burial mounds or Roman roads can be found. (Specialist maps also exist for interests such as history, geology and leisure pursuits.)

Southwest England

1. DARTMOOR
National Park

Covers 365 sq miles (945 sq km). A short drive from Exeter, Plymouth and South Devon coast. M5 motorway reaches as far as Exeter; A30 from Exeter to Okehampton runs along the park's northern edge; A38 Exeter to Plymouth along the southern edge. The B3212 from Exeter cuts right across the roof of the moor via Postbridge and Two Bridges. Viewpoints (with or close to parking) include Haytor Rocks and Hound Tor, Whitchurch Common. Lanes are heavily congested in summer and some are too narrow for caravans and wide vehicles. For walkers and pony trekkers there are about 180 sq miles (466 sq km) of open moorland to explore. Chagford and Manaton are excellent walking centres. Viewpoints for walkers include Buckland Beacon, Chinkwell Tor and Kestor Rock. Guided walks are regular features during holiday season (details from any local tourist information centre or DNP office, Tel: Bovey Tracey 832093). Some 40 sq miles (104 sq km) of the northern moor are used as military firing range. Warning notices mark danger area and red flags fly on firing days. Details of firing times are displayed locally.
☐ Map ref 3A3.

2. EXMOOR
National Park

Covers 265 sq miles (686 sq km). The M5 motorway passes within a dozen miles of the park as the crow flies. Westbound visitors turn off at Bridgwater (A39) or Taunton (A358), to enter park at Dunster. The main park information centre is at Dulverton. Tel: Dulverton 23665. Others (closed in winter) at Lynmouth, County Gate and Combe Martin. One of the most spectacular drives is along the A39 from Minehead up Porlock Hill and then high above the sea to Lynton and Lynmouth. In general there is freedom to walk anywhere on commons and open moorland. Also miles of well signposted and waymarked walks (park information centres have useful booklets on where to walk). Watersmeet, Horner Woods, Badgworthy Water and the Chains are good walking areas, but best is the section of the long-distance footpath around the South-west Peninsula, which begins at Minehead and follows the national park coastline of hog-backed cliffs and hanging woods to Combe Martin.
☐ Map ref 3A2.

Southwest England

3. CORNWALL
Area of Outstanding Natural Beauty

Not one area but a patchwork of isolated fragments which together represent the finest coast and countryside within the county. Apart from Bodmin Moor, they are all spread along the coast at different points. Most of West Penwith (the 'toe' of Cornwall) is included; so is the Lizard. Other areas include Morwenstow, the cliffs from Dizzard down to Pentire Point, Padstow to Watergate Bay, St Agnes, Portreath, and the estuaries and river valleys between Falmouth and Looe.
□ Map ref 2B3.

4. DORSET
Area of Outstanding Natural Beauty

The Isle of Purbeck, the central downlands as far east as Blandford and the whole of West Dorset combine to form the third largest AONB in this, the least spoiled county in the whole of Southern England. This is the Wessex of Thomas Hardy's novels; heaths, chalk downs, combes and vales crossed by tunnelling country lanes and bounded by a splendid coast which includes Lulworth Cove, Durdle Door, the Chesil Beach and the fossil-studded cliffs of Charmouth and Lyme Regis. The South-west Peninsula long-distance footpath follows the coast from end to end.
□ Map ref 4B4.

5. EAST DEVON
Area of Outstanding Natural Beauty

Takes in the Devon coast (with small gaps at Sidmouth and Seaton) between Exmouth and the Dorset border, and its hinterland as far north as Honiton. Its most outstanding features are cliffs of red sandstone and the high inland commons behind Budleigh Salterton, of which Woodbury Common is best for walks and views. For a day out by the sea, try Branscombe (pebble beach, NT cliffs,

good village pub, though busy on summer weekends).
□ Map ref 3B3.

6. ISLES OF SCILLY
Area of Outstanding Natural Beauty

Smallest of all the AONBs, but also possibly the most beautiful. A cluster of tiny granite islands lying in the Atlantic some 28 miles (40km) off Land's End. Utterly peaceful, with bays and coves of dazzling sands and a mild Gulf Stream climate which favours the commercial cultivation of daffodils and other spring flowers. Tresco Abbey is famous for its sub-tropical gardens and 'Valhalla' of ships' figureheads from old wrecks. Boat trips to the out islands for picnics and bird-watching are popular. Tourist information centre, Tel: Scillonia 22536. Day trips to the Scillies are operated by steamer and British Airways helicopter from Penzance.
□ Map ref 2AZ.

7. MENDIP HILLS
Area of Outstanding Natural Beauty

A long swell of grey limestone hills rising abruptly above the dykes and watermeadows of the Somerset Levels. The limestone is riddled with stalactite-hung caverns, once the home of Stone Age man. Wookey Hole and Cheddar caves are the most famous.
□ Map ref 4B3.

8. NORTH DEVON
Area of Outstanding Natural Beauty

Covers virtually the whole of Devon's Atlantic coast between Ilfracombe and Hartland point. Includes the sandhills of Braunton Burrows, the wooded cliffs around the show village of Clovelly, and the rugged headlands of Bull Point, Morte Point, Baggy Point and Hartland. The South-west Peninsula long-distance footpath provides continuous access.
□ Map ref 3A2.

9. QUANTOCKS
Area of Outstanding Natural Beauty

The Quantock Hills offer a foretaste of Exmoor, which lies to the west, but they have a character of their own: a 12 mile (19km) ridge of hills rising to a height of 1261ft (383m), composed of red sandstone and covered with heather, bracken and tangled woodlands. Sea views, bracing walks, and the possibility of seeing red deer. Holford, just inside the AONB, is rich in memories of the poets Wordsworth and Coleridge.

☐ Map ref 3B2.

10. SOUTH DEVON
Area of Outstanding Natural Beauty

Includes the entire South Devon coast between Plymouth and Brixham, together with the valley of the River Dart as far as Totnes (river cruises ply in summer between Dartmouth and Totnes), and the fertile South Hams countryside beside the River Avon. Marvellous cliff walks from Thurlestone to Bolt Head, and from Prawle Point to Start Point (part of the South-west Peninsula long-distance footpath).

☐ Map ref 3A4.

Avon

The heart of Avon is an urban complex composed of Bristol, Bath and the seaside resort of Weston-super-Mare. But there is also much of interest for country-lovers, especially in the limestone landscapes of the Cotswolds. The beautiful Georgian city of Bath is an ideal springboard for days out in Avon. West Country Tourist Board, Tel: Exeter 76351.

11. AVON GORGE
National Nature Reserve

This woodland reserve stretching along the west side of the Avon over Clifton Bridge is one of the most important reserves on lowland carbo-niferous limestone. Oak predominates in association with ash, birch, small-leaved lime, beech and sycamore. Towards the north of the reserve yew and holly grow together and among the various species of whitebeam is the rare Bristol whitebeam, found nowhere else in the world except along the Avon Gorge. Woodland flowers and ferns thrive on the lime soils and autumn brings a good range of fungi, including poisonous fly agaric. The Iron Age hill-fort of Stokeleigh Camp lies within the reserve. The reserve is managed by the NCC by agreement with the NT. Visitors are welcome but must keep to footpaths and mown grass areas.

☐ Start at stone arch beside A369 Bristol to Portishead road. Clifton, Bristol. Map ref 4B2.

12. BROCKLEY COMBE
Nature trail

This waymarked nature trail leads through Brockley Combe, a deep winding gorge cut through carboniferous limestone. The woods are a mixture of oak, ash, beech and sycamore, sweet chestnut and yew. Other features include turkey oak and a handsome avenue of lime trees. Look out for woodland and grassland butterflies and for four kinds of fern growing by the path. Leaflet from Brockley Combe Fruit Stall.

Tel: Avon Wildlife Trust: Bristol 313396.

☐ Near Brockley, three miles (5km) NW of Congresbury. Map ref 4A2.

13. CASTLE FARM MUSEUM
Folk Museum

A rare and largely unrestored long house or farmhouse dating from the 16th century is the focal point of this museum which is also part of a working farm. Later buildings date from the 18th century and contain a dairy, cheese loft and granary. Old domestic and agricultural tools are also on show. Open three afternoons a week, mid-June to mid-Sept. Check opening times. Tel: Marshfield 469.

Southwest England

☐ At Marshfield, eight miles (13km) W of Chippenham off A420. Map ref 4B2.

14. NORTON ST PHILIP
Historic inn

The George inn is an excellent example of a country inn which started as an abbey hospice. The stone building of 1397 was partly burned down, however, and only the ground floor of the present inn survives from this 14th-century structure. The half-timbered upper storeys were added about 1500, since when the inn has been used by, among others, Cromwell, the Duke of Monmouth and Judge Jeffreys.

☐ Approximately five miles (8km) SE of Bath at junction of A366 and B3110. Map ref 4B3.

Cornwall

The coast is Cornwall's glory. Wild and rugged where it faces the Atlantic, its savage cliffs of slate and granite interspersed with magnificent surf beaches. Softer and gentler on the south coast, with wooded creeks and sheltered fishing harbours. The Isles of Scilly, just over the horizon beyond Land's End, are an additional bonus of shell sand beaches and granite seascapes. West Country Tourist Board, Tel: Exeter 76351.

15. BOSCASTLE
Coastal village

A village on the rugged coast of North Cornwall which matches the beauty of its surroundings. In effect it is almost two villages: one nestles on top of the cliffs, the other is clustered around a tiny but dramatic harbour in a twisting creek sheltered by the cliffs. A narrow street of white-washed cottages, Fore Street, runs steeply downhill to a ruined castle *motte* or mound that marked the founding of a town here early in the 12th century. The harbour – which prospered for more than a century after the building of a break-water in 1740 – is owned by the NT.

☐ On B3263, three miles (5km) N of Tintagel. Map ref 2B3.

16. BOTALLACK TIN MINE
Industrial archaeology

Cornwall has many relics of tin mining but few are more dramatically sited than this former mine on the very edge of the cliff. The workings – for copper as well as tin – extended far under the Atlantic Ocean and in places were 1200ft (366m) deep. The mine ceased to function during the 19th century after 100 years or so of dangerous productivity. The former manager's house is now a restaurant but otherwise the ruins, including engine house and stack, are balanced precariously on a narrow platform just above the sea, suggesting rapid abandonment once the precious deposits were exhausted or no longer economic to work. Care should be taken when exploring.

☐ Off B3306, one mile (1.6km) NW of St Just. Map ref 2A4.

17. BUDE
Sea coast and canal

Once a busy port, Bude is now primarily a beach resort renowned for surfing. Bude Canal was constructed between 1819 and 1826 to carry beach sand inland for farmers to balance the acidic soil. Today it is used by pleasure boats, fishermen and towpath walkers. Ebbingford Manor, just by the canal, is a typical Cornish manor dating from the 12th century with a walled garden. Open from June to Sept. Tel: Bude 2808. Nearby, Bude Historical and Folk Exhibition, housed in an old forge, shows a history of the canal. Open daily in summer.

The cliffs at Bude reveal spectacular contortions and folds in the rock strata. When the tide is out you can walk along the beach to the beautiful Coombe Valley, returning along the cliffs, a good seven mile (11km) walk. Several interesting nature trails start from the picnic site and car park in the valley. Walks are signposted at the entrance to Stowe Wood on the Duckpool road, just past Stowe Farm.

☐ On the A3073. Map ref 2B3.

18. CADGWITH
Coastal village

Cars are best left in the car park above this tiny village which is down a narrow valley and is crowded in summer. To the south-west of the village is the Devil's Frying Pan – reached via a steep cliff path which enables you to look down into this natural cauldron formed by the cave roof falling in. When the sea is rough the water below looks like hot fat.

The Poltesco Cadgwith nature trail starts from Ruan Minor taking the walker along a circular trail of three miles (4.8km) through a wooded valley with a cascading stream, past caves and cliffs. You can see the remains of an 18th-century serpentine rock factory.
□ On Lizard peninsula, reached by minor road off A3083 from Helston. Map ref 2A4.

19. CHARLESTOWN SHIPWRECK CENTRE
Maritime history

Charlestown is a small working port which has hardly changed since it was built in 1791. The Shipwreck Centre, near the harbour, illustrates the history and anatomy of Cornish shipwrecks and contains the wreck of the *Grand Turk*. Open 10 days at Easter, then only Thur and Sun until May to Sept when open daily. Also Thur and Sun in Oct. Tel: St Austell 3332.

China Clay has been mined in this area for about 200 years and is still loaded from the narrow harbour. Nearby at Carthew, two miles (3.2km) from St Austell, is the Wheal Martyn Museum in which you can see working waterwheels, a 220ft (67m) clay kiln and the trappings of clay works. Open summer only. Tel: St Austell 850362.
□ Charlestown is two miles (3.2km) E of St Austell, off A390. Map ref 2B4.

20. CHYSAUSTER
Prehistoric Village

A 'village' of nine houses which were inhabited in Late Iron Age and Roman times. The houses, roughly oval in shape, have immensely thick walls with inner rooms opening on to a central courtyard. The rooms were originally roofed with stone or thatch but are now open to the sky. Archaeologists disagree over how Chysauster's first inhabitants lived, although they probably worked the tin deposits in the

Chysauster: this settlement is one of the most remarkable Iron Age survivals in the British Isles.

valley below. What is certain, however, is that the village is one of the most remarkable survivals of Iron Age settlement in the British Isles. Open standard DoE hours.
□ Three miles (4.8km) N of Penzance. Signposted off minor road between B3311 and the Penzance to Zennor road at New Mill. Grid ref SW 473340; OS map 203. Map ref 2A4.

21. CORNISH SEAL SANCTUARY
Wildlife

Do not be deterred by the approach through a new bungalow estate. The sanctuary itself has an idyllic setting overlooking the wooded banks of the tidal Helford River. Sick, injured and orphaned Atlantic seals are cared for in five spacious pools before being returned to the wild. An unrivalled opportunity to see these gentle wild

Southwest England

mammals at close quarters. A splendid day out for all the family, but especially for children. Open daily, all year.
□ At Gweek, near Helston. Map ref 2A4.

22. COTEHELE
Historic house and garden

Romantic medieval house, now belonging to the NT, perched on the steep banks of the Tamar. House contains armour, furniture, tapestries. Beautiful terraced gardens lead down to ponds, quay and watermill with blacksmith's and wheelright's shops. Open daily except non-Bank Holiday Mons, Apr to Oct. Ring for winter opening times

for garden and hall only. Tel: St Dominick 50434.
□ Near St Dominick, eight miles (12km) SW of Tavistock off A390. Map ref 3A3.

23. DAPHNE DU MAURIER'S CORNWALL

For many people the romance of Cornwall and its lawless seafaring history are indivisible from Daphne du Maurier's novels. Her stories – *Rebecca, Jamaica Inn, Frenchman's Creek* – are steeped in the magic of Cornwall, whose coves, creeks and lonely moors can still conjure up visions of the days when smuggling was the mainstay of

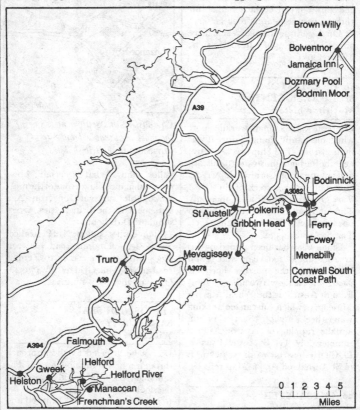

Daphne du Maurier's Cornwall: the country of Rebecca, Jamaica Inn and Frenchman's Creek stretches from wild mysterious Bodmin Moor to Helford River. Day Out 23

many a Cornish community.

For a day out in du Maurier's Cornwall, where better to begin than the little port of Fowey where the authoress herself first fell in love with Cornwall at the age of five. She lived for a while at a house just below Bodinnick Ferry, and later moved to Menabilly, about one mile (2km) west of Fowey, where she lived for 26 years. Menabilly is thought to be the model for Manderley in *Rebecca*. It is not open to visitors, but a splendid walk from Fowey along the Cornwall South Coast Path passes within half a mile (1km) of the house as it rounds Gribbin Head to Polkerris, setting for *The House on the Strand*.

Look at the OS map of Truro and Falmouth (Sheet 204) and you will see, just west of Helford, a narrow finger of the Helford River, called Frenchman's Pill. Nowadays the inlet is better known as 'Frenchman's Creek', after du Maurier's novel of the same name. To visit this secluded creek, take the road from Gweek to Manaccan and turn off to the left where the sign says 'Kestle'. You will then have to leave your car and walk the last few hundred yards. Alternatively, there are regular boat trips to Frenchman's Creek and the lovely Helford River from Falmouth harbour during the holiday season. Manaccan has a church with a fig tree growing from the tower and a good village pub, the New Inn. In the old days, contraband run ashore at spots like Frenchman's Creek was often smuggled further inland before being distributed to other parts of the country. A popular hiding place was the wild and empty expanse of Bodmin Moor, not far from the Devon border. This is the setting for *Jamaica Inn*, and at Bolventor the granite-built 18th-century Jamaica Inn still offers hospitality to travellers on the A30 road from Penzance to London. Nearby is the granite tor of Brown Willy, at 1375ft (418m), the highest point on the Moor, and Dozmary Pool, traditionally the site where King Arthur received his legendary sword Excalibur.
□ Map ref 2B4.

24. FAL ESTUARY
Cornish estuary

This beautiful mingling of blue tidal waters, secluded creeks and deep oak-wood valleys is best explored by boat from Falmouth or St Mawes. Details of sea and river trips from Falmouth Tourist Information Office. Tel: Falmouth 312300. The area is formed by the five main tributaries of the River Fal, which converge upon a four mile (6.4km) long drowned valley, or ria, called Carrick Roads. There are passenger ferries from Falmouth to Truro, St Mawes and Flushing, and a car ferry at King Harry Ferry. Pendennis Castle (AM) and St Mawes Castle (AM) face each other across the estuary. Both were built by Henry VIII and are open to the public daily. St Mawes has an exceptionally pretty harbour and waterfront and mild, sun-trap climate. Some two or three miles (4km) north of St Mawes is St Just in Roseland church, its churchyard a sub-tropical profusion of palm trees and exotic shrubs on the banks of a peaceful tidal creek.
□ Map ref 2B4.

25. GLENDURGAN GARDEN
Valley garden, spring flowers

Exotic trees and shrubs and a laurel maze planted in 1833. Many magnolias, tree ferns and good rhododendrons spreading down the valley to the idyllic NT hamlet of Durgan, on the sheltered shores of Helford River. At its best with early spring flowers in bloom, when it is probably the loveliest garden in Cornwall. Open Mar to Oct, on Mon, Wed and Fri. Tel: Mawnan Smith 250780.
□ Four miles (6.5km) SW of Falmouth on road to Helford Passage. Map ref 2B4.

26. KERNOW FOREST
Forest walks, industrial past

Cardinham Woods have picnic place, walks and trails. The picnic place is by a clear stream fringed with alder and slopes of the forest rising behind. The

Riverside walk is easy and follows the stream; the Panorama trail is more strenuous with fine views down Glynn Valley; the Silvermine trail leads to Hurstocks lead mine, worked in the early 19th century. The path is steep in places. The old chimney and engine house ruins at mine are unsafe. All walks start from picnic place where leaflets are on sale from a dispenser. Distances vary from one mile (1.6km) to 3½ miles (5.6km).

□ Two miles (3.2km) NE of Bodmin. Access from A38 Bodmin to Plymouth road. Map ref 2B3.

27. KYNANCE COVE
Cliffs and caves

The Lizard is a flat, heathery plateau, ringed by dramatic cliffs, rock stacks, coves and caverns. Kynance Cove (NT) is popular with sightseers in summer. The cliffs are streaked with multi-coloured serpentine rock which is made into ornaments by local craftsmen.

On the path down to the cove you can see jagged outcrops of rock caused by the diagonal jointing of the serpentine. The caves can only be seen at low tide and exploration can be dangerous. Some have curious names: Ladies' Bathing Pool, Devil's Letter Box. From the beach you can see Asparagus Island, named after the plant which grows there.

Following the Cornwall Coast Path to the Lizard you can see how the rock changes from serpentine to schist. The lighthouse is open to the public. Tel: The Lizard 290431.

□ On Lizard peninsula, reached by toll road off A3801. Map ref 2A4.

28. LANHYDROCK HOUSE
Historic house and garden

A great Jacobean house two-thirds gutted by fire in the late 19th century, and rebuilt to cater for house-party life on the grand scale. All is now on show, from the kitchen to the billiard room, and the butler's pantry to the boudoir. A final bonus is the long gallery in the wing: one of the finest long galleries in England, with a barrel-vaulted ceiling. The parkland extends to the River Fowey with fine formal gardens. House open daily, Apr to late Oct, gardens all year. Tel: Bodmin 3320.

□ 2½ miles (4km) SE of Bodmin off B3268 to Lostwithiel. Map ref 2B3.

29. LAUNCESTON
Market town

This market town grew like many others around the Norman castle which was both its protector and its customer. Its dominating site over the River Kensey had drawn earlier settlers, though; Celtic and Saxon settlements preceded the Norman castle. The castle still dominates the town which is built on a number of hills.

Its long history is reflected in a jumble of architectural styles, never more jumbled than in the White Hart, a former coaching inn with a front entrance formed by the Norman doorway of an old priory. There is also a gateway surviving from the old town walls; 16th-century St Mary Magdalene Church carved out of the granite which is local to Cornwall but whose hardness makes it so rare in church buildings; and some fine Georgian houses in partly-cobbled Castle Street. Launceston is still an important market town, with markets on Tues and Sat. The livestock market is on Tues.

The castle is open standard DoE hours plus Sun mornings Apr to Sept.

□ 13 miles (21km) NW of Tavistock on A30/A388; Map ref 3A3.

30. LOE POOL
Lake and pebble bar

Between Porthleven and Gunwalloe stretches a great shingle bank thrown up by the sea. Behind it lies Loe Pool, the largest freshwater lake in Cornwall. The bar itself is composed mainly of rounded flints and is 600ft (182m) wide. The wooded Loe is encircled by footpaths, the round trip being six miles (9.6km) long. There are several access points where you can park and then walk to the pool. Among them,

Penrose Hill car park, signposted off the B3304 as you approach Porthleven. Swimming in the Pool is forbidden.
□ Near Porthleven. Map ref 2A4.

---

31. LOOE
Fishing port

Joined by a long stone bridge, the twin towns of East and West Looe share the same colourful river-mouth harbour and an international reputation as a shark fishing centre. All claims for world records in shark fishing must be channelled through the Shark Angling Club of Great Britain, whose HQ overlooks the quayside where the shark boats weigh their fearsome catch. Boats can be hired for shark fishing trips but it is advisable to book well in advance. Details from Tourist Information Centre, Tel: Looe 2072. Advisable to park in West Looe car park as streets are very narrow and congested. A four mile (6km) cliff walk leads west to Polperro.
□ 16 miles (26km) W of Plymouth on A387. Map ref 2B4.

---

32. MEVAGISSEY
Fishing village

Fishing is still important here, though the old pilchard fleet has been replaced by shark-angling boats to attract the tourists. The village itself, and its sturdy inner and outer harbours, are as picturesque as any on this coast. The Folk Museum at East Quay occupies an 18th-century boat building workshop and displays local crafts, fishing, seafaring, farming, china clay and copper mining. Open daily, Easter to Sept. Tel: Mevagissey 3568. Nearby Dodman Point, crowned by an Iron Age fort, gives sweeping coastal views, west to the Lizard and east towards Fowey and Polperro.
□ On B3273, about five miles (8km) S of St Austell. Map ref 2B4.

---

33. PERRANPORTH
Atlantic beach

Perran beach stretches for three miles (4.8km) to Ligger Point with its ancient wells, once believed to possess miraculous powers. Encroaching dunes, said to cover the lost city of Langarrow, lure surfers and caravan dwellers. The army uses the area north of Penhale Sands. St Piran's Oratory, one of the earliest known seats of Christianity, was dug out of the sand in 1835. Now in need of maintenance, it is protected from the sand by a concrete shell. White stones mark the path to the church across the dunes. St Piran's Round, near Rose, 1½ miles (2.5km) east of Perranporth, is an ancient enclosure where, until quite recently, Cornish mystery plays were still performed. To the south is a cliff walk around Cligga Head, starting behind Droskyn Castle Hotel in Perranporth.
□ Five miles (8km) S of Newquay off A3075. Map ref 2A4.

---

34. PORTH HELLICK DOWN
Prehistoric site

Around 50 chambered tombs from the Neolithic or Bronze Age can be found in the Isles of Scilly – all on St Mary's, the largest of the islands. The best preserved is probably one of a group of five on Porth Hellick Down in the south-east of the island. The tomb is still roofed and contained within a mound 40ft (12m) in diameter. The central chamber is reached through a curving passageway 14ft (4.3m) long. Access is available at any reasonable time.
□ Porth Hellick Down is reached by a footpath off A3110 and the tomb is at grid ref SV 929108; OS map 203. Map ref 2A2.

---

35. RIVER CAMEL
Cornish estuary

Camel is Cornish for 'crooked river'. The wide sandy estuary merges with the Atlantic between two noble headlands: Pentire Point (NT) to the east and Stepper Point to the west. Across the mouth lies a sand bar called the Doom Bar. The entire estuary is a splendid recreational playground. You can surf at Polzeath, swim safely at Daymer Bay, sail at Rock (dinghies on hire to competent sailors), fish for bass, or take a boat cruise from the picturesque fishing port of Padstow, one of the few havens on this wild Atlantic coast. There is a passenger

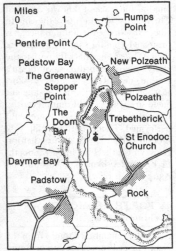

The Camel estuary, holiday play-ground on Cornwall's rugged coast

ferry between Rock and Padstow, and parking at Padstow Quay, Rock, Daymer Bay and Polzeath. A pleasant walk along the sands will take you from Rock to Daymer Bay and onto Polzeath over the clifftop turf of the Greenaway. A slightly more strenuous walk runs from Polzeath out to Pentire Head and the Rumps, where Atlantic seals, ravens, and sometimes basking sharks, may be seen. Until 1863 St Enodoc's church was buried but now it stands, re-excavated and functioning, amid the dunes and golf course on the east side of the Camel estuary.

☐ Map ref 2B3.

36. ST AUSTELL
Industrial landscape

China clay has been quarried from open pits north of St Austell since the mid-18th century. Two hundred years later great holes have been opened up and vast conical heaps of glistening white spoil built around them, often nicknamed the 'Cornish Alps'.

☐ Main workings N of St Austell, around granite outcrop of Hens-barrow, along the A391. Map ref 2B4.

37. ST MICHAEL'S MOUNT
Causewayed isle

Fairytale fortress home of Lord St Levan, perched on a pyramidal granite island that dominates Mounts Bay from wherever you look at it. At low tide you can walk across the sandy causeway from Marazion in ten minutes. At high tide there is a ferry. The castle (NT) is 12th-century, with later additions. For opening times, Tel; Marazion 710507.

☐ Marazion, three miles (4.8km) E of Penzance. Map ref 2A4.

38. SEAL ISLAND
Nature walk

Though not a designated nature trail, the four miles (6.4km) of the Cornwall Coast Path from St Ives westward towards Zennor provides a good chance of sighting wild Atlantic seals. In fact the nearer of the two rocky islets just beyond Carn Naun Point is known locally as 'Seal Island'. This beautiful walk also offers magnificent cliff and granite moorland scenery, ravens, seabirds and clifftop wild flowers.

☐ Map ref 2A4.

39. SENNEN COVE
Sandy beach

At Sennen the granite cliffs give way to the pounding surf and finely-powdered white shell sands of Whitesand Bay. Sennen is the 'last village in England', only about one mile (1.6km) from Land's End. You can walk along the Cornwall Coast Path to Land's End and see the isolated Longships light-house and infamous Seven Stones Reef.

☐ Near Land's End, reached by minor road off A30. Map ref 2A4.

40. TINTAGEL CASTLE
Sea castle

The sea-girt peninsula of Tintagel

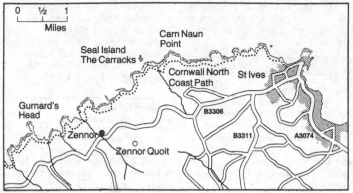

Seal Island and Zennor: the Cornwall Coast Path westward towards Zennor from St Ives provides sightings of seals and seabirds. Zennor has stone-walled fields which go back to the Iron Age. Days Out 38, 44

Head has been almost cut off from the mainland, so the ruins of King Arthur's Castle must now be reached by a dizzy footbridge. The castle, which dates from the 12th century, some 600 years later than the legendary King Arthur, is open daily.

□ About 3½ miles (5.6km) SW of Boscastle on B3263. Map ref 2B3.

41. TRELISSICK GARDENS
Stately garden

Situated at the head of Falmouth harbour, this garden has glorious views and many exotic trees and shrubs, particularly a collection of over 100 species of hydrangea. Open Apr to Oct daily. Tel: Devoran 862090.

□ Near Truro, on B3289 overlooking King Harry Ferry. Map ref 2B4.

42. TRESCO ABBEY
Sub-tropical garden

No part of the British Isles has a milder climate than this, and so, ever since Augustus Smith started to make a garden here in the mid-19th century, the collection of rare plants from many parts of the world has grown in extent and interest. All types are grown, woody and herbaceous, but Tresco is particularly notable for its succulent plants and species from the southern hemisphere. Open daily throughout the year except Sun. Tel: Scillonia 22849.

□ On Tresco, Isles of Scilly. Reached by ferry from St Mary's. Map ref 2A2.

43. TREWITHEN
Spring garden

Magnificently landscaped garden containing camellias, magnolias and rhododendrons. Open daily, except Sun, Mar to Sept, afternoons only. Tel: Grampound Road 882764.

□ Probus, near Truro. Off A390 S of St Austell. Map ref 2B4.

44. ZENNOR
Moorland village, prehistoric tomb

A tiny Cornish hamlet with a moorland stream, wayside museum and church renowned for its carving of a mermaid. The surrounding pattern of tiny, stone-walled fields goes back to the Iron Age. Above, on the windswept granite moors, is Zennor Quoit, a chambered tomb dating from around 3000 BC. Below the village, about two miles (3.2km) to the west along the Coast Path, is Gurnards Head, one of the wildest headlands in Cornwall. It is crowned by a fine Iron Age promontory fort. The South-west Peninsula Coast Path provides continuous access along the cliffs.

Southwest England

□ On B3306 between St Ives and St Just. Zennor Quoit is off the B3306 at Grid ref SW 454385; OS map 203. Map ref 2A4.

Devon

Glorious Devon claims two splendid coastlines: North Devon has wild cliffs and Atlantic surf; South Devon offers sheltered estuaries and a mild climate. In between lie the heights of Dartmoor, idyllic river valleys, rolling farmlands, and Exeter, the county town. West Country Tourist Board, Tel: Exeter 76351.

45. ALSCOTT FARM MUSEUM
Farm museum

Old farm tractors, ploughs, barn machinery and a cider press. Also some dairying equipment. North Devon's agricultural past is recalled in a selection of photographs. Open daily, noon till dusk, Easter to end Sept. Tel: Shebbear 206.
□ At Shebbear, 6 miles (9.6km) NE of Holsworthy. Access from A388 or A3702 via minor roads. Map ref 3A3.

46. APPLEDORE
Maritime history

Fascinating little town with long history of ship-building and glorious position overlooking the mouth of the sandy Taw and Torridge estuary. Hinks Yard specialises in building wooden working replicas of ships of old. Also in Appledore is the North Devon Maritime Museum. Open daily, Easter to Sept. Tel: Bideford 6042.

Five miles (8km) south of Appledore the famous 'Long Bridge of Bideford' crosses the Taw on 24 arches of differing widths. The bridge is 677ft (206m) long and was built in the 15th century.
□ Three miles (5km) N of Bideford on B3236. Map ref 3A2.

47. ARLINGTON COURT
Nature trails and heronry

Handsomely furnished Regency house (NT), with extensive grounds containing nature trails, lake and heronry. Gardens open daily except Mon throughout year. House open daily, Apr to Oct. Tel: Shirwell 296.
□ Seven miles (11km) NE of Barnstaple on A39. Map ref 3A2.

48. BARNSTAPLE
Ancient market town

Claims to be the oldest borough in the country with a charter granted in 930 by King Alfred's grandson, King Athelstan, giving Barnstaple the right to have a market. This still flourishes now in the 19th-century vaulted Pannier Market building – a commercial centre for North Devon. Interesting buildings include the colonnaded 17th-century Queen Anne's Walk (once the trading place or exchange between merchants and shippers) and the bridge over the River Taw which dates from the 12th century.
□ Nine miles (14km) NE of Bideford on A39. Map ref 3A2.

49. BERRY HEAD
Country park

Prominent limestone headland to the east of Brixham with park and nature trails as well as sweeping coastal views over Torbay.
□ Map ref 3B3.

50. BICKLEIGH MILL FARM
Rural life

A living example of farming and country life in Devon at the turn of the century, complete with horse-drawn equipment working the land and rare breeds of goats and cows milked by hand. There is also an agricultural and crafts museum adjacent to the farm situated in an old watermill where you can see, among other things, a maker of corn dollies at work and observation bee hives. Open daily, afternoons only, Jan, Feb, Mar, and all day Easter to Christmas. Tel: Bickleigh 419.
□ Off A396 about four miles (6.4km) S of Tiverton. Map ref 3B2.

51. BICTON
Formal gardens and farm museum

Lots of family attractions at Bicton, including rides on miniature railway. For garden enthusiasts, the main attraction is the large formal gardens with terraces and pools made in the mid-18th century. Also a 19th-century pinetum, conservatories, an 'American' garden and farming museum. Open daily, Apr to Oct. Tel: Colaton Raleigh 68465.

□ Colaton Raleigh, off A376 S of Newton Poppleford. Map ref 3B3.

52. BRAUNTON
Sand dunes and strip fields

This large North Devon village has two exceptional features in the vicinity: the rolling dunes of Braunton Burrows, and the Great Field between the village and the dunes. The Great Field is a relic of a medieval open field that covers some 350 acres (141 hectares) and is still shared by several farmers. The former strips of medieval farming, grouped together in blocks or furlongs, can be traced within the field. Braunton Burrows extends north from the Taw and Torridge estuary for 3½ miles (5.6km). Its rolling sand hills spread across over 2000 acres (809 hectares), making this one of the largest dune systems in the British Isles. There are two military training areas (watch for red warning flags) and a nature reserve at the southern end. Visitors are requested to keep to the paths to protect the fragile vegetation. Spartina and marram grass, samphire and orchids grow here. Many sea shells are found here. There is a gemstone and shell museum in Croyde village. Open Mar to Oct, restricted opening in winter. Tel: Croyde 890407.

□ Access from A361 and B3231. Map ref 3A2.

53. DARTINGTON HALL
Landscape garden

Peaceful stone-built 14th-century hall with tiltyard around which a modern landscape and flower garden have been created since 1926. Many fine old trees and shrubs including rhododendrons and camellias. Superb in springtime, with crocus carpets under the trees. Henry Moore's sculpture of a reclining woman occupies a key position. Open all year. Tel: Totnes 863291.

□ Two miles (3.2km) N of Totnes, off A384 S of Buckfastleigh. Map ref 3A3.

54. DAWLISH WARREN
South Devon estuary

Dawlish Warren is a mile-long (1.6km) sand spit, almost blocking the mouth of the River Exe. Dunes swarm with holiday-makers in summer with parking for 2000 cars! The mudflats to the north are a National Wildfowl Reserve. To reach the beach of red sand you have to cross Brunel's railway.

□ Minor road off A379, 12 miles (20km) S of Exeter. Map ref 3B3.

55. EGGESFORD FOREST
Forest walks

Flashdown Woods is the site of the first trees planted by the Forestry Commission in Britain in 1919. About one mile (1.6km) south of Eggesford station, an information point near the forest office gives details of three forest walks. Home Valley Walk and Hilltown Trail, both one mile (1.6km), start from the cark park and picnic site. (Leaflets from dispenser.) To reach Heywood Walks and Flashdown, turn off the A377 opposite Eggesford station, keeping right at the two junctions. The longest walk is 2½ miles (4km), but there are shorter routes through the Douglas fir plantations.

□ Off A377 midway between Exeter and Barnstaple. Map ref 3A2.

56. FARWAY COUNTRYSIDE PARK
Country park

This privately owned country park affords superb views over the surrounding Devon hills and the terrain itself, though rugged in places, is very

Southwest England

picturesque and unspoiled. There are hillside and woodland picnic areas, a viewpoint, waymarked nature trails (leaflets available at shop and cafeteria) and a longer walk to a recently purchased area of the park, where there are a number of prehistoric mounds. There is a rare-breeds farm, an animal sanctuary and a pets' enclosure; there are pony rides and donkey carts, facilities for pony-trekking and a herd of roe deer; on rainy days visitors may picnic – but not smoke! – in the Farm Barn and in 1981 a new grass skiing centre is to open. Open 12 to 26 Apr, then Sun and May Day only; daily (except Sat), Spring Bank Holiday to end Sept. Further details, Tel: Farway 224 or 367.
□ Four miles (6.4km) S of Honiton along the A375, then two miles (3.2km) along the B3174 Seaton road. Farway is signposted. Map ref 3B3.

57. GRIMSPOUND
Prehistoric village

Dartmoor is scarcely the most propitious location for farming even nowadays with all the aids of 20th-century technology. How much more difficult it must have been in the Bronze Age when this settlement existed. Its size is marked by a line of stone rubble from what were the outer walls. Within the four acres (1.6 hectares) of this compound are the remains of some 20 huts and several cattle pens. Parts of the outer wall have been reconstructed.
□ 7½ miles (12km) NW of Ashburton off minor road which leads S of B3212. Grid ref SX700809; OS map 191. Map ref 3A3.

58. HARTLAND POINT
Coastal scenery

Here in this windswept, westernmost Devon parish the flat fields suddenly fall away to form the most savage coast in the whole of South-west England. 'A sailor's grave by day and night', Hartland Point has a lighthouse (open to the public; Tel: Hartland 328) to warn shipping away from the jagged ribs and tusks of carboniferous rock that tear the waves to ribbons at the base of these fearsome cliffs. The rock formations and contorted strata assume the most extraordinary shapes, and the force of the Atlantic can be gauged at Hartland Quay, three miles (4.8km) away along the North Devon Coast Path. The old quay was swept away during a gale in 1806. There is a hotel here in the old Harbour Master's house. Hartland Point is now NT.
□ Minor road off A39, signposted to lighthouse. Map ref 2B2.

59. HAYTOR GRANITE RAILWAY
Industrial archaeology

In the 19th century, Dartmoor granite was used to build bridges, wharves and other heavy engineering works. One busy quarry lay on the eastern fringe of the Moor near Haytor Vale. To get the stone to the coast, a granite railway was built, with rails of stone. Parts of the old track still survive on the Moor northwest of Haytor Vale, below the popular viewpoint of Haytor Rocks.
□ W of minor road leading from Haytor Vale to B3344 near Manaton. Map ref 3A3.

60. HEDDON VALLEY
Nature trail

The NT owns nearly 1000 acres (405 hectares) of woodland, moorland and meadow around Trentishoe in the Exmoor National Park. Here the Devon Trust for Nature Conservation has devised a beautiful and interesting nature trail which follows the little River Heddon down Heddon's Mouth Cleave to the sea. Look out for lichens, liverworts and pennywort on the stone walls, and birds such as dippers, herons and buzzards. The circular walk (two miles, 3km) begins and ends near Hunters Inn Hotel.
□ Four miles (6km) W of Lynton (off A39 at Parracombe). Map ref 3A2.

61. HEMBURY WOODS
Woodland wildlife

These beautiful coppice woodlands

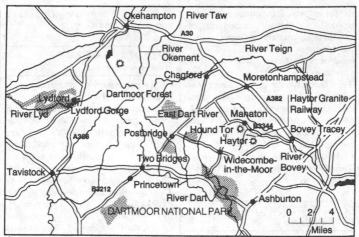

Dartmoor: the great moor with its weird weathered granites such as Hound Tor has an old railway with rails of stone at Haytor, spectacular Lydford Gorge and the celebrated Tom Cobleigh village of Widecombe-in-the-Moor. Days Out 63, 59, 66 and 80 respectively

(NT) lie in the valley of the River Dart. They once produced charcoal for the local copper mines but this practice ceased with the decay of the Devon mining industry. The wood is full of interesting flowers and mosses, including cow-wheat and yellow pimpernel. There are paths running through the wood down to the river. The wood is mainly oak but there is also willow, hazel, beech, sycamore, alder and buckthorn, and several species of butterflies and dragonflies. Ferns thrive in this damp habitat, and alder grows along the riverbanks.

☐ The wood lies N of Buckfast. Travel N along A38 past Buckfastleigh, and take left turn to Buckfast. Map ref 3A3.

62. HOLSWORTHY
Old market town

A market town still dominated by agriculture and especially on Thursdays with the weekly livestock market. A general market also takes place with stalls in the market square and adjoining streets on Wednesdays. There are some pleasant old cottages and essentially this is a place which has not outgrown its origins as a market centre.

☐ Nine miles (14km) E of Bude at junction of A3072 and A388. Map ref 3A3.

63. HOUND TOR
Weathered rocks, abandoned dwellings

In the vicinity of this characteristically weatherbeaten granite outcrop are the remains of several rectangular buildings which have been laid bare by excavation. Situated at about 1100ft (335m) above sea level, these dwellings probably date from the early 12th century and could not survive a climatic deterioration which set in at a later date. The 1:50,000 and 1:25,000 OS maps for Dartmoor repay careful study as they show innumerable cairns, hut circles and other ancient sites.

☐ In Dartmoor National Park, off minor road between Widecombe-in-the-Moor and Manaton, four miles (6.4km) W of Bovey Tracey. Map ref 3A3.

64. KENT'S CAVERN
Lair of the cave bear

This vast limestone cave system is one of the oldest known dwelling places in the British Isles. Guided tours reveal a half-mile (0.8km) wonderland of floodlit stalactites and stalagmites and the skull of a former prehistoric resident – the Great Cave Bear. For opening times and admission charges, Tel: Torquay 24059. A larger exhibition of discoveries from the cave, including a sabre-toothed tiger skull, can be seen at the Torquay Natural History Society Museum, in Babbacombe Road.

□ Ilsham Road, Wellswood, near Torquay (off B3199 behind Anstey's Cove). Map ref 3A3.

65. LUNDY ISLAND
Wildlife haven

Lundy looms out to sea off the North Devon coast, a great granite mass, three miles (5km) long by half a mile (1km) wide, with high cliffs, bays and combes. The island was bought in 1969 by the NT in conjunction with the Landmark Trust. Some of the place-names – Kittiwake Gully, Seals' Rock, Gannet's Bay – give you an idea of the wildlife to be seen. Unfortunately, few of the puffins which gave Lundy its name have remained. (*Lunde* is Norse for puffin.) Several animals have been imported: Soay sheep, Sika deer, Lundy ponies and feral goats. Boats from Ilfracombe throughout the year. Tel: The Landmark Trust, Barnstaple 73333.

□ 11 miles (18km) NW of Hartland Point. Map ref 2B2.

66. LYDFORD GORGE
Woods and waterfalls

On the western fringe of Dartmoor the leaping River Lyd plunges down a deep and narrow chasm (NT) to the leafy woods below. A mile-long (1.6km) footpath follows the river, with steep cuts in the rock, past foaming falls to gentle trout pools set among banks of ferns and wild garlic. The gorge is open daily, Apr to Oct. The falls are at their most spectacular after heavy rain. In the 17th century this was reputedly the lair of an outlaw family, the Gubbinses. Lydford town, now only a grey moorland village, is still dominated by its grim Norman castle keep.

□ Just off A386, midway between Tavistock and Okehampton. Map ref 3A3.

67. LYNTON AND LYNMOUTH
Coast walk

The waters of the East and West Lyn, tumbling down from Exmoor through deep wooded valleys, merge at Watersmeet (NT), and enter the sea at Lynmouth. This picturesque little harbour resort has now recovered from the 1952 flood disaster which destroyed nearly 100 houses in the town. From

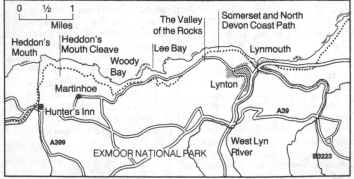

Lynton and Lynmouth: picturesque twins on the North Devon coast, the first a starting point for the extraordinary Valley of the Rocks and coastal walking beyond, the second for exploration of the valley of the fast running Lynn. Day

Lynmouth an old-fashioned cliff railway, opened in the 1890s, rises sedately to the clifftop town of Lynton, starting-point for a spectacular stretch of the long-distance South-west Peninsula coastal footpath. The route passes through the Valley of the Rocks, with its rugged skyline and wild goats, and continues through hanging woods to Heddon's Mouth. Hunter's Inn at the head of Heddon's Mouth Cleave is a convenient lunchtime stop. Total distance, Lynton to Hunter's Inn and back, about 12 miles (19km).

☐ Lynton is on A39, midway between Barnstaple and Minehead. Map ref 3A2.

68. MORWELLHAM QUAY
Industrial archaeology

In the last century these tiny docks leading off the Tamar were a thriving port, shipping copper ore from the mines up in the hills, notably the famous Devon Great Consols mine. The harbour decayed after the closure of the mines but it has now become the site for a fascinating outdoor museum of industrial archaeology as well as a nature trail, open all year. Tel: Tavistock 832766 for further information.

☐ Two miles (3.2km) off A390 between Tavistock and Gunnislake. Map ref 3A3.

69. PLYMOUTH
Sailing and boating

Plymouth Sound provides five sq miles (12.8 sq km) of sheltered waters. Even if it's blowing a gale outside the Sound, it is usually safe for sailing inside and the Hoe forms a natural grandstand for watching the club racing on summer evenings and at weekends. There are also plenty of slipways for launching boats and sailing boats can sometimes be hired from the Plymouth Sailing School. Fine views and coastal walks around Rame Head on the Cornish side of the Sound, and the beautiful woodlands of the Mount Edgecumbe estate.

☐ Map ref 3A4.

70. PLYMTREE
Ancient church

Where else but in Devon could a village have such a name as this? Built of the local brownish sandstone, this church is impeccably maintained, and harbours, as so often in this county, a spectacular screen, with its original colouring most delicately restored. The set of old benches is complete.

☐ 10 miles (16km) NE of Exeter off B3176 (nearest intersection on M5 motorway is junction 28). Map ref 3B3.

71. RIVER DART
Boat and rail trips

The best way to explore this beautiful wooded river valley is by boat. River trips from the historic port of Dartmouth to Totnes, 11 miles (17.7km) upstream, take about 75 minutes and there are daily sailings each way during the holiday season. On the way you pass two pretty villages: Stoke Gabriel, which has a 1000-year old yew tree in the churchyard, and Dittisham, famous for plums, salmon and thatched cottages.

Or you can take a journey into nostalgia by steam train along the old Buckfastleigh line for seven miles (11.2km) beside the Dart. Return trip from Buckfastleigh to Totnes by Dart Valley Railway takes about one hour. Tel: Buckfastleigh 2338.

Dartmouth itself is full of colour and maritime romance. The 15th-century castle (AM) is open standard hours. The most picturesque part of the town is Bayard's Cove with its ruined stronghold and cobbled quay (AM). The 17th-century Butterwalk in Duke Street is also of interest.

☐ Map ref 3A4.

72. ROSEMOOR GARDEN
Woodland garden

Beautiful garden in wonderful woodland setting in the Torridge Valley. Famous for its ornamental shrubs and old-fashioned roses. Also rhododen-

Southwest England

drons, conifers, flowering trees. Unusual plants for sale. Open daily Apr to Oct. Tel: Torrington 2256.

□ Great Torrington, one mile (1.6km) SE of Torrington on B3220 to Exeter. Map ref 3A2.

73. SALCOMBE
Scenic estuary

Salcombe is a yachting haven which has the distinction of being England's most southerly resort. It enjoys a very mild climate that is almost Mediterranean, and some of the loveliest views in the British Isles. No great rivers run down to the sea at Salcombe. The estuary, which broadens inland once past the hanging woods and sandy coves at its narrow entrance, is a drowned river valley. Its tidal creeks, splayed like the fingers of a hand, empty at low water, leaving narrow channels and miles of gleaming mudflats. There are fishing trips, cruises and boats for hire, both at Salcombe and at the head of the estuary at Kingsbridge. A passenger ferry runs from Salcombe pier to East Portlemouth, and another runs in summer to South Sands and Kingsbridge. Best viewpoint is from Sharpitor (NT), a house high above the mouth of the estuary, with six acres (2.4 hectares) of luxuriant sub-tropical woodland gardens and a small museum. (Gardens always open; museum open Apr to Oct.) Beyond Sharpitor the finest stretch of the South Devon Coast path leads to the mica-schist crags of Bolt Head, one mile (1.6km) farther on, and along the 400ft (120m) cliffs to Bolt Tail and Hope Cove. Total distance from Sharpitor: about six miles (9.6km).

Another good walk is along the South Devon Coast path from East Portlemouth to Prawle Point and Lannacombe. Here there is a raised beach. The 'shelf' was once below high water mark. The original cliffs, up to 300ft (91m) high, can be seen half a mile (800m) inland, complete with caves.

□ S of Kingsbridge on A381. Map ref 3A4.

74. SEATON
Pebbles and landslips

The beach here is mostly pebbles. Look out for semi-precious stones like beryls and agates. A narrow-gauge electric tramway runs along the west bank of the River Axe to Colyford and Colyton, daily in summer and limited service in winter. Tel: Seaton 21702. Bird-watching on Axe estuary (waders, wildfowl) is best in autumn and winter. There are good walks over the cliffs to Beer, where the chalk unexpectedly reappears to form Beer Head. Fishing and boat trips from Seaton and Beer. Axmouth, across the bridge on the B3174, was once a flourishing port but a major landslip on the east bank in the 12th century caused the river to silt up. From Axmouth you can follow the South Devon Coast path eastwards to Lyme Regis along Dowlands Cliff, scene of the grand landslip of 1839. This area is now a nature reserve. The walk is hard going, with no way off.

□ On B3174, six miles (10km) SW of Axminster. Map ref 3B3.

75. SHAPTOR WOODS
Woodland walks and wildlife

Shaptor Woods is in one of Devon's most beautiful valleys, just within the Dartmoor National Park. It is owned and managed by the Woodland Trust who have added new public paths. The walk from Furzeleigh Cross takes you on a circular route through a variety of trees from mature beech to the twisted oak so characteristic of Dartmoor. Energetic walkers should try the climb to Shaptor Rock for panoramic views of the countryside. Birds include tree pipits and wood-warblers. Tel: The Woodland Trust, Grantham 74297.

□ Near Bovey Tracey, five miles (9km) NW of Newton Abbot. Map ref 3A3.

76. SLAPTON LEY
Nature reserve

Here the road from Dartmouth to Torcross runs along the rim of a long

Tree pipit (left) and wood warbler, two of the birds to look for on a walk through Shaptor Woods in the Dartmoor National Park, Devon

pebble beach, with the sea on one side and a reed-rimmed freshwater lake called Slapton Ley on the other. This 460 acre (186 hectares) private nature reserve is rich in wildlife, particularly sea and marsh birds (reed warbler, water rail), dragonflies and rare plants. Open all year, with $1\frac{1}{2}$ mile (2.4km) walk along the inner shore of the Ley, starting from Slapton village.

☐ On A379 between Dartmouth and Kingsbridge. Map ref 3A4.

77. TIVERTON MUSEUM
Farm museum

The Agricultural Hall in this museum is a mini-museum in itself, with a substantial collection of implements and tools, including rarities such as the 'Norwegian harrow', thought to be the only one of its kind in existence. There is a 17th-century cider press, a variety of vermin- and man-traps and an exhibition of wagons and carts. Open all year, except Sun, Bank Holidays and Christmas week. Tel: Tiverton 2446.

☐ St Andrew's Street, Tiverton. On A396, N of Exeter. Map ref 3B2.

78. TORBAY
Scenic tour

This popular seaside area, stretching from Torquay to Brixham, is the starting point for a 25 mile (40km)

drive into Dartmoor which dramatically illustrates how climate and altitude affect the landscape of the British Isles.

To see this for yourself leave Torbay on the A385 to Totnes – an architecturally rich old town in itself and one well worth exploration. From Totnes follow the signs for Buckfastleigh where you join the A38 to Ashburton. Shortly before Ashburton, turn left on to the B3357 which climbs onto Dartmoor itself.

By the time you reach Two Bridges and Princetown you have not travelled much more than 25 miles (40km) since leaving the coast, but the countryside is radically different. Intermediate stages at which to observe these landscape changes are Skinner's Bridge, between Totnes and Buckfastleigh, and New Bridge (over the River Dart) on the B3357 west of Ashburton. In the Torbay area itself the Torre Abbey gardens feature exotic sub-tropical flowers and shrubs that flourish in the bay's mild climate.

☐ Map ref 3A3. *Also see map overleaf.*

79. WESTWARD HO!
Pebble ridge

This holiday resort was named in 1863 after the novel by Charles Kingsley. Its sandy beach, pounded by surf, is backed by a three mile (4.8km) ridge of large grey pebbles. The ridge is two

Southwest England

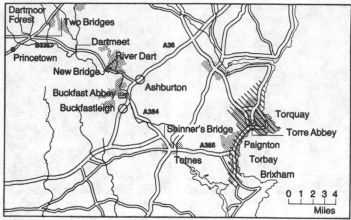

Torbay: from here the visitor can make a 25 mile (40km) scenic drive into Dartmoor. Day Out 78

miles (3.2km) long, 50ft (15m) wide and 20ft (6m) high and it is moving inland at a rate of about a yard (1m) a year. Behind the ridge is the famous Royal North Devon Golf Course and Northam Burrow, some 650 acres (244 hectares) of flat common land. Across this common is Bideford Bar and the River Torridge estuary. The Somerset and North Devon Coast Path runs along the coast from the promenade of Westward Ho! The path climbs to Cornborough Cliff and Abbotsham Cliff with breathtaking views.

☐ By road via Northam or signposted footpath. Map ref 3A2.

80. WIDECOMBE-IN-THE-MOOR
Moorland village

Widecombe Fair, destination of Tom Cobleigh in the famous song, is on the second Tuesday of September. Tourists throng to this granite village deep in the heart of Dartmoor's most rugged moorlands. (Many of the finest tors – Haytor, Hound Tor, Chinkwell, Honeybag and Bowerman's Nose – are within a few miles of Widecombe.) The village church with its tall granite tower, built around 1500, is known as the 'Cathedral of the Moor'. Inside you can read about the day the Devil came

to Widecombe during a Sunday service in 1638!

☐ Minor roads off A38 or B3357, five miles (8km) NW of Ashburton. Map ref 3A3.

Dorset

Almost all of Dorset is still intensely rural. Behind its extraordinary coast of shingle banks and fossil-studded cliffs lie broad vales, quiet villages, rolling prehistoric chalklands, and a host of handsome old towns which include Shaftesbury, Sherborne, Blandford, and the county town of Dorchester. West Country Tourist Board, Tel: Exeter 76351.

81. ABBOTSBURY
Village and swannery

Mellow stone and thatched cottages line the long main street of this beautiful village near the Chesil Beach. Many of the cottages are listed buildings, recently restored with great sensitivity, together with the village pond, which provides an idyllic foreground to Abbotsbury's thatched monastic tithe barn. The barn is 276ft (84m) long, one of the largest in the country. Together with an old stone gateway; it is all that remains of the great 12th-century Benedictine Abbey. It was the monks who built the prominent 15th-century chapel on St Catharine's Hill, high 'above the village, to serve as a landmark for sailors. The hill itself is terraced with Bronze Age lynchets.

To the south of the village (follow the signs) is Abbotsbury Swannery, sanctuary for hundreds of mute swans, whose ancestors have nested here since Plantagenet times. Their home is the brackish western waters of the Fleet, the long lagoon behind the Chesil Beach. Extensive reed beds provide an ideal habitat for marsh birds – and thatch for Abbotsbury's rooftops. Ringed plovers and little terns frequent the shingle beach. A fine example of a duck decoy can also be seen, together with a lofty pole commemorating the great storm of 1824 which drowned the swannery under 20ft (7m) of water. The Swannery is open daily, May to Sept (small admission charge). Also well worth a visit are Abbotsbury Sub-tropical Gardens, to the west of the village on the B3157. The gardens are full of exotic plants and trees, and are at their best when the azaleas and magnolias bloom. Open mid-Mar to Sept, weekdays and Sun afternoons.

☐ About seven miles (11km) NW of Weymouth on B3157. Map ref 4B4.

82. ACKLING DYKE
Roman road

This was the name given to the Roman road from Dorchester to Salisbury. It can be traced quite clearly in several places but never more easily than south-east of Handley (grid ref SU 015164) where it survives as a huge *agger* or bank some 40 to 50ft (12 to 15m) wide and 5 to 6ft (1.5 to 2m) high.

☐ 12 miles (19km) SW of Salisbury off A354. Map ref 4B4.

83. ARNE RESERVE
Bird-watching

Arne reserve covers 1000 acres (404 hectares) of land on the west shores of Poole Harbour. It is one of the last remnants of the heathland which was once extensive in southern Britain. The three main types of heather – ling, cross-leaved heath and bell heather – grow on the reserve and the lesser-known Dorset heath is also found here. The rare Dartford warbler breeds on the heath as do many other bird species such as meadow pipits, stonechats and nightjars. A public footpath from Arne village leads to Shipstal Point where there is a nature trail (open May to Sept). Access to the rest of the reserve is by permit, obtainable from the RSPB Warden, Syldata, Arne, Wareham.

☐ Near Wareham. Map ref 4B4.

84. ASHMORE
Hilltop village

A classic example of a nucleated village with all roads leading to a perfectly circular pond. Its hilltop location at 700ft (213m) above sea level in an area of early settlement – Cranborne Chase – prompted the celebrated interpreter of English landscape, W.G. Hoskins, to suggest that the village site has been inhabited continuously since pre-historic times. But the first certain evidence of its existence comes in the Domesday Book of 1086 which recorded the village as *Aisemara* meaning 'ash-mere' – the pond where ash trees grow.

☐ Approximately eight miles (13km) SE of Shaftesbury off B3081 road. Map ref 4B3.

85. BROWNSEA ISLAND
Nature reserve

Brownsea, the largest island in Poole Harbour, is a haven of wild heathland, woodland and quiet beaches. A walk of about 1½ miles (2km) guides you through the southern part (excluding the Dorset Naturalists' Trust Nature Reserve). Places of special interest are signalled by 26 posts along the way. At the start of the walk is a vantage point over the DNT Reserve lagoon with its wading birds, wildfowl and terns. There are red squirrels in the woods as well as pheasants and peacocks. Boats from Poole Quay or Sandbanks. Tel: Poole Tourist Information, Poole

Southwest England

5151.

□ In Poole Harbour, 1½ miles (2km) SE of Poole near Sandbanks. Map ref 4B4.

86. CERNE ABBAS
Prehistoric site

Nobody knows for certain how old he is and nobody knows why he is there at all, but the Cerne Abbas 'giant' is certainly a remarkable figure, for his size if nothing else: 180ft (55m) high and formed by a one foot (0.3m) trench cut into the chalk of the Dorset hills. But even more remarkable (and more puzzling) features should be apparent to even short-sighted non-archaeologists. Why is he wielding an enormous 120ft (37m) long club? And why are his sexual organs so explicit?

Most experts date the giant as 1800 years old and representing the god Hercules, and many believe it became a fertility symbol; May Day celebrations, also associated with fertility rites, were certainly held on the hill until quite recently. But there are many other theories and legends surrounding the giant, who is now in the care of the NT. In 1979 this care included the rejection of an idea canvassed locally that the giant should don a modesty loin-cloth. As with the Uffington White Horse and other chalk-cut figures, it is traditionally scoured every seven years. The giant in his full-sized glory is best seen from a distance: from the lay-by specially provided on the A352 road just north of Cerne Abbas. But footpaths lead to the giant himself from the village via the churchyard and the ruined abbey.

□ Cerne Abbas is 5½ miles (9km) N of Dorchester on A352. Map ref 4B4.

87. CHESIL BEACH
Pebble beach

This unique beach stretches for about 16 miles (25.7km) from Burton Bradstock to Portland. No one knows why the pebbles that form the huge sea wall are so well graded: small pebbles to the west and larger ones to the east towards Portland. The pebble bank, mostly flint and chert, encloses a lagoon called the Fleet, which ends at Abbotsbury. The beach is excellent for beachcombing but swimming is dangerous.

□ Best viewed from Abbotsbury Hill on B3157 from Bridport. Map ref 4B4.

88. CHARMOUTH
Historic inn

The Queen's Armes is housed in an unusually complete example of a medieval house with much original timbering. It was here that Charles II made plans to escape to France after the Battle of Worcester. After the Restoration the inn had a chapel where nonconformists could worship in safety. Most of the other houses in this small resort on the Dorset coast date from the Regency period but of greater interest to geologists are the nearby cliffs which contain numerous and important fossils.

□ A little over one mile (1.6km) E of Lyme Regis on A35. Map ref 4A4.

89. CRANBORNE MANOR GARDENS
Romantic garden

Early Tudor house with framework of early 17th-century garden almost completely replanted in the 19th century and largely remodelled since 1950. Trees, shrubs, herb garden, herbaceous plants and a collection of old-fashioned roses. Open occasionally from spring to autumn. Tel: Cranborne 248.

□ Near Cranborne village, on B3078, 18 miles (30km) N of Bournemouth. Map ref 4B4.

90. FORDE ABBEY
Historic house

A Cistercian abbey converted into a private house in the mid-17th century by Edmund Prideaux, Cromwell's attorney-general. The result is a rambling and fascinating mixture of monastic remains and 17th-century alterations, strung out along one side of an immense lawn. The highlights are the tower and great hall built by Abbot Chard shortly before the monastery was dissolved in 1539, and Prideaux's saloon, approached by a carved staircase of the same date and rich with panelling, plasterwork and tapestries. The house and garden are generally open on Sun, Wed and Bank Holiday afternoons from May to Sept.

☐ Four miles (6.4km) SE of Chard off B3167 or B3172. Map ref 4A4.

91. GOLDEN CAP
Fossil cliffs

This sandstone capped bluff (NT) is the highest cliff on the south coast at 625ft (190m), and is rich in fossils. There are also many fossils in the rock exposed by the massive landslip which took place in 1908 at Black Ven, west of Charmouth. Black Ven is a nature reserve, closed to the public. To see some of the spectacular prehistoric specimens found in this area visit Dorset County Museum, High West Street. Open weekdays and Sat. Tel: Dorchester 2735. Or the Philpot Museum, Bridge Street, Lyme Regis, which is a local history museum with local fossil finds. Open Easter to Sept, daily. Also Barney's Fossil Shop and Museum in Charmouth High Street. If you have seen enough fossils and would like an edible souvenir of Dorset, visit Moore's Biscuit Factory on the A35 at Morecombelake, where they make traditional Dorset Knob biscuits. Open all year, Mon to Fri. Tel: Chideock 253.

☐ Near Lyme Regis. Approach along Dorset Coast Path from Charmouth, 3 miles (4.8km), or from Seatown, 1 mile (1.6km), or from behind at Morecombelake, on A35. Map ref 4A4.

92. HARDY'S DORSET
Literary landscape

Thomas Hardy was born in Dorset in 1840, lived there most of his life and died at Max Gate, his home on the outskirts of Dorchester, in 1928. During his lifetime he established himself as one of the greatest writers of all time with his powerful 'Wessex'

novels. To this day his home county is still talked of as 'Hardy's Wessex'.

Hardy took the name of Wessex from the ancient kingdom of the West Saxons and used it, like other place-names in his stories, as a thin disguise to blur the true identities of his Dorset locations. Part of the enjoyment of a literary pilgrimage to Hardy's Wessex lies in deciphering the fictional names and unearthing the real towns and villages. But the greatest pleasure is that today, though half a century has passed since Hardy died, much of Dorset has changed so little that keen readers will have little difficulty in recognising the rural scenes he immortalised in his novels.

The area covered by most of Hardy's works is about 50 miles by 35 miles (80km by 56km), with Dorchester, the county town and 'capital' of the Hardy Country, at its centre. From here you could spend several days exploring Hardy's world. The day out we have selected is based on a Hardy Trail devised jointly by the West Country Tourist Board and the Southern Tourist Board, whose special Hardy Trail leaflet is available at the Tourist Information Centre, Antelope Hotel, South St, Dorchester. Tel: Dorchester 67992. The names shown in brackets are those used by Hardy in his novels. **Dorchester (Casterbridge).** The town is rich in its associations with Hardy and his novels. The County Museum in the High Street contains the finest Hardy source collection in the world, and a memorial room with a reconstruction of the author's Max Gate study. Hardy's statue stands at Top o'Town. The King's Arms Hotel and White Hart Hotel both feature in *Far From the Madding Crowd*. The Antelope Hotel, St Peter's Church, Maumbury Rings (a Roman amphitheatre) and Grey's Bridge over the Frome all feature in *The Mayor of Casterbridge* – as also does nearby Maiden Castle.

Stinsford (Mellstock). Featured in *Under the Greenwood Tree*. Hardy's heart is buried in Stinsford churchyard, in the grave of his first wife.

☐ Two miles (3km) E of Dorchester.

Higher Bockhampton (Upper Mellstock). Here stands Hardy's Cottage, the pretty thatched cottage in which he was born and where he wrote *Under the Greenwood Tree* and *Far From the Madding Crowd*. Acquired by the NT in 1947. Gardens open Apr to Oct, 11.00 to 6.00; interior by arrangement with tenant, Tel: Dorchester 2366.

☐ Three miles (5km) S of Dorchester, ½ mile (1km) S of A35.

Puddletown (Weatherbury).

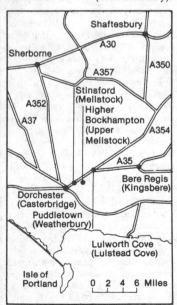

The heartland of Hardy's Dorset

Where Fanny Robin was buried in the churchyard and Troy spent a night in the porch in *Far From the Madding Crowd*. About one mile (1.5km) northwest of Puddletown is Waterston Manor (Weatherbury Farm). Puddletown Heath (Egdon Heath) is part of the great heath, now much fragmented, which once stretched from Bockhampton to Poole Harbour. Hardy's cousin, Tryphena Sparks, was a student-teacher at Puddletown village school.

☐ On A35 midway between Dorchester and Bere Regis.

Bere Regis (Kingsbere). Where Tess and her family set up their four-poster bed outside the church in *Tess of the d'Urbervilles*. Splendid church contains tombs of the real Turbervilles.

☐ At junction of A35 and A31, between Dorchester and Bournemouth.

Wool. Woolbridge Manor Hotel (Wellbridge Manor) was the honeymoon home of Tess and Angel Clare in *Tess of the d'Urbervilles*.

☐ Five miles (8km) S of Bere Regis.

Lulworth Cove (Lulstead Cove). Troy swam out from here in *Far From the Madding Crowd*. Today the beauty of the cove attracts madding crowds in summer.

☐ 4½ miles (7km) S of Wool on B3071.

West Stafford. Tess and Angel Clare were apparently married in West Stafford Church in *Tess of the d'Urbervilles*. Nearby, in the lovely water-meadows of the Frome (Valley of the Great Dairies), is Stuart's Weir (Shadwater Weir), where Eustacia and Damon were drowned in *The Return of the Native*. West Stafford also has a pleasant village pub, the Wise Man, which provides excellent bar snacks.

☐ 2½ miles (4km) E of Dorchester.

■ Total distance of round trip from Dorchester: about 35 miles (56km). Map ref 4B4.

---

93. ISLE OF PORTLAND
Rocky peninsula

This bleak limestone peninsula, scarred by quarrying for Portland stone, is of great geological interest. Portland Bill has a large area of raised beach, rich in shells. The old lighthouse on Portland Bill is now a bird-watching station. Near the lighthouse is a large sea cave, inaccessible from the land, called Cave Hole. The tidal race off the Bill is one of the fiercest in Europe, caused by the tides meeting between here and the Shambles sandbank to the south-east. Portland Bill lighthouse is open to the public, most afternoons. Tel: Portland 820495. There are two castles. One is a ruin. The other, Portland Castle, built by Henry VII, overlooks the harbour. Open to the public, Apr to Sept daily, and Sun afternoon.

□ Take A354 from Weymouth. Map ref 4B4.

94. KIMMERIDGE BAY
Fossils and marine life

A sheltered bay at the foot of green hills, backed by low cliffs of crumbling shale. The cliffs are full of fossils but there is constant danger from the falling rocks. The beach also is an unattractive stretch of grey sand and shale. So why come here? There are many reasons, one of the main ones being the clear, shallow water and its wealth of marine life – now protected as the Purbeck Marine Wildlife Reserve – which you can explore with mask and flippers. (Further details from Dorset Naturalists' Trust, Tel: Parkstone 24241.) The Romans had a thriving trade here, making jewellery from the wafery slabs of shale. Today the new industry is oil, with a 'nodding donkey' pumping on the clifftop to the west of the bay. On the opposite arm of the bay is a ruined 18th-century watchtower built by the Clavell family, and a fine stretch of the Dorset Coast Path leading to Chapman's Pool. Coast walks to the west are restricted when the Army firing range is in use, but the path is open for all but about six weekends a year as well as from late July to mid-Sept. Tel: Range Officer, Bindon Abbey 462721 ext 819 between 8am and 5pm. South-east of Kimmeridge is Smedmore House, ancestral home of the Mansel family for six centuries. Doll collection, walled garden, fine coastal views. Open summer, Wed only. Tel: Corfe Castle 480717.

□ Kimmeridge village is on a minor road off the Corfe Castle to Worbarrow road. Toll road to bay; small charge for parking. Map ref 4B4.

95. LULWORTH COVE
Coast walk

A five mile (8km) walk along the finest stretch of the Dorset Coast Path from Ringstead Bay to Lulworth Cove takes you past Burning Cliff (NT), where in 1826 the oil shales of the Kimmeridge beds smouldered for several years, up White Nothe and past the Purbeck limestone arch of Durdle Door. Beside Lulworth Cove is Stair Hole where the sea has broken through the limestone to create another arch. Lulworth's natural harbour was formed when the sea breached the outer rock wall and eroded the softer clays and chalk of the cliffs behind. Parking on B3017.

□ Map ref 4B4.

96. MAIDEN CASTLE
Prehistoric hill-fort

The most dramatic hill-fort in England. The ramparts may seem deceptively simple when viewed from the main road but they are astonishingly steep and massive when approached on the ground. The triple ramparts and ditches are at their most complex at the two gates and protected a town rather than a mere fort. It was stormed by the Romans, probably in AD 45, and although later superseded by nearby Dorchester it was used in the 4th century as the site of a Romano-Celtic temple, the foundations of which can still be seen. Finds from extensive excavations on the site can be seen at Dorset County Museum in Dorchester. Open weekdays and Sats. Tel: Dorchester 2735.

The 45 acres (18 hectares) of the castle are open to the public at all times and the area's protected status means that it is rich in the natural wildlife of chalk downland. A footpath follows the highest rampart and a complete 1½ mile (2.5km) circuit of the fort can be completed in an easy 45 minutes. Many will prefer to linger, however. It is a spectacular spot for picnicking.

□ One mile (1.6km) S of Dorchester, signposted off A354 road to Weymouth. Map ref 4B4.

97. MILTON ABBAS
Planned village

An 18th-century planned village of considerable charm. It was created when Joseph Damer, the first Earl of Dorchester, obliterated the original village in order to enlarge the park of his new mansion. The 'new' village was built a short distance away with identical four-square cob and thatch cottages facing onto a green. The country house itself, known as Milton Abbey and incorporating the hall of the original 15th-century abbey, is now a school and stands next to a fragment of the abbey church, also 15th-century.

□ Nine miles (14.5km) SW of Blandford Forum, off A354 road to Dorchester. Map ref 4B4.

98. PARNHAM HOUSE
Historic house and garden

Mellow mansion of Ham Hill stone dating from 16th century with additions by John Nash. Now the home of distinguished craftsman John Makepeace, whose furniture workshops are also open to view. Extensive gardens in leafy valley beside the River Brit, with formal terraces, cascade, Italian garden, pleasant riverside walks and picnic area. Open Sun, Wed and Bank Holidays, Apr to Oct. Tel: Beaminster 862204.

□ On A3066, ¾ mile (1km) S of Beaminster, five miles (8km) N of Bridport. Map ref 4A4.

99. POOLE HARBOUR
Natural harbour

The 95 mile (153km) coast of Poole Harbour, part of the drowned valley of the ancient Frome-Solent River, is one of the longest natural harbour shorelines in the world. Poole itself became prominent during the 15th century when the channel serving nearby Wareham silted up, and it is now a busy port. A vehicle and passenger ferry runs from Sandbanks to Shell Bay on the Isle of Purbeck. There is also a passenger ferry to Brownsea Island within the Harbour.

Among Poole's many old buildings are the 16th-century Scaplen's Court, High Street, which houses the local history museum. The Maritime Museum is in the old town cellars, Paradise Street. The Guildhall Museum is in Market Street. From the Guildhall there are guided tours round the historic precinct. Book in advance. For all these, Tel: Poole 5151.

For good views of the Harbour and the Purbeck Hills visit Compton Acres gardens at Canford Cliffs on the B3065. Open daily Apr to Oct. Tel: Canford Cliffs 708036.

□ Map ref 4B4.

100. SHAFTESBURY
Market town

Its old name was Shaston and this is perpetuated in the novels of Thomas Hardy. The town stands on the edge of a 700ft (216m) plateau with outstanding views over the Blackmore Vale towards Somerset. The hill is dramatic within the town, too, with Gold Hill a picturesque echo of life in pre-motor car Britain; it is cobbled and lined by tiny cottages, some thatched and some tiled but virtually all stepped up or down on one another to adjust to the steep gradient. One pities the houses in Shaftesbury's days as a coaching stop on the main London to Cornwall route. Little remains of the abbey which was once here.

□ 17 miles (27km) SW of Salisbury on A30. Map ref 4B3.

101. SWANAGE BAY
Sea coast

Swanage lies at the end of a valley of Wealden clay which the sea has carved away to form the bay. It is protected from further erosion by the hard limestone of Peveril Point, to the south. Swanage, formerly an Anglo-Saxon port, was used to ship marble quarried from the Purbeck hills. You can see working quarries south of the town, near Durlston Bay, where the whole Purbeck rock series is exposed. Many early prehistoric specimens were found here, including dinosaur tracks, now in the Natural History Museum, London. Following the Dorset Coast Path south you come to Dancing Ledge, a platform of rock with its own natural swimming pool. To the north are the chalk stacks of Old Harry Rocks. Studland Heath nature reserve has a mile-long (1.6km) woodland trail and another through the sand dunes, both starting from the car park, off Ferry road, in Studland village.

□ Swanage, Isle of Purbeck, via A351 from Corfe Castle. Map ref 4B4.

102. WEYMOUTH
Coast path walk

This lively resort and cross-Channel port can also be the base for an unusual walk along one of the Countryside Commission's waymarked long-distance footpaths. The Dorset Coast Path forms a 72-mile (116km) stretch of the mammoth South-west Peninsula Coast Path. But whereas most long-distance paths are strictly linear,

The official long-distance footpaths of England and Wales. The walk described below is part of the longest – the 515 mile (825km) South West Peninsula Coast Path

running from A to B, the Dorset path also includes an alternative inland section that offers the possibility of a circular walk based on Weymouth. Depending upon whether you wish to walk in a clockwise or anti-clockwise direction, you begin near the ruins of Sandsfoot Castle or the suburb of Overcombe (where the A353 turns away from the coast) respectively.

Assuming you are walking in a clockwise direction the path – way-

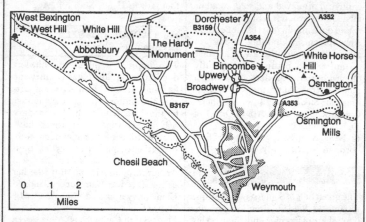

Weymouth: base for an unusual circular walk along stretches of long-distance footpaths

marked by the official acorn symbol – takes you parallel with the extraordinary Chesil Beach to Abbotsbury and then West Bexington before turning inland. Then via Limekiln Hill, White Hill, the Hardy Monument, Upwey, Bincombe, Green Hill, East and West Hills, White Horse Hill, Osmington and Osmington Mills before rejoining the coastal path at Osmington Mills and turning back towards Weymouth.

The length of this walk is over 30 miles (48km), so its entirety would be beyond a day's walk for most ramblers. But it can easily be broken up into smaller sections. A feature of the inland section is that it mainly follows the line of the prehistoric Dorset ridgeway and is accordingly rich in prehistoric remains such as tumuli and earthworks; it passes close to Maiden Castle, for instance. But for many people perhaps the greatest attraction of all is the peace and charm of the Dorset countryside.
☐ Map ref 4B4.

103. WORLDWIDE BUTTERFLIES, COMPTON HOUSE
Butterflies and moths

Stately home for butterfly enthusiasts. British and foreign species are bred in captivity, displayed and sold, dead or alive. In the grounds, visitors can walk round dark muslin tents like a Bedouin encampment, containing a host of caterpillars munching away at their favourite food plants. The recently opened butterfly gardens show which plants attract butterflies. Also Lullingstone Silk Farm is now based here. Car park. Open daily, Apr to Oct. Tel: Yeovil 4608.
☐ Near Sherborne (on A30 Sherborne to Yeovil road). Map ref 4B3.

Somerset

The green hills of Somerset – Mendips, Quantocks, Poldens, Brendons and the lion's share of Exmoor – fill much of this cream and cider county of rich pastures. The low-lying 'Levels' add another dimension, as do their encircling towns: Taunton, Wells and Glastonbury. West Country Tourist Board, Tel: Exeter 76351.

104. BARRINGTON COURT
Historic house and garden

Mellow stone 16th-century house (NT). Gardens by Gertrude Jekyll in 1920s. Aquatic plants in moat; formal iris garden; herbaceous borders. Open Wed only, all year. Tel: Ilminster 2242.
☐ Three miles (4.8km) NE of Ilminster off B3168. Map ref 4A3.

105. BREAN DOWN
Scenic viewpoint

This narrow limestone headland, jutting out into the Bristol Channel in a quiet and isolated corner of the Somerset coast, is a noted viewpoint (300ft, 91m) in a lowland landscape. A passenger ferry runs across the Axe estuary from Weston-super-Mare to Burnham-on-Sea. The Woodspring Museum, Burlington Street, Weston-super-Mare is housed in old workshops of the Edwardian Gaslight Company. There is a Victorian seaside holiday display plus local natural history and much more. Open all year, weekdays. Tel: Weston-super-Mare 21028.
☐ Minor road off B3140 to Brean, footpath to Head. Map ref 4A3.

106. CADBURY CASTLE
Archaeological site

This impressive prehistoric hill-fort dominates the low-lying countryside for miles around. Iron Age ramparts ring the hilltop, strongest contender for the site of King Arthur's legendary seat of Camelot. Excavations have proved that the fortifications were strengthened and a 'feasting hall' built at about the time of the historical Arthur, around AD 500. But whether or not this was Camelot – if indeed Camelot ever existed – may never be known.
☐ At South Cadbury, off A303, seven miles (11km) NE of Yeovil. Map ref 4B3.

107. CHARTERHOUSE
Archaeological site

The area around this village on the open plateau top of the Mendips has been associated with lead mining since Roman times. The Romans had a small town here and a road led to Old Sarum but a small oval amphitheatre is all that survives of this Roman community. It was much later lead working that gave the landscape its present character with rumpled ground, spoil heaps and the remains of circular buddles or washing pits.
☐ Three miles (5km) N of Cheddar on minor roads off B3371 and B3134. Map ref 4A3.

108. CHEDDAR GORGE
Caves

The famous limestone cliffs of Cheddar Gorge tower 450ft (130m) above the winding road. Gough's Cave, open all year, plunges a quarter of a mile into the hills. Its stalactite chambers were once the home and burial place of Stone Age man. Cox's Cave and waterfalls are closed to the public in winter. Tel: Cheddar 742343 for details. Black Rock Nature Reserve at the head of the Gorge has a 1½ mile (2.4km) circular walk from the B3135 at Black Rock Gate. Managed by the Somerset Trust for Nature Conservation, it winds through woodland, limestone scree and rough downland grazing.
☐ On S edge of Mendip Hills. Take B3135 out of Cheddar. Map ref 4A3.

109. CULBONE
Interesting church

Hidden in the woods not far from Porlock, in the Exmoor National Park, the church at Culbone is said to be the smallest in England in regular use – just 33ft (10m) by 12ft 8in (3.8m). The only way to reach it is to follow the North Somerset coast path from Porlock Weir – a pleasant and easy two mile (3.2km) walk. Coleridge wrote *Kubla Khan* at the farmhouse just above the church.
☐ Map ref 3A2.

110. DUNSTER
Historic village

This village is best known for its castle but contains much else of interest. The octagonal 17th-century Yarn Market in the wide main street is one of the most attractive market buildings in the country. The Luttrell Arms takes its name from the family which has owned the castle since the 14th century and was once the guest house of a Cistercian monastery at Cleeve. The core of the inn is a 15th-century Gothic hall with a hammerbeam roof.

In Dunster there are also an old watermill, a packhorse bridge, a mainly Perpendicular-style priory church, a 12th-century dovecote and a Butter Cross, in addition to the castle, which although dating from the 13th century was extensively rebuilt in the last century. The castle is open during the summer but opening times vary according to season. Tel: Dunster 314.
☐ Two miles (3km) SE of Minehead near junction of A396 and A39; OS map 181. Map ref 3A2.

111. EBBOR GORGE
National Nature Reserve

Two waymarked walks lead through these beautiful Mendip valley woods. The short, half mile (1km) round trip route goes through lofty ash woods full of ferns, mosses, fungi and badger setts. Stout shoes are essential for the longer route – 1½ miles (2.4km) – which involves a strenuous climb up through the gorge itself, where scree slopes, crags and caverns of carboniferous limestone are among geological features to be seen. Keep to paths and please do not enter caves. Display centre at car park where walk starts. Tel: Nature Conservancy Council, South West Region, Taunton 83211.
☐ Near Wookey Hole, three miles (4km) NW of Wells. Map ref 4B3.

112. LEIGH-UPON-MENDIP
Old church

The late-Gothic towers of some Somerset churches are among the great

Southwest England

sights of England: at least a dozen are practically faultless. Leigh-upon-Mendip (pronounced 'lie') is especially moving, for it stands high, and you can feel how all the local effort went into the raising of this superb grey limestone tower. The attached church is tiny, but has old benches, tie-beam roofs and, happily, no Victorian glass.

□ Located in a tangle of roads between Frome and Shepton Mallet, off A361 or 1367. Map ref 4B3.

113. MARTOCK
Country town with fine old church

In atmosphere Martock is more village than town. Almost every building, from the 15th-century church to the humblest cottage, is built of the local honey-gold Ham Hill stone. The church contains one of the ecclesiastical glories of Somerset: a timber roof with 750 carved panels, supported by flying angels also carved in wood.

□ On B3165, signposted on A303 midway between Ilchester and Ilminster. Map ref 4A3.

114. MEARE LAKE VILLAGE
Archaeological site

The broken ground of these fields beside the River Brue may not appear particularly impressive at first sight, but it reveals the site of a village that flourished amid the protecting marshes in late Iron Age and Roman times. Excavation has revealed the foundations of scores of huts and the overgrowing peat has preserved dugout canoes, baskets, wooden bowls and other relics now displayed in the Castle Museum, Taunton.

□ Three miles (5km) NW of Glastonbury, beside the River Brue. Grid ref ST445422; OS map 182. Map ref 4A3.

115. MINEHEAD
Cottage architecture

This is almost two towns in one. One is the popular holiday resort with a vast holiday camp; the other is the old village or Higher Town which has probably the best examples of mud-built cottages in England. There is also a 17th-century fishermen's chapel next to the harbour. Minehead is an excellent centre for Exmoor National Park. Steam railway enthusiasts (and others) will enjoy the reopened line between Minehead and Bishops Lydeard; Tel: Minehead 4996.

□ Between Lynton and Bridgwater on A39. Map ref 3B2.

116. MONTACUTE HOUSE
Historic house and garden

One of the finest Elizabethan houses in England, built of golden stone from nearby Ham Hill (fine views). In the Long Gallery, said to be the longest in England, is a National Portrait Gallery exhibition of paintings of the period 1530 to 1630. Also fine heraldic glass and furniture. The house and its splendid formal garden, with topiary and gazebo, belong to the NT. Open daily, afternoons Apr to Oct (except Tues). Tel: Martock 823289.

□ At Montacute, on A3088 four miles (6.4km) W of Yeovil. Map ref 4A4.

117. NEROCHE FOREST
Forest walks

The Castle Neroche picnic place is 900ft (274m) up on the site of former earthworks and near the ruin of an 11th-century castle. It has fine views of Taunton Vale, Bristol Channel and the Mendips. Forest walks cross many streams and pass through mixed woodland with over ten different tree species. Access via by-road off A303 W of Broadway. Prior's Park picnic place is six miles (9.6km) south of Taunton on B3170. It is in former parkland about 800ft (244m) above sea level set among oak, larch and beech.

□ Near Taunton. Map ref 3B2.

118. NETHER STOWEY
Quantock village

An ideal centre for exploring the Quantock Hills. Numerous paths and trails, including the three mile (4.8km) Quantock Forest Trail, starting two miles (3.2km) south-west of Nether Stowey. Wordsworth's former home is now a hotel but Coleridge's Cottage, owned by the NT, is open Apr to Sept (except Fri and Sat). Tel: Bridgwater 732662.

☐ Seven miles (11.3km) W of Bridgwater on A39. Map ref 3B2.

119. QUANTOCK INTERPRETATION CENTRE
Wildlife

The interpretation centre is housed in the restored stables of the 17th-century manor house of this ancient hamlet on the eastern slopes of the Quantock Hills. There is a nature trail through the grounds with their woods and lake which were landscaped in the 18th century but are now being returned to the kind of vegetation more characteristic of the Quantocks. Trail leaflets and a series of booklets describing the fauna and flora of the Quantocks are available at the Interpretation Centre. Tel: Somerset Naturalists' Trust, Taunton 45412.

☐ Fyne Court, Broomfield, four miles (7km) W of North Petherton. Map ref 3B2.

120. SEDGEMOOR
Reclaimed fen battlefield

The reed-choked wilderness which once hid the fugitive King Alfred from the Danes has been reclaimed and converted into lush pasturelands crossed by slow rivers and drainage ditches, known locally as 'rhines'. But much of this part of lowland Somerset is still below sea level, and winter flooding drowns the fields, attracting large flocks of ducks and wild swans. The whole area is rich in marsh and meadow flora. Withies, or willow wands, are grown and woven by local craftsmen to make beautiful baskets. The Battle of Sedgemoor, the last major battle on English soil, was fought about half a mile (0.8km) NW of Westonzoyland church in 1685, crushing the Duke of Monmouth's rebellion against James II. After the battle, 500 rebel prisoners were locked up in Westonzoyland church tower. Among the most interesting of the surrounding towns and villages is Somerton, once the capital of the West Saxons, now a well preserved market town of red-tiled, grey stone houses, with a wide square, an octagonal market cross and a church embellished with a fine 15th-century tie-beam roof.

☐ Map ref 4A3.

121. SELWORTHY BEACON
Scenic viewpoint

A magnificent viewpoint for Exmoor, the North Devon coast and Bristol Channel. This 1013ft (304m) moorland summit can be reached by coastal footpath from Minehead via North Hill, three miles (4.8km), or more steeply from the village of Selworthy, (NT), one of the prettiest villages in England. Above the village are the remains of Bury Castle, an Iron Age hill-fort.

☐ On minor road off the A39, four miles (6.4km) W of Minehead. Map ref 3B2.

122. SIMONSBATH
Farming landscape

The Exmoor estate of the Knight family centred on Simonsbath is still very much a part of the contemporary landscape, yet it is well over 150 years since John Knight purchased 15,000 acres (6070 hectares) of desolate upland moor and within a generation transformed it into good agricultural land. A boundary wall 29 miles (46km) long fenced in the 15 Knight farms, and the wall, farms, shelter belts of conifers and high earth banks enclosing the rectangular fields are still there to emphasise Knight's success in taming the former upland wilderness.

☐ Around Simonsbath, at junction of B3223 and B3358. Map ref 3A2.

123. SOMERSET RURAL LIFE MUSEUM
Country life

Apart from craft tools relating specifically to Somerset trades such as cider-

making, peat digging and the withy industry, this museum has given over two rooms to showing the life of one typical Victorian farmworker, who began work aged 12 and earned three shillings a week for a six-day week. Open Easter to end Sept, Mon to Fri; Sat; Sun afternoon. Shorter winter openings. Tel: Glastonbury 32903.
□ Abbey Farm, Chilkwell Street, Glastonbury. On A361. Map ref 4A3.

124. STOGURSEY
Ancient village

Stogursey was one of many medieval new towns that failed. It was created after the Norman Conquest and given a castle and a fine priory. Of these, apart from the 12th-century church, only a moat and a dovecote remain. However, Priory Farm not only occupies the site of the old priory and bears its name but was largely built from the former monastic stone. The town had made little headway over the centuries when in the 19th century its fate as an urban centre was sealed by being by-passed by the railway. Today it remains a village with a wide main street that was once a market-place.
□ 10 miles (16km) W of Bridgwater between the Quantocks and the sea, off the A39. Map ref 3B2.

125. WOOKEY HOLE
Limestone caverns

Subterranean birthplace of the River Axe, home of the legendary 'Witch of Wookey' and former refuge of Paleolithic man, who sheltered in these caves during the closing phases of the Ice Age, when mammoth, woolly rhinoceros, wolf and bear roamed the Mendip Hills. Visitors can explore the first three floodlit chambers, see the underground lake formed by the Axe, and the 'Witch of Wookey' stalagmite. In 1912 excavations revealed the skeleton of a woman, together with a sacrificial knife and a stalagmite crystal ball. Open daily. Tel: Wells 72243.
□ Two miles (3.2km) NW of Wells on minor road between A371 and B3139. Map ref 4A3.

Southern England

126. CHICHESTER HARBOUR
Area of Outstanding Natural Beauty

A peaceful expanse of creeks, saltings and tidal water centred on the picturesque and historic village of Bosham. The harbour includes about 50 miles (80km) of shoreline while the total area of the AONB covers 47 sq miles (75 sq km). Although Bosham is the largest village on the water's edge, there are several other attractive hamlets such as Emsworth, Dell Quay, Itchenor and Birdham – see map.

Sailing. The Harbour offers a well sheltered stretch of water for a day's sail with a boatyard in almost every village and plenty of launching sites. Plenty of waterside pubs, too, for both sailors and those who want to watch the hundreds of craft going to and from their moorings.

Bird-watching. During the winter months many small wading birds come to these waters. They include sanderling, dunlin, large pied oystercatchers, ringed plovers and several different kinds of gull. On the mudflats huge flocks – maybe as much as a tenth of the world's population – of brent geese feed on the seaweed between November and March; on the saltings you should see curlew, redshank ·and shelduck.

East Head, at the southern end of the harbour, is a particularly good place for bird-watching.

Walks. There are miles of footpaths around the harbour. These are detailed not only on OS map 197 but also in an excellent Harbour Guide published by the Chichester Harbour Conservancy (Tel: Birdham 512301). This guide describes the history of the villages and the area's flora and fauna, as well as offering advice to would-be sailors, anglers and walkers. Itchenor is a good starting point for walks, particularly in summer months when a ferry operates to Bosham (weekends Apr to mid-July; then daily until mid-Sept). The ferry is for walkers and cyclists only. (See Day Out 221 – Selsey

Chichester Harbour: a haven for yachtsmen, anglers, ramblers and bird-watchers. Days Out 126, 221

Southern England

– for details of a nature trail around East Head.)

Angling. In addition to the tidal waters of the Harbour itself, the Chichester Canal is also popular with anglers. The canal joins the harbour at Birdham but is no longer used for commercial traffic.

☐ Chichester Harbour is SW of Chichester off A27 or A286. Map ref 5B4.

127. EAST HAMPSHIRE
Area of Outstanding Natural Beauty

A seemly spread of well farmed countryside, spacious downs and beech-wooded hillsides extending eastwards from Winchester to join the Sussex Downs AONB. A village tour of the area could include Selborne, birthplace and home of the 18th-century naturalist Gilbert White; Hambledon, the cradle of the game of cricket; and East Meon in the delightful Meon Valley. The total area of the AONB is 243 sq miles (391 sq km).

☐ Map ref 5A3.

128. ISLE OF WIGHT
Area of Outstanding Natural Beauty

This covers almost all the coast and hinterland in the south and west of the island, from Shanklin to the Needles and along the Solent shore to Gurnard Bay near Cowes. It also includes a small pocket of coast between East Cowes and Ryde, and a large expanse of countryside reaching from Newport, the island 'capital', to the chalk downs which end at Culver Cliff. Its total area is 147 sq miles (235 sq km).

☐ Map ref 5A4.

129. KENT DOWNS
Area of Outstanding Natural Beauty

This follows the North downs from Westerham on the Surrey border to the Channel coast at Folkestone. It shares, with the Surrey Hills AONB, the North Downs Way long-distance footpath and has many pretty villages such as Charing and Chilham. The area includes two country parks, Trosley near Wrotham and Camer Park near Meopham, and is exceptionally rich in historic houses. Its total area is 528 sq miles (845 sq km).

☐ Map ref 7B1.

130. NORTH WESSEX DOWNS
Area of Outstanding Natural Beauty

Largest of all the AONBs with a total area of 1086 sq miles (1738 sq km) spreading beyond Berkshire into Wiltshire, Oxfordshire and Hampshire. Southern chalk down scenery at its best: a rolling sea of smooth grassy hills scattered with tumuli and prehistoric hill-forts. It contains probably the finest stretch of the Ridgeway long-distance footpath, from Streatley to Avebury and its famous prehistoric stone circle. Other sights and places of interest include the Uffington White Horse, Silbury Hill, Barbury Castle (Iron Age hill-fort) and the West Kennet Long Barrow. Here, too, are the breezy summits of Inkpen Hill with its sinister gibbet, and Warbury Hill, at 974ft (297m) the highest chalk down in England. Savernake Forest and the peaceful Kennet and Avon Canal offer a change of scene from the dry and open chalk hills.

☐ Map ref 5A2.

131. SOUTH HAMPSHIRE COAST
Area of Outstanding Natural Beauty

This consists of the Solent coast between Christchurch Bay and Southampton Water plus the hinterland of Beaulieu River. Places to visit include Buckler's Hard, the stately home at Beaulieu, and the country park on the Lepe and Calshot foreshores. The latter covers 122 acres (49.5 hectares) of clifftops and beaches three miles (5km) south of Fawley. The AONB covers 48 sq miles (78 sq km).

☐ Map ref 5A4.

132. SURREY HILLS
Area of Outstanding Natural Beauty

London's weekend country playground. Suburbs lap against its northern edges but the beech groves, bluebell woods and chalkland slopes of the North downs form a continuous *cordon sanitaire* of unbroken countryside from Kent to Guildford, which contains Leith Hill – at 965ft (294m) the highest point in south-east England – Box Hill and the picturesque villages of Shere and Abinger. West of Guildford the Surrey Hills AONB is different in character, with sandy heaths and commons, wooded hills and many beauty spots, including Frensham Ponds, and the Devil's Punchbowl near Hindhead. Ideal countryside for gentle walks and picnics, much of it protected by the NT. The total area of the AONB is 258 sq miles (414 sq km).
□ Map ref 7A1.

133. SUSSEX DOWNS
Area of Outstanding Natural Beauty

Superlative rolling chalk downland, from the Hampshire border through West Sussex to the sheer white cliffs of Beachy Head in East Sussex. Marvellous views from Ditchling Beacon, 813ft (250m), on the Downs behind Brighton. In addition to bracing coastal walks over Seven Sisters there are many famous sights and places of interest: castles at Lewes and Arundel; stately homes and gardens such as Firle Place and Glynde Place (both near Lewes), and Petworth; the Saxon figure of the Long Man of Wilmington, three miles (4.8km) north-west of Eastbourne, cut in the downland turf; and the smugglers' village of Alfriston with its 15th-century Star Inn. For horse-riders as well as walkers, the South Downs Way long-distance footpath provides a high-level route over the roof of the Downs from Beachy Head to the Hampshire border, a distance of 80 miles (129km). The total area of the AONB is 623 sq miles (981 sq km), which provides the naturalist with some rare examples of flora and fauna.
□ Map ref 7B2.

Berkshire

A county bounded in the north by the River Thames and including part of the North Wessex Downs AONB – the largest in the country. Attractions include Windsor, with its castle and park, and the Thames itself from Maidenhead to the Goring Gap. Thames and Chilterns Tourist Board, Tel: Abingdon 22711.

134. COMBE HILL
Iron Age England

At just under 1000ft (297m) this is the highest chalk hill in England. Almost inevitably, in an area rich in hill-forts, it is therefore crowned by Iron Age fortifications. The hill-fort is known as Walbury Hill and encloses a large area – 82 acres (33 hectares) – but otherwise is remarkable mainly for its views over the Kennet Valley. However the fort is crossed by a trackway, probably prehistoric, which can be followed south-east towards another hill-fort known as Beacon Hill (grid ref SU 457572) and the Seven Barrows burial mounds next to the A34 – a distance of just over six miles (9.6km) from Walbury Hill. On the same trackway barely half a mile (800m) north-west from Walbury Hill is the extraordinary Combe Gibbet – a gallows first erected in the 17th century on a long barrow. OS map 174 shows other prehistoric relics in this area such as tumuli and ancient field systems as well as 20th-century footpaths.
□ Five miles (8km) SE of Hungerford on minor road to Inkpen. Map ref 5A3.

135. COURAGE SHIRE HORSE CENTRE
Farm museum

Shire horses and their history are on display here, with harnesses, photographs, farrier's shop and agricultural implements. Open daily Mar to Oct,

except non-Bank Holiday Mons. Tel:
Littlewick Green 3917.
☐ At Maidenhead Thicket three miles
(4.8km) W of Maidenhead off A4. Map
ref 7A1.

136. GORING GAP
River valley

The Thames cuts through the chalk
escarpment at Goring in a beautiful
wooded valley. Roads such as the A329
and B4009 offer glimpses of the river
between Wallingford and Pangbourne, but it is seen more dramatically from viewpoints such as 500ft
(150m) Streatley Hill, a prominent
spur of chalk overlooking the meandering river. The 15 miles (24km) between
Wallingford and Pangbourne offer
recreations for most tastes. There are
attractive villages, riverside walks and
fishing; castle remains at Wallingford;
a wildlife park at Basildon (for opening
hours, Tel: Upper Basildon 325); and
Basildon Park. The latter is a Georgian
house with fine grounds recently
opened by the NT: open afternoons
only Apr to Oct, daily except Mon and
Tues but all day Bank Holiday Mons.
Tel: Pangbourne 3040. And, of course,
on this highly attractive stretch of the
Thames there is boating on the river
itself; ask tourist office about boats for
hire.
☐ Goring is eight miles (13km) NW of
Reading via A329. Map ref 5A2.

137. HURLEY
Riverside village and inn

The southern banks of the Thames here
offer an attractive setting for picnicking and gentle strolls by the water's
edge. The village itself was the site of a
Benedictine Priory with which not only
the church but the inn, Ye Olde Bell,
can claim a connection. The Norman
parish church was originally part of the
priory while the inn was first founded in
the 12th century as a hospice attached
to the priory. A new half-timbered inn
was built on the site of the earlier
hospice towards the end of the 16th
century and parts of this are still well
preserved. A few remains of the priory,

including a dovecote, can also be seen
in the village.
☐ Four miles (6.4km) E of Henley off
A423. Map ref 7A1.

138. LAMBOURN
Racehorses and antiquities

An attractive village, with a large
Norman church and many Georgian
houses, on the Berkshire downs but
now best known for racehorse training.
Many famous stables are situated in
Lambourn or neighbouring Upper
Lambourn with the result that these
villages and the surrounding downland are some of the best places in the
British Isles to see thoroughbred horses
in action. The prehistoric Ridgeway
path passes four miles (6.4km) to the
north of Lambourn through an area
which has many antiquities. The most
famous are probably the Lambourn
Seven Barrows, a group of round
barrows about two miles (3.2km)
north of the village (grid ref SU
328828). But there is also a long barrow
(SU 326833) and a small Iron Age hill-
fort known as Alfred's Castle (SU
277827).
☐ Six miles (9.6km) N of Hungerford
on B4000, near junction 14 on M4.
Map ref 5A2.

139. MUSEUM OF ENGLISH RURAL LIFE
Agricultural history

The museum is part of the Institute of
Agricultural History at the University
of Reading and has been open to the
public since 1955. The permanent
exhibition contains early agricultural
tools and machinery from all over
England, dating mainly from the 19th
and early 20th centuries. Open
throughout the year, Tues to Sat
except Bank Holidays. Tel: Reading
85123, ext 475.
☐ At Whiteknights, Reading, on
A327. Map ref 5B2.

140. WINDSOR GREAT PARK
Royal parkland and gardens

The hunting territory of kings is now a

picnicking ground for the masses. The park is vast, stretching through 4800 acres (1942 hectares) from the River Thames to Virginia Water. Tucked away in the south-east corner of the park, near Englefield Green, are two outstanding gardens within one mile (1.6km) of each other. The Savill Garden began as a bog garden and grew into a general ornamental garden with flowering shrubs, trees, herbaceous plants, roses and alpines. The Valley Gardens are larger. They are located around Virginia Water and were developed in the 'natural' style with shrubs and a heather garden in attractive woodland. Both gardens are open daily Mar to Dec. Tel: Egham 35544.

□ Off A30 between Egham and Virginia Water. Map ref 7A1.

East Sussex

The Sussex coast draws many visitors with a string of resorts of which the most famous are Brighton, Eastbourne and Hastings. Other Attractions include the South Downs (with long-distance footpath), Rye, Lewes, Battle and the Bluebell Railway. South-East England Tourist Board: Tunbridge Wells 40766.

141. ASHDOWN FOREST
Ancient forest

The Romans knew it as the Forest of *Anderida* and in those days it covered most of south-east England. It still extends over some 14,000 acres (5668 hectares) of sandy heathland and woodland between roughly East Grinstead, Uckfield and Crowborough. By the 16th century it was the centre of the British iron industry whose demand for charcoal denuded the forest of many more trees. The area is best explored on foot or via the minor roads which cross the forest, e.g. around Nutley and Wych Cross off A22. Places of interest include the Beacon, a 792ft (238m) viewpoint west of Crowborough; a Forestry Commission picnic area and forest trail adjacent to Gravetye Manor, a Jacobean mansion (now a

hotel) south of East Grinstead; and Nutley Mill, open afternoons on last Sun of month, Easter to Sept, one mile (1.6km) north of Nutley on unclassified road.

□ SE of East Grinstead, N of Uckfield, W of Crowborough off A22 or A26. Map ref 7B2.

142. BURWASH
Jacobean mansion and watermill

A 'linear' village along a wide and tree-lined street. Among many lovely houses, the most renowned within the village is the 17th-century Rampyndene with elaborate carving and a high roof. The most famous house, though, lies a short distance outside the village: Bateman's (NT), a Jacobean stone mansion, was Rudyard Kipling's home from 1902 to 1936 and is now preserved as he left it. In the grounds of Bateman's is an 18th-century watermill, itself a listed building and now restored to working order. The house is usually open daily Mar to Oct, except Fri, but hours vary, so it might be best to check. Tel: Burwash 882302.

□ Burwash is approximately halfway between Hastings and Tunbridge Wells on A265 with Bateman's half a mile (0.8km) S of the village. Map ref 7B2.

143. DITCHLING COMMON
Country park

There are ponds, fishing and bridleways as well as the customary fare of picnic places and walks in the 183 acres (74 hectares) of the scrub-covered common land of this country park.

□ Two miles (3.2km) N of Ditchling on B2112. Map ref 7B2.

144. EASTBOURNE
Coastal and downland walk

As with Weymouth this is a seaside resort which can serve as the base for an unusual circular walk along stretches of a long-distance footpath – in this case, the South Downs Way. An 18 mile (29km) circuit, waymarked

Southern England

throughout, can be achieved by using the alternative coastal and inland sections at the eastern end of the South Downs Way (see map). The going over the chalk downlands is relatively easy

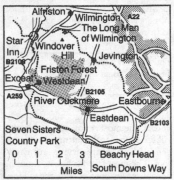

Eastbourne: the base for a walk over the South Downs via Beachy Head and Seven Sisters country park

and the views, over the sea and the Weald, are excellent. Roughly halfway around the circuit is Alfriston, a pretty village in the Cuckmere valley with a fine 14th-century church and the 15th-century Star Inn. Also *en route* is the Seven Sisters Country Park (see Day Out 152).

In a clockwise direction from Eastbourne, the route takes you over the Beachy Head clifftops to the Cuckmere valley; crosses the main coast road, the A259, at Exceat near the country park where there is a car park; continues through West Dean and Friston Forest to Alfriston; and returns along a bridlepath over Windover Hill, Jevington and Eastbourne golf course. Smaller stretches, of course, can be undertaken and alternative starting points devised. OS map 199 details the footpaths.

□ The South Downs Way begins (or ends) at the western end of Eastbourne, near where the sea front turns away from the coast to climb up to Beachy Head. Map ref 7B2.

145. FOREST WAY
Linear country park

Part of the old railway line between Groombridge and East Grinstead has been converted into a linear country park 9½ miles (15.5km) long. The route is open throughout the year and can be used by cyclists and horse-riders as well as walkers; it is even smooth enough for prams and push-chairs. The Forest Way skirts the northern edges of Ashdown Forest and follows the valley of the River Medway; the wildlife is therefore varied. OS maps 187 and 188 cover the route of the Way and further information can be obtained from East Sussex CC county estates department. Tel: Lewes 5400 (weekdays only).

□ Access is possible at several points including S off A21 ½ mile (800m) SE of East Grinstead; at Forest Row on A21; off B2026 N of Hartfield; and off B2110 SW of Groombridge. Map ref 7B2.

146. GREAT DIXTER
Romantic flower garden

The half-timbered 15th-century manor house was reconstructed early this century by Sir Edwin Lutyens, who also laid out the gardens as a series of enclosures which contain many rare plants as well as topiary and a famous 'long border'. Open daily, except non-Bank Holiday Mons, Apr to Oct. Tel: Northiam 3160.

□ 12 miles (19km) N of Hastings at Northiam off A28. Map ref 7C2.

147. HASTINGS
Country park

This 500 acre (203 hectare) park is comprised of wooded glens, ghylls, heathland, cliffs and beach. It is backed by farmland and faces out over the English Channel; Fairlight Glen is designated as an area of special scientific interest. There are five nature trails, for which leaflets are available from Hastings Tourist Information Bureau and the Interpretative Centre at Fairlight. The park is open daily throughout the year; the interpretative centre is open Thurs, Sat and Sun afternoons from May to Sept. Tel: Pett 2140. The main entrance to the free car park is just off Fairlight Road; there are three picnic areas.

□ The country park is just E of the Old Town of Hastings and stretches along the coastline for about three miles (6.8km). Map ref 7C2.

148. LULLINGTON HEATH
Wildlife refuge

A national nature reserve for keen naturalists only. A steep walk (20 min) brings you to one of the best examples of chalk heath vegetation. It includes an unusually large variety of plants: not only chalk-loving species such as salad burnet and dropwort, but those usually associated with more acid soils, such as heather and tormentil. Left to itself, the grassland would quickly revert to scrub, so there is management in the form of grazing by New Forest ponies and sheep, and mowing. Where gorse and scrub has grown up, however, this provides a good habitat for birds and insects. Visitors should keep strictly to the three public rights of way across the reserve and keep dogs on a lead. A leaflet is available but no other public facilities. For further information, contact Nature Conservancy Council. Tel: Lewes 6595.
□ Off A2105 at Jevington, three miles (4.8km) N of East Dean. Map ref 7B2.

149. PEVENSEY
Roman and Norman fortress

Perhaps best remembered as the place where William the Conqueror landed in 1066. Pevensey was also the site of one of the Romans' Saxon Shore Forts (see map) and enough of those fortifications survived for the site to be used again by the Normans who erected their own castle keep within the Roman walls. Now the remains of both castles stand guard over a harbour that – like those other Roman sea forts in Kent other than Dover – has long since silted up with the result that they are one mile (1.6km) inland. The castle ruins are open during standard DoE hours and on Sun mornings Apr to Sept.
□ Four miles (6.4km) NE of Eastbourne near junction of A259 and A27. Map ref 7B2.

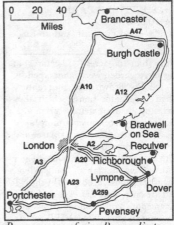

Pevensey: one of nine Roman Forts of the Saxon Shore. Days Out 149, 166, 183, 195, 479

150. RYE
Medieval town and coastal walk

An ancient Norman Cinque Port which is now two miles (3.2km) inland. It is a highly picturesque town on a hill above Romney Marsh with steep, cobbled streets that still convey a medieval air. One of the old gates, the 14th-century Landgate, survives to add to the general feeling of antiquity, much admired by 20th-century visitors. Among many fine buildings are the 15th-century Mermaid Inn and Lamb House (NT), once the home of Henry James.

There is a fine walk along the dyke, keeping the sea at bay, from Rye Harbour to Winchelsea Beach. A nature reserve is run here by the local authorities with a good mix of sea and land birds, particularly little tern. It is open to the public. Tel: Rye 3862. Return to Rye via Camber Castle which stands on the marshes some 1½ miles (2.4km) inland. One of Henry VIII's coastal defences, the castle is now being restored by the DoE but is not yet open to the public. The walk is roughly seven miles (11km) long: OS map 189.
□ Rye is 10 miles (16km) NE of Hastings on A259 and A268. Map ref 7C2.

Southern England

151. SHEFFIELD PARK GARDENS
Landscaped gardens and steam railway

More than 100 acres (40 hectares) of this large garden were landscaped by 'Capability' Brown in the 18th century when the Tudor house which they surround was also extensively remodelled. In the 19th century two more lakes, plus a considerable amount of tree and shrub planting, were added while the 20th century has seen an even greater influx of exotic plants. The gardens, but not the house, are owned by the NT and are open daily Easter to mid-Nov, except non-Bank Holiday Mons and Sun mornings. Tel: Dane Hill 790655 or 790338. The house is separately owned and open afternoons Wed, Thur and Sun, Easter to Oct. Tel: Dane Hill 790531. A short distance away from the house and gardens is a terminus for one of the best-known privately operated steam railways, the Bluebell Line. This operates from Sheffield Park to Horsted Keynes daily during June to Sept; Wed and weekends in May and Oct; weekends in Mar, Apr and Nov; Sun only during Dec to Feb; plus Bank Holidays. Tel: Newick 2370.
□ Five miles (8km) NW of Uckfield on A275 between East Grinstead and Lewes. Map ref 7B2.

152. SEVEN SISTERS
Chalk cliffs and unspoilt estuary

This is now the name not only of the famous line of chalk cliffs culminating in Beachy Head (532ft, 161m) but also of a country park. The cliffs are remarkable for their sheer vertical drops. Originally they extended further south, but over the years the sea has undercut the base of the cliffs. Because the chalk has vertical joints, chunks are broken off by the undercutting to leave the dry 'hanging' valleys and sheer cliffs which now form part of Britain's protected 'Heritage Coast'. Look out for the horizontal lines of flint in the chalk.

In addition to the downland adjoining the cliffs (AONB), the country park contains the meandering valley of the River Cuckmere as it approaches the sea – one of the few remaining undeveloped river estuaries in south-east England. Some of the river's meandering loops now form ox-bow lakes, cut off from the Cuckmere's course to the sea. The wide variety of habitats – chalk, shingle, open water, salt marsh, meadowland, downland and scrub supports equally diverse wild life.

The park offers almost unlimited scope for picnicking and an information centre is housed in a splendid old barn. Open daily from Easter to last weekend in Oct, then weekends only. Tel: Alfriston 870280. There is a nature trail, fishing, bridleways, footpaths (including a stretch of the South Downs Way, see Day Out 144) and a forest walk. The latter is a 2¾ (4.4km) circuit through Friston Forest, climbing the escarpment on broad downland rides through young mixed beech and pinewoods. It offers fine views towards Beachy Head where, of course, the views are magnificent.
□ Off A259 three miles (5km) E of Seaford. Map ref 7B2.

153. WINCHELSEA
Failed medieval 'new town'

The present sleepy town set on a hill above the marshes was created when an earlier town had been swallowed up by the sea. Edward I decided to lay out a new town in the 1280s and the inhabitants of Old Winchelsea were allowed burgess plots to recompense them for their loss. Today the grid-iron plan of the town still serves as a reminder of medieval planning. The unfinished parish church of St Thomas, a chancel without a nave, also stands as a memorial to the 14th century when New Winchelsea's prosperity ebbed away in favour of neighbouring Rye. The town was never finished on the intended grand scale, with only 12 of the 39 quarters of land between the roads ever built over. Some streets have vanished to become grazing ground for sheep, although their lines remain visible to the present day. A degraded sea cliff below Strand Gate shows how far the sea has retreated from this once thriving port, leaving it stranded some two miles (3.2km) inland. The Old Court House is now a local history museum; open during summer only.

☐ Two miles (3.2km) SW of Rye on A259. Map ref 7C2.

Greater London

Innumerable tourist attractions with famous gardens at Kew, Hampton Court, Chiswick and in some of the royal parks. London Tourist Board, Tel: 01-730 0791.

154. HAM HOUSE
17th-century house and garden

A fascinating example of an Elizabethan mansion converted and enlarged into a 'formal house' by Charles II's gross but able minister, the Duke of Lauderdale. One has the feeling that the clock stopped in 1700. Matching apartments for the Duke and Duchess on the ground floor, and a state apartment for a monarch above, all still contain an extraordinary amount of their original contents and decorations. None of the rooms is large; the house was designed for a few people to pass elaborate compliments to each other in a setting of intimate formality. The garden is being restored to its original 17th-century form, although it will take some years for this process to be completed. The gardens are open daily throughout the year; the house is open daily except Mon and most Bank Holidays. Tel: 01 940 1950.

☐ One mile (1.6km) SW of Richmond off A307 road to Kingston or by towpath walk from Richmond through Petersham meadows. Map ref 7A1.

155. STAINES RESERVOIRS
Bird-watching

This is the best place in the London area for watching winter wildfowl. The birds themselves seem undisturbed either by bird-watchers or by the planes from Heathrow a few miles away. If you visit in October you stand a chance of seeing a black-necked grebe and in the later winter months there are usually wigeon, shoveler, goldeneye, tufted duck and pochard, with perhaps smew and goosander.

☐ Immediately north of Staines, off A30 with access from a footpath off B378. Map ref 7A1.

156. TRENT PARK
Country park

The country park closest to north London with 680 acres (275 hectares) of wood and parkland including bridleways for horse-riding as well as footpaths, fishing and golf.

☐ 1½ miles (2.4km) W of Enfield off A111. Map ref 7B1.

Wigeon, (left) and Tufted duck, both of which are common winter visitors at Staines Reservoirs

Southern England

A large county stretching from the sea to London's commuter belt. Its attractions include river valleys such as the Test and Itchen; towns such as Winchester, Lymington and Portsmouth; stately homes at Beaulieu and Stratfield Saye; and the Solent sea coast. Southern Tourist Board, Tel: Eastleigh 616027.

157. AVINGTON
Village and trout fishing

A small village in the Itchen valley with a 17th-century mansion once occupied by Charles II and Nell Gwynn, and a stillwater fishery which has become famous for its development of fast-growing rainbow trout. Avington Trout Fishery is open daily, Apr to Sept, and offers fishing on three lakes plus a stretch of a tributary of the Itchen. The current British record – a 19lb 8oz (8.8kg) fish – came from these waters. Tel: Itchen Abbas 312.
□ Four miles (6.4km) NE of Winchester off B3047. Map ref 5A3.

158. BREAMORE COUNTRYSIDE MUSEUM
Farm museum

This exhibition in the grounds of an Elizabethan Manor House is arranged according to the year's farming calendar, from ploughing in the winter to root-crop harvesting in the autumn. As well as a collection of hand-tools, there are vintage tractors and several stationary engines used to work barn machinery. Indoor displays include a farm worker's cottage before electricity. There is also the Breamore Carriage Museum set in the 17th-century stables of the house with a selection of 19th-century carts, carriages and chaises. The museum (and house) are open daily, afternoons, except non-Bank Holiday Mons and Fris, Apr to Sept. Tel: Breamore 468.
□ At Breamore House, Breamore, nine miles (14km) S of Salisbury on A338. Map ref 5A3.

159. BUCKLER'S HARD
18th-century riverside village

The sheltered waters of the Beaulieu river near Buckler's Hard offer fine sailing, with the river remaining navigable as far north as Palace House, the home of Lord Montagu at Beaulieu on the edge of the New Forest. One of Lord Montagu's predecessors had intended to turn Buckler's Hard itself into a port, but it never really developed that way. However, the present Lord Montagu is developing the village into something like an adjunct of Beaulieu. Cars, for instance, are channelled towards car parks where individuals (as well as cars) have to pay entrance fees to the village whether they wish to stay for a few minutes or a full day. Nevertheless, Buckler's Hard remains an attractive, largely 18th-century riverside village with the restoration being carried out with evident care. The shipyard which once built ships for the Napoleonic wars is also being restored and there is a Maritime Museum, open throughout the year. Tel: Buckler's Hard 203. The 'free' way to see the village is to walk there from Beaulieu along the riverside path. Non-sailors can join cruises which operate May to Sept.
□ Five miles (8km) NE of Lymington off B3054. Map ref 5A4.

160. BUTSER ANCIENT FARM
Iron Age agriculture

Within the 1400 acres (463 hectares) of open downland and forest which comprise the Queen Elizabeth country park, there is one section of special interest: Butser Ancient Farm Demonstration area, a unique project begun in 1972 to investigate the Iron Age, basing its research on a reconstruction of a farm building dating from 300 BC. Its most impressive feature is probably Pimperne House, the largest reconstruction anywhere of an Iron Age structure. There are also crops and livestock appropriate to the period. On the lower slopes of 889ft (274m) Butser Hill, there are regular demonstrations of sheep management, including sheep-rearing and sheepdog handling. Other features of the country park are forest walks, bridleways and views. The park is open daily throughout the year but the reception centre is open daily only from Apr to Oct. During Nov the centre is closed Mon and Sat; from Dec to Feb it is open only on Sun. The farm demonstration area is open from May to Sept during afternoons, plus Sun and Bank Holiday mornings. Tel: Horndean 595040.

☐ Two miles (3.2km) S of Petersfield on A3 to Horndean. Map ref 5B3.

161. DANEBURY
Hill-fort with nature trail

The Iron Age hill-fort lies within relatively modest ramparts, but the site is an important one: excavations have shown a complex history dating back to the Bronze Age. Now its ramparts and central area of 13 acres (5.3 hectares) are dotted with trees – and 20th-century picnickers. A nature trail winds round the fortifications; leaflets should be available from an 'honesty box' at the site.

☐ 4½ miles (7km) S of Andover signposted off minor road between A343 and A30. Map ref 5A3.

162. HILLIER ARBORETUM
Trees and shrubs

The largest collection in the world of trees and shrubs from temperate regions. There are also dwarf bulbs, camellias, azaleas, magnolias and a bog garden in this arboretum which was founded by Harold Hillier of the well known nursery firm. Open throughout the year Mon to Fri plus weekend and Bank Holiday afternoons from Apr to Oct. Tel: Braishfield 68787.

☐ At Ampfield, three miles (4.8km) E of Romsey off A31. Map ref 5A3.

163. HURST CASTLE
Sea castle

This castle was built in the 16th century by Henry VIII to command the narrowest entrance to Southampton Water. It stands at the end of a shingle spit from the mainland, barely half a mile (0.8km) from the shores of the Isle of Wight. The castle can be reached either by walking along this 1½ mile (2.4km) long spit known as Hurst Beach or, during the summer, by ferry from Keyhaven. The castle is open standard DoE hours plus Sun mornings Apr to Sept.

☐ Four miles (6.4km) SE of Lymington off B3058. Map ref 5A4.

164. MOTTISFONT ABBEY
Priory garden

Originally a 12th-century Augustinian priory, although the house itself underwent major changes in the 18th century. The grounds, which are bordered by the River Test, include old roses, a knot garden and a pleached avenue – a tree-lined walk where the branches are arched over and interlaced. The grounds are open afternoons Tues to Sat, Apr to Sept; the house Wed and Sat afternoons only, same months. NT. Tel: Lockerley 40757.

☐ 4½ miles NW of Romsey off A3057. Map ref 5A3.

165. NEW FOREST
Old hunting forest

This is the largest expanse of unenclosed land in the south of England. Once a royal hunting forest, it covers 145 sq miles (371 sq km) the bulk of which is managed by the Forestry Commission. The FC provides over 140 car parks and picnic places, controlled camping areas and forest walks. Details of facilities and leaflets available from Lyndhurst Information Centre at public car park in village. Open Easter to Sept, Tel: Lyndhurst 2269. Recommended guide book: *Explore the New Forest*. Ponies, cattle and pigs graze the open forest, and there are four species of deer. Among forest highlights are the Bolderwood Woodland Walks from Bolderwood car park on by-road from Lyndhurst via Emery Down; Blackwater, Tall Trees and Brock Hill walks, all starting

Southern England

off the southern stretch of the Ornamental Drive (see map), two miles (3.2km) west of Lyndhurst off A35; Ober Water walks from White-

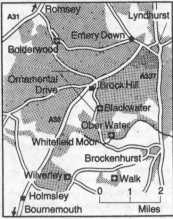

New Forest: waymarked walks and picnic places open up the ancient forest of kings

field Moor car park on by-road two miles (3.2km) west of Brockenhurst; and Wilverley Walk (2¾ miles, 4.4km) from Wilverley Plain car park on Brockenhurst to Holmsley road. OS 1:25,000 Outdoor Leisure map for the New Forest is invaluable

☐ The forest is SW of Southampton and NE of Bournemouth. Map ref 5A4.

166. PORTCHESTER
Roman and Norman sea fort

The best preserved of the Roman sea forts, with its walls and gateways from about AD 300 the most perfectly intact in northern Europe. The site is an excellent example of the continuity of settlement within the British Isles. Even before the Romans, there is evidence of prehistoric occupation in the form of a rampart. And after the Romans came the Normans who used the Roman walls to enclose a splendid castle and church, both dating from the 12th century. The keep of the castle is open standard DoE hours plus Sun mornings Apr to Sept. Beyond its moat the grassy compound within the castle walls forms what must be one of the

most richly historic settings for cricket anywhere in England. (See also Day Out 149 for map of all the Roman Saxon Shore Forts.)

☐ Half a mile (0.8km) S of A27 between Portsmouth and Fareham. Map ref 5A4.

167. ROMSEY
Norman abbey and river valley

Romsey Abbey dates from the 10th century and although it was changed and enlarged by the Normans it contains some carving which is believed to have survived from Saxon times. The abbey dominates this little market town but it is not the only building of either distinction or antiquity. Near the abbey is King John's House, a 13th-century house built possibly as a hunting lodge for exploring the New Forest. Nowadays, the sportsmen who head towards Romsey are more likely to be anglers since the town stands on the banks of the River Test, generally recognised as the supreme trout fishing water in the country. Market days in Romsey are Friday and Saturday. Just south of the town is Broadlands, the 18th-century former home of Lord Palmerston and the late Lord Mountbatten. The house stands in grounds landscaped by 'Capability' Brown and is open daily Apr to Oct except non-Bank Holiday Mons. Tel: Romsey 516878.

☐ Six miles (9.6km) NW of Southampton on A3057. Map ref 5A3.

168. SELBORNE
Literary village

This village is firmly associated with the naturalist Gilbert White (1720–93), and Selborne Hanger or Hill, where he made many of the observations recorded in his most famous work, *The Natural History of Selborne*, is now protected and owned by the NT. White's former home, The Wakes, is a museum dedicated to the life and works of both White and the Antarctic explorer Captain Oates; it is open afternoons Tues to Sun, plus Bank Holiday Mons, from Mar to Oct. Tel:

Selborne 275. Three miles (5km) up the road is an even more famous literary shrine: Chawton, the final home of novelist Jane Austen. Here, too, there is a museum in the former family home. Tel: Alton 83262 for details.

☐ Selborne is four miles (6.4km) SE of Alton on B3006; Selborne Hill is SW of B3006 between Selborne and Newton Valence. Map ref 5B3.

169. SILCHESTER
Abandoned Roman city

Calleva Atrebatum was a Roman regional capital in Hampshire and one of the few Roman towns of any size to remain deserted – the modern village of Silchester is smaller than its predecessor and on a separate site a short distance to the west. The Roman walls of flint bonded with blocks of chalk still exist, however, and enclose 120 acres (49 hectares) of farmland with a tiny medieval church standing close to the former eastern gate of the town. Although no buildings other than the walls are visible, the lack of later development means that the foundations of all the Roman buildings, including a church, remain intact beneath the surface. Outside the walls near the eastern gate (where a farm, like the church, incorporates some of the Roman wall) a hollow in the ground marks the site of the former amphitheatre. A small museum exists half a mile north of the modern village of Silchester.

☐ Between Reading and Basingstoke in a tangle of lanes off A340 and A33. Map ref 5A3.

170. WAGGONERS' WELLS
Hammer ponds

The ponds are a reminder that this stretch of apparently unspoilt countryside was once part of a thriving iron industry. Wakeners' Wells, as they were originally called, were the site of an iron foundry as long ago as the 16th century with the water being stored in the ponds to power the wheels and hammers of the foundry. Now they are owned by the NT, along with large tracts of the surrounding land including Ludshott Common and Bramshott Chase. Leaflets describing NT nature trails are available from post office and newsagent in Grayshott village.

☐ 1½ miles (2.4km) SW of Hindhead between the A3 and B3002. Map ref 5B3.

171. WELLINGTON
Parkland fun and dairy museum

A park covering nearly 600 acres (243 hectares) and what seems at first glance almost as many interests. The park is on the Duke of Wellington's estate and it contrives to offer both unspoilt woodland and parkland (nature trails, bridleways, fishing etc) and a developed leisure area (crazy golf, adventure playground, model boats, miniature steam railway etc). There is also a lake with facilities for rowing and canoeing. A national dairy museum displays a collection of past dairy equipment and, like the park, is open daily Mar to Oct, weekends Nov to Feb. Tel: Heckfield 444 or Basingstoke 882882. The Wellington stately home, Stratfield Saye House, and its grounds are 2½ miles (4km) away and open Easter to Sept. Tel: Turgis Green 602.

☐ Seven miles (11km) S of Reading near junction of A33 and A32. Map ref 5B3.

Isle of Wight

Separated from the mainland by the Solent. Coastal resorts include Shanklin, Ryde and Ventnor. Isle of Wight Tourist Board, Tel: Newport 524343.

172. ALUM BAY
Cliffs of many colours and long-distance trails

This bay, just north of the Needles, is famous for its sand cliffs which are striped vertically in 21 different colours ranging from chocolate brown to strawberry pink. Local shops sell souvenirs as it is dangerous for visitors to scramble up the cliffs to collect their own. A chair lift operates from the cliffs to the beach in summer. The Needles, a line of jagged chalk sea stacks with a lighthouse (not open to the public), are best seen from the Coastguard station on the headland south-west of Alum Bay. Also nearby is Tennyson's Down, named after the poet who walked here regularly from his home in Freshwater.

The Isle of Wight County Council has devised a 15 mile (24km) Tennyson Trail from Alum Bay to Carisbrooke through forest and downland with fine sea views. It is one of seven long-distance trails on the island; all are waymarked and described in excellent leaflets available from tourist information offices. OS map 196 shows the paths, but even better is the county council's own footpath map, 'Long Distance Trails and other Public Rights of Way'. For details of all walks on the island – from a 60 mile (96km) coastal path, to six short nature trails – contact the tourist board. Tel: Newport 524343.
□ Four miles (6.4km) S of Ryde on A3055. Map ref 5A4.

173. BRADING
Roman villa

The fine mosaic pavements which have survived and which can be seen here indicate that it was something approaching a country house. But the manner in which the buildings are grouped around an open courtyard is a reminder that this, like most villas, was essentially the centre of a farm or estate with the 'courtyard' probably the equivalent of a superior farmyard. The villa is open daily in summer. In Brading itself the old town hall preserves stocks, a whipping-post and a bull-baiting ring.
□ Four miles (6.4km) S of Ryde on A3055. Map ref 5A4.

174. BRIGHTSTONE
Forest walk

The Brightstone Jubilee Walk was laid out by the Forestry Commission in 1969 to commemorate the 50th anniversary of the forest. The full walk – waymarked by green stakes – is 2½

miles (4km) but short cuts shown by red and blue stakes reduce this to respectively one or 1¾ miles (1.6 or 2.8km). The walk passes over open downland as well as woodland with some fine views. An FC leaflet is available describing the wildlife which might be seen along the route. Details from tourist board. Tel: Newport 524343.
□ Trail starts at NT car park at the top of Brightstone Down, 1¼ miles (2km) N of Brightstone near junction of B55 and B58. Map ref 5A4.

175. COWES
Yachting and a royal house

The yachting centre of the British Isles – some would say the world – with the headquarters of the Royal Yacht Squadron housed in Cowes Castle. Yachts of all shapes and sizes can be seen here throughout the year, but most especially during the eight days of Cowes Week beginning each year on the first Saturday in August. Unevenly numbered years – 1981, 1983 etc – are best of all, since in those years around 20 national teams from all over the world compete for the Admiral's Cup. Cowes itself is divided into two halves, east and west, by the Medina estuary. One mile south-east of East Cowes is Osborne House, said to have been Queen Victoria's favourite residence, and open to the public Mon to Sat, Easter to early Oct. Tel: Cowes 292511 for further information.
□ Cowes is at the northern tip of the Isle of Wight on the A3021 (to East Cowes) and A3020 (to West Cowes). Map ref 5A4.

176. FIRESTONE COPSE
Woodland trails

Three waymarked paths lead from a car park and picnic area through mainly conifers and some oak and beech to Blackridge Brook with fine views of Wootton Creek. The main walk – waymarked in green – is 1¾ miles (2.8km). Another, shown by yellow markers, is one mile (1.6km) while the third, with blue markers, is only ¼ mile

(0.4km). The Forestry Commission also provides picnic areas in small glades in a young beechwood.

□ SE of Wootton Bridge ¾ mile (1.2km) along minor road to Havenstreet. Map ref 5A4.

177. ROBIN HILL
Country park

This extends over 80 acres (32 hectares) of down, woodland and meadow. Much of the park remains in its natural state, providing an excellent habitat for wildlife of all kinds. The water gardens, on which work began in 1978, create an interesting addition for botanical enthusiasts. There is a walk through the 10 acre (four hectares) animal enclosure while for children there are a 'jungle house', a commando-style assault course and, in high season, donkey and pony rides. Open daily from Mar to Oct; during July and Aug it is open until midnight – for barbecues. Leaflet available. Tel: Newport 527352.

□ The park is situated at Downend, about three miles (4.8km) SW of Newport. Map ref 5A4

178. ST CATHERINE'S POINT
'Riviera' vegetation and lighthouse

Running eastwards from this most southerly point of the island for some six miles (9.6km) to Ventnor is a remarkable ledge just above sea level. This ledge is composed of a series of landslips and is so sheltered that a variety of semi-tropical trees and shrubs have flourished to give the area an almost Riviera flavour. The landslip is featured (and explained) in the Geology Museum at Sandown Public Library. Open Mon to Sat. Tel: Sandown 402748. At St Catherine's Point itself is a castellated lighthouse nicknamed the 'cow and calf' because of the smaller matching fog signal tower standing beside it. The lighthouse is open to the public at certain times. Tel: Niton 730284.

□ Six miles (9.6km) SW of Ventnor off A3055. Map ref 5A4.

179. YAFFORD MILL
Mill museum

The present mill at Yafford dates from the 19th century, although the foundations suggest the possibility of medieval origins. It was fully working until 1970 and was principally a grist mill for grinding animal foodstuffs. It now contains a collection of agricultural tools in common use until the 1950s. There is also a collection of Isle of Wight waggons, in the process of being restored and repainted in traditional livery. One unique feature of Yafford Mill is its Seal Pool, specially constructed below the millrace, as a centre for the Grey Seal. Open daily Easter to Oct, but afternoons only Sun. Tel: Brighthouse 740610.

□ W of Shorwell on B3399 five miles (8km) SW of Newport. Map ref 5A4.

Kent

Known as 'The Garden of England' but landscapes range from the North Downs to Romney Marsh with long stretches of coastline. Attractions also include Canterbury Cathedral, the moated Leeds Castle near Sevenoaks, the country home of Sir Winston Churchill at Chartwell, and Knole. South-East England Tourist Board, Tel: Tunbridge Wells 40766.

180. BARFRESTON
Norman church

The small Church of St Nicholas was built partly of flint and partly of limestone imported from Caen, a vehicle for more delicate carving than the tougher sandstone of Kilpeck (Day Out 414). However, the stone is not so durable and the church is therefore much more restored – yet it is more authentic than Dalmeny and Leuchars, the two Scottish examples of this type. The principal pleasures are external, especially the very rich south door and the unusual wheel window at the east end, also profusely adorned.

□ Ten miles (16km) SE of Canterbury on minor roads off A2. Map ref 7C1.

Southern England

181. BEDGEBURY PINETUM
Coniferous trees and village

Nearly 100 acres (40 hectares) of hill and valley planted by the Forestry Commission and the Royal Botanic Gardens, Kew, as a national collection of coniferous trees. With more than 200 species, the Pinetum claims to have the most comprehensive collection of coniferous trees in Europe. It is beautifully landscaped with many broad-leaved trees to improve the pictorial effects and to increase autumn leaf colour. The Pinetum is open throughout the year. Tel: Goudhurst 211392. The nearby village of Goudhurst is one of the most attractive in the county, with not only fine houses, inns and a 15th-century church but also a thatched pond shelter for ducks and swans.
□ The Pinetum is at Bedgebury, two miles (3.2km) S of Goudhurst on B2079; Goudhurst is 10 miles (16km) E of Tunbridge Wells. Map ref 7B2.

182. CHIDDINGSTONE
Half-timbered village

The church has 13th-century origins and a fine Perpendicular tower, but the houses facing the church are the real glory of this village which is largely owned by the NT. A row of outstanding half-timbered buildings date from the 16th and 17th centuries. Chiddingstone Castle is an 18th-century restoration of a much earlier manor house. it is open daily except Mon, Mar to Oct. Tel: Penshurst 870347. Also nearby is Penshurst Place, a country house renowned for its medieval hall and Tudor garden. Tel: Penshurst 870307.

□ Five miles (8km) NW of Tunbridge Wells off B2027 or B2176. Map ref 7B2.

183. DOVER
Roman lighthouse and Norman castle

The castle high on the clifftops to the east of the town dates from shortly after the Norman Conquest, though many additions and alterations were made in succeeding centuries. It is an impressive structure with walls 100ft (31m) high and up to 21ft (7.5m) thick. The hilltop site also shows evidence of occupation from even earlier times, most notably the 40ft (12m) high remains of a Roman lighthouse which stands beside a Saxon church within the castle. Dover was one of the Roman forts of the Saxon shore (*Dubris*) and the site continued to be important in controlling the biggest harbour on the shortest sea crossing to France. The castle is open standard DoE hours (plus Sun mornings Apr to Sept) and affords stunning views of the channel.

Other interesting buildings in Dover include Crabble Watermill in Lower Road and a well preserved Roman house in New Street. Both are open to the public during summer months, although opening days and times differ. For details, telephone respectively Dover 201066 or Dover 203279.
□ The castle is to the E of the town. Map ref 7D2.

184. DUNGENESS
Bird-watching

The RSPB has a 1190 acre (482 hectare) reserve on this vast and unique foreland of windswept shingle, which is on one of the main flight paths

The Straits of Dover are surprisingly shallow. Not even at their deepest would they drown St Paul's Cathedral

for migrating birds. Here, almost in the shadow of Dungeness nuclear power station, 270 different species of bird have been recorded. Flooded gravel pits attract wintering ducks and waders. Breeding species include little tern, wheatear, ringed plover and great crested grebe. The area is also famed for its loudly croaking marsh frogs and typical flowers of the shingle shore. The reserve is open all year on Wed, Thur, Sat and Sun, and a small charge is made for admission. Visitors should report to warden's house at reserve entrance (Boulderwall Farmhouse, Dungeness Road, Lydd, Kent TN29 9PN). A leaflet is available.
☐ Lydd is eight miles (13km) E of Rye on B2076. Map ref 7C2.

185. EYNSFORD
Roman villa with chapel

An attractive forded village on the River Darent with the remains of a castle including a ditch and flint-rubble walls. Also nearby are Lullingstone Castle, largely rebuilt in the 18th century but with some Tudor elements, and Lullingstone Villa, the finest Roman villa within easy reach of London. The villa was discovered only in 1949 under the sludge and hill-wash of 15 centuries. Its history, well told in an imaginative museum on the site, reflects the experience of many villas whereby original farmhouses were rebuilt as grander country mansions. But the villa also contains the only Christian chapel to have been found in any Roman villa within Britain. Open daily all year, although hours vary. Tel: Farningham 863467.
☐ Midway between Sevenoaks and Dartford on A225. Map ref 7B1.

186. HEVER CASTLE
Gardens with statuary

This delightful little castle, dating from the 13th century and once the home of Anne Boleyn, acquired its garden in the early years of this century when it was bought by William Waldorf Astor, 1st Viscount Astor of Hever. Part of it, in Italian style, was specially designed for the display of a large collection of Roman statues and antiquities. Other features are a grotto garden with many fountains, a rose garden, herbaceous borders, a rock garden, water lilies in two moats, a set of chessmen cut from yew, a maze and a vast landscaped lake overlooked by a colonnaded piazza. The castle and gardens are usually open afternoons on Tues, Wed, Fri (except Good Friday), Sun and Bank Holiday Mons. Tel: Edenbridge 862205.
☐ Three miles (5km) SE of Edenbridge off B2026. Map ref 7B2.

187. HIGH ROCKS
Picnics and rock-climbing

To the west of the elegant spa town of Tunbridge Wells is an area of heathland rising to the impressive sandstone outcrop known as High Rocks. It is an ideal spot for walks and picnics or to watch rock-climbers performing on the vertical crags. Similar rock faces occur at Harrison's Rocks in neighbouring Groombridge and at Barle's Rocks, Eridge, where on payment of a fee visitors may use the grounds of the Bowles Outdoor Pursuits Centre. Open daily all year. Tel: Crowborough 4127.
☐ High Rocks is two miles (3.2km) W of Tunbridge Wells S of A264. Map ref 7B2.

188. HOLLINGBOURNE
Downland walk

There are several interesting old buildings in the village of Hollingbourne but none are so old as the Pilgrim's Way which traverses the nearby North Downs. In fact, this ancient trackway from Winchester to Canterbury was used long before Christianity established itself at Canterbury or anywhere else in the British Isles. Today it forms part of the long-distance North Downs Way and Hollingbourne can be the base for a short seven mile (11km) circuit incorporating this and other footpaths (see map overleaf). Follow first waymarked Greenway path to Har-

Southern England

Hollingbourne: a walk along the North Downs

rietsham, turn left at Harrietsham Church and climb to where the waymarked Pilgrim's Way path crosses the road. Return along this to the Pilgrim's Rest Inn and Hollingbourne. The walk straddles the borders of no fewer than three OS maps – 178, 188 and 189.

□ Hollingbourne is on B2163, one mile (1.6km) NW of junction M20 and A20 E of Maidstone. Map ref 7C1.

189. HOO PENINSULA
Roman field patterns and heronry

This peninsula between the Thames and the Medway can claim a survival of Roman land management known as 'centuriation'. This involved land being parcelled out in blocks measuring approximately 1500 by 750 yards (142m by 71m) and many academics believe the field patterns around the village of Cliffe in particular have remained unchanged in these dimensions since Roman times. The peninsula also has an RSPB reserve with the largest heronry in the United Kingdom. Over 200 pairs breed here in the reserve in mixed woodland and scrub on the edge of the North Kent marshes. A nature trail starts from Northward Avenue in High Halstow. Tel: RSPB Reserves Dept, Sandy 80551.

□ Cliffe and High Halstow are both approx five miles (8km) N of Rochester on the B2000 and A228 respectively. Map ref 7C1.

190. IGHTHAM MOTE
Moated house

A medieval moat-encircled house hidden in the woods of the Kentish Weald. It grew round a courtyard from the early 14th till the early 16th century, starting with the great hall, and ending with the chapel. It was never at all grand; and the mellow and peaceful mixture of stone, brick and half-timbering that resulted is irresistible. The surrounding grounds are simple with an upper lake feeding the moat itself. Open Fri afternoons throughout the year and Sun afternoons Apr to Sept. Tel: Sevenoaks 62235.

□ Six miles (9.6km) SE of Sevenoaks off A25 or A227. Map ref 7B1.

191. KNOLE
Country house and deer park

The house is one of the largest in England. It was begun in 1456 by Thomas Bourchier, Archbishop of Canterbury, and greatly extended in the early 17th century by the Sackville family to whom it had been granted by Elizabeth I. There is a series of fine state rooms containing rare furniture, rugs and tapestries dating largely from the 17th and 18th centuries. The house is now owned by the NT and is open daily Wed to Sat plus Sun afternoons and Bank Holidays from Apr to Nov, although hours are shorter in Oct and Nov. Since last admission to the house is one hour before closing, it might be prudent to check hours. Tel: Sevenoaks 53006. (The garden is open only on the first Wed of each month from May to Sept but it is for its park rather than its garden that Knole is renowned.) The 1000 acre (400 hectare) park which surrounds the house is well wooded with oak, chestnut and beech. Vast herds of deer roam freely around the park, so maintaining a practice which has been in existence ever since the house was established. The park is open daily throughout the year and is free for pedestrians.

□ One mile (1.6km) SE of Sevenoaks off A225 to Tonbridge. Map ref 7B1.

192. LAMBERHURST
Abbey and romantic garden

This village is on a busy road but amid some delightful Wealden scenery. It is an altogether unlikely place to have been an important industrial centre yet such it was during the 16th and 17th centuries. A faint echo of those times comes from following the little River Teise west of Lamberhurst to Furnace Mill, an 18th-century corn mill (not open to the public) erected on the site of a watermill that once served a major iron foundry. The mill though is no longer on the river.

A little further west, however, the Teise was dammed to form a 'hammer pond' which now survives as a natural-looking lake close to the remains of Bayham Abbey. The ruins of the 12th-century abbey are among the most notable in south-east England; they are open standard DoE hours plus Sun mornings, Apr to Sept. Also close to Lamberhurst, and worth a visit, are the new reservoir at Bewl Bridge and Scotney Castle Garden, 1½ miles (2.4km) south-east of the village on A21.

At the latter the garden is set around a partly-ruined 14th century moated castle. In the 19th century the ruins were used to create a picturesque landscape with native and exotic trees and shrubs which are particularly memorable in autumn. An unusual ice-well, thatched with heather and used in the days before refrigerators, is a feature of the garden which is open daily except Mon and Tues, Apr to Oct. Tel: Lamberhurst 890306.
□ Seven miles (11km) E of Tunbridge Wells on A21. Map ref 7B2.

193. MEDWAY RIVER
River and estuary sailing

The river has a non-tidal part, with several locks, running deep into the heart of Kent. It is navigable to just beyond Tonbridge and is pleasant motor cruising country for those who are in no hurry. At Allington Castle, just north of Maidstone, the river becomes tidal to Sheerness off the Thames estuary. From a wiggling river, close to green fields and villages, it thus opens out into a wide delta of marshes, mud flats and creeks. This provides wonderful dinghy sailing water with all the room in the world at high tide, and a testing channel and twisting creeks to tack through at low water. The easiest access to the tidal reaches is the slipway at Upnor just north of Strood and Rochester. There is also a country park at Eastcourt Meadows bordering the estuary at Gillingham.
□ Map ref 7C1.

194. PARK WOOD
Woodland wildlife

One of the best examples of mixed woodland in East Kent, Park Wood nearly fell victim to the chain saw. Now, owned and managed by the Woodland Trust, visitors are welcome and its trees – hornbeam, oak, beech, and chestnut coppice – are secure. It is an ideal habitat for woodland song-birds such as blackcap, willow warbler and chiffchaff. There is also rich ground plant and insect life. Fur further information, Tel: Grantham 74297.
□ On A252 SW of Chilham which is five miles (8km) SW of Canterbury. Map ref 7C1.

195. RICHBOROUGH
Roman fort and port

To the Romans it was *Portus Rutupis* and the main port of entry and departure between Britain and mainland Europe. The invading forces landed not far from Richborough where one of their sea forts was later built. It guarded the south-east entrance of the then navigable Wantsum Channel – the stretch of water which made the Isle of Thanet an island – while another fort and port, Reculver, near what is now Herne Bay, controlled the northern approach.

The Wantsum Channel has long since vanished – a combination of natural silting and monastic reclamation that was completed by the 18th century. Richborough is now inland but it remains one of the greatest monuments to the Roman age with high flint walls dating from the 3rd century. The greatest mystery of Richborough is the huge mortar emplacement cross within the fort. Suggestions vary as to its function but it could be the foundations of a monument to mark the original invasion, or a lighthouse. It could even have been both: a monument ornamented with marble, later stripped to assume a more functional purpose.

There is a small museum on the site which, like the remains, is open standard DoE hours plus Sun morning Apr to Sept. Tel: Sandwich 612013. Some Roman remains also exist at Reculver but they are less notable.

☐ Two miles (3.2km) NW of Sandwich on minor roads off A257. Map ref 7D1.

196. SALMESTONE GRANGE
Monastic remains

The word 'grange' was used to denote an outlying farm of a monastery. In this case it was a Benedictine grange of St Augustine's Priory at Canterbury which played an important role in the reclamation of the Wantsum Channel (see also Richborough). Salmestone Grange is now maintained as a sanctuary for wild flowers. Open every afternoon May to Sept or by appointment. Tel: Thanet 21136.

☐ In Nash Road, Margate. Map ref 7D1.

197. SANDWICH
Medieval port and nature reserve

One of the Cinque ports, Sandwich survived the silting up of the Wantsum Channel (see also Richborough) but not for long. The River Stour which divides Pegwell Bay from Sandwich Bay also began to silt up from the 15th century, thus eroding Sandwich's importance as a commercial port. It still has a quay but today it serves only the occasional fishing vessel and pleasure craft.

Two miles (3.2km) north-east of the town to the south of the Stour is an NT nature reserve covering more than 200 acres (81 hectares) of coastal saltings and dunes. Access either via New Downs Farm or along the beach by toll road from Prince's Golf Club; for details, leaflets etc, contact Kent Trust for Nature Conservation, 125 High Street, Rainham, Kent. Tel: Medway 362561.

☐ Five miles (8km) NW of Deal. Map ref 7D1.

198. SISSINGHURST CASTLE
Romantic garden

The Sissinghurst Castle garden was made by Sir Harold Nicolson and his wife, Vita Sackville-West, between 1930 and her death in 1962, around the remnants of an Elizabethan house and two cottages. It consists of a series of enclosures, skilfully integrated, but each with its own distinctive design and planting. Plant associations have been studied with exceptional care. The garden's justified fame makes it vulnerable to serious overcrowding at weekends. It is open afternoons daily except Mon, Apr to mid-Oct. Tel: Sissinghurst 712850.

☐ The garden is one mile (1.6km) E of Sissinghurst off A262. Map ref 7B2.

199. TENTERDEN
Weatherboarded houses

A market town stretched out along a wide grass-verged main street typical of towns that once served as centres for large sheep markets (compare the high streets of Marlborough or Thame, for instance). But long before it was a main street or market-place it was a drovers' road for taking sheep to and fro between Romney Marsh and Thanet. Tenterden is remarkable for its large number of houses with exquisitely maintained white timber weatherboarding, reflecting the continuation of both a local style and local prosperity. Steam railway services are being revived over a short stretch of track from Tenterden during the summer. Tel: Tenterden 2943.

☐ Tenterden is 10 miles (16km) SW of Ashford on A28. Map ref 7C2.

200. TOYS HILL
Viewpoint and woodland walks

This is the highest point in Kent with good views of the Weald. The woods are mainly beech, many of which are pollarded and are very old, with oak, birch and pine. Wood and heathland walks lead from the car park.
□ 2½ miles (4km) S of A25 at Brasted. Map ref 7B1.

201. WYE
Nature reserve

The Wye National Nature Reserve forms one of the finest examples of grass and woodland habitat on the North Downs and is particularly rich in butterflies. Over 25 species occur in the reserve, especially over the open grassland where chalkland flowers such as salad burnet, wild thyme and rockrose and several kinds of orchid abound. There are also some fine trees of the chalk: yew, whitebeam, and magnificent beech. There is a nature trail and information centre. Tel: Wye 812791.
□ Four miles (6.4km) NE of Ashford off minor road between Wye and Hastingleigh. Map ref 7C2.

Surrey

Much beautiful countryside remains in London's commuter country, notably around the North Downs. Attractions include villages such as Chiddingfold and Shere; Guildford; viewpoints such as Box Hill and Leith Hill near Dorking; and Runnymede. South-East England Tourist Board, Tel: Tunbridge Wells 40766.

202. ABINGER HAMMER
Industrial archaeology and walks

Few places in the countryside of Kent or Surrey reveal their unexpected industrial past as explicitly as this attractive hamlet at the southern foot of the North Downs. The word 'hammer' comes from its days as a centre of the Wealden iron industry. Rivers were dammed to form ponds from which water was released with sufficient power to drive the wheels of watermills which operated the heavy hammers of local iron works. They are still known as hammer ponds (as at Abinger and nearby at the delightful Friday Street) or furnace ponds (as at Cowden in Kent). Sometimes, too, the remains of old furnaces can still be found, but far more widespread is the survival of the wood furnace or forge as applied to farms, woods or streams. At Abinger Hammer another clue to its industrial past is an old clock in the main street depicting a blacksmith at his trade.
□ Abinger Hammer is 4½ miles (7km) W of Dorking on A25; Friday Street is on minor roads south of Abinger Hammer. Map ref 7A1.

203. ALICE HOLT FOREST
Forest and wildlife trails

A former royal hunting forest straddling the Surrey–Hampshire border with associations going back through naval history to Roman times. Attractions include picnic places, forest and wildlife trails and coarse fishing. Arboretum trail, starting at Lodge Enclosure picnic place, is suitable for wheelchairs; Goose Green Trail leads into oak woodland planted in 1820; and Abinger Ranmore Forest Walk is on lip of North Downs escarpment with views to Dorking, Leith Hill and over the Weald. There is an information centre ¼ mile (400m) SE of A325 at Bucks Horn Oak – take road to Duckenfield. The centre is open weekdays throughout the year and weekend afternoons during the summer. Tel: Bentley 3135.

□ Four miles (6.4km) S of Farnham off A325 as described above. Map ref 5B3.

204. CLAREMONT
Landscape garden

The earliest surviving English landscape garden, begun by Vanbrugh and Bridgeman before 1720 and extended and 'naturalised' by Kent. The NT completed the restoration of these lovely gardens in 1979. They now include a lake, which has an island with a pavilion, a grotto and a turf amphitheatre as well as viewpoints and avenues in true 18th-century style. Open every day. (Claremont House, not NT, is an 18th-century Palladian mansion, now a school, open only on the afternoons of first weekend of the month, Feb to Nov. Tel: Esher 67841.)

□ ½ mile (0.8km) SE of Esher, E of A307. Map ref 7A1.

205. DEVIL'S PUNCHBOWL
Viewpoint and nature trails

Below the magnificent viewpoint of Gibbet Hill, standing at 894ft (272m), the sandy heathlands of the Surrey 'Highlands' are trenched with deep combes such as the spectacular Devil's Punchbowl with its steep slopes covered in gorse and pine. Numerous footpaths criss-cross Hindhead Commons (NT) and there are opportunities to see four species of deer. The Punchbowl nature trail (NT) starts from the southern rim, marked by orange signposts, covering 2½ miles (4km). The Gibbet Hill nature trail starts from the car park on the A3, marked by white signposts, and covers nearly two miles (3.2km); a leaflet is available from café in car park or for 10p plus s.a.e. from the Hon. Sec., Hindhead Committee, Littleshaw, Hindhead, Surrey. Note the contrast in the scenery between the sandstone ridge and its heathland and the neighbouring chalkland of the South and North Downs.

□ Off A3 or A287 from Hindhead which is 13 miles (21km) SW of Guildford on A3. Map ref 5B3.

206. FRENSHAM COMMON
Antiquities and country park

Prehistoric remains are rare in Surrey, partly because of the development of villages and towns as commuter bases for London. But on the crest of Frensham Common there is a line of barrows. Also on Frensham Common, an area of some 900 acres (364 hectares), is a country park. The area is generally flat, apart from three significant ridges. The outstanding features of the park are its extensive heather heathlands and the Great and Little Ponds. The Great Pond has a sandy beach area around the shoreline and provides opportunities for boating and fishing. The park is open daily throughout the year. General enquiries, Tel: Godalming 4104; Country Park Ranger service, Tel: Frensham 2416.

□ Main car park is off A287; four miles (6.4km) S of Farnham; smaller car parks are accessible from minor roads leaving A287. Charges are made for car parks Sun and Bank Holidays only. Map ref 5B3.

207. LEITH HILL
Views and walks

This sandstone escarpment is the highest point in south-east England at 965ft (295m). The NT owns part of the hill, including five acres (two hectares) near the summit where there is an 18th-century tower open to the public in good weather. From the top of this tower there are panoramic views over the surrounding woods and farmland.

An Iron Age hill-fort, Anstiebury Camp, can be seen on the eastern side of Leith Hill (grid ref TQ 153440). The village of Coldharbour is an attractive base for the ascent of Leith Hill. Cars can also be parked one mile (1.6km)

south-west of Coldharbour at Starveall Corner. Leith Hill is more sprawling than Box Hill and therefore usually less crowded.
□ Four miles (6.4km) SW of Dorking on minor roads. Map ref 7A1.

208. POLESDEN LACEY
Edwardian garden and Regency villa

The 18th-century landscape garden was extended in 1906 with herbaceous borders, a rose garden, hedges and beechwalks. The gardens are open daily throughout the year. The house, like the garden, is now owned by the NT. Originally a Regency villa, the house was also somewhat remodelled in Edwardian times. Between Apr and Oct the house is open daily except Fri and non-Bank Holiday Mons; in Mar and Nov it is open weekend afternoons only. Tel: Bookham 52048. Footpaths lead from the house through beechwoods to Ranmore Common, one mile (1.6km) to the south. The Common offers good walking along the escarpment of the North Downs.
□ Three miles (5km) NW of Dorking off A246. Map ref 7A1.

209. WINKWORTH ARBORETUM
Trees and shrubs

More than 100 acres (40 hectares) of trees and shrubs, begun in 1938. Spectacular autumn colours are best seen in mid-Oct, but the Arboretum is open throughout the year. Tel: NT regional office at Bookham 53401.
□ On E side of B2130, three miles (5km) SE of Godalming. Map ref 5B3.

210. WISLEY
Kaleidoscope of garden styles

The Royal Horticultural Society's Garden covers 60 acres (24 hectares) and almost every style of gardening, from formal to informal. It is especially renowned for its rock garden, heather garden, woodland garden and collection of rhododendrons and azaleas. It also has magnificent mixed borders, two rose gardens, demonstration gardens, trial grounds and splendidly stocked greenhouses. There are fruit and vegetable gardens in which new varieties are tested. There are also lakes, a formal canal pool and a walled garden. Open daily throughout the year, except Christmas Day. Tel: Ripley 2163.
□ One mile (1.6km) NE of Ripley on A3. Map ref 7A1.

211. WITLEY COMMON
Heathland nature trails

These 377 acres (153 hectares) of west Surrey heathland have a wide range of wildlife, much of which can be seen from three trails. The blue route in the central part of the common passes through woods, glades and heathland. The red route takes you by wet and dry heath, and woods of pine and birch. A more specialised trail, the orange route, pays particular attention to the effects of management on neighbouring Milford Common. Leaflets available from NT information centre which is open Apr to Oct. Tel: Wormley 3207.
□ Half mile (0.8km) SW of Milford between A3 and A286. Map ref 5B3:

West Sussex

The South Downs cross the county which also includes such well known coastal resorts as Bognor and Worthing. Other attractions include Arundel Castle, Goodwood House and Chichester with its cathedral, harbour and Roman Palace at nearby Fishbourne. South-East England Tourist Board, Tel: Tunbridge Wells 40766.

212. BRAMBER
Norman settlement

A small country town on the River Adur, which still has the model plan of a Norman settlement with castle and church connected by the main street. The castle, now in ruins, was destroyed during the Civil War and the town has suffered unduly and unjustly through being located on a main road. Some fine timber-framed buildings remain to help the town retain something of its old charm.

□ Five miles (8km) inland from Shoreham on A283. Map ref 7A2.

213. CISSBURY
Prehistoric fort and flint mines

On the highest point of a spur of the South Downs two miles (3.2km) inland from Worthing lies one of the largest Iron Age hill-forts in the country (grid ref TU 139080). The huge single rampart and ditch encloses 60 acres (24 hectares), and it is estimated that 60,000 tons of chalk rock went into the raising of the earthwork. At the western end of the fort and around the southern entrance the groundds heavily pocked with bumps and hollows — evidence of Neolithic (New Stone Age) flint mines second in importance only to those at Grimes Graves in Norfolk.

□ $\frac{3}{4}$ mile (1.5km) E of Findon off A24. Map ref 7A2.

214. FISHBOURNE
Roman palace

Nearby Chichester was an important Roman town, *Noviomagus*, which still partly reflects its original grid layout. But even this does not explain why Fishbourne should be the site of a Roman villa of such magnificence that it is more aptly described as a palace. This is the largest Roman dwelling ever found in the British Isles, with around 100 rooms rich with mosaics and gaily painted friezes. A formal garden in the Roman style has also been recreated on its original site. The history of the palace, which was laid out about AD75, is excellently displayed in a fine museum on the site, open daily Mar to Nov. Tel: Chichester 785859.

□ One mile (1.6km) W of Chichester off A27. Map ref 5B4.

215. HIGHDOWN
Chalk garden

This garden was made in the first half of the 20th century in a disused chalk quarry, and on the rather barren chalk down in front of it. Thanks to the skill of its creator, the late Sir Frederick Stern, in choosing the right plants, the quarry is now almost completely covered with growth, and the down has been converted into a well stocked garden which includes some very unusual plants and fine specimen trees. Open daily Apr to Oct; weekdays only Nov to Mar. Tel: Worthing Borough Council for details, Worthing 37111, ext 96.

□ At Goring-by-Sea W of Worthing on A259. Map ref 7A2.

216. LEONARDSLEE
Woodland garden

A wonderful collection of rhododendrons, azaleas, magnolias, camellias, acers and other exotic shrubs and trees in a well wooded valley with lakes. It is superbly landscaped and the autumn foliage colour is particularly good. It is usually open Wed, Thur, Sat, Sun and Bank Holiday Mons late April to early June, then weekends only in Oct. Tel: Lower Beeding 212.

□ In Lower Beeding $4\frac{1}{2}$ miles (7km) SE of Horsham on A281. Map ref 7A2.

217. MARDEN-STOUGHTON FOREST
Europe's finest yew trees

Marden-Stoughton forest, run by the Forestry Commission, is a stretch of fine beech woodland on the South Downs. It offers a beautifully secluded picnic area and a $1\frac{1}{2}$ mile (2.4km) walk through young beech and yew towards a viewpoint on Bow Hill. From here – weather permitting – there is a panoramic view towards the south coast from Worthing to the Isle of Wight. But it also overlooks Kingley Vale, an NCC nature reserve covering 361 acres (144 hectares) and protecting what is widely regarded as Europe's finest yew forest. The oldest yews (some are at least 500 years old) are found in a grove at the foot of the valley known as Kingley Bottom. A nature trail winds through the reserve throughout the year and trail leaflets are available at the trail start from either an honesty box or a field museum (open weekends

Southern England

only, Easter to Oct). Tel: East Marden 286. The area around Marden-Stoughton and Kingley Vale is rich in history with an Iron Age fort (Goosehill Camp) just below the forest viewpoint among several prehistoric relics such as earthworks, tumuli and the sites of ancient flint mines. There is also the site of a Roman building. OS map 197.

□ Marden-Stoughton forest is eight miles (13km) NW of Chichester; access to picnic area and woodland walk is via car park off B2146 between Stoughton and East Marden. Access to Kingley Vale is a ¾ mile (1.2km) walk N of a car park just W of West Stoke which is two miles (3.2km) W of Mid Lavant off A286. Map ref 5B4.

218. MIDHURST
Historic inn

The Spread Eagle inn was described by Hilaire Belloc as 'that old and most revered of all the prime inns of this world'. Whether or not everyone would go quite this far is doubtful, but it is certainly one of the most interesting inns in England, let alone Sussex. The building consists of two parts: a half-timbered house with lattice windows dating from 1430, once used as an Elizabethan hunting lodge; and a stone and brick addition of 1650. In the 18th century it became a coaching inn in an attractive market town with many beautiful houses. Just outside the town is Cowdray Park, a well known centre for polo.

□ 10 miles (16km) N of Chichester at junction of A272 and A286. Map ref 5B3.

219. NYMANS
Romantic garden

Rare plants from many parts of the world, including camellias, azaleas, magnolias, rhododendrons and eucryphias, are arranged here with great skill in a series of linked gardens in the manner advocated by Gertrude Jekyll and William Robinson in the early years of this century. There is also an exhibition on the history of the garden which is now owned by the NT. Open daily except Fri and non-Bank Holiday Mons from Apr to Oct, although hours vary. Tel: Handcross 400321.

□ At Handcross on B2114 six miles (9.6km) S of Crawley just off A23. Map ref 7A2.

220. PETWORTH
Country house and deer park

A picturesque small town right next to a large house and, in fact, almost overshadowed by the large gateway to the house. Petworth House (NT) was rebuilt in the late 17th century with 19th-century alterations. A great deal of rebuilding occurred in the town itself during the 17th century but some houses survive from even earlier times in the narrow streets set around a tiny market-place. Set around the house is a large deer park   one of the first to be landscaped by 'Capability' Brown. The park is open all year but the house, which contains a fine collection of paintings, is open on afternoons only Apr to Oct except Fri and non-Bank Holiday Mons. Tues is 'connoisseur's day' with more rooms open but higher charges. Tel: Petworth 42207.

□ 5½ miles E of Midhurst on A272 and A283. Map ref 5B3.

221. SELSEY
Sandy beaches and nature trail

This peninsula was where the South Saxons first settled. For over 1000 years the area was a political and administrative unit known as the Hundreds of Manhood. Most visitors to the area head for the miles of sandy beaches between Selsey Bill, the southernmost point, and West Wittering. A 1½ mile (2.4km) waymarked nature trail starts from West Wittering around the beach and sand dunes to East Head, a spit of land jutting into Chichester Harbour which in the winter especially is the haunt of many birds. The trail, which is open all year, starts at the far end of the car park; leaflets are available either locally or from the NT. Tel: NT regional office at Bookham 53401. (NB: the dunes are very vulnerable to erosion so please keep to beach or marked paths.) See map on page 41.

□ The Selsey peninsula is S of Chichester via B2145; West Wittering is six miles (9.6km) SW of Chichester off B2179. Map ref 5B4.

222. SINGLETON
Open-air museum

A small village with a mainly Saxon church sheltering under the South Downs in general and 818ft (250m) Linch Down in particular. The village itself has strong racing connections with nearby Goodwood but is now probably best known as the site of the Weald and Downland Open-Air Museum. Among many historic buildings saved by being re-erected on this 40 acre (16 hectare) site are houses from the 14th to 16th centuries, an Elizabethan treadwheel, a market hall, and a 19th-century blacksmith's forge. The buildings and the setting are sufficiently attractive to mitigate the slight air of artificiality. Pleasant walks through the parkland and woods pass at one point a reconstruction of a charcoal burner's settlement. Open daily June to Aug; daily except Mon in Apr, May, Sept and Oct; Sun only Nov to Mar. Tel: Singleton 348.

□ Six miles (9.6km) N of Chichester on A286. Map ref 5B4.

223. SLINDON EARTHAM WOOD
Forest walk along Roman road

This pleasant woodland setting includes not only a picnic area among beech trees but also a forest walk of some two miles (3.2km) along part of Stane Street, the Roman road which ran from Chichester to London Bridge. The walk is one of two woodland walks which start from the picnic area.

□ Seven miles (11km) NE of Chichester and ¾ (1.2km) W of Benges Corner off A285. Map ref 5B4.

224. UPPARK
17th-century country house

Lost on top of the Downs, and mellowed to a silvery pink by the sea breezes, this original 17th-century brick house was redecorated and filled with beautiful things owned by the Fetherstonhaugh family in the 18th century. In Regency days Sir Henry Fetherstonhaugh, after a fling with Emma Hart (Nelson's Lady Hamilton), married his dairy-maid. She and her sister inherited the house and lived there for 50 years without touching it. Lovingly and conservatively restored by recent owners (now NT), the gently faded rooms have exquisite contents, including the best doll's house in England. Open Wed, Thur, Sun and Bank Holiday Mons from Apr to Sept. Tel: Harting 317.

□ Four miles (6.4km) SW of Petersfield off B2146. Map ref 5B3.

225. WAKEHURST PLACE
Exotic garden species

In 1965 this garden was leased from the NT by the Royal Botanic Gardens as an overflow garden, particularly for rhododendrons, pines and exotic species which do not thrive in the rather poor soil at Kew. A watercourse links several ponds and lakes in the picturesque way which makes Kew Gardens themselves so attractive. Open daily throughout the year, except Christmas Day and New Year's Day. Tel: Ardingly 892701.

□ 1½ miles (2.4km) NW of Ardingly on B2028. Map ref 7B2.

Wiltshire

A rural county with rolling chalk downs sporting several 'white' horses, Wiltshire is rich in prehistoric remains, notably around Stonehenge and Avebury. Other attractions include the village of Castle Combe; Longleat and Wilton House; Salisbury Cathedral; and the market towns of Devizes and Marlborough. West Country Tourist Board, Tel: Exeter 76351.

226. AVEBURY
Prehistoric monuments

This small village is richer with

prehistoric monuments than any other place in the country (see map). Although Avebury itself can become busy at summer weekends, the sites are sufficiently scattered to enable most visitors to avoid the crowds.

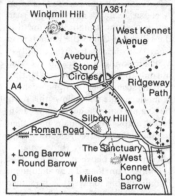

Avebury, Wiltshire, epicentre of an area which is particularly rich in prehistoric monuments

At the heart of the antiquities, and encompassed by the village, is a huge ring-earthwork or henge covering 28½ acres (11.5 hectares): a circular embankment with a deep ditch and standing stones which was a Bronze Age sanctuary. To the south runs The Avenue, 50ft (15m) wide and flanked by standing stones. Many of these stones survive, but by no means all. The Avenue originally ran for a mile (1.6km) to a smaller site, known as the Sanctuary, now next to the A4 opposite a transport café. Only the sites of the stones which once stood here can now be seen but there are several round barrows close by.

Also within a short distance and an easy walk of Avebury are West Kennet Long Barrow, the largest Neolithic chambered tomb in England and Wales; the mysterious Silbury Hill, the largest prehistoric mound in Western Europe at 130ft (40m) high; Windmill Hill, the site of a Neolithic settlement established around 3700 BC and topped by three concentric ditches; the route of the prehistoric Ridgeway track (now a long-distance footpath); a stretch of Roman road which is clearly

visible as a grassy bank running across a field off the A361; and many round barrows.

In Avebury itself there is a museum covering the antiquities of the area. This is open standard DoE hours plus Sun mornings Feb to Nov. Among other attractions of Avebury are a folk life museum in a converted 17th-century thatched barn and a lovely Tudor-Elizabethan manor house (open May to Sept). In short, Avebury is a marvellous base for an extraordinary day's exploration of the past, with gentle walks and splendid views over the Downs. OS map 173 covers the area.

☐ 10 miles (16km) S of Swindon on A361. Map ref 5A2.

227. BOWOOD GARDENS
Landscape gardens

Large 18th-century landscape garden and lake by 'Capability' Brown with Italian style terraces added in the 19th century. There are also 50 acres (20 hectares) of rhododendrons – best in late May or early June – fine rockwork, cascade with grottoes, daffodils naturalised in the park, an arboretum, a pinetum and a rose garden. The house itself is largely 18th-century and features work by architects such as Robert Adam. Over half the house is now open to the public. Open afternoons daily except non-Bank Holiday Mons, Easter to Sept. Tel: Calne 812102.

☐ At Studley, three miles (4.8km) SE of Chippenham on A4. Map ref 4B2.

228. BRADFORD-ON-AVON
'Wool' town with Saxon church

An attractive town which was a thriving centre of the Wiltshire wool trade until this began to decline in the last century. It is still dominated by the old Abbey Mill (now offices) but of greater antiquity are St Lawrence's, one of the most complete Saxon churches in the country, and a medieval bridge with an 18th-century chapel on it. The town has many attractive little alleyways and in a street called Dutch Barton (reflecting the important role played by Dutch spinners in establishing the wool trade here) are some old weavers' cottages. Across the river to the south is Barton Farm Country Park with a spectacular 14th-century tithe barn among several historic buildings alongside the River Avon. South-west of the town is the 15th to 16th-century Westwood Manor, open Wed afternoons, Apr to Sept. Tel: NT regional office at Bourton (Dorset) 224.

☐ Six miles (9.6km) SE of Bath on A363. Map ref 4B3.

229. CHISELBURY CAMP
Hill-fort on a medieval road

This hill-fort is on an ancient routeway, possibly used in prehistoric times, certainly used up to coaching days and now the preserve of walkers and horseriders (see map). It is part of the old Exeter road south-west of Salisbury. Whereas the modern A30 runs along the valley of the River Nadder, the old road followed the chalk ridgetop – now a marvellous stretch of 'green road' running some 13 miles (21km) from Harnham, just south of Salisbury, until rejoining the modern road at the foot of Whitesheet Hill east of Shaftesbury. The route passes several tumuli as well as Chiselbury Camp, an almost perfectly circular hill-fort with a single embankment. Grid ref SU 018281; OS map 184.

☐ Chiselbury Camp is eight miles (13km) SW of Salisbury off A30 or on the old medieval road as described above. Map ref 4B3.

230. CHUTE CAUSEWAY
Roman road

A classic example of a Roman road which was not straight. Just north of the village of Chute the Roman road from Winchester to Mildenhall in Wiltshire swings in a great arc to avoid not only the slopes of Haydown Hill but also the steep valley of Hippenscombe. A modern lane still follows this route but it is not quite the curve it appears to be on maps. The Romans built their uncharacteristic diversion through a series of nine short but separate alignments between $\frac{1}{4}$–$\frac{3}{4}$ mile (400m–1.2km) long. These alignments remain visible today. It is presumed that the diversion was made because the route was primarily a civilian one and therefore likely to carry heavy goods traffic. Where routes were essentially for military use they paid less respect to contours.

☐ Seven miles (11km) NW of Andover on minor roads. Map ref 5A3.

231. GREAT CHALFIELD
Medieval manor

The church, farm buildings and manor add up to one of the most perfect medieval groups to survive in England. Great Chalfield Manor (NT) was built about 1470–80, and its mellow but modest cluster of roofs and gables, all

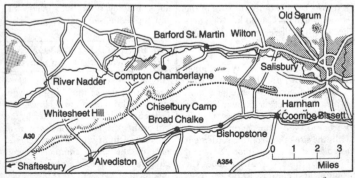

Chiselbury: the old coaching road now forms a marvellous 'green' route for walkers and horse-riders. Day Out 229

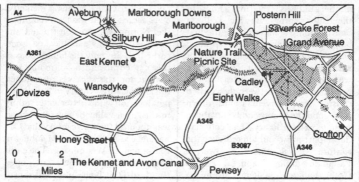

Wiltshire: here within a few miles are the varied attractions of prehistoric Avebury, Dark Age Wansdyke, medieval Savernake Forest and the 18th-century Kennet and Avon Canal. Days Out respectively 226, 240, 237 and 232

gathered round a central great hall, is still redolent of medieval hospitality. The house gently decayed into partial ruin until it was lovingly restored at the beginning of this century. The house is usually open on Wed only from mid-Apr to late Sept. Tel: NT regional office at Bourton (Dorset) 224 for details.

□ 2½ miles (4km) NE of Bradford-on-Avon off B3109. Map ref 4B2.

---

232. KENNET AND AVON
Canal with lock 'staircase'

One of the most scenic canals in England. This linked the River Avon with the River Thames at Reading, but it was no match commercially for the Great Western Railway and fell into decay earlier this century. In places the canal has completely dried up with broken-down locks, but over the last 20 years it has gradually been restored to life by painstaking volunteers. The most spectacular reclamation currently being undertaken is that of the 'staircase' of 29 locks contained in a two mile (3.2km) stretch of the canal west of Devizes, an attractive old market town with some fine houses and churches.

The lock staircase is the longest range of locks in England and lifts the canal a total of 231ft (70m). East of Devizes the canal flows less dramatically through the Vale of Pewsey with old wharves and canal inns (as at

Honey Street, west of Pewsey) providing occasional reminders of a busier past. Popular now with fishermen, but there are also some boat trips. Tel: Kennet DC public relations office, Devizes 4911 for details or enquire locally.

□ The 29-lock 'staircase' lies W of Devizes off A361. Map ref 4B3.

---

233. LACOCK
Showpiece village with 'abbey' house

A beautiful village now entirely owned by the NT – a state of affairs which can attract crowds during the summer and weekends (although less so than at nearby Castle Combe) but which safeguards its appearance. There are, for instance, no intrusive urban features such as TV aerials or yellow traffic lines. Lacock has many claims to attention and preservation, for hardly a building in the village is later than 18th century. The buildings reflect many styles, but blend together with a mellow charm. Particular buildings of note are a 14th-century tithe barn, the 15th-century half-timbered Sign of the Angel, the 14th-century Church of St Cyriac, a packhorse bridge and, of course, Lacock Abbey.

This country house, on the edge of the village in meadows running down to the River Avon, is also owned by the NT. It was originally a medieval nunnery but was turned into a house in the 16th century by Sir William Sharrington. He moved in on the first floor only and, apart from pulling down the church, left the ground floor as the nuns had lived in it. This part has scarcely been touched since, and the resulting contrast between the vaulted cloisters and convent rooms down below and the country house up above is quite extraordinary. The country-house part grew and altered over the centuries – a Renaissance tower, a Palladian dining room, a rococo Gothic hall, and final embellishments by W.H. Fox Talbot, who invented photography. The house and grounds are open afternoons except Tues, June to Sept; afternoons except Tues and non-Bank Holiday Mons in Apr, May and Oct. Tel: NT regional office at Bourton (Dorset) 224.

☐ Three miles (4.8km) S of Chippenham, off A350. Map ref 4B3.

234. MALMESBURY
Market town

This town on the southern edge of the Cotswolds has benefited from two sources and periods of prosperity. The first was the foundation of a Benedictine abbey in the 12th century; a fragment of the abbey church remains today and, although partly in ruins, contains some elaborate and outstanding carving. The second period of prosperity came in the 17th and 18th centuries when the town became established as a weaving centre. A late medieval octagonal market cross overlooks the small market square and, with its intricate carvings, the 40ft (12m) high cross is regarded as one of the two finest examples of its type in England – the other being at Chichester.

☐ 10 miles (16km) N of Chippenham on A429. Map ref 4B2.

235. OLD SARUM
Abandoned city

This hill-top predecessor of modern Salisbury was first occupied by Iron Age man (who left the outer ramparts); taken over by the Romans as their city, *Sorviodonum*; and it was then rebuilt by the Normans, who constructed the inner earthworks and the first great cathedral. But only the foundations of this cathedral and a Norman castle remain for the site was abandoned during the 13th century in favour of a new location with a better water supply in the Avon valley below. However it was not until the 19th century that Old Sarum ceased to return Members of Parliament to Westminster. The cathedral and castle ruins are open standard DoE hours plus Sun mornings Apr to Sept.

☐ Two miles (3.2km) N of Salisbury, off A345. Map ref 4B3.

236. SALISBURY PLAIN
British prairie-land

Britain's prehistoric heartland has many places of interest other than world-famous Stonehenge. Follow the meandering waters of the Avon from Salisbury along narrow lanes among the water meadows and through sleepy villages like the Woodfords, Wilsford and Durnsford. The chalk streams of the Vale of the Wylye (north-west of Salisbury) and the River Bourne (north-east of Salisbury) also offer quiet retreats for anglers or picnickers. The ancient Ridgeway offers miles of breezy walking with splendid views across the Vale of Pewsey. Army activity in several areas of Salisbury Plain can mean that access is often restricted, but warning notices indicate danger areas.

☐ Salisbury Plain is N of Salisbury with Stonehenge two miles (3.2km) W of Amesbury and Imber eight miles (13km) S of Devizes. Map ref 4B3.

237. SAVERNAKE FOREST
Woodland walks

An ancient forest that, although still large, is only a fraction of its former size. It is not quite as 'natural' as it looks since many fine avenues of beech were planted under the direction of 'Capability' Brown in the 18th century. The finest of these is the Grand Avenue, a three mile (4.8km) road through the heart of the forest. However, the trees of Grand Avenue are ageing badly and their future is in doubt. The Forestry Commission is considering closing the road to cars as well as felling the trees. Halfway along Grand Avenue is a junction known as Eight Walks where eight routes radiate in strict geometric fashion. Although there is only one statutory footpath through the forest (north from Cadley Church) walkers and horse-riders – upon purchase of a permit – are in practice allowed general access to the forest. The FC has provided a picnic site and nature trail at Postern Hill (east of A346 one mile or 1.6km south of Marlborough) but picnicking is also possible in the many glades accessible from the minor roads through the forest.

☐ ½ mile (0.8km) SE of Marlborough between A4 and A346. Map ref 5A3.

---

238. STEEPLE ASTON
'Wool' church

The Church of St Mary the Virgin is one of a number of churches, characteristic also of the Cotswolds, which were entirely rebuilt in the 15th century through the generosity of rich clothiers and wool merchants. The exterior is spectacular, with quite a regal tower, two big porches and an array of huge pinnacles and gargoyles. The very lofty interior is also sumptuous, with vaulted aisles and a nave roof of silvery oak in vault form, best seen with one's back to the east window.

☐ Four miles (6.4km) E of Trowbridge on minor road off A350. Map ref 4B3.

---

239. STOURHEAD
Landscaped garden

A supremely beautiful example of 18th-century landscape gardening with additional planting of exotic trees and shrubs in the following century. The main garden is around a large artificial lake, surrounded by temples, a rustic cottage, a grotto, a stone bridge and other eye-catching features. Even the little hamlet of Stourton, with its church, is incorporated in the design. The garden (NT) is open throughout the year. The Palladian house around which the garden was developed is open every afternoon except Fri from May to Aug; Mon, Wed and weekend afternoons in Apr, Sept and Oct. Tel: NT regional office at Bourton (Dorset) 224 for further information. Vulnerable to crowds.

☐ In the village of Stourton, three miles (4.8km) NW of Mere off B3092. Map ref 4B3.

---

240. WANSDYKE
Dark Age earthworks

This is the greatest of the English dykes and is believed to have stretched originally for some 50 miles (80km) from east of Marlborough to the Bristol Channel near Portishead. It is probably best preserved where it runs across the Marlborough Downs, roughly parallel with the A4 two miles (3.2km) to the north. The dyke is a single bank with a ditch on the northern side, indicating that it was built to keep out invaders from the north. It originates from the early Dark Ages, around AD 500, and thus pre-dates Offa's Dyke by nearly 300 years. Several tumuli, long barrows and other ancient earthworks are visible along this stretch of the dyke. See map on page 69.

☐ Off A361 three miles (5km) S of the A361/A4 junction near Avebury or off unclassified roads near the villages of Allington, Alton Barnes and East Kennet. OS map 173 clearly indicates the course of the dyke. Map ref 4B3.

Wales

241. BRECON BEACONS National Park

The nearest national park to London, and one which is well served by roads: the M4 passes close to the southern edge; the M50 to Ross-on-Wye (then A40 to Abergavenny and Brecon) speeds visitors from the Midlands and North. Several south-north roads cut through the park. The A470 climbs 1440ft (443m) at Storey Arms, passing close to the 2906ft (886m) summit of Pen-y-Fan, highest of the Beacons. Storey Arms is one of several fine viewpoints with or near car parks. Others are Black Mountain, Sugar Loaf, and Llangorse Common. Pony-trekking is popular and most of the hill-tops are common land, ideal country for ridge walkers. Offa's Dyke long-distance footpath follows the eastern boundary of this park in Powys. There is a country park at Craig-y-Nos north of Ystradgynlais and national park information centres at Brecon, Abergavenny and Llandovery, plus the excellent Brecon Beacons Mountain Centre near Libanus. Tel: Brecon 3366. Sightseeing attractions include Brecon Cathedral; the fortified manor house of Tretower, Llanthony Priory ruins; Carreg Cennen castle; and Llangorse lake.

□ Map ref 9D2.

242. PEMBROKESHIRE COAST National Park

This is a difficult park to see by car, since its prime attractions – cliffs, bays, headlands, estuaries – can only be fully appreciated on foot. However, there are numerous viewpoints with car parking, such as Newgale Sands and Wooltack Point. The B4329 from Haverfordwest to Cardigan crosses the Preseli Hills which are included in the park, as are the oakwood shores of the Cleddau estuary (best explored by boat). There are park information centres in Dyfed at Haverfordwest, Fishguard, Tenby, St David's, Pembroke, Milford Haven and Kilgetty plus an excellent information centre and countryside unit at Broad Haven, which organises talks and summer walks with wildlife themes. Tel: Broad Haven 412. Most of the park is private farmland with no public right of access, but the magnificent Pembrokeshire Coast long-distance footpath runs the entire length of the park from Amroth to St Dogmaels, a distance of 168 miles (269km). Its scenic highlights include Strumble Head; the views of Ramsey, Skomer and Stockholm islands; Stackpole Head and St Govan's Head (with its ancient chapel); and the rock stacks and seabird colonies of Flimston Bay.

□ Map ref 9A2.

Wales

243. SNOWDONIA
National Park

Main roads encircle all major upland areas and there are spectacular, though often crowded, scenic routes through the passes of Nant Ffrancon, Llanberis and Aberglaslyn, as well as gentler drives such as along the beautiful Mawddach estuary.

A popular feature of this park is the steam trains which puff laboriously into the hills on narrow-gauge lines. One is the precipice-hugging rack and pinion railway which runs from Llanberis to the top of Snowdon. For those who prefer climbing the hard way, the mountains of Snowdonia provide some of the most challenging rock faces in the British Isles. Not only is there Snowdon – at 3560ft (1085m) the highest peak in England and Wales – but there are a host of other summits: Tryfan, Cnicht, Crib Goch, the Carneddau, the Glyders and more.

The Central Council of Physical Recreation's Plas y Brenin mountaineering centre is at Capel Curig; Tel: Capel Curig 214 (office) or 280 (bookings). In the southern half of the park there are several different routes to the 2927ft (892m) summit of Cader Idris. Bala, Betws-y-Coed, Llanberis, Capel Curig and Dolgellau are all favourite walking centres. Pony-trekking and angling are also popular. Apart from the peaks and passes themselves, sightseeing attractions include Harlech Castle, the waterfalls of Betws-y-Coed, and Llyn Tegid (or Bala Lake), the largest natural lake in Wales. There are tourist information centres and/or park offices at Blaenau Ffestiniog, Aberdovey, Bala, Dolgellau, Harlech, Llanberis, Conwy and Llanwrst.
□ Map ref 8C2.

244. ANGLESEY
Area of Outstanding Natural Beauty

Apart from a few gaps – one of which is filled by the nuclear power station at Wylfa Head – this comprises the whole of the island's rich coastline of cliffs, rock stacks, dunes, shingle ridges, salt-marshes, coves and gleaming sands. There are plenty of beaches, with safe bathing and sheltered spots for picnics, and the island, which forms part of the county of Gwynedd, is a paradise for bird-watchers, with seabirds, waders and wildfowl much in evidence. The dunes of Newborough are a National Nature Reserve, and there are other bird sanctuaries at Cemlyn Bay (visitors may view from the road) and Puffin Island, near Penmon. Total area: 134 sq miles (347 sq km).
□ Map ref 8C1.

245. GOWER PENINSULA
Area of Outstanding Natural Beauty

An unspoilt peninsula in West Glamorgan between Swansea and the Lough-or estuary with beautiful bays and limestone cliffs on the south coast, culminating in the distinctive saurian profile of Worm's Head. There are cliff walks plus caves to explore. The north coast has vast salt-marshes, cockle beds and tidal sands alive with oyster-catchers and other wading birds, and a National Nature Reserve at Whitford Burrows. (See map with Days Out 359 and 360.) Total area: 118 sq miles (306 sq km).
□ Map ref 9C2.

246. LLYN (or LLEYN)
Area of Outstanding Natural Beauty

The Land's End of North Wales. A rugged peninsula in Gwynedd, largely treeless, its small green fields quartered by furzy hedgerows and dominated by the bare triple summits of Yr Eifl (The Rivals), 1850ft (500m). The peninsula is bounded by a succession of cliffs, headlands, coves, bays and sandy beaches, including the 'Whistling Sands' of Porth-oer. The AONB includes nearly all the north coast, the south coast as far east as Llanbedrog, and the offshore islands of Bardsey and St Tudwal's. Total area: 97 sq miles (251 sq km).
□ Map ref 8B2.

Wales

Part of the county of Gwynedd. Anglesey is separated from the mainland by the Menai Strait. The island's coastline is an AONB while inland there are many prehistoric sites. Beaumaris has a fine medieval castle overlooking the Menai Strait which is crossed by bridges near Bangor. North Wales Tourism Council, Te,: Colwyn Bay 56881.

247. ABERFFRAW
Sand dunes and history

This quiet hamlet stands on the shallow tidal estuary of the River Ffraw which has an enormous warren of dunes at its mouth and a stark, single-arched bridge spanning the river. For over 400 years in the Dark Ages Aberffraw was the capital of North Wales but its buildings betray no clue to past glory or importance. One mile (1.6km) west of the village is a quiet rocky beach where you will find cowrie shells, curlews and the church of St Cwyfan on an islet in the bay. At low tide you can walk out to the church which was restored in 1893 on 7th-century foundations; an annual service takes place in June. Two miles (3.2km) north-west of Aberffraw is Barclodiad-y-Gawres, a 4000-year-old tomb ornamented with megalithic murals; it is open to the public on afternoons from June to Sept, weekends and Wed. Grid ref SH 329707; OS map 114.
□ 12 miles (19km) W of Menai Bridge on A4080. Map ref 8B1.

248. BLACK POINT
Headland and monastic remains

On this most easterly peninsula of Anglesey – curiously named since it is composed of greyish carboniferous limestone – are the remains of Penmon Priory (AM), a 13th-century Augustinian monastery. In addition to the monastic buildings themselves there is a gigantic stone dovecote dating from about 1600 and a Dark Age carved cross in the Deer Park. From Black Point, with its lighthouse and warning bell, there are five views across the sweep of Lafan Sands and Conwy Bay towards Snowdonia. Half a mile (800m) offshore is Puffin Island, but there is normally no public access to this island, also known as Priestholm.
□ Four miles (6.4km) NE of Beaumaris via B5109. Map ref 8C1.

Some common Welsh place-names and their English meanings

Modern form	Meaning
Aber	River mouth
Afon	River
Bettws	Chapel
Cwm	Corrie
Fach	Little
Hafod	Summer dwelling
Hendre	Winter dwelling
Llan	Church
Llyn	Lake
Nant	Valley

249. BRYN CELLI DDU
Prehistoric tomb

This late Neolithic chambered tomb (AM) is one of the most impressive in the British Isles and is certainly the best preserved in Wales. It dates from about 1600 BC and was raised over the relics of an earlier henge or circular embanked monument. The giant stones that form the burial chamber are covered by a grassy mound that is only a fraction of its former size. Inside the burial chamber is an upstanding monolith that rises almost to the roof. The chamber can be visited and is normally unlocked during standard

DoE hours; if not, the key is available during those hours from the nearby farmhouse. Grid ref SH 508702; OS map 114.

☐ One mile (1.6km) E of Llanddaniel Fab church off a minor road between this church and the A4080. The tomb is 800 yards (700m) down a signposted lane that also leads to a farm; cars have to be left on the road. Map ref 8C1.

250. CHURCH BAY
Pebbles and seabird isles

This remote sand and rock beach, sheltered by 100ft (30m) cliffs, is an excellent place to look for shells and pebbles. There is a footpath running along the cliffs to Carmel Head, a windswept headland covered with gorse and the occasional stunted pine. From here you can see the Skerries: a cluster of islets and reefs formed by a low tract of land which became submerged. They were first used to support a lighthouse in 1714. The present lighthouse is open to the public; Tel: Holyhead 2320 or 2329. Boats can sometimes also be hired from Holyhead or Cemaes Bay to see seals and seabirds which live on and around the Skerries.

☐ Five miles (8km) SW of Cemaes Bay, W off A5025 at Llanrhuddlad or Llanfaethlu. Map ref 8B1.

251. DIN LLIGWY
Ancient village

A thick wall here encloses substantial foundations of circular and rectangular stone houses to form one of the most impressive sites of early settlement in the British Isles (grid ref SH 497861; OS map 114). Some of the walls are still 6ft (1.8m) high. The fortified village, overlooking sandy Lligwy Bay, was occupied by native Britons during Roman times, certainly as late as the 4th century. Short walks from Din Lligwy are Capel Lligwy, a 12th to 16th-century chapel, and Lligwy Cromlech, a Neolithic and Bronze Age tomb topped by an enormous capstone weighing some 28 tons.

☐ ¾ mile (1.2km) N of Llanallgo along a minor road to Lligwy; Din Lligwy is a 500 yard (450m) signposted walk off this minor road. OS map 114 shows all locations clearly. Map ref 8C1.

252. HOLYHEAD MOUNTAIN
Viewpoint and wildlife

Although only 720ft (222m) high this is one of the best viewpoints in Wales, embracing the Lake District, the Isle of Man, the mountains of Mourne and Wicklow in Ireland and Snowdonia. Holyhead Mountain is 2½ miles (4km) from Holyhead, along the minor road heading west through the village of Llaingoch. There are several paths to the summit. One starts from the road leading to South Stack Lighthouse. It is signposted to Hut Circles (AM), the remains of an Iron Age settlement which was occupied until the 3rd or 4th centuries AD. Further up the path is Caer y Twr, an Iron Age hill-fort.

The South Stack headland forms part of an RSPB reserve which is not only prodigal in its birds and flowers, but in the beauty and variety of its surroundings. The high headlands and cliffs are covered in late spring and early summer by masses of cliff plants, including the blue spring squill, stonecrop and scurvey grass. This is also the time when the seabirds come to the cliffs to breed: guillemot, razorbill, puffin, chough, raven and jackdaw all make use of the ledges and holes in the ragged cliffs.

The heathland of Penrhos Field Common behind the headland is a place of heath and bog plants and a haven for birds such as stonechat and linnet, as well as a variety of butterflies. Grey seals can often be seen along the coast, particularly in Golgarth Bay.

Access to the reserve is via public footpaths. Further information from resident summer RSPB warden or RSPB Wales Office, 18 High Street, Newtown, Powys. A leaflet for a nature trail along South Stack Steps is available locally from NW Wales Naturalists' Trust, 154 High Street, Bangor, Gwynedd.

☐ W of Holyhead. Map ref 8B1.

Wales

253. NEWBOROUGH WARREN
Sand dunes and forest

A well surfaced road through miles of coniferous trees leads to a sheltered car park and picnic spot behind the sandy shore of Llanddwyn Bay. To the west is the 'island' of Llanddwyn with its lighthouse and ruined 15th-century church perched on an outcrop of rocks which are among the oldest in Wales. Eastwards is the miniature 'Sahara' of Newborough Warren with five sq miles (12.95 sq km) of sand dunes, some rising to over 100ft (31m), now largely covered by conifers. The dunes are a National Nature Reserve and there is an information point and exhibition at the car park. This is also the starting point for a one mile (1.6km) trail through dunes to a medieval house exposed by blown sand.

☐ SW of Newborough nine miles (14km) SW of Menai Bridge on A4080. Map ref 8B1.

254. PARYS MOUNTAIN
Industrial landscape

In the 18th century it was the biggest copper mine in the world; in the 20th century it is an almost lunar landscape which, on a fine day, glistens with orange, brown and reddish hues. It is a copper mountain still, although the old workings scoured gigantic holes out of the mountain such as the 'Great Pit' on the south-western slopes. The feeling of devastation is intensified by the crumbling remains of old engine houses; the remnants of 'settling pits' where copper was extracted by precipitation from the metal-bearing waters draining the workings; disused mine shafts; and the stump of an old windmill on the mountain's 600ft (185m) crest. The massive quays and jetties of nearby Amlwch Port are another clue to the area's once equally massive commercial importance. NB: the old mountain workings should be explored with care and are not recommended for families with young children.

☐ Two miles (3.2km) S of Amlwch off B5111. Map ref 8B1.

Clwyd

Largely mountainous county with holiday resorts such as Rhyl and Colwyn Bay in the north. Its many castles include Chirk, Denbigh, Ewloe, Flint, Hawarden and Ruthin. Rivers include the Dee as well as the Clwyd. English architectural influence can be seen in the east around Wrexham and Chester. North Wales Tourism Council, Tel: Colwyn Bay 56881.

255. BANGOR-IS-Y-COED
River walks and angling

This ancient crossing point of the River Dee is a tiny piece of Wales lying on the English side of the river. Bangor-on-Dee, as it is known, is said to have been designed by Inigo Jones. The village has an excellent racecourse and one of the earliest monasteries in Britain was founded here in the 5th century. Stand on its 17th-century red sandstone bridge and watch the salmon fishermen at work in the gliding waters – fishing permits are available in the village. Basket-weaving continues in the village – an echo of earlier times

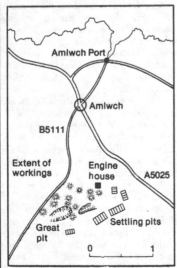

Extent of the Old Parys mountain copper mine workings near Amlwch, Anglesey

when fishing was carried out in flimsy coracles. There are attractive walks along the meandering Dee.

☐ Four miles (6.4km) SE of Wrexham on A525. Map ref 8D1.

256. CLOCAENOG FOREST
Woodland walks and picnics

Bod Petrual visitor centre is a converted keeper's cottage with an exhibition presenting the forest in its ecological and historical setting. The visitor centre is unmanned and usually open during the summer only. Further information from the Forestry Commission, Tel: Ruthin 2579. Near the centre is a picnic area set among pine trees and beside a lake. The picnic area is the starting point for a series of waymarked walks from just $\frac{1}{4}$ mile to $2\frac{3}{4}$ miles (400m to 2.8km) in length.

☐ Seven miles (11km) SW of Ruthin off B5105 at Pont Petryal. Map ref 8D1.

257. CORWEN
Market town with historic inn

The Owain Glyndwr Hotel stands in the square of this small market town near the confluence of the Alwen and Dee. It was originally a monastery in the grounds of the church and later became a coaching inn on the route to Holyhead. In 1789 an extension was built to house the first public Welsh Eisteddfod. Leaflets are available locally for a town trail. North-east, on a hill overlooking Corwen, is the town's predecessor: Caer Drewyn, an Iron Age hill-fort, which still has some remains of its stone walls and houses (grid ref SH 088443; OS map 125). The modern Corwen caters for tourists – notably with fine angling in the Dee – but is also a centre for farmers. Fair Day the third Tuesday of every month and the September Ewe Sale attracts thousands of sheep for sale.

☐ 10 miles (16km) W of Llangollen on A5. Map ref 8D2.

258. ERDDIG
Country house and park

A house cleverly presented by the NT to show the servants' point of view as much as the masters'. The public enter by the back door, by way of the blacksmith's and joiner's workshops, stable yard, laundry, kitchen, servants' hall and butler's pantry. All retain many of their original contents and fittings, and the servants' hall and corridor are lined with portraits and photographs of generations of servants, commissioned by the Yorkes, their amiable but eccentric employers. The main house is remarkable less for its architecture than for its contents, which include splendid furniture and mirrors commissioned for Erddig in the early 18th century. In the grounds is a country park with picnic sites, an industrial trail and an agricultural museum. Open daily (except Mon other than Bank Holidays) Apr to Oct. For information about the house, Tel: NT office, Betws-y-Coed 312.

☐ One mile (1.6km) S of Wrexham off A483. Map ref 8D1.

259. GRESFORD
Stately parish church

It has to be admitted that what is acclaimed by architectural connoisseurs as the best parish church in Wales belongs both in style and in spirit to nearby Cheshire. Wholly Perpendicular, and of buff-coloured sandstone throughout, it has a stately west tower, a good deal of old glass, and original woodwork in fine profusion: stalls with misericords, screen with restored loft, and cambered tie-beam roofs everywhere, with angels and many carved bosses. A delight. (If locked, ask for the key at the vicarage.)

☐ Three miles (4.8km) N of Wrexham off A483. Map ref 8D1.

260. LLANGOLLEN
Natural and man-made landscapes

This attractive town is often crowded with visitors and never more so than for the International Musical Eisteddfod. It stands on the Dee (which is crossed by a 14th-century bridge) at the heart of some remarkable scenery where the

Wales

works of man have complemented the natural beauty of the Dee Valley (see map). A tourist information centre (Tel: 860828) near the bridge will provide information about the features

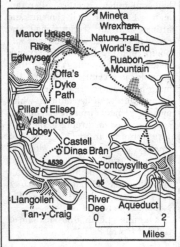

Llangollen: an area which is rich in natural and man-made features. Days Out respectively 260, 265 and also 263

of the town. Among these is Plas Newydd, the black-and-white timbered home for 50 years of 'the ladies of Llangollen'. Lady Eleanor Butler and Miss Sarah Ponsonby were a pair of 18th-century eccentrics who made their home a tourist attraction even in their own day. Other features of the surrounding area are:

River Dee. Some of Britain's finest incised meanders can be found near Llangollen. They were formed when the river continued to cut down its bed as the surrounding mountains were uplifted by crustal forces. The depths of the incisions can be appreciated from viewpoints such as the Horseshoe Pass and Castell Dinas Brân (see below). In two places the river has broken through the neck of its meander to leave its former course high and dry. One such abandoned meander is south-east of Llangollen along the valley now followed by the minor road to Tan-y-Graig; the other is north of

the town at Pentrefelin. There are attractive river (and canalside) walks.
Canal. Telford's Shropshire Union Canal flows into the town – see also Day Out 263 – and there is now a canal exhibition centre at the town's wharf. Open Easter to Sept, Tel: Llangollen 860702. Also canal cruises.
Castell Dinas Brân. On a hill towering over the town from the northern banks of the Dee is the Hill of Brân, some 900ft (274m) high, and crowned by the ruins of a castle. This was a stronghold of Welsh princes before the English conquest making it one of the few Iron Age hill-forts to have been occupied in medieval times. A steep climb but spectacular views over the Vale of Llangollen and the splendid white escarpment of Eglwyseg Mountain with its great apron of screes. See also Day Out 265 for a walk incorporating the Hill.
Valle Crucis Abbey. Founded in the late 12th century. These ruins to the north of Llangollen reflect an unusual mixture of traditional Cistercian styles with native Welsh craft tradition. The effect is diminished by some restoration work and an unsightly adjacent caravan site, but the Abbey is still worth seeing.
Eliseg's Pillar. Erected in the 9th century, this is one of the most elaborate inscribed records of its kind surviving from pre-Norman Britain. It stands in a field close to the abbey ruins. □ 10 miles (16km) SW of Wrexham on A5, A539 and A542. Map ref 8D2.

261. LLANRHAEADR
Church with outstanding stained glass

A charming church, not well known but full of interest. Excellent woodwork, including north porch and hammer-beam roof with angels. But the great treasure is the exceptionally well preserved Jesse window, executed in 1533, with perhaps the most enjoyable late-Gothic stained glass in Britain – Fairford and King's College Cambridge not excepted. The rich colours are, principally, ruby, clear blue, green, yellow and white.

A Jesse Window is a picture window that depicts the descent of Christ through the Royal House of Israel – the line of David who was the son of Jesse. 'And there shall come forth a rod out of the root of Jesse and a flower shall rise up out of his root' – Isaiah II, 1 and 2.

□ 2½ miles (4km) SE of Denbigh on A525. Map ref 8D1.

262. MOEL FAMAU
Country park

A vast area – 2374 acres (961 hectares) – of open moorland extending in the Clwydian Hills. There are three hill-forts, but the main feature of the park is the Jubilee Tower, built in 1810 to commemorate George III's Jubilee. Offa's Dyke long-distance footpath passes through the park. There is a Forestry Commission picnic site and car park and a waymarked nature trail. Formerly the ancient lands of the lordship or manor of Ruthin, the park is an important leisure area throughout the year and is popular in winter with skiers and tobogannists. Open daily throughout the year.

□ Six miles (9.6km) W of Mold, signposted off A494. Map ref 8D1.

263. PONTCYSYLLTE AQUEDUCT
Sensational canal architecture

A masterpiece, even by Thomas Telford's standards. The engineering skill which carries the Llangollen arm of the Shropshire Union Canal over the River Dee 127ft (39m) below is complemented by its graceful exe-cution and beautiful setting. It can be seen from the A5 approaching Llangollen but perhaps better still from the small bridge carrying road traffic over the Dee between Froncysyllte and Trefor. To see a barge crossing the aqueduct high above you – or, indeed, to cross the 1007ft (301m) long aqueduct by boat – is an extraordinary sensation. Walkers with heads for heights can join the towpath from Trefor. See map and Day Out 260 for more about the canal.

□ 4½ miles (7.2km) E of Llangollen off A5 or A539. Map ref 8D2.

264. RUTHIN
Half-timbered market town

There are more important market centres in North Wales – Denbigh and Mold, for instance – but Ruthin is architecturally the most interesting market town in the area. It grew around a castle, now a hotel which specialises in medieval banquets; Tel: Ruthin 2664. But it is the lesser buildings which now give Ruthin most of its appeal. Many are outstanding examples of half-timbering and, dating from the 15th to 17th centuries, reflect the town's prosperity in the wool trade. Most of the oldest buildings are grouped around the market square which, set on top of a hill, still forms the heart of the town. A town trail takes visitors past the most interesting buildings; a leaflet is available locally.

□ Seven miles (11km) SE of Denbigh at junction of A525 and A494. Map ref 8D1.

265. WORLD'S END
Walk to an unspoilt valley

This is the exotic name given to the head of the steep and beautiful wooded valley of the River Eglwyseg north of Llangollen. A minor road leads there off A542 but it is best appreciated on foot. A section of the long-distance Offa's Dyke Path follows the valley and can be used as part of an 11 mile (17.6km) walk based at Llangollen. Follow the waymarked Offa's Dyke Path north of Llangollen, past Castell Dinas Brân under towering Eglwyseg Rocks to World's End – look out for a Tudor manor house in the valley. Return along the escarpment's crest to Pontcysyllte Aqueduct and back to Llangollen along the canal towpath. There is also a one mile (1.6km) nature trail at World's End during the summer – details from North Wales Naturalists' Trust, Tel: Bangor 51541, or enquire in Llangollen tourist information centre. OS map 117 details the paths in this area; see also map with Day Out 260.

□ Five miles (8km) N of Llangollen. Map ref 8D1.

Wales

The largest Welsh county, stretching from Mid Wales to the Pembrokeshire Coast National Park in the south-west. Tourist centres include Aberystwyth, Cardigan, Carmarthen, Haverfordwest, Pembroke, St David's, Tenby. Many castles. Mid Wales Tourism Council and South Wales Tourism Councils each cover parts of Dyfed.

266. ABERAERON
Regency-style village

Unusually for a Welsh village, this was laid out and built to a set plan – in the early 19th century. It not only reflects the prevailing Regency architecture of that time but does so with such style that it has been suggested that John Nash himself participated in its design. Certainly he was living in the area at the time and certainly the small two-storey houses in the squares and terraces around the harbour are like miniature versions of Nash's houses in London and elsewhere. The village once had a lively ship-building industry, but the harbour is now almost totally devoted to yachting.
□ 12 miles (19km) NW of Lampeter on A482 and A487. Map ref 9C1.

267. BORTH
Sand dunes with nature trail

Borth straggles for two miles (3.2km) along a sandy beach backed by a high bank of pebbles, ending in a spit of sand dunes at the mouth of the River Dovey. At low tide evidence of a submerged forest can be seen. Behind the village, which attracts many summer visitors, is Borth Bog (Cors Fochno). This contains many rare plants but can be dangerous to walkers who stray off the paths. The Nature Conservancy Council's waymarked Ynyslas Nature Trail runs through the sand dunes to the north which is part of the NCC Nature Reserve covering nearly 4000 acres (1619 hectares) of sandbanks and saltings in the estuary. These are important feeding grounds for thousands of waders, mallard and other wildfowl. A trail leaflet is available. Tel: NCC at Bangor 4001.

One mile (1.6km) north of Trerddol on the A487, overlooking Borth Bog and the Dovey estuary, is Pantglas picnic area among oak and beech trees. This is also the start of a ¾ mile (1.2km) forest walk along the sheltered slopes planted with young conifers.
□ Six miles (9.6km) N of Aberystwyth on B4572. Map ref 8C2.

268. BOSHERSTON
Lily ponds and coastal walks

Sand dunes building up at nearby Broad Haven Bay cut off three streams from the sea to form the Bosherston Pools or Lakes: nearly three miles (4.8km) of water famed for their water-lilies (best seen in June) and their coarse fishing. The pools also attract a wide variety of birds including heron.

Bosherston: the starting-point for a walk along the clifftops and a visit to ancient St Govan's Chapel. Days Out 268 and 291

The village can also be the starting point of a marvellous 10 mile (16km) walk along part of the long-distance Pembrokeshire Coast Path (see map). Head south to St Govan's Head – detouring to see the medieval cliff-side chapel (see Day Out 291) and the Huntsman's Leap, 130ft (40m) above the sea. Then follow the coast path westwards via Elegug Stacks or Stack Rocks to the rock arch known as the Green Bridge of Wales. Return to

Bosherston inland via Merrion and use the B4319 to fill the gap in the otherwise waymarked circuit. OS map 158 details the paths on this walk. NB: this walk is *not* possible when firing is taking place on the tank range. Check to see if red flags are flying, ask locally or Tel: Castlemartin 321.

□ Four miles (6.4km) S of Pembroke. Map ref 9B2.

269. BRECHA FOREST
Walk and picnic area

A 1¾ mile (2.8km) waymarked forest walk through an attractive wooded valley begins at a picnic area set among red oaks beside a stream on the east side of the village of Abergorlech.

□ 16 miles (26km) NE of Carmarthen on B4310. Map ref 9C1.

270. BROAD HAVEN
Cliffs and sandy beach

Not the Broad Haven close to Bosherston (above) but a tiny village with an extensive sandy beach backed by cliffs showing evidence of the coal measures of the Pembrokeshire beds to be seen in the spectacular folding of the rocks. Both Broad Haven and neighbouring Little Haven were once coal mining centres. In the large car park is the Countryside Unit of the Pembrokeshire Coast National Park – Tel: Broad Haven 412 – a focal point for a wide range of walks, excursions and lectures. One such walk is from Broad Haven to Rickets Head, four miles (6.4km) to the north for sweeping views of St Bride's Bay. At low tide on Newgale Beach you may be able to see the ebony-like tree-stumps of a submerged forest.

□ Six miles (9.6km) W of Haverfordwest on B4347. Map ref 9A2.

271. CALDY ISLAND
Island monastery

The limestone hill of Caldy was once part of the Coedrath Forest but the island, which is 1½ miles (2.4km) long, was severed from the mainland by the rising sea level. Celtic monks founded a monastery here as early as the 6th century. The Normans handed the island over to the Benedictines in the 12th century. Various ownerships followed the dissolution of the Monasteries before it was taken over in 1929 by an order of Cistercian monks who farm the island today. The monks sell clotted cream and Caldy perfume made from local flowers to visitors but allow only men in the monastery. Non-sexist attractions on the island include its churches, the old priory and the views from near the clifftop lighthouse (not open to the public). Seals and many seabirds have colonies on the island but are best seen by taking a boat trip around the island.

□ About 20 minutes by boat from Tenby harbour. Frequent summer service. Map ref 9B2.

272. CAREW
Castle and last Welsh tidal mill

This hamlet has two buildings of outstanding interest: a castle dating from the 13th century and the last remaining tidal mill in Wales. There is a fine 11th-century cross at the castle entrance but otherwise it is the setting as much as the building that gives Carew Castle much of its appeal. This same riverside setting increases the attraction of the Carew French Mill, as it is known. The present building is 19th-century but there has been a mill on this site since Elizabethan times. It works by storing water brought by the incoming tide in the mill-pond and then releasing water from the pond on the ebbing tide to turn the waterwheels. The mill is open daily Apr to Sept (but only afternoons on Sun) and there is a picnic site by the mill-pond.

□ Four miles (6.4km) E of Pembroke on A4075. Castle and mill on the S bank of the Carew River. Map ref 9B2.

273. CARREG CENNEN
Castle with spectacular views

In spite of its apparent isolation Carreg Cennen Castle was once of great strategic importance during the Norman advance into south-west Wales. The site is magnificent – there

Wales

was a castle here long before the present late 13th or early 14th-century building – with a precipitous drop on one side down to the valley floor and overlooking the Black Mountain. It was largely demolished in the 15th century but its situation is so dramatic that the ruins retain a great romantic appeal that is enhanced by its links with the caves in the rock beneath. Open standard DoE hours plus Sun morning, Apr to Sept.
☐ 4½ miles (7km) SE of Llandeilo. Map ref 9C2.

274. CEMAES HEAD
Cliff walks and estuary

Cemaes Head rises to 550ft (167m) with spectacular folding in the cliffs around the headland. It is the first (or last) highlight for walkers on the Pembrokeshire Coast Path which has its northern terminus at nearby St Dogmael's. The headland can only be reached by foot along the clifftop path. Just south of the headland is an almost dry valley called Pwll Granant which runs into the Teifi estuary. This is an overflow valley formed by meltwater in the Ice Age. The Teifi estuary itself is a drowned valley almost closed by a sandbar. At St Dogmael's the ruins of a 12th-century abbey (AM) can be seen in the grounds of the vicarage.
☐ Three miles (4.8km) NW of St Dogmael's via B4546 and paths. Map ref 9B1.

275. DALE PENINSULA
Walks and sailing

The peninsula is almost an island, separated from the mainland by a deep valley. The village of Dale itself has a sheltered muddy sand and shingle beach and is a popular sailing centre. The village is said to be the sunniest place in Wales and is noted for its early crops. It is a six mile (9.6km) walk around the peninsula on part of the Pembrokeshire Coast Path; leaflets are available locally from national park offices or the Countryside Unit at Broad Haven. The Griffin Inn at Dale is the base for the walk which passes

Mill Bay, where Henry Tudor landed in 1485 to claim the English crown; an Iron Age promontory fort at Great Castle Head; Dale Point; St Anne's lighthouse (open to the public), Tel: Dale 314; and views over Milford Haven.
☐ 12 miles (19km) SW of Haverfordwest on B4327. Map ref 9A2.

276. DINAS FOREST
Nature trail for bird-watching

A beautiful oakwood valley with a 1½ mile (2.4km) public nature trail managed by the RSPB. Plentiful woodland birds and flowers here, including buzzard, raven, redstart and pied flycatcher. There is a chance, too, of seeing the rare red kite. The trail is open throughout the year and starts from the warden's hut at Troedrhiwgelynen, Rhandirmywn. A leaflet is available from RSPB Reserves Dept, Tel: Sandy 80551.
☐ W of Rhandirmwyn about 11 miles (18km) N of Llandovery off minor road to Ystradffin. Map ref 9C1.

277. DINAS ISLAND
Wildlife and walks

Not an island but a small promontory on the North Pembrokeshire coast, Dinas offers some beautiful and exciting walks. It is about three miles (4.8km) right round the 'island' but shorter walks of just over a mile (1.6km) start from Pwllgwaelod on the west or Cwm-yr-Eglwys to Dinas Point. Dolphins and porpoises may sometimes be seen from the point and there are always plenty of birds and flowers along the cliffs. A very good leaflet is produced by the West Wales Naturalists' Trust on the natural history of the 'island'. Available at tourist information centres or contact the Trust, Tel: Haverfordwest 5462.
☐ Four miles (6.4km) E of Fishguard off A487. Map ref 9B1.

278. DOLAUCOTHI
Trails round Roman gold mines

Here, in the wooded Cothi valley, is

one of the most remarkable yet least known survivals of Roman Britain: the Roman gold mines of Dolaucothi. The evidence of gold workings during the 19th and early 20th centuries are more evident, but two short waymarked trails explore surprisingly extensive remains of Roman mining. Perhaps the most interesting feature of all is the Roman aqueduct which can still be seen, as a channel running for seven miles (11km) along the valley to collecting basins on the hill slopes above the mine.

The gold which once left this far outpost of Rome for the Imperial Mints in France and Italy is no longer mined commercially, so that the healing powers of nature have done much to restore the ravages of man. The result: a quiet, beautiful and evocative place.

An exhibition of the Roman mines can be seen in the museum at Abergwili, near Carmarthen, where a leaflet is also available. Close to the mines at Pumsaint and easily spotted are a picnic site and three waymarked trails of $\frac{1}{2}$ mile (800m) to two miles (3.2km) which start at Ogofau Lodge on the Cwrt y Cadno road.

The trails, run by the NT, pass through woodland, steep in parts, and enable visitors to see remnants of the aqueduct systems and old opencast workings. A booklet is available from an information office at the site during the summer or from the NT at 22 Alan Road, Llandeilo, Dyfed, SA19 6HV. Visitors, especially those with young children, are advised to stick to the waymarked paths.

☐ The goldmines are clearly signposted off A482 at Pumsaint, eight miles (13km) SE of Lampeter. Map ref 9C1.

279. DRE-FACH FELINDRE
Wool museum and trail

This area was one of the most important centres of the Welsh woollen industry from 1860 to 1930. The Museum of the Woollen Industry, a branch of the Welsh Folk Museum, was established in part of a working mill to show details of this rural trade with exhibitions of tools and machinery used in carding, spinning, weaving and finishing cloth. Open Mon to Sat, Apr to Sept; Tel: Felindre 370453. A circular 'factory trail' showing other aspects of the woollen industry can be undertaken from here; details from the museum, or Wales Tourist Board booklet, *A Glimpse of the Past*, price 65p by post (for address see appendix).

☐ Four miles (6.4km) E of Newcastle Emlyn off A484. Map ref 9B1.

280. DYLAN THOMAS'S WALES
Laugharne village

Thomas was born in Swansea in 1914 and lived there longer than anywhere else. But he is most identified with Laugharne in Dyfed where he lived for four years until his death in 1953 and where he is buried. Laugharne is an attractive village with a castle, quaint cottages and Georgian houses. Much of the atmosphere of the village is apparent in his greatest work, *Under Milk Wood*, even though the setting for the play – a 'cliff-perched town at the far end of Wales' – is more likely to have been New Quay on Cardigan Bay. Thomas is buried in the churchyard at Laugharne and his home, the Boathouse, is usually open daily Easter to Oct, but check times. Tel: Laugharne 420.

☐ 12 miles (19km) SW of Carmarthen on A4066. Map ref 9B2.

281. HAFOD
Pioneer landscaping and forest trails

In the 18th century, as the field enclosure movement was reaching its zenith in lowland Britain, a few pioneering landowners made brave attempts to 'improve' the upland landscapes where soil and climate were at their least propitious. The soils were not only generally thinner but were intensely leached by heavy rain and rapid drainage over the steep slopes.

Despite these unfavourable circumstances the 18th century brought an improved climate and increased demand for farm produce and wool as the population grew which en-

Wales

couraged attempts at upland 'improvement'. In Wales the most notable pioneer was Thomas Johnes with his country house, formal gardens and 'natural' landscaping of the Ystwyth valley at Hafod, inland from Aberystwyth.

More than four million trees were planted, mainly larch but also oak and beech in more sheltered places, in a valley where the original wood cover had been destroyed by lead mining. Although some of the deciduous trees were quite foreign to the Welsh hillsides, the arboriculture was on the whole a success and Johnes's Hafod estate became one of the wonders of Wales. Among those lured by its fame was J.W. Turner who has left us with a painting of the now demolished house.

Remnants of the Hafod estate survive today under the protection of the Forestry Commission. These include laid-out terraces, exotic trees and the estate church. There is also the Jubilee Arch erected over the road (now the B4574) by Johnes as his tribute to the Golden Jubilee of George III. By the arch there is now an FC picnic place which is also the starting point for three forest trails between $\frac{1}{2}$ and $1\frac{1}{2}$ miles (800m to 2.4km) long. In theory, leaflets should be available at the 'honesty boxes' at the start of each trail but a more certain way of obtaining a copy is to call at an FC visitor centre; the nearest is at Bwlch Nant-yr-Arian (see Day Out 289). □ Jubilee Arch is two miles (3.2km) SE of Devil's Bridge on B4574; the estate church and site of Haford House are two miles (3.2km) W of Cwmystwyth off B4574 to Ysbyty Ystwyth.

282. KIDWELLY
Castle, dunes and forest

Kidwelly stands at the confluence of Gwendraeth Fawr and Gwendraeth Fach. The estuary is crossed by a fine 14th-century bridge but otherwise only the layout of the town's streets indicates its medieval origins. It grew up around the castle which still dominates the town, commanding marvellous views over the river estuary. The towers and gatehouse of the castle (AM) are particularly well preserved; it is open standard DoE hours, plus Sun mornings Apr to Sept. South-west of the town is Pembrey Forest, a five mile (8km) expanse of sand backed by dunes and a pine forest; forest trails begin from a picnic place near where the A484 crosses the railway near Pembrey.
□ Eight miles S of Carmarthen on A484. Map ref 9B2.

283. LLANGRANNOG
Village and clifftop walks

This tiny and picturesque village, nestling in a narrow coastal valley, is sometimes called the Polperro of Wales. Its houses straggle down to a narrow sandy beach which is dominated by a bizarre 50ft (15m) sea stack. The cliffs rise steeply on either side and provide miles of coastal walks: northwards to the imposing 540ft (164m) headland of Ynys Lochtyn (NT) with two tiny sandy coves and prehistoric earthworks, or southwards to the sandy beaches of Penbryn.
□ 11 miles (18km) NE of Cardigan on B4334 or B4321 off A487. Map ref 9B1.

284. LLYS-Y-FRAN
Country parks

Llys-y-Fran reservoir lies in a wooden valley in the foothills of the Preseli Mountains and is now a country park. Its main recreation is fishing – the reservoir is well stocked with rainbow and brown trout – and permits are available either from the warden's office at the cafeteria (open daily from Whitsun to end Sept) or from the Welsh Water Authority at Meyler House, Haverfordwest. Limited boating facilities are available as well as a picnic area. The park is run by Dyfed County Council, which also operates as a country park the landscaped grounds and woodlands surrounding Scolton Manor, NE of Haverfordwest off B4329. Tel: Clarbeston 457.
□ Llys-y-Fran is eight miles (13km) NE of Haverfordwest and is signposted off B4329. Map ref 9B2.

285. MANORBIER CASTLE
Norman sea castle

A romantic moated Norman castle standing on the north slope of a valley, about $\frac{1}{2}$ mile (800m) from the shore. The well preserved remains give a good idea of life at the castle with a dovecote, fishpond, mill, park and orchard. Open Easter and Whitsun to Sept. Tel: Manorbier 394. Below the castle, which is privately owned, the valley falls into a small sand and shingle bay cut along a fault in the old red sandstone cliffs. Some of the cliffs have nearly vertical strata giving a striped effect when the different coloured beds are exposed. The cliffs (NT) can be approached via the A4139. Old Castle Head, to the east, is used by the Ministry of Defence: no access is allowed when in MoD use. On Priest's Nose, the headland on the east of Manorbier Bay is the King's Quoit, a ruined cromlech or burial chamber.
□ $5\frac{1}{2}$ miles (9km) W of Tenby off B4585. Map ref 9B2.

286. MWNT
Sandy cove with cliffs

A remote cove with a delightful sandy beach, surrounded by steep shale cliffs. At the foot of the conical hill, rising 250ft (75m) to the north, is an ancient whitewashed church, one of the oldest in Wales. There are old lime kilns near the beach. Car parking at top of cliffs with a steep path down to the beach. (NT.)
□ Four miles (6.4km) N of Cardigan by minor road off A487. Map ref 9B1.

287. PLWMP
Rare farm animals

The West Wales Farm Park consists of some 60 acres (24 hectares) of parkland housing a large collection of rare and indigenous farm animals. Species of cattle, for example, include Belted Welsh, White Park and Gloucester. Open daily mid May to Sept. Tel: Rhydlewis 317.
□ On A486 five miles (8km) S of Newquay. Map ref 9B1.

288. PRESELI HILLS
Prehistoric remains

Stone rocks from these hills were used at Stonehenge and started an as yet unresolved argument as to whether they were taken all the way to the Salisbury Plain by ice or by man. The hills bear their own traces of prehistoric man, notably the Gors Fawr stone circle (grid ref SN 135294 off A478) and the exposed stones of a former burial chamber known as Pentre Ifan cromlech (grid ref SH 099370 off A487).

A six mile (9.6km) trail along a prehistoric routeway through the hills has been devised by the Pembrokeshire Coast National Park. It starts from Croesfihangel and passes many prehistoric remains as well as the site believed to have been used to quarry the materials for Stonehenge. The walk is not waymarked, but a national park leaflet (available from park offices) details the trail and is the best source of information.
□ The hills are a long range running roughly east-west to the south of Fishguard and Pembroke and crossed by the A478, B4329 and B4313. Map ref 9B1.

289. RHEIDOL FOREST
Mountain trails and abandoned mines

The Bwlch Nant-yr-Arian Forest Visitor Centre in sheltered heather glades on western edge of Cambrian Mountains has an exhibition which interprets local landscape. The centre is open from Easter to Oct on weekdays and Sat afternoons. Tel: Ponterwyd 694. Also here is a picnic area and the start of a trail which follows old lead-mine paths along the rim of the valley, crosses an open ridge and returns through larch and spruce woodlands by a small lake: $1\frac{1}{2}$ miles (2.4km). Nearby, too, is the old Llywernog Silver Lead Mine at Ponterwyd open daily Easter to Oct. Tel: Ponterwyd 620.
□ 10 miles (16km) E of Aberystwyth on A44. Map ref 9C1.

Wales

290. ST DAVID'S
Cathedral city close to spectacular cliffs and beaches

Britain's smallest cathedral city offers much to appeal to many different interests both in the city itself and in the surrounding countryside of this most south-westerly tip of Wales. Among these attractions are:

St David's. A medieval cathedral built on a site chosen by the patron saint of Wales in the 6th century. Next to it are the imposing ruins of the Bishop's Palace, open standard DoE hours plus Sun mornings Apr to Sept.

Beaches. Many small coves are tucked between the cliffs but the biggest beach is Whitesand Bay, a magnificent stretch of sandy beach enclosed by dramatic cliffs. Popular with families and also for surfing. Also known as Porth-mawr. Overlooked by summit and viewpoint of Carnllidi.

Cliffs. The waymarked long-distance footpath follows the clifftops. It can be used for circular all-day walks based on St David's but even short stretches are highly rewarding, offering magnificent views with many seabirds to be seen on the islands and rocks offshore. A promontory fort at St David's Head is among several prehistoric sites.

☐ 13 miles (21km) NW of Haverfordwest on A487. OS map 157 covers the area. Map ref 9A2.

291. ST GOVAN'S CHAPEL
Cliff-face chapel

This tiny stone-built chapel lies in a cleft of the rocks on the cliff face of the Castlemartin peninsula (see map with Day Out 268). The building as it exists today is remarkable enough, given its position just above the high tide mark and its 13th-century construction. But it also has a rude stone altar and rock-cut cell which tradition assigns to the 5th-century saint of its name. Certainly the site and the well below the chapel are typical of early Celtic religious foundations. A footpath leads down to the chapel by 52 stone steps from the clifftop. NB: there is no access when the Castlemartin firing range is being used.

☐ Five miles (8km) S of Pembroke off B4319 via Bosherston. Map ref 9B2.

292. SKOMER ISLANDS
Bird-watching, views and nature trails

These are a group of islands just off the mainland between Milford Haven and St Bride's Bay. The name of Skomer is also given to the largest of the islands, a grey mass of igneous rock which is a National Nature Reserve with one of the finest seabird colonies in north-west Europe including fulmar, shag, kittiwake, puffin, guillemot, gulls and Manx shearwater. Grey seals can also be seen. Daily boat trips from Easter to Sept from Martin's Haven, near Marloes, according to demand. The crossing takes about 20 minutes. Tel: St David's 241 for further information about boat trips to Skomer. A landing fee is payable to the warden.

There are no visitor facilities on the island other than a 2¼ mile (3.6km) nature trail; a booklet published by the West Wales Naturalists' Trust is available from Lockley Lodge Information Centre at Martin's Haven. Tel: Dale 234. Also worth visiting on the island is an Iron Age promontory fort.

Skokholm is an important bird observatory and has a lighthouse but it is not open to the public. Nor is there access to Grassholm, the smallest and most distant of the islands. In contrast Gateholm is so close to the mainland that it can be reached on foot at low tide from Marloes Sands – the starting point of a 2½ mile (4km) waymarked nature trail, details of which are available locally or from the West Wales Naturalists' Trust. Tel: Haverfordwest 5462.

☐ Martin's Haven is 15 miles (24km) SW of Haverfordwest via B4327. Map ref 9A2.

293. TREGARON
Drovers' roads and wildlife

Every other Tuesday cattle and sheep fill the market place and streets of this little town beneath the Cambrian mountains. Tregaron remains an important market town, although its fortunes have suffered along with those of the hill farmers whom it serves. Its past importance is illustrated by the number of old drovers' roads that led through here over the mountains to England – see Day Out 345 for a motoring tour of the Cambrian Mountains on some of these roads.

But some former drovers' roads remain in their traditional form and have recently encouraged a new growth ‘ industry: pony-trekking. Other interests which can be pursued here are angling in the upper Teifi (and its tributaries) and the study of wildlife which exists north of the town in the great Bog of Tregaron, a four mile (6.4km) wilderness which is now a National Nature Reserve.

Cors Tregaron, as the Bog is also known, is one of the oldest and most scientifically studied peat bogs in Britain. It contains in a semi-fossilized form a complete record of the vegetation of this remote Welsh valley from the Ice Age to the present day. Permits must be obtained to visit it to see the large variety of rare bog plants, such as sundew and butterwort. This NCC reserve is also interesting to the bird-watcher since this is the largest overwintering station for Greenland's whitefronted goose. For further information, contact the NCC. Tel: Bangor 4001.
□ 11 miles (18km) NE of Lampeter on A485 or B4343. Map ref 9C1.

Gwent

A hilly county in south-east Wales, its attractions include Chepstow, Tintern Abbey in the Wye Valley and Abergavenny. South Wales Tourism Council, Tel: Carmarthen 7557.

294. CAERWENT/CAERLEON
Roman remains

Caerwent was the site of the only walled civilian town in Roman Wales. The city of *Venta Silurum* was built to house – and civilise – the conquered natives. But the settlement did not retain its importance after the Romans' departure and it suffered badly at the hands of Irish raiders. Nevertheless there are substantial remains of the old Roman walls, in places up to 17ft (5m) high, and the village's main street follows the old Roman lines. Rome's military settlement in this part of the Empire was nine miles (14km) west at Caerleon. Here there are some fine remains of a large Legionary Fortress, despite the suburban sprawl of modern Caerleon and neighbouring Newport. By far the most notable of these remains is a superb amphitheatre, excavated in 1928 on a site rich in Arthurian legend; it is open standard DoE hours plus Sun mornings Apr to Sept.
□ Caerwent is five miles (8km) SW of Chepstow off A48; Caerleon is one mile (1.6km) NE of Newport. Map ref 4A2.

295. CWMCARN
Forest drive

A seven mile (11km) 'scenic drive' has been devised by the Forestry Commission and Countryside Commission in a side valley off Ebbw Vale. Picnic places, adventure play areas, forest or mountain walks and viewpoints are clearly marked along the route which is open Easter to Oct. There is an admission charge to the drive along twisting roads through mixed coniferous woodland with exceptional views of both the Bristol Channel and Brecon Beacons. Leaflet available from Forest Office at Abercarn. Tel: Newbridge 244223.
□ Access from A467 S of Abercarn, approx six miles (9.6km) N of junction 27 on M4. Map ref 9D2.

296. LOWER WYE VALLEY
Wooded river gorge

After leaving the Herefordshire plain the Wye finds its way to the sea barred by the limestone and coal-bearing rocks of the Forest of Dean plateau. In its dramatic escape to the sea, the river has cut a deep gorge through the plateau. By swinging from one side of the valley to another and by eroding any softer rocks it may encounter, the

Wales

Wye has created a series of loops and U-turns.

These loops and gorges are set against a frame of wooded hillsides and picturesque villages.. Here, on the Welsh side of the border, lies Tintern, dominated by the magnificent ruins of its Cistercian abbey, the inspiration for one of Wordsworth's finest poems. And further up the river stands the lovely red sandstone castle of Goodrich, with the village crouched at its feet. The result is some of the most spectacular and accessible   scenery in lowland Britain.

Even the main road following the river valley from Chepstow to Ross-on-Wye produces stunning views. A good map, however, reveals not only smaller roads but a large number of nature or forest trails and footpaths, notably the Wye Valley Walk and Offa's Dyke long-distance path.

Above Tintern the river becomes non-tidal and this combined with softer rocks allows the valley to broaden and expand until it meets the Monnow at Monmouth. Above Monmouth the dual carriageway A40 allows swift access to Symonds Yat via a beautiful wooded valley which straddles the England-Wales border.

At Symonds Yat a bluff of resistant rock has diverted the river northwards in an ever-widening loop. Once started this loop must extend as the current of the river is directed towards the extending bank. In time a way will be found through the rock. Once this happens the loop will be sealed off and a temporary 'ox-bow' lake will form until this in turn is silted up. No need to hurry, though: it won't happen in your lifetime. The car park nearest Symonds Yat is crowded at peak times, but there is alternative parking (and a pleasant walk) at the Biblins picnic area and forest trail, one mile (1.6km) to the south.

There are many other things to see in this popular touring area. Among them, and including some lesser known spots are the Kymin (NT hill east of Monmouth off A1436); Bargain or Whitestone Woods off A466 between Llandogo and Tintern; Wynd Cliff (off A466 north of St Arvans); and Chepstow Castle.

OS map 162 and the Wye Valley and Forest of Dean 1:25,000 Outdoor Leisure Map detail minor roads, footpaths including the Offa's Dyke and Wye Valley Walks, nature trails and picnic sites. See also Tintern Forest (below).

☐ Between Chepstow and Ross-on-Wye. Map ref 4A2.

---

297. TINTERN FOREST
Woodland trails, views and picnics

This forest covers a large tract of woodland in south-east Wales. The former station at Tintern (now restored) houses an exhibition and is a central point for walks in the forest. Leaflets are available for unguided walks and a programme of guided walks is also organised. Details from the visitor centre. Tel: Tintern 566. There is a picnic area at the station. Among other features of the forest are:

St Pierre Wood. Picnic place at edge of beechwood overlooking Severn estuary and with good views of the Severn Bridge. Fairly level forest walk through young beechwoods and with a variety of plants growing on carboniferous limetone. In summer this is a good area for butterflies. Distance $1\frac{1}{4}$ miles (2km). About one mile (1.6km) NW of A48 at Pwllmeyric on by-road to Shirenewton.

Priscau Bach. Picnic place and forest walks. Picnicking alongside Mounton Brook. Three walks climbing up steep wooded slopes with fine views over Tintern Forest. Longest is $1\frac{1}{2}$ miles (2.4km). On B4235 W of Chepstow.

Lower Wyndcliff. Picnic place with attractive view over horseshoe bend of River Wye. Alongside main Wye Valley road A466 about three miles (4.8km) from Chepstow. Also Lower Wyndcliff 365 Steps picnic place in woodland overlooking Severn Estuary.

Upper Wyndcliff. A viewpoint which is on a by-road off A466 $\frac{1}{2}$ mile (800m) north of St Arvans or reached by 365 steps from Lower Wyndcliff picnic place. A nature trail starts from Upper Wyndcliff car park and leads to Eagle's Nest viewpoint 700ft (213m) above Wye Gorge with fine view of confluence of Severn and Wye rivers.

Industrial history trail. Along the valley bottom to Pont-y-Saeson linking remains of sites which formed an industrial complex based on water power from 1556 to 1901. Trail starts from Tintern Sawmills car park. From Chepstow turn left immediately before Royal George Hotel in Tintern. Car park is about ¼ mile (400m) up on right.
□ Map ref 4A2.

298. TREDEGAR
Restoration house and park

Tredegar House is a 17th-century building – with 18th-century additions which is widely regarded as the finest Restoration house in Wales. Two rooms are open to the public on afternoons other than Mon and Tues, Apr to Sept, and restoration work is continuing on other parts of the house. The park and woodland around the house now form a country park with a children's farm and fishing or boating on the lake. Tel: Newport (Wales) 62568.
□ Three miles (4.8km) SW of Newport near junction of M4 and A48. Map ref 4A2.

299. WHITE CASTLE
Moated castle

The white plaster coating on the masonry which gave the castle its name has now virtually disappeared. But the inner bailey is still surrounded by a steep-sided moat which makes this castle, though quite small, one of the more interesting of those that survive from the days when the Marcher lords were struggling to control the Welsh. It formed a triangle of defensive fortifications with Grosmont and Skenfrith castles. Grosmont and Skenfrith are open any reasonable time, White Castle standard DoE hours.
□ Seven miles (11km) NE of Abergavenny off B4521 or B4233. Map ref 9D2.

Gwynedd

Dominated by Snowdonia National Park but also with Llyn Peninsula AONB. Tourist centres include Bala, Caernarfon, Conway and Harlech. It is a county of many castles but landscapes of mountains, rivers, lakes and sea are the main attractions. Other features include railways, old slate mines and the Italianate village of Portmeirion near Porthmadog. North Wales Tourism Council, Tel: Colwyn Bay 56881.

300. ABERGYNOLWYN
Mountain scenery

This small quarrying village on the Dysynni river, which flows from the ice-scoured Talyllyn Lake, three miles (4.8km) to the north-east, is a good base from which to explore the scenery around 2928ft (903m) Cader Idris. Two miles (3.2km) north-west of the village is Castell-y-Bere, the ruins of a 13th-century castle built by Llewellyn the Great. This offers good views of the sharp crag of Bird Rock where cormorant and guillemot nest six miles (9.6km) inland. South-westwards (three miles, 4.8km) are the beautiful Dolgoch Falls (125ft, 37m) and the terminus of the Talyllyn narrow-gauge railway which carries passengers seven miles (11km) to the coast and the railway museum at Tywyn. Tel: Tywyn 710472 for information about

Wales

the railway. In Abergynolwyn itself the village museum at 14 Water Street (no telephone) has more than 200 items illustrating the life of a mining community. It is open summer only, Mon to Sat plus Bank Holidays.

□ 10 miles (16km) SW of Dolgellau on B4405. Map ref 8C2.

---

301. BODNANT GARDEN
Terraces and woodland

A very large garden (NT) overlooking the Conwy Valley with views of Snowdonia, terraces in the Italian style made in the early 20th century, an 18th-century pavilion, water-lily pools and exotic planting. There is also an extensive woodland garden with a vast collection of rhododendrons, other shrubs and trees as well as rock gardens, herbaceous perennials and naturalised bulbs. The garden is open daily from mid-Mar to Oct. Tel: Ty'n-y-Groes 460.

□ Eight miles (13km) S of Llandudno on A470. Map ref 8C1.

---

302. BONT NEWYDD
Nature trail and waterfall

The Coedydd Aber Nature Trail winds among the ancient woods and crags of the Aber valley to the Aber Falls or Rhaeadr Fawr, climbing gently from 150 to 700ft (46 to 216m) above sea level. On the higher slopes there is a mixture of oak, birch and hazel; in more sheltered places wych elm, ash, alder, blackthorn and sallow may also be seen with a good selection of spring flowers such as primroses, wood anemones, wood sorrel and bluebells. Watch for woodland birds such as woodpecker, nuthatch, tree creeper and warblers, and by the riverside, dipper and grey wagtail. Raven and buzzard can be seen near peaks. At the falls note the rich flora of mosses and liverworts, kept damp by the spray. Coedydd Aber is a National Nature Reserve. The distance from the car park at Bont Newydd to the falls is about two miles (3.2km). Sensible clothes and shoes are advised as the path may be wet and slippery. Further information can be obtained from the Nature Conservancy Council. Tel: Bangor 4001.

□ ¾ mile (1.2km) SE of A55 on minor road from Aber between Bangor and Conwy. OS map 115. Map ref 8C1.

---

303. BLAENAU FFESTINIOG
Railways and quarrying

Quarrying for slate was centuries old in North Wales before it reached its peak during the 19th century. It enhanced neither the health of its workers nor the natural beauty of the landscape. But, ironically, the narrow-gauge railways and tramways that linked the quarries with the ports have outlived the quarries to become attractions in themselves, taking tourists through the 'unspoilt' countryside.

The Festiniog railway is one of the most famous of the 'Great Little Trains of Wales' (see overleaf), and currently hauls passenger services throughout the year from Porthmadog on the coast to Tanygrisiau just over a mile (2km) south of Blaenau Ffestiniog. Work is now in progress thanks partly to an EEC grant – on the final lap into Blaenau Ffestiniog itself. One mile (1.6km) to the north of the town, on the A470, the Llechwedd Slate Caverns are taking visitors by train through old slate tunnels to vast subterranean caverns up to 200ft (62m) high. A new incline has recently been opened which takes visitors to the lowest depths of the mines.

There are also exhibitions devoted to the industry both at Llechwedd and at another neighbouring quarry-turned-working museum now known as the Gloddfa Ganol Mountain Tourist Centre. Both are open daily from Easter to Oct, and both can be chilly underground. Tel: Porthmadog 2340 for details of Festiniog rail services and Tywyn 710472 for details of other 'Great Little Trains of Wales'. Tel: Blaenau Ffestiniog 306 for information about Llechwedd's opening hours, and Blaenau Ffestiniog 664 about Gloddfa Ganol.

□ 10 miles (16km) SW of Betws-y-Coed on A470. Map ref 8C1.

304. CAERHUN
Roman Wales

Here was the site of *Canovium*, a Roman fort commanding the Conwy river three miles (4.8km) further upstream than the site chosen 12 centuries later for the castle and 'new town' of Conwy. The outline of the Roman walls can still be seen in meadowland close to the river. Mountain walkers can experience a more arduous reminder of the Roman presence in North Wales by following the footpath that traces the route of the old Roman road west from Caerhun over the mountains to Aber. It is a route dotted with cairns and earthworks but also, and less evocatively, electricity pylons. The Roman road eventually led to *Segontium*, the Roman predecessor of another great 'new' medieval settlement – Caernarfon. *Segontium* was a large fort; a museum, and its remains to the east of the modern town, are open standard DoE hours. OS map 115 shows the route of the Roman road clearly.
□ Three miles (4.8km) S of Conwy off B5106. Map ref 8C1.

305. CLOGAU
Gold mine

Clogau mine provided the gold for the Queen's wedding ring, but the heyday of the mine was in the latter half of the 19th century. By a small car park is an interpretative display board which illustrates a short walk along the banks of the river where prospectors used to pan for gold. There is also a summary of the history of the mine. Visitors wanting to find out more should go to the Forestry Commission Maesgwm Visitor Centre – see next entry.
□ At Bontddu four miles (6.4km) NE of Barmouth on A496. Map ref 8C2.

306. COED-Y-BRENIN FOREST
Mountains, rivers and waterfalls

A network of over 50 miles (80.5km) of attractive paths, tracks and forest roads take walkers into the heart of the forest. There are six car parks and two picnic areas as well as a number of forest trails and waymarked walks. Maps and guides are available from the Maesgwm Visitor Centre (Forestry Commission) which also has an exhibition on life and work in the forest, the extraordinarily rich formations and the Clogau gold mines. The centre is open daily, from Easter to 30 Sept. Tel: Ganllwyd 226. Best starting points for walks are the Dolgefeiliau and Tyn-y-Groes picnic places and the Arboretum car park. Three miles (5km) to the south, in the NT estate of Dolmelynllyn, is Rhiadr Ddu or Black Waterfall, one of the most spectacular falls in Wales. Path leads from Dolmelynllyn village hall for about two miles (3.2km) and is steep in places.
□ Maesgwm Forest Visitor Centre is eight miles (13km) N of Dolgellau off A470. Map ref 8C2.

307. COED YDD MAENTWROG
Nature trail and lake

The Coed Llyn Mair nature trail may be followed either from Tan-y-Bwlch station (on the Festiniog Railway) or from the car park near Llyn Mair, a small artificial lake visited by black-headed gull, mallard and grebe among other birds. It goes through oak woodlands and meadows with dry-stone walls. At one point on the trail, there is a display of nest-boxes showing different patterns to suit the needs of various birds. There is a good view of the lake from the trail which is $1\frac{1}{2}$ miles (2.4km) long, but it is open only from Easter to Sept 30. A leaflet is available from kiosk at north point or 'honesty box' at south car park. Further information from the Nature Conservancy Council. Tel: Bangor 4001.
□ Off B4110 two miles (3.2km) W of Maentwrog. Map ref 8C2.

308. CRICCIETH
Castle and caves

Criccieth Castle was a native stronghold, later strengthened by Edward I. Its remains (AM) stand on a grassy headland overlooking Tremadog Bay with panoramic views of the sea and mountains. Beneath the castle – open standard DoE hours plus Sun mornings Apr to Sept – are sand and pebble beaches. About a mile (1.6km) east of the castle is Black Rock, pitted with caves which can be seen at low tide or reached by boat. Walk to Black Rock along the beach or follow sign alongside railway line to Black Rock Halt. 1½ miles (2.4km) west of Criccieth is Llan-

ystumdwy where Lloyd George spent his early life. His grave is there and a memorial museum is open weekdays in summer. Tel: Criccieth 2654.
□ Nine miles (14km) W of Porthmadog on A497. Map ref 8C2.

309. CWM IDWAL
Glacial landscape

For a chance to understand the workings of a former glacier, walk a

The Great Little Trains of Wales

Among railway buffs the name of Richard Trevithick is almost as revered as that of George Stephenson. Some 20 years before Stephenson's *Rocket* became the first locomotive to haul regular passenger services, Trevithick's steam engine was hauling loads for an iron works at Merthyr Tydfil in South Wales.

With such a history it is scarcely surprising that Wales has retained a strong bond with the age of steam. It is mostly in mid and north Wales, however, that steam has enjoyed a renaissance over the last 10 years. So many railways have been revived that now they have banded together to promote themselves as 'The Great Little Trains of Wales'. So successful have they been that more than a million passengers each year travel the old lines that were either declining or in some cases abandoned altogether before this second age of steam.

The clue to much of their appeal lies in the word 'little'. For these are mostly narrow-gauge railways, winding their way up and through the mountains on routes which in some cases were originally used to haul slate from quarries to ports. The result: wonderful views of the Welsh mountain and coastal scenery without the hassle of traffic jams.

Each of the 11 railways in this loose-knit alliance operates its own time-tables but general tourist tickets are available for use on several of the lines over a seven-day period. For information about these tickets or the little trains generally contact local tourist

information centres or Tel: Tywyn 710472. Otherwise contact the individual railways themselves.

Festiniog Railway. 12¼ miles (20km) from Porthmadog to Tanygrisiau with plans to extend it to its original terminus at Blaenau Ffestiniog. Originally a slate line – it started as early as 1836 as a horse-drawn tramway – this line was closed in 1946 before its triumphant reopening by enthusiasts. Operates from mid-Feb to mid-Nov. Tel: Porthmadog 2340. (See also Day Out 303.)

Talyllyn Railway. 7¼ miles (11½km) from Tywyn to Nant Gwernod. This line has operated continuously since 1865 and was the first in Britain to be saved from closure by volunteers. There are fine walks past waterfalls from the intermediary station at Dolgoch. Trains run Easter to mid-Sept. Tel: Tywyn 710472. (The railway museum at Tywyn is open during rail season or by request.)

Vale of Rheidol Railway. 11¾ miles (19km) from Aberystwyth to Devil's Bridge. The only 'little train' operated by British Rail and the only one originally built for tourists. Easter to early Oct. Tel: Aberystwyth 612377.

Llanberis Lake Railway. Two miles (3.2km) along eastern shore of lake from Padarn Park, near Llanberis. It is part of the old slate line from the now closed Dinorwic quarry. Another link with those days is the North Wales Quarrying Museum close to the terminus. Easter to Sept.

rugged $1\frac{1}{4}$ mile (2km) nature trail (NCC) open throughout the year around Cwm Idwal. This cwm or corrie was scoured out of the surrounding mountain by Ice Age glaciers. It has been famous since the 17th century for the rich variety of plants and birds which can be seen. The trail starts at the western end of Llyn Ogwen, just south of Ogwen Cottage Mountain School on the A5,

following a well worn trail to the lake of Llyn Idwal. Cross the stepping stones to the right and climb to the ridge which gives a splendid view north of the glacial trough of Nant Ffrancon with the A5 running through it. Walk to the head of the lake, noting the hummocky ice-deposited moraines and the cliffs of the Devil's Kitchen with its waterfall. Pass the ice-smoothed climbing cliff of Idwal Slabs and return to base over ⟫⟫⟫

Tel: Llanberis 549.

Welshpool & Llanfair Railway. $5\frac{1}{2}$ miles (8.8km) from Llanfair Caereinion to Sylfaen with ambitions to complete the old route into Welshpool. Originally established as a passenger line, the rolling border hills rather than mountains give it a character of its own. Easter to mid-Oct. Tel: Llanfair Caereinion 441. (See also Day Out 343.)

Snowdon Mountain Railway. $4\frac{3}{4}$ miles ($7\frac{1}{2}$km) from Llanberis to the summit of the highest mountain in England and Wales – 3561ft (1085m), Snowdon. The ascent takes an hour with predictably magnificent views. Accommodation on the rack and pinion trains is limited so that passengers may have difficulty finding room during the peak season. Note, too, that high winds can sometimes cause services to be halted at Clogwyn – three-quarters of the way to the summit. Easter to early Oct. Tel: Llanberis 223. (NB: for the next easiest way to the summit, see Day Out 322.)

Fairbourne Railway. Two miles (3.2km) from Fairbourne to Barmouth Ferry. This line has the smallest gauge of all – just 15 inches (38cm); even children can tower over its miniature trains. The line runs along a fine beach with excellent views over the Mawddach estuary. Easter to mid Oct. Tel: Fairbourne 362.

Bala Lake Railway. $4\frac{1}{2}$ miles (7.25km) from Llanuwchllyn to Pont Mwnwgl-y-llyn near Bala along the eastern shore of the largest lake in Wales, Llyn Tegid or Bala Lake. A

narrow-gauge track was laid here along a route once used by the Great Western for its services between Barmouth and Ruabon and thence to London. Easter to mid-Oct. Tel: Llanuwchllyn 666.

Brecon Mountain Railway. Two miles (3.2km) from Pant, near Merthyr Tydfil, where Trevithick was such a pioneer. The line runs into the magnificent scenery of the Brecon Beacons. Future construction will take the railway – the only narrow gauge 'Little Train' in South Wales – a further $3\frac{1}{2}$ miles (5.6km) into the national park. The terminus is, at present, at Pontsticill on the shore of Taf Fechan reservoir. Daily, May to Oct, with limited winter service. Tel: Merthyr Tydfil 4854.

Don't forget, too, the trains of British Rail – not merely because they might also disappear if they are not used but because they are attractive in their own right. The Conwy Valley Line from Llandudno Junction to Blaenau Ffestiniog is timetabled to connect (by coach for the time being) with the Festiniog Railway but is worth the trip anyway. So, too, is the Cambrian Coast Line from Aberystwyth to Pwllheli. Aberystwyth itself is linked by the Mid Wales Line to Shrewsbury. The Heart of Wales Line follows a spectacular route from Shrewsbury to Swansea via Llandrindod Wells. British Rail also provides tourist tickets for use over particular periods; for details, contact British Rail or tourist information centres.

more moraines to the starting point. OS map 115 covers the area and a trail leaflet is available; details from the Nature Conservancy Council. Tel: Bangor 4001.

☐ Four miles (6.4km) W of Capel Curig off A5. Map ref 8C1.

310. CWM PENNANT
Hidden mountain valley

To see an unspoilt upland valley almost in the heart of Snowdonia's highest mountains visit the hidden Cwm Pennant. Travel along the picturesque River Dwyfor to the crag of Craig Isallt, a tough igneous intrusion which even the glaciers failed to breach. Behind the crag is lonely and beautiful Cwm Pennant with its scattered sheep farms encircled by a majestic sweep of frost-shattered summits and ice-eroded slopes. For the fit and energetic a scramble from the valley head one mile (1.6km) to the col offers an unusual view of Snowdon.

☐ Four miles (6.4km) NE of A487 at Dolbenmaen. Map ref 8C2.

311. DINAS DINLLE
Seaside hill-fort

This is a type of hill-fort more common in Scotland and Ireland than Wales or England: perched on the very edge of the sea. Inland the twin ramparts of the 3½ acre (1.4 hectare) fort can still be seen, but on the western side they are heavily eroded by the sea. Its style of construction places it clearly in the Iron Age, but pottery and coins have been found from the second and third centuries AD. The fort has given its name to a three mile (4.8km) stretch of sandy beach which it overlooks. As well as offering good bathing and ample car-parking this beach is a centre for sea angling, canoeing and surfing.

☐ 4½ miles (7km) SW of Caernarfon off A499. Map ref 8B1.

312. GREAT ORME
Cliffs with nature trail

Great Orme's Head is the larger of two great masses of carboniferous lime-stone on the North Wales coast near the seaside resort of Llandudno, the other being Little Orme's Head to the east. The Great Orme has both a cable car and a tramway to take visitors towards its 700ft (213m) summit with its fine views.

The headland itself can be explored either by car along Marine Drive (a toll road starting from Llandudno Pier) or via a nature trail (starting from the café in Happy Valley). The trail totals five miles (8km) and covers geology, wildlife, historical and archaeological sites. An excellent leaflet is available from an information kiosk at the pier.

☐ Immediately NW of Llandudno. Map ref 8C1.

313. HARLECH
Sea castle

Now a massive ruin, Harlech Castle (AM) was built by Edward I in 1283 on a rocky promontory overlooking the sands of Morfa Harlech and the Glaslyn estuary. Originally the castle was on a sea cliff but the sea has retreated leaving the castle stranded half a mile inland. Climb the 143 steps up to the top of the gatehouse to get excellent views of Snowdon, the Lleyn Peninsula, Tremadog Bay and south to Cader Idris. Open standard DoE hours plus Sun mornings Apr to Sept. The sands and estuary of Morfa Harlech form a nature reserve mostly used by flocks of wildfowl wintering from Northern Europe. It is not open to the public.

☐ Nine miles (14km) N of Barmouth on A496. Map ref 8C2.

314. LLANBEDR
Farm trail

The workings of a typical Welsh hill farm are explained by boards strategically sited along the two mile (3.2km) Cefn Isaf Farm Trail within the Snowdonia National Park. Open all year. Trail starts 1½ miles (2.4km) east of Llanbedr. See map with Day Out 321.

☐ Llanbedr is four miles (6.4km) SE of Harlech on A496. OS map 124. Map ref 8C2.

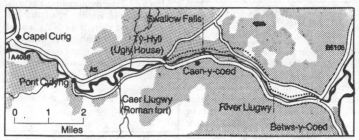

*Llugwy Valley: a mountain river in varied and dramatic moods. Day Out 315
and also 326 and 327 for forest walks*

315. LLUGWY VALLEY
Mountain river

To see a mountain river in all its moods follow the valley of Llugwy between Capel Curig and Betws-y-Coed, a distance of just over 7 miles (11km). A good starting point is the attractive group of cottages at Pont Cyfyng, one mile (1.6km) south-east of Capel Curig – cross the bridge south of the A5 road. Here the river is terminating a stage of gorges, deep pools, rapids and 'white water'; follow the minor road eastwards where the river glides easily through alluvial meadows, swinging into meanders and leaving grassy gravel terraces above its floodplain, on one of which the Romans sited their fort of Caer Llugwy. Cross the A5 at the picturesque Tŷ-Hyll (Ugly House) and follow the river by path or minor road on its northern bank to Betws-y-Coed. But detour along the A5 itself to see the magnificent drop of the river at the famous Swallow Falls, between Tŷ-Hyll and Betws-y-Coed. (See map.)

□ Capel Curig and Betws-y-Coed are on the main A5 road between Llangollen and Bangor. OS map 115. Map ref 8C1.

316. MOCHRAS
Wildlife on a man-made peninsula

Also known as Shell Island since at least 100 varieties of shell and many unusual pebbles can be found here. The best time to hunt for shells is during the big tides in Jan, Feb, Aug and Sept. It is not a natural island but a man-made peninsula, created by the Earl of Winchelsea in the 19th century who diverted the river to reclaim the land. The channel silted up to form the high, grassy dunes which are now a haven for tern, oyster catcher, sandpiper, all kinds of gulls and even buzzard. Shelduck nest in the rabbit holes. There are many wild flowers, including orchids and wild dwarf roses. If you arrive early in the morning you can often see seals, particularly if the sea is calm. The 'island' is open to the public on payment of a toll and reached by a causeway which is covered at high tide.

□ W of Llanbedr off A496 seven miles (11km) N of Barmouth. Map ref 8C2.

317. PENRHYN CASTLE
Neo-Norman castle

This is 19th-century romanticism and social climbing at its most extravagant. Dawkins Pennant, whose fortune came from slate quarries and sugar plantations, established his family in the landed aristocracy by building an enormous neo-Norman castle on a splendid site looking along the North Wales coast below Snowdonia. Everything is elaborately Norman, down to the drawing-room sofas and dining-room wallpaper. A four-poster bed of solid slate advertises the family quarries. All designed with the utmost panache and obvious enjoyment by Thomas Hopper in 1824–34. Now owned by the NT it is open daily Apr to Oct, but opening times vary. Tel: NT regional office; Betws-y-Coed 312.

□ One mile (1.6km) E of Bangor at junction of A5 and A55. Map ref 8C1.

Wales

318. PORTHMADOG and PORTMEIRION
Contrasting coastal villages

Once a great port for the slate industry the sheltered harbour of Porthmadog at the foot of Snowdonia is a good centre for an unusual day out on water or land. The double estuary of the Afon Glaslyn and the Afon Dwyryd offers an intriguing day's sailing: when the tide is in, it is a sheltered lake, while, when the tide is out, you sail a winding channel through some 10 sq miles (26 sq km) of clean sands. These sands provide fine beaches, but they can be dangerous in view of the fact that they are estuarial. And for après sail, or simple land-lubbers, there are the attractions of the picturesque Festiniog Railway (see page 98) and the idyllic Italianate village of Portmeirion.

Created on a rocky headland by Welsh architect Clough Williams-Ellis, Portmeirion, with its colonnaded buildings, piazzas, bell towers, exotic gardens and fountains, is a real showpiece. The village is open to visitors daily Apr to Oct; Tel: Penrhyndeudraeth 453.

□ Five miles (8km) E of Criccieth on A487 at western end of a toll road. Map ref 8C2.

319. PORTH NEIGWL
Beach and clifftop viewpoint

This four mile (6.4km) stretch of beach, backed by cliffs of boulder clay, is also known as Hell's Mouth and is virtually inaccessible except at either end. On a stormy day, when waves pound the shore, you can see the full force of Atlantic erosion. There are spectacular views from the headland of Trwyn y Ffosle (NT) at the south-eastern end of the beach. Note how the tiny River Soch turns away from the sea (its channel is blocked with blown sand) and instead follows a rocky gorge, cut by glacial meltwaters before reaching the sea at Abersoch. Plas-yn-Rhiw is a 16th-century NT-owned house with gardens, stream and waterfall, overlooking the bay to the north-west of Hell's Mouth. Open

Mon and Tues by appointment only. Tel: Rhiw 219. For the beach of Porth Neigwl itself there is an NT car park south-west of Llanengan which is reached on minor roads south-west of Abersoch. The headland of Trwyn-y-Ffosle is off a minor road south from Abersoch.

□ 1½ miles (2.4km) SW of Abersoch. Map ref 8B2.

320. PORTH-OER
Whistling sand

This lovely beach is famous for its 'whistling sand': a strange phenomenon which is caused by the spherical shaped grains of sand rubbing together when you walk upon them. The beach is also good for bathing, with rock pools to explore at low tide, and sea angling.

□ Two miles (3.2km) N of Aberdarm near Methlem. Map ref 8B2.

321. ROMAN STEPS
Ancient trackway

More than 2000 slabs of rock or flagstones here mark out a route across a col in the mountains known as the Harlech Dome. Were they laid by the Romans as their name suggests? Certainly the route lies near their inland fort at Tomen-y-Mur near Lake Trawsfynydd, so it is plausible to argue that the Romans used the route. But the stones themselves were more likely to have been laid in medieval times to provide a land supply route for

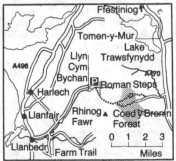

Roman Steps: a mountain mystery not far from the Llanbedr farm trail. Days Out respectively 321, 314

Harlech Castle. Later it would have been used by packhorse teams. Now the Steps provide an interesting walk for ramblers – see map.

□ Four miles (6.4km) E of Harlech along minor road to Llyn Cwm Bychan where there is a car park. Map ref 8C2.

322. SNOWDONIA
1: The easiest way up Wales's highest mountain: 3561ft (1085m) Snowdon

The easiest way up Snowdon is by the Snowdon Mountain Railway from Llanberis. The second easiest way, however, is by foot and follows a very similar route – see map. A broad and easy-angled track follows the same north-west ridge although there are boggy sections along the five miles (8km) and 3000ft (925m) of ascent. Stout shoes or boots are essential. As late as early June a snowbank can remain across the top of this approach. Whatever the month, avoid the mountain if snowy conditions prevail and you lack the necessary equipment and experience. An excellent information centre at Llanberis – open all year – can provide detailed walking information. Tel: Llanberis 765.

Start from the Royal Victoria Hotel in Llanberis where signposts direct you along an initial 20 minutes stretch of tarmac road – the signposts are in English as well as Welsh. Near a viewpoint over Ceunant Mawr (Large Waterfall) the tarmac road is in fact the steepest of the whole ascent. Continue up it to pass between two houses. There are a few more scattered houses to be passed on both sides before reaching the top of the immediate hill. Here a gate crosses the road. Go through it and continue up a gentle incline to a signpost saying 'Path to Snowdon'. This is the Llanberis track proper and the route from here on is obvious, if a little rough and rocky.

The building of Halfway House (refreshments) can be seen well ahead, the path becoming barer and wider beyond. At 2521ft (775m) it passes beneath the rack-and-pinion railway to the edge of Cwm Glas Bach – with

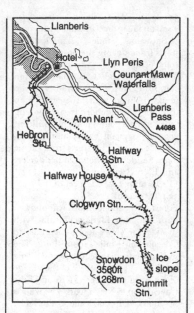

Snowdon: the two easiest ways to reach the summit

splendid views of mountainside and the Llanberis Pass below. About 600ft (185m) higher is Bwlch Glas ('the green col') just above path and railway and worth visiting to look down into Cwm Dyli. It is up here that the Llanberis Track meets two other paths: the Snowdon Ranger route on the right and the Pen-y-Gwryd path on the left. Another quarter of an hour's steep climbing alongside the railway completes the ascent which usually takes three hours or so.

□ Llanberis is six miles (9.6km) SE of Caernarfon on A4086. OS map 115. Map ref 8C1.

323–327. SNOWDONIA
2: Five days out in the forest

Snowdonia Forest Park covers 23,400 acres (9473 hectares) of spectacular scenery within the larger Snowdonia National Park. The park embraces the forests of Gwydyr and Beddgelert amid the foothills of Snowdon. Its centre is at Betws-y-Coed on the River Llugery and it includes:

Wales

323 Beddgelert Forest
Trail on fairly level ground with views of Snowdon, ¾ mile (1.2km) long. It starts from a camp site on west side of A4085 one mile (1.6km) north of Beddgelert; leaflet available from camp site. Also a forest walk 1½ miles (2.4km) long with a steep climb through rhododendrons and young forest to viewpoint giving magnificent view of Gwynant Valley and lake, 1½ miles (2.4km). This starts from picnic place beside A498 between Beddgelert and Llyn Gwynant.
□ OS map 115. Map ref 8C1.

324 Tŷ Canol
Forest walk along short waymarked path on the Llyn peninsula with spectacular views across the coast to Caernarfon, ¼ mile (400m) long. The walk starts from the car park and picnic site ¾ mile (1.2km) north of the village of Lithfaen on B4417 extension of the Caernarfon to Nefyn road. The walk is waymarked, but no leaflet is available.
□ OS map 123. Map ref 8B2.

325. Gwydyr Uchaf
One mile (1.6km) west of Llanrwst on the B5106 near Gwydyr Castle is Gwydyr Uchaf Forest Visitor Centre. Open daily Easter to Sept; Tel: Llanrwst 640578. Nearby – and signposted is a picnic place at the edge of a meadow by 17th-century chapel and Dower House overlooking the Vale of Conwy. Also in Gwydyr Forest are 10 waymarked walks through varied landscape of woodlands, meadows, crags, stream sides and hidden lakes with spectacular views of Snowdonia. These vary in length from ¾ mile (1.2km) to 5¼ miles (8.4km) and start in the vicinity of Betws-y-Coed. A leaflet describing all 10 walks is available at the visitor centre.
□ OS map 115. Map ref 8C1.

326 Garth Falls walk
A smooth paved path with handrails which winds through mature open forest with ferns and shrubs alongside a stream. It has been designed for handicapped and elderly people; the path, which is 300 yards (274m) long, ends by a waterfall where there are picnic tables and seats. There are descriptive texts in braille. The walk starts at the west end of Betws-y-Coed from a small car park near Miner's Bridge. Walks for groups of handicapped people can be arranged via the Head Forester. Tel: Llanwrst 640578.
□ Map ref 8C1.

327 Cae'n y Coed
This is a picnic place on grassy slopes with scattered birches just below the forest edge, off the A5 west of Swallow Falls, 1½ miles (2.4km) from Betws-y-Coed. Arboretum Walk, steep in places, starts from the picnic place and climbs up through a hillside arboretum with a collection of 48 exotic tree species. There are fine mountain and valley views across the forest to Moel Siabod. A leaflet is available locally.
□ OS map 115. Map ref 8C1.

---

328. TRE'R CEIRI
Spectacular hill-fort

This is one of the most exciting prehistoric sites in the British Isles: a fortified town on a narrow mountain top some 1800ft (549m) high with dramatic views over Snowdonia, the Llyn peninsula and across to Anglesey. Partly because of its remoteness and partly because it was built of local stone, the remains of this settlement are more substantial than is customarily the case with Iron Age hill-forts.

The five acre (two hectare) site was protected not only by ramparts but was also completely walled. Some parts of this wall are still six feet (1.8m) high. The walls of many huts can also be seen at Tre'r Ceiri which is on the most easterly summit of a mountain known as Yr Eifl. In all more than 150 huts were built here and excavation has produced rich finds of pottery, mainly from around AD 150, indicating that Tre'r Ceiri thrived well into Roman times. A footpath leads towards this mountain fortress from the B4417 road between Llanaelhaearn and Llithfaen. It is a steep ascent which emphasises Tre'r Ceiri's strength and weaknesses: easy to defend but impossible for peaceful agricultural settlement.
□ Approx one mile (1.6m) W of Llanaelhaearn off B4417. Grid ref SH 34447; OS map 123. Map ref 8C2.

Mid-Glamorgan

Small and largely industrial county with many mining valleys. Attractions: castles at Caerphilly and Bridgend. South Wales Tourism Council. Tel: Carmarthen 7557.

329. BRIDGEND
Norman castles and priory

More an industrial than a market centre these days but its position near three valleys – Ogmore, Garw and Llynfi – has left it with three nearby Norman castles. Coity Castle is two miles (3.2km) north-east of Brigend off A4061; New Castle is near the town centre on A4063; and Ogmore Castle 2½ miles (4km) south-west on B4524. The latter is particularly interesting with its 13th-century structure built on earlier earthworks and ditches. Ogmore also has some ancient stepping stones leading to its remains across the River Ewenny. A fourth ancient building near Brigend is Ewenny Priory, a 12th-century monastery which had military defences with walls and towers.

All four buildings are under the care of the DoE; Coity and Ogmore are open standard hours, Ewenny weekdays only, New Castle similar days but different times. The Wales Tourist Board say that if it is locked during recognised opening hours (detailed in the DoE booklet, *Historic Monuments*) the key for New Castle is available at Farm Cottage, 18 Llangewydd Road, Bridgend, while that for Ogmore is at the farmhouse opposite the castle.
□ 16 miles (26km) W of Cardiff on A48. Map ref 9C2.

330. CAERPHILLY
Moated castle

A town known for its cheese – although this is no longer made here – and its castle. The latter is partly in ruins but its design was one of the finest in Europe with particularly elaborate water defences: not one but two moats. Similarly there is an inner and outer

ward within the central keep. The castle dates from the 13th century and just survived attempts by Cromwell to blow it up. However one tower is still leaning at a dizzy angle from that particular blast. Open standard DoE hours plus Sun mornings Apr to Sept.
□ Seven miles (11km) N of Cardiff on A469. Map ref 9D2.

331. DARE VALLEY
Country park on reclaimed land

More than 470 acres (193 hectares) of open moorland and wooded valley have been largely reclaimed from derelict land which once contained six collieries: a good example of the pioneering work which is in progress to make the South Wales valleys green again. The landscaped country park offers ample scope for picnicking and walking. Leaflets giving details of mountain and forest walks and an industrial trail are available from the visitor centre which is open daily throughout the year and has a permanent warden service. Tel: Aberdare 874672.
□ Park is signposted off B4277, two miles (3.2km) S of Aberdare. Map ref 9D2

Powys

The only landlocked county in Wales. The Severn, Usk and Wye all rise from its mountains. Brecon Beacons National Park is in the south. Many castles in the borderland of the Welsh Marshes, also the best stretches of Offa's Dyke. Other attractions include the city of Brecon with its outstanding cathedral. Mid Wales Tourism Council, Tel: Machynlleth 2401.

332. BLACK MOUNTAINS
Mountain drive and ancient priory

A spectacular drive of about 17 miles (27km) through the Black Mountains over Hay Bluff is on the B4423 road from Llanfihangel Crucorney to Hay-on-Wye – it becomes unclassified north of the ruins of the 11th-century

Wales

Augustinian priory of Llanthony. The priory was built on the site of a ruined chapel dedicated to St David and was originally consecrated as a hermitage. From these humble beginnings it grew into one of the finest priories in Wales and its still substantial remains are a fine reminder of its former splendour.

The road beyond the priory climbs up the attractive Vale of Ewyas to a high pass (1778ft, 533m), known as the Gospel Pass, on the road over Hay Bluff. The views northwards are glorious with wooded foothills, the great curve of the Wye near Hay-on-Wye, Radnor Forest and the Clee Hills.

□ N of Abergavenny. OS map 161. Map ref 9D2.

333. BRECON AND ABERGAVENNY CANAL
Canal walks and boating

One of the most beautiful canals in the British Isles. It was built between 1797 and 1812 along the Usk Valley from the outskirts of Brecon eastwards to Pontymoile, one mile (1.6km) south of Pontypool, where it joined the Monmouthshire canal, and where a canal exhibition has just been established by Torfaen Museum Trust. Tel: Ebbw Vale 790437. Thirty-three miles (53km) of the canal are still open to traffic, including the most attractive stretch of all – through the Brecon Beacons National Park between Brecon and Abergavenny.

Yet even here there are reminders of the canal's earliest industrial functions: limekilns at Gilwern, Govilon and Goytre, wharves and warehouses at several points including Llanfoist, where one of the tramroads or waggonways which fed the canal with coal or limestone had its terminus. The canal largely followed the contours of the Usk Valley, but there are still a few locks as well as other examples of canal architecture such as aqueducts and cottages.

The canal is no longer used commercially but is becoming increasingly popular with leisure craft. Boat trips operate during the summer from Goytre Wharf among other places (details from tourist information centres) and boats can be hired at Govilon, Gilwern, Llanfoist, Llanover and Pontypool. These places also provide access points for privately-owned boats, but prospective holidaymakers here should note that the canal is one of the shallowest in the country with a depth at places not much more than two feet (60cm).

The canal often runs some distance away from villages through the wooded slopes of the valley and as such offers attractive walking along its towpath as well as boating along its waters. A typical walk might be from Llangattock. Take the towpath south-east to Llanellen via Gilwern, Govilon and Llanfoist to see the scenic glories and the industrial echoes of the canal. Cross Usk Bridge and walk two miles on the high road to Abergavenny, taking the bus back to Crickhowell and the completion of a nine mile (14km) walk.

□ OS map 161. Map ref 9D2.

334. BUILTH WELLS
Farming centre

This town, near the confluence of the Wye with the Irfon, is famous not only for the medicinal waters suggested by its modern name but also for livestock. It is one of the great farming centres of Mid Wales with a weekly cattle and sheep market held on Mon and the Royal Welsh Agricultural Society's annual show being staged here every July. Its position close to the mountains and several salmon rivers draws pony-trekkers and anglers, but architecturally it is undistinguished. Tourist information is available over Easter and from Spring Bank Holiday to Sept at Grove car park. Tel: 3307.

□ Six miles (9.6km) S of Llandrindod Wells on A483 and A470. Map ref 9D1.

335. CEFNLLYS
Abandoned medieval town

Within an arm of the River Ithon faint hollows that were once streets and mounds that were the sites of medieval

houses may still be discerned in a scrawny, rock-strewn pasture which was once a town. The town of Cefnyllys grew up around a castle built in this exposed part of the Welsh Marches by the powerful and richly-endowed family of the Mortimers. Markets were held here in the 14th century and by 1360 Cefnllys is on record as a borough. Now even the castle has disappeared, although its site, too, can still be explored and is shown on OS map 147.
□ Two miles (3.2km) E of Llandrindod Wells, best approached via minor road SE off the A483 near Crossgates. Map ref 9D1.

336. CEMMAES
Angling

On the banks of the Dyfi – the best of the Mid Wales rivers known for their sea trout, known locally as sewin. Other rivers where sewin can also be caught are the Dysynni, Rheidol and Ystwyth. But for information about day or visitors' permits to fish in the Dyfi from south of Machynlleth to north of Cemmaes contact the New Dovey Fishery Association, Tel: Machynlleth 2721.
□ Eight miles (13km) NE of Machynlleth on A470. Map ref 8C2.

337. ELAN VALLEY
Reservoirs and rapids – an upland drive and walks

There are now four reservoirs adjacent to each other in the Elan Valley. The oldest, Craig Goch, was completed in

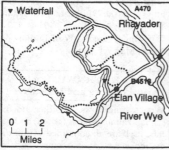

Elan Valley: former drovers' roads reveal its man-made beauty

1904, but the landscapes created by these flooded valleys remain quite distinct from natural lakes. There has not been time for the banks to erode into gentle curves and where there were once hillside depressions, the water now laps in long thin fingers.

The high plateau of central Wales has been eroded by the Severn, Wye and their tributaries into deep and wide valleys. These valleys, allied to high rainfall and the impervious nature of the rock, make the area an ideal place for collecting and storing water for the ever-growing thirst of the Midlands.

The minor road that leads northwest away from the outskirts of Rhayader – *not* the main A470 road – climbs towards the northern end of Craig Goch reservoir via an attractive little valley, dotted with rapids, waterfalls and open woodland. The road then divides: the right fork to continue along an old drovers' road to Devil's Bridge or the left fork to run alongside the shores of two other reservoirs, Pen-y-garreg and Garreg Ddu before reaching the Caban Coch reservoir. At Caban Coch the road again divides: one branch leads to the Claerwen reservoir opened in 1952 and the other heads back towards Rhayader past Elan.

The Craig Goch dam itself can be quite spectacular. When the water level is high a white curtain of overspill water cascades over the 120ft (36.5m) high dam wall. In contrast, in very dry summers, the remains of old farms or villages may be revealed if water levels are extraordinarily low. For walkers there are some attractive paths alongside some of the reservoirs, although as yet there are no established picnic areas.

Rhayader itself is a market town – livestock market on alternate Weds – at the meeting of many roads. Once these were old drovers' routes used to drive sheep from the Welsh hillsides to markets in the English Midlands and even London. Now some of these old 'green roads' have been upgraded into roads for (small) motor traffic and these are mostly the routes suggested

Wales

above for driving round the reservoirs; see map and also Day Out 345 for a more extensive drive on old drovers' roads. But some drovers' roads remain green and these have encouraged the development of pony-trekking in the Rhayader area.

☐ The Elan reservoirs begin three miles (5km) S of Rhayader off B4518. OS map 147. Map ref 9C1.

338. HAFREN FOREST
Headwaters of the Severn

The forest takes its name from Afon Hafren, Welsh for River Severn, which has its source here. A series of trails starts from the Forestry Commission's Nant Melen picnic place at Rhyd-y-Benwch in the heart of the forest overlooking meadows and with a panoramic view stretching from the headwaters of the Severn to Plynlimon Mountains beyond. The shortest trail is known as the Cascades Trail and follows the tree-lined bank of the Severn for one mile (1.6km) passing several waterfalls. A leaflet available at the picnic place details this and other walks including one to the source of the Severn. Hafren walks are for the serious walker in remote and wild country which is often rough and wet.

☐ The picnic place is seven miles (11km) W of Llanidloes on minor roads following signs for Old Hall. OS map 136. Map ref 9C1.

339. HAY-ON-WYE
Town of books

Its position in the Wye valley beneath the Black Mountains attracted first the Romans, who built a fort nearby, and then the Normans who built a castle. Nowadays it is best known for the second-hand bookshops which line the streets of Hay. Even what little remains of the castle has been partly adapted for second-hand books. For the local farming population, though, the town remains a market centre – market days are Mon and Thur – while anglers are drawn to the waters of the Wye itself.

☐ 18 miles W of Hereford on B4348. Map ref 9D1.

340. KNIGHTON
Walks along Offa's Dyke

The Welsh name is much more revealing about the attractions of this small town on the River Teme. In Welsh it is Tref-y-Clawdd: 'the town on the dyke'. For here is Offa's Dyke, the great 8th-century earthwork erected to protect the expanding kingdom of Mercia from the Welsh. North of Knighton is one of the best preserved stretches of the Dyke with the bank as

Knighton: northwards runs one of the best-preserved parts of Offa's Dyke

high as 30ft (9m) and the ditch as deep as 15ft (4.5m) in places. The Dyke is followed by a long-distance footpath. Offa's Dyke Association Centre is open all year at the Old School, Knighton. Tel: 528573.

☐ 15 miles (24km) W of Ludlow on A488. Map ref 9D1.

341. LAKE VYRNWY
Nature reserve and lake drive

Woods, meadows, heather moors rising to almost 2000ft (600m) and the lake itself are all contained within the 16,000 acres (6500 hectares) of this superb valley on the catchment of the Upper Vyrnwy. Water birds include dipper, kingfisher, wagtail and sand-piper. Sparrowhawk, buzzard and raven are common, and merlin breed on the moors. Mammals include the rare polecat and it is also a fine area for butterflies. Spectacular mountain drives lead from Bala to this man-made lake – a reservoir built in the 19th century to provide water for Liverpool – which is encircled by the B4393.

The Vyrnwy visitor centre is at Llanwddyn at the SE corner of the lake. Open: weekends from Easter to Spring Bank Holiday; daily from then till end Sept. Party visits all year round. Enquiries to the warden, Lake Vyrnwy Estate Office, Llanwddyn, via Oswestry, Powys. Tel: Llanwddyn 246. The centre provides leaflets and information about the forest, moorland walks, nature trails, bird hides and the lake itself.

☐ Eight miles (13km) W of Llanfyllin. Map ref 8D2.

342. LLANDRINDOD WELLS
Spa town with fishing

Waters for fishing rather than for medicinal purposes are increasingly this town's prime attraction, although the elegant streets and hotels remain as a legacy of its spa days. Fishing is popular not only in the Ithon but also a 14 acre (5.7 hectares) lake which is stocked with several species, including carp.

☐ Six miles (9.6km) N of Builth Wells on A483. Map ref 9D1.

343. LLANFAIR CAEREINION
Steam railway

An attractive little town at the western end of the narrow gauge Welshpool and Llanfair Light Railway. Just under six miles (9.6km) of the line has been reopened leaving the eastern terminus currently at Sylfaen, three miles (4.8km) from Welshpool, the ultimate destination for the enthusiasts who have brought the line back to life. Steam services operate daily from early June to early Sept and at weekends and Bank Holidays from Easter to early June and early Sept to early Oct; Tel:

Llanfair Caereinion 441. Around Llanfair are the attractive valleys of the Banwy and Vyrnwy.

☐ Eight miles (13km) W of Welshpool on A483. Map ref 8D2.

344. LLANIDLOES
Market town and mining trails

This somewhat remote town on the upper Severn – just 10 miles (16km) from its source – has had a long history as a market centre for the surrounding villages and hill-farmers. This is demonstrated by its early 17th-century market hall, which is regarded as one of the finest in Wales.

The half-timbered building provided arcaded space on the ground for stall-holders while the first floor was used for town hall offices. Now the latter houses a Museum of Local History and Industry; open Easter and from Spring Bank Holiday to Sept. No tel, but the tourist information centre (also open daily, summer only) can be reached at Llanidloes 2605.

Markets are still an important feature of the town, with livestock markets being held on alternate Fris and general markets every Sat. But the town also had a period when it was a centre of lead-mining.

The biggest and most profitable mine was the Van Lead Mine, three miles (5km) north-west of Llanidloes off B4518. Now not much more than a lone chimney on the hilltop, the remains of an incline running down from the mine and the great heaps of grey spoil are left to indicate that Van was once a revered name in mining circles.

The remains of the smaller Bryn Tail lead mine can be seen along the course of a 2½ mile (4km) scenic trail around part of the lake formed by Clywedog Reservoir 3½ miles (5.6km) north-west of Llanidloes off B4518. Leaflets for the trail can be obtained from 'honesty boxes' in the car park at Clywedog Dam, by post from the Forestry Commission or from the tourist information centre.

☐ 15 miles (24km) SW of Newtown on A470. OS map 136. Map ref 9C1.

Wales

345. LLANWRTYD WELLS
Mountain drive

This small town stands at the head of an old drovers' road – the Abergweryn Pass – over the Cambrian mountains to Tregaron. This follows the valley of the Irfon (a popular fishing river) with attractive Forestry Commission picnic areas and scenic walks signposted along the way. The road itself makes a dramatic drive and forms part of a tour of the Cambrian Mountains by drovers' roads devised by the Wales Tourist Board in their *Going Places* touring guide (price £1 by post). These roads (see map) are suitable only for cars. Other drovers' roads remain in their original 'green' form and have helped to establish pony-trekking here. Just outside the small town itself a wool factory can be visited to see a final stage in the process which began with the sheep being driven over the mountains to markets. Tel: Llanwrtyd Wells 211.
☐ 13 miles (21km) SW of Builth Wells on A483. Map ref 9C1.

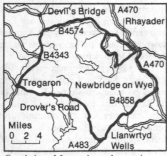

Cambrian Mountains: the scenic route which follows the old drove roads. Day Out 345

346. NEW RADNOR
Failed medieval town

This was one of the scores of new towns that were founded in the two centuries after the Norman Conquest. It was established about the year 1250 to take over the functions of Old Radnor three miles (5km) to the south-east. A huge grassy castle *motte* or mound stands at the head of the main street to signify its intended importance. But the town never developed a full urban life, although it is possible to trace out in the hedges of adjacent fields the lines of streets that were never completed.
☐ Seven miles (11km) NW of Wington on A44. Map ref 9D1.

347. NEWTOWN
Market town

This town's English name means what it says: it was developed as a new town by the English. Roger de Mortimer built it in the 13th century on the site of a small village called Llanfair Cedewain on a loop of the Severn. It was established to command an important route between the two countries after the defeat of Llywelyn, last of the Welsh princes, at Abermule, five miles (8km) to the north-east. Little remains of either Llywelyn's Dolforwyn Castle (AM) – west of Abermule – or Newtown's medieval origins. But there are attractive riverside walks, a livestock market on Tues and a fine former coaching inn, the Bear, with timbered gables and a wooden gallery supported by pillars at the first-floor level.

Robert Owen, a native of Newtown and a pioneer of the co-operative ideal (see Day Out 889) is buried in the old churchyard. A memorial museum has been dedicated to his life and work and houses manuscripts, books and a 'behaviour indicator' for workers. Open daily May to Sept; no tel.
☐ Eight miles (13km) SW of Montgomery on A489 or A483. Map ref 8D2.

348. PARTRISHOW
Tudor church

On a hillside, but embowered in trees, is one of the most secluded churches in Britain, serving no visible parish, yet alive. The great feature of this little Tudor church is its silvery oak screen, which, despite the Order in Council of October 1561 prohibiting them, preserved (with the aid of discreet restoration) its beautiful rood loft. Partrishow needs seeking out, but it is well worth the effort. If locked, the key

is available from an adjacent farm.
□ Six miles (9.6km) N of Abergavenny (see map). Map ref 9D2.

Partrishow church is well hidden, but this map will help you locate it

349. PISTYLL RHAEADR
Waterfall

Generally regarded as the finest waterfall in Wales because of its great height (240ft, 72m) and almost unbroken descent (the highest fall plummets vertically in a 100 foot (30.5m) leap, while the lower falls beneath a natural arch and a footbridge). On the border with Clwyd, the falls can be crowded in summer since the approach road is very narrow. By following the path to the right on leaving the small car park it is possible to reach the clifftop and thence the rolling Berwyn Hills.
□ Four miles (6.4km) NW of Llanrhaeadr-yn-Mochnant on minor road off B4580 W of Oswestry. Map ref 8D2.

350. POWIS CASTLE
Converted castle with terraced gardens

Perhaps the finest example of a fascinating type of British country house: the medieval castle, adapted and made increasingly comfortable over the centuries. Little survives of the original castle except its exterior, towering up from a spectacular hilltop site near Welshpool. Inside, the long gallery is Elizabethan, and the late 17th-century staterooms include a frescoed staircase and a bedroom prepared and decorated for Charles II, with a bed in an alcove protected from the vulgar by a carved balustrade. The hillside garden was laid out with terraces and topiary in about 1700, and there is also some modern planting both on the terraces and woodland. The garden and the castle, restored and part-redecorated with commendable taste in the 1890s, are usually open on afternoons other than Mon and Tues from Easter to Sept; Tel: NT at Betws-y-Coed 312.
□ One mile (1.6km) S of Welshpool – pedestrian access from High Street (A490), cars from A483 to Newtown. Map ref 8D2.

351. PRESTEIGNE
Half-timbered buildings

The Radnorshire Arms is a fine timbered building, once a private residence, which dates from 1616. It became an inn in 1792 and was a posting house in the first half of the 19th century. The Duke's Arms is older but less distinguished architecturally. Despite its small size, Presteigne was the county town of the old county of Radnorshire and being near Herefordshire its architecture is typical of the borderland area known as the Marches with English styles such as half-timbering mingling with Welsh traditions. Market day is Wed. Three miles (5km) south-west of the town is Burfa Camp or Castle, an Iron Age hillfort incorporated into Offa's Dyke (Grid ref: OS 284610).
□ 12 miles (19km) W of Leominster on B4362. Map ref 9D1.

352. RADNOR FOREST
Moorland walking

A remarkable mountain dome of Silurian grits and limestones, rising to breezy moorland summits with delightful names – the highest point at 2166ft (649m). The area provides invigorating but rugged walking off the beaten track with great panoramic views over the Welsh borderland. On

Wales

the eastern side is the beautiful Harley Valley with its classic example of overlapping spurs incised by the river; to the south is the wonderfully named waterfall of 'Water-break-its-neck'. Since there are no roads fit for cars in this mountain massif it remains an unspoilt wilderness area – the ancient name 'forest' refers to the unenclosed moorland, not to the new Forestry Commission plantations.

☐ Eight miles (13km) SW of Knighton between A488, A44 and B4372. OS map 148. Map ref 9D1.

353. TRETOWER
Fortified house

As the Welsh borderland became more peaceful, dwellings became less fortified. The gradual process of change can be seen at Tretower where a 13th-century tower remains from a motte-and-bailey castle. This was followed a century later and 200 yards away by Tretower Court, still retaining something of a fortified flavour but also beginning to show elements of a stately or country home. A stone gateway protects the house which overlooks an open courtyard. Both Court and Castle are open standard DoE hours.

☐ Three miles (4.8km) NW of Crickhowell on A479. Map ref 9D2.

354. YSTRADFELLTE
Walks by waterfalls

Narrow limestone gorges, thick with woodlands, have been formed where small rivers descend over hard ledges to the fault-guided and glacially over-deepened Vale of Neath. The best concentration of waterfalls is in the gorge of the Mellte south of Ystradfellte. Riverside walks lead south from a car park and picnic area about one mile (1.6km) south of the village. The paths can be slippery – so wear suitable shoes – but they are also spectacular. In little more than two miles (3.2km) you pass four falls: from north to south, Scwd Clyn-gwyn, Scwd Isaf Clyn-gwyn, Scwd y Pannwr and (on the sister river Hepste) Scwd yr Eira. Also approximately one mile (1.6km) south

of Ystradfellte the Mellte disappears down a pothole to reappear a short distance away. Other potholes exist for experienced cavers. The nearest tourist information centre for leaflets, etc is at Dan-yr-Uguf Showcaves, Abercraf. Open all year. Tel: Abercraf 284.

☐ Six miles (9.6km) NE of Glyn Neath on minor road to Defynnog. Falls are signposted off both Defynnog road and the A4221 from Glyn Neath to Abercraf. Map ref 9D2.

South Glamorgan

A mostly industrial county set around Cardiff. Attractions: Cardiff Castle, Llandaff Cathedral, Castell Coch. South Wales Tourism Council, Tel: Carmarthen 7557.

355. KENFIG BURROWS
Beach with nature trail

This is a wilderness of sand dunes behind a magnificent five mile (8km) stretch of sandy beaches which themselves make the area a great attraction. They are also recognised by the NCC as a Site of Special Scientific Interest for animals, flowers and coastal birds. A three mile (4.8km) nature trail starts from Kenfig and a booklet is available from the Glamorgan County Naturalists' Trust, 104 Broadway, Cowbridge, South Glamorgan. Beside Kenfig Pool stand the ruins of Kenfig Castle – the medieval town of Kenfig was buried beneath the sand 600 years ago – and Sker House. The Burrows can be reached only on foot – from Margam Sands, Kenfig or Porthcawl. See also Day Out 358.

☐ NW of Porthcawl. Map ref 9C2.

356. ST FAGAN'S
Folk museum

St Fagan's Castle is an Elizabethan mansion within the walls of a medieval castle. What makes it even more interesting nowadays, however, is the Welsh Folk Museum housed within the 'castle' and its grounds. Many examples of typical Welsh vernacular architecture have been re-erected in the grounds, often saving them from destruction. They include a 15th-century farmhouse, a 17th-century thatched barn, medieval cottages, a toll house and even a cockpit. Woollen and corn mills are also there, in working order, and on weekdays and most Bank Holidays craftsmen give demonstrations of their traditional skills. Open all day weekdays and Sun afternoons throughout the year except over Christmas, New Year and May Day Bank Holidays. Tel: Cardiff 561357 or 569441.

□ Four miles (6.4km) W of Cardiff city centre off A48 or A4119. Map ref 9D2.

West Glamorgan

The Gower Peninsula (AONB) is the highlight of an otherwise largely industrial county. Also Pennard and Weobley Castles. South Wales Tourism Council, Tel: Carmarthen 7557.

357. AFAN ARGOED
Country park and forest walk

This park lies within the spectacularly beautiful Afan Valley, with its forested hills, steep valleys, fast flowing streams and long-ranging views. The Countryside Centre contains the excellent Welsh Miners' Museum with its exhibits of local history, industry and wildlife: visitors can even wander through a recreated coal mine. Museum and Centre are open daily, Easter to Sept, and weekend afternoons only from Oct to Easter.

There are picnic areas, waymarked walks and nature trails in the park, which is also the halfway point of the Coed Morgannwg Way, a 23 mile (37km) forest walk from Craig-y-Llyn (on A4061 Rhondda to Hirwaun road) to Margam Park (see next entry), with fine views of the Brecon Beacons to the north and South Wales coast in the opposite direction. The walk follows ancient Roman earthworks and passes Bronze and Iron Age settlements, Dark Age hill-forts and defensive ditches. Leaflets and information on walks and other activities in the park, including fishing and bird-watching, are available from the Countryside Centre. Tel: Cymmer 564.

□ Eight miles (13km) NE of Port Talbot beside A4107. Map ref 9C2.

358. MARGAM
Country park with abbey and museum

A large country park near the Kenfig Burrows sand dunes (see Day Out 355), with facilities for a wide variety of interests. Within its 794 acres (322 hectares) of park and woodland is an outstanding 18th-century Orangery; the magnificent Tudor-Gothic style mansion known as Margam Castle; a rhododendron garden, which is at its best in May; the remains of an old Cistercian abbey; the ruins of a fine twelve-sided Chapter House; a large herd of fallow deer; waymarked walks and picnic areas; a landscaped lake; and pony riding. The park is open every day except Mon, Apr to Oct, and every day except Mon and Tues, Nov to Mar. Tel: Port Talbot 87626. Near Margam Church, which occupied the site of the Abbey of Margam, founded in 1174, is a museum (AM) containing inscribed early Christian stones. Open all year Wed, Sat and Sun afternoons.

□ Two miles (3.2km) E of Port Talbot on A48 (leave M4 at exit 39). Map ref 9C2.

359. OXWICH
Coastal trails

Oxwich Sand Trail starts at the high tide mark and covers about half a mile (800m). A leaflet is available from the Oxwich Reserve Centre at the car park in Oxwich. Tel: Gower 320. The dunes and marshes inland are a National Nature Reserve closed to the public. Oxwich Point offers a good view of the Bristol Channel. Other interesting places near Oxwich include two forest walks starting from the car park opposite the entrance to Penrice Castle, one mile (1.6km) north of Oxwich; Three Cliffs Bay, where faults in the rock have caused an impressive natural arch; and Pennard Castle, a

Wales

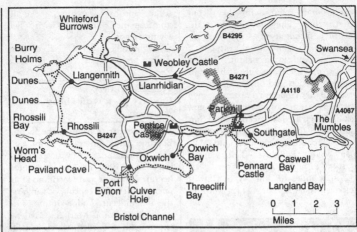

Whiteford Burrows
B4295
Swansea
Burry Holms
Weobley Castle
Dunes
Llangennith
B4271
Llanrhidian
A4118
Dunes
Parkmill
A4067
Rhossili Bay
Rhossili
The Mumbles
B4247
Penrice Cas
Southgate
Worm's Head
Oxwich Bay
Caswell Bay
Paviland Cave
Oxwich
Pennard Castle
Port Eynon
Culver Hole
Threecliff Bay
Langland Bay
Bristol Channel
0 1 2 3
Miles

Gower Peninsula: one of the most beautiful areas of Wales in otherwise industrial West Glamorgan. Days Out 245, 359, 360

crumbling sand-stream ruin which can be reached by footpath half a mile (800m) south of Parkmill. See map.
□ 10 miles (16km) W of Swansea off A4118. Map ref 9C2.

360. RHOSILI
Coastal walks and views

At the south-westernmost tip of the beautiful Gower peninsula the tiny village of Rhosili is an ideal centre for walks to explore the superb coastal scenery (see map). A three mile (4.8km) NCC nature trail starts from Rhosili car park and traverses cliffs with limestone flora. It is open all year and leaflets are available from the Oxwich Reserve Centre (see previous entry). To the north is the splendid curve of Rhosili Bay where smooth sands are backed by a three mile (4.8km) coastal hill walk to the hermit's cell of Burry Holms. To the west is the islet of Worms Head which can be reached at low tide. To the south is a four mile (6.4km) walk along 200ft (61m) high cliffs to the spectacular rock formations of Culver Hole, passing secluded Mewslade Bay and Paviland Cave, believed to have been a dwelling for prehistoric man; the cave can be entered at low tide.
□ 15 miles (24km) W of Swansea at end of B4247. OS map 159. Map ref 9C2.

Lower Middle England

361. THE CHILTERNS
Area of Outstanding Natural Beauty

Most of the AONB falls within Oxfordshire and Buckinghamshire, but in the east it extends into Hertfordshire with an outlying pocket in Bedfordshire, and in the west it joins up with the North Wessex Downs AONB, forming a long swathe of hilly countryside traversed by the ancient Ridgeway long-distance footpath. Beechwoods and bluebells, chalk hillslopes and downland scarps are among the chief glories of the Chiltern landscape, with the additional delights of the upper Thames from Marlow to Henley, Pangbourne, Goring and Wallingford. Area 312 sq miles (800 sq km).
□ Oxfordshire and Buckinghamshire. Map ref 5B2.

362. THE COTSWOLDS
Area of Outstanding Natural Beauty

Gloucestershire contains the lion's share of the Cotswolds, but this second largest of AONBs also spreads into the adjoining counties of Avon, Wiltshire, Oxfordshire, Hereford and Worcester. A justly celebrated range of hills, rising in a green crest above the Severn Vale (glorious views from Birdlip Hill). Clear streams steal through the valleys, and beside them, mellow stone towns and villages built of Cotswold stone. There are noble churches endowed by rich medieval wool merchants (Northleach has one of the finest), stately Palladian houses at Badminton and Painswick, and historic Sudeley Castle at Winchcombe. Area 588 sq miles (1520 sq km).
□ Map ref 4B2.

363. MALVERN HILLS
Area of Outstanding Natural Beauty

This imposing miniature mountain range of ancient rocks provides one of the finest ridge walks in England. The area extends over 40 sq miles (104 sq km). The paths are good and access is easy with bus stops and cark parks along the roads below. There are enormous views: westward to Wales, and eastward to the Cotswolds and chequerboard farmlands of the Vale of Severn. Worcestershire Beacon 1394ft (425m), highest of the Malvern summits, can be reached from Great Malvern, past St Ann's Well on well marked paths, or from the car park at West Malvern. Many gently graded paths wind round the northern slopes. The southern hills (Herefordshire

Lower Middle England

Beacon) are best climbed past the massive Iron Age hill-fort of British Camp where the A449 crosses the range. The fort's ramparts wind round a ridge of the Malverns enclosing an area of 32 acres (13 hectares). A *motte*, or mound, at the very top was added in the 11th or 12th century. For the complete walk along the summit ridge start by climbing to North Hill from the North Malvern Road clock tower in Great Malvern, a beautifully situated spa town, continuing southwards by way of Worcestershire Beacon, Wyche Cutting, Ragged Stone Hill and Chase End Hill, before descending for the last time to complete a nine mile (14.4km) walk. You will need OS map 150.

☐ Great Malvern is seven miles (11km) SW of Worcester on A449. British Camp is three miles (5km) SW

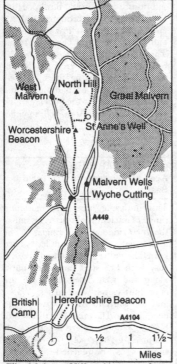

The Malvern Hills: this area of Outstanding Natural Beauty offers magnificent ridge walks and sweeping views

of Great Malvern on A449. Good but steep paths lead from a large roadside car park. Map ref 4B1.

Bedfordshire

The rambling river Ouse drains much of the county's flat acreage. In the south there are the breezy heights of Dunstable Downs and Whipsnade Zoo. Dunstable and Luton are industrial, while Bedford, the county town, has miles of riverside walks, gardens and water meadows. Thames and Chilterns Tourist Board, Tel: Abingdon 22711.

364. DUNSTABLE DOWNS
Chalk hills

This largely open stretch of downland on the north-eastern fringes of the Chilterns takes its name from the nearby town sited at the junction of Roman Watling Street and the older Icknield Way. The town (now rapidly merging with neighbouring Luton) was the site of an important 12th-century priory of which the nave and west front still survive. Part of the Downs is protected by the NT; part of them forms a 'natural' setting for the animals of Whipsnade Zoo. There are good walks with fine views. Nearby Ivinghoe Beacon (NT) is reached by a narrow road just outside Ivinghoe village. From its summit, nearly 800ft (244m) high, there are good vistas of the Chilterns and the Downs. The Coombe at Ivinghoe is a classic feature of chalk country – a dry valley.

☐ The Downs are two miles (3.2km) S of Dunstable off B4540 or B4541. Ivinghoe is on the B489 SW of Dunstable. Map ref 5B2.

365. EATON BRAY
Chalkstone church

The Church of St Mary the Virgin is constructed of the local Totternhoe chalkstone from the nearby Chilterns. The plain exterior gives no hint of the delights of the interior, entered through a door enriched with beautiful foliated ironwork over 700 years old.

The north arcade of the nave, with its splendidly crisp stiff-leaf capitals, is one of the most exquisite examples of Early English architecture in a village church: a miniature Wells Cathedral.
□ Four miles (6.4km) SE of Leighton Buzzard off A4146. Map ref 5B1.

366. LUTON HOO
Stately home

Most people go to see the house, designed by Robert Adam in 1767, with its unique collection of Russian imperial family treasures and Fabergé jewels. It also has paintings by Rembrandt and Titian, magnificent tapestries and furniture. Its setting is superb – the park was landscaped by 'Capability' Brown in the 1770s. There are two lakes, a rose garden and some fine cedars. The rock garden is a delight. There are fine views over the Lea Valley. Open from Easter to end Sept daily, except Tues and Fri. Tel: Luton 22955.
□ Thirty miles (48km) N of London off M1 at junction 10. Entrance by Park Street gates on A6129. Map ref 6A2.

367. STOCKGROVE PARK
Country park

This small park of 33.5 acres (13.5 hectares) stands on chalk and clay and is composed mainly of woods and open parkland. There is a free car park, picnic areas and lake fishing. Open daily throughout the year. Visitor centre, Tel: Dunstable 608489.
□ 2½ miles (4km) N of Leighton Buzzard off A418. Map ref 5B1.

368. WOBURN
Stately home

Few people need reminding that this is the home of the Duke of Bedford's family whose 18th-century abbey building was one of the first country mansions to become a stately home catering for 20th-century tourists. The house has a magnificent collection of old masters and French and English furniture and silver. Its collections of paintings by Canaletto and Sir Joshua Reynolds are outstanding. Among the outside attractions is one of the largest drive-through game reserves in Europe. In the deer park surrounding the house there are lakes which offer coarse fishing. Information and opening times, Tel: Woburn 666.
□ 8½ miles (13.7km) NW of Dunstable on A50. Map ref 5B1.

369. WREST PARK
French-style garden

The oldest part of this garden was made at the beginning of the 18th century. A long canal pool has the mansion at one end and a handsome pavilion at the other. The vista is closed in by blocks of woodland criss-crossed by allées with statues and other ornaments at the intersections. Later 'Capability' Brown landscaped the surrounding park, and in the 19th century formal terraces were added. The house, in Louis XV style, was built in 1836 and is resplendent with vases, mirrors, and white, gold and mahogany panels. Open Sat, Sun and Bank Holiday Mons from Apr to Sept. Tel: Silsoe 60152.
□ On A6 at Silsoe between Bedford and Luton. Map ref 6A2.

Buckinghamshire

The Chilterns run across the south of the county. To the north lies the rich agricultural region of the Vale of Aylesbury. Aylesbury, where six routes meet, is the county town. Watling Street and the Icknield Way run through the county. Thames and Chilterns Tourist Board, Tel: Abingdon 22711.

370. ASCOTT
Garden of evergreens

Originally a hunting lodge, the house is mainly 19th-century, having been enlarged in its original half-timbered style of the early 1600s. It contains French and Chippendale furniture and paintings by Rubens, Stubbs and Gainsborough. The gardens were

planted with evergreens so that the estate would look its best when it was being used in winter. There is an unusual sundial garden set out in topiary, a large circular pool and an orchard of flowering cherries. The 30 acres (12 hectares) of gardens have views across the Vale of Aylesbury to the Chilterns. The house (NT) is open from 2 to 6pm on Wed and Thur Apr to Sept, and also Sat in July and Aug. The gardens open only on last Sun of every month. Tel: Wing 242.
□ ½ mile (800m) E of Wing SW of Leighton Buzzard on S side of A418. Map ref 5B1.

371. BLACK PARK
Country park

Woodland with bridleways and nature trail. It also has a lake for fishing, canoeing, swimming and sailing model power-boats. Leaflets for the nature trail are available at car park honesty box for 10p. Open daily throughout year although car parks close at dusk.
□ Two miles (3.2km) NE of Slough off N side of A412. Map ref 5B2.

372. BURNHAM BEECHES
Forest walks and drives

This ancient wood with its gnarled and pollarded beech trees is owned and managed by the City of London Corporation which rescued it from destruction in 1880. This, and Epping Forest in Essex, are considered the prototypes of all country parks. There are many delightful paths and six miles (9km) of forest drives. The woods are especially lovely in late autumn. From Lord Mayor's Drive, which runs south-west from Farnham Common, it is possible to see the remains of a prehistoric camp and the Druid Oak, estimated to be 400 years old.
□ Three miles (5km) N of Slough off A355 W of Farnham Common. Map ref 7A1.

373. CHEQUERS
A walk passing Chequers

Since 1917 this 16th-century house in the Chilterns has been the country home of the Prime Minister of the day. The house is not open to the public, but a public footpath crosses part of the estate and can be used to form part of a rewarding nine mile (14.6km) circular walk though the surrounding woods and hills. For part of the way, too, you follow the Ridgeway long-distance footpath which incorporates the pre-historic Ridgeway and Icknield Way routes between the Marlborough Downs and Ivinghoe Beacon. But for the purposes of this more modest outing make Wendover your base. From here you climb Bacombe Hill and Coombe Hill – with spectacular views from the chalk escarpment - before descending

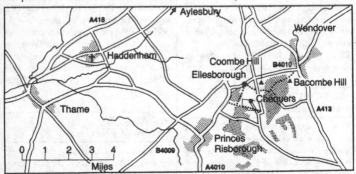

Chequers: the country home of the Prime Minister of the day is featured in this attractive walk through the woods and hills of Buckinghamshire. Haddenham with its traditional cottages and well preserved green lies a few miles to the west of Chequers. Days Out 373, 378

through woods and crossing roads (including the Chequers drive) to where the Ellesborough footpath turns off. Follow this, then right again by the path from Ellesborough to the B4010 below Coombe Hill and back to Wendover.

☐ Wendover is five miles (8km) SE of Aylesbury at the junction of A413 and A4011. Map ref 5B2.

374. CHESHAM BOIS
Woodland wildlife refuge

This area of woodland stretching along both sides of the road was bought in 1978 by the Woodland Trust, and is open to the public. It is a splendid refuge for the wildlife between the towns of Chesham and Amersham, and a fine example of the dense high forest of the Chiltern beechwoods. Tel: Woodland Trust, Grantham 74297.

☐ About one mile (1.6km) S of Chesham on A416. Map ref 7A1.

375. CLIVEDEN
A view of the Thames

The present Cliveden House dates from the mid-19th century and is the third to have been built on this site overlooking one of the most famous and beautiful stretches of the Thames. There is a particularly fine view of the river from the boat house. Cliveden was the centre of political and intellectual life in England between the wars, when Nancy, Lady Astor, American wife of the 2nd Viscount, held court there. The hall and dining-room are said to be the finest parts of the house. The panelling, the marble chimneypiece and painted overdoors in the dining-room came from the Château d'Asnières, near Paris, in 1897, and are considered equal in quality to the finest Louis XV decoration still surviving in France. The landscape gardens have terraces, wooded walks, lavish flower borders, rose garden, an open air theatre and an assortment of temples and statues in the fashion of earlier centuries. The water garden was designed by Lord Astor in the 1890s. Cliveden is now owned by the NT. The house is open Sat and Sun afternoons from Apr to end Oct. The gardens are open every day. Tel: Burnham 5069.

☐ Near Cookham three miles (5km) N of Maidenhead off B476. Map ref 7A1.

376. EMBERTON PARK
Country park

The park lies in the Ouse Valley near the small town of Olney, home of the poet William Cowper. It was created on 174 acres (70.4 hectares) of sand and gravel workings. It has four areas of sailing water. The main lake, Grebe Lake, is suitable for dinghies or canoes, although there are no boats for hire. There is a one mile (1.6km) nature trail. Permits for fishing are obtainable from park office. Other facilities include a pitch and putt course, cafeteria, picnic areas, camping and caravan park, observation tower and children's adventure play-ground. The park is open daily throughout the year; park office open daily Apr to Oct, Tel: Bedford 711575. The Cowper Museum in Olney's Market Square has his furniture, effects and first editions of his Olney hymns.

☐ Four miles (6.5km) N of Newport Pagnell on A509. Map ref 5B1.

377. GAYHURST
Elegant estate church

The church's neighbour in this small hamlet on the River Ouse is the beautiful Elizabethan house which featured in the Gunpowder Plot. One of the conspirators was taken from here to the Tower of London. The church was built in 1728, with no expense spared, using fine ashlar masonry throughout. It has an elegant interior with beautiful plaster ceilings and good plain glazing, mostly original. The pulpit is a two-decker and the tester is a whopper, with marquetry on its underside. There are handsome wrought-iron communion rails, gilded reredos and one outstanding monument.

☐ Three miles (5km) NW of Newport Pagnell on B526. Map ref 5B1.

Lower Middle England

378. HADDENHAM
Cottages of mud

A sprawling village with a well maintained and preserved centre and village green. Many of the houses and cottages are built of mud or, to be more precise, wichert-chalk marl compressed with straw. As such it is one of the best examples of this traditional form of cottage construction in this part of the country. St Mary's church is of 13th-century origin with a Norman font and medieval glass in the north chapel. The water of the village pond laps at its walls.

☐ Three miles (5km) NE of Thame on A418. Map ref 5B2.

379. HAMBLEDEN VALLEY
Chiltern valley

One of the most beautiful of the deep, wooded valleys which dissect the southern slopes of the Chilterns. Here the landscape of bluebells, cherry blossom and flint-built villages is rural England at its best. Starting at the Thames, at Mill End with its 14th-century mill, the visitor can follow the tiny chalk stream up its valley past the pretty village of Hambleden to the hidden hamlet of Fingest. This is cradled in chalk hills, overlooked by a splendid windmill and thick beech-

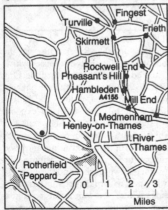

Hambleden Valley: this gem of a valley cuts into the wooded southern slopes of the Chilterns

woods, interspersed with the gorse commons of Turville Heath. Grey's Court (NT), an Elizabethan house which for generations obtained its water by donkey-power, is open to the public from Apr to Sept. It stands three miles (5km) west of Henley-on-Thames on a minor road to Rotherfield Peppard.

☐ Three miles (4.8km) NE of Henley-on-Thames, off the A4155. Map ref 7A1.

380. LANGLEY PARK
Country park

Woodland and parkland with facilities for camping. There are also rhododendron gardens, bridleways, a nature trail and a farm trail. Explanatory leaflets are available at car park honesty boxes for 10p. Open daily throughout the year although car parks close at dusk.

☐ Three miles (5km) W of Uxbridge off S side of A412. Map ref 7A1.

381. STOWE HOUSE
Classical landscape garden

Only the grounds and garden buildings are open to the public – and then only during the Easter and summer holidays of Stowe School, although students of architecture and landscape gardening are welcome during term-time – but they are among the wonders of Europe, providing an extraordinary and magical example of the 18th-century English aristocracy's determination to model their parks on the landscape paintings of Claude and Poussin. The leading landscape designers of the day, 'Capability' Brown, who worked here as head gardener for 10 years, and William Kent, laid out the grounds, first as a semi-formal garden, but later in the new style with lakes, secret glades and turf-clad vistas, temples, statues, obelisks, a Palladian bridge and almost everything else you can think of. The gardens cover 250 acres (101 hectares) and have six lakes and 32 temples. The great palace of the Dukes of Buckingham and Chandos, in the centre of it all, became a public

school in the 1920s. Tel: Buckingham 3650.
☐ Three miles (5km) NW of Buckingham off A422. Map ref 5B1.

382. WADDESDON MANOR
Park and garden

The house was built between 1874 and 1889 by Baron Ferdinand de Rothschild in the style of a 16th-century French château. The furniture includes pieces made for Louis XVI and a writing table made for Marie Antoinette. There are French, Dutch and Italian paintings as well as works by Gainsborough and Reynolds. The extensive grounds have a collection of sculpture from Italy, the Netherlands and France. There are lawns, terraces, many rare trees, a herd of Japanese Sika deer and tropical birds in the aviary. Open Wed to Sun in afternoons, gardens from 11am, from late Mar to late Oct. Tel: Waddesdon 293.
☐ On A41 six miles (9.6km) NW of Aylesbury. Map ref 5B2.

383. WEST WYCOMBE PARK
Palladian house and park

A Palladian house set in an 18th-century landscape park with classical temples. Built by Sir Francis Dashwood, founder of the infamous Hell Fire Club, it has magnificent ceiling paintings, tapestries and furniture. Centre piece of the park is a 10 acre (4 hectares) lake shaped like a swan with a cascade at its head. One of the temples, the Temple of Apollo, has the motto of the Hell Fire Club, 'Fay ce que voudras' (Do as you please), on a panel over the arch. Open frequently. Tel: High Wycombe 24411.
☐ On A40 W of High Wycombe. Map ref 7A1.

Gloucestershire

The centre of the county is dominated by the Cotswolds, the west by the wide, fertile Vale of Severn, beyond which lies the Forest of Dean. Gloucester with its cathedral is the county town. Cheltenham is stylish with Pump

Room and Promenade. Villages of warm Cotswold stone epitomise a tranquil rural England. Heart of England Tourist Board, Tel: Worcester 29511.

384. BIBURY
Trout water village

A small but notable Cotswold village on the River Coln. The river is a well-known trout water. A trout farm here is open to the public during late Mar to Oct afternoons. Arlington Row is a picturesque group of weavers' cottages which were converted in the 17th century from a 14th-century wood store. They are administered by the NT. Arlington Mill, from the same period, is now a museum featuring mill machinery and old agricultural implements. This old corn mill is open daily Mar to Oct and weekends during the rest of the year. Tel: Bibury 368. The church has Saxon origins but reflects the additions and alterations of many different periods. The village, described by William Morris as the most beautiful in England, can be crowded in the summer months.
☐ Seven miles (11km) NE of Cirencester on A433. Map ref 4B2.

385. CHIPPING CAMPDEN
Cotswold market town

The name begins to tell the story: 'Chipping' derives from the Anglo-Saxon *cheapen* meaning to buy and is now always associated with a marketplace. This market town thrived on the medieval wool trade and signs of the prosperity it brought are everywhere, from the mostly 15th-century church to the early 17th-century almshouses. The stone-arched market hall also dates from the 17th century and stands in the centre of the town which, like other market towns such as nearby Moreton-in-Marsh and Broadway, is set around a wide main street. But unlike these, Chipping Campden has been spared the rush of 20th-century traffic using this street as a main trunk highway. It becomes quite busy with visitors during summer weekends, but they do not diminish the town's appeal. The age of its many excellent buildings gives the Cotswold stone a particularly mellow charm.

☐ Five miles (8km) NE of Broadway on B4081 and B4035. Map ref 5A1.

386. CIRENCESTER
Capital of the Cotswolds

Self-styled 'Queen of the Cotswolds', it can claim a longer pedigree than most of its rivals to this title. As *Corinium Dobunorum* it was the largest Roman town outside London with a defended enclosure of 240 acres (97 hectares). It was also the meeting-point of the Fosse Way, Akeman Street and one of the two Ermine Streets. Hardly anything remains to be seen of the Roman city on the ground but finds from archaeological excavations are displayed in a local museum. Cirencester prospered again in the Middle Ages as one of the most important centres of the wool trade in Britain. The most remarkable legacy of this period, in a town which is generally built of the ever-attractive Cotswold stone, is the beautiful Church of St John the Baptist overlooking the market-place. Particularly interesting is the three-storey porch which was added to the church in around 1500 by the local guilds. It served not only as an entrance to the church but also provided rooms for the traders on its upper floors. This close link between secular and religious worlds at the market-place is not unparalleled in Britain but rarely, if ever, has it been expressed so memorably.

☐ Sixteen miles (26km) NW of Swindon. Map ref 4B2.

387. COTSWOLD FARM PARK
Rare breeds of farm animals

Cotswold Farm Park, created in 1970, contains the most comprehensive collection of rare breeds of British animals on display in the country. There are little Soay sheep, the last survivors of the prehistoric domestic sheep of Europe; the 'Seaweed Eater', a rare Orkney breed and a relic of Scottish croft sheep; striped 'Iron Age'

pigs; fluffy Sebastopol geese and Wild White Park cattle thought to have been brought to Britain by the Romans. The farm, covering 1000 acres (404 hectares), is a member of the Rare Breeds Survival Trust and is now important as a breeding farm as well as a show-place. There are occasional demonstrations of Shire horses and what are believed to be the only working oxen in Britain using traditional methods. For those interested in crop husbandry there are farm trails as well as seasonal activities such as harvesting, sheep-shearing and ploughing, especially at summer weekends. There is also a picnic area. Open daily from end Apr to end Sept. Tel: Guiting Power 307.

☐ Near Guiting Power off B4077 about five miles (8km) W of Stow-on-the-Wold. Map ref 5A1.

388. DEERHURST
Saxon church and chapel

Here on the banks of the Severn between Tewkesbury and Gloucester are two outstanding Saxon buildings. The parish church of St Mary was certainly in existence by the beginning of the 9th century. Although it was extended in the 10th century, some of the building is thought to date from as early as the 7th century. But even this would not have been the first building on the site: recent archaeological investigations have suggested that it was first the site of a Roman villa. Barely a hundred yards away from the church stands Odda's Chapel, a tiny Saxon chapel built in 1056 but only rediscovered towards the end of the last century since years earlier it had become part of a timber-framed farmhouse. It was only in the 1960s that the chapel was disentangled from the farmhouse and came under the care of the Department of the Environment.

☐ Two miles (3.2km) SW of Tewkesbury off B4213. Map ref 4B1.

389. DYMOCK
Poets' village

This village was the home of a group of

poets who made their mark on the literature of the early 1900s. Robert Frost, Lascelles Abercrombie, Rupert Brooke, John Drinkwater, Wilfred Gibson and Edward Thomas lived here between 1911 and 1914. Some of their best known work first appeared in a quarterly which was published from the village. This included Brooke's sonnet *The Soldier*: 'If I should die, think only this of me . . .' The First World War, in which Brooke and Thomas were to die, caused the break up of the Dymock Poets. Little Iddens, the cottage where Frost lived, and the Old Nail Shop where Gibson lived, can still be seen. Three miles (4.8km) from the village are ancient Dymock Woods, 1500 acres (607 hectares) where wild daffodils bloom in spring.

□ S of Ledbury on B4216. Map ref 4B1.

390. FOREST OF DEAN
Forest, rivers and industrial history

Few other British forests retain the character of the mysterious primeval forest which once covered the land better than the Forest of Dean, 50 sq miles (129 sq km) of broadleaved and coniferous woodlands and open country between the Severn and the Wye. This former royal hunting forest, managed by the Forestry Commission, is criss-crossed by hundreds of miles of lanes, paths and bridleways; dotted with dozens of car parks and picnic places. It is rich in the relics of a long industrial history and is endowed with some of the most spectacular river scenery in the British Isles (the Wye Valley is designated an AONB). It also reflects a powerful history in its great buildings and castles – Tintern Abbey, one of the most beautiful ruins in Britain; Goodrich Castle on its high spur above the Wye; and the massive Norman walls of Chepstow Castle, which guards the mouth of the river.

Forest. Highlights include Abbotswood forest trail with superb views of the Black Mountains and over the Severn Valley to the Cotswolds; a circular scenic forest drive; and the

wilderness trails which identify different uses of land, passing through forest, fields, farm, former mine workings and two nature reserves. The latter start from Plumb Hill on A4136 two miles (3.2km) SW of Mitcheldean.

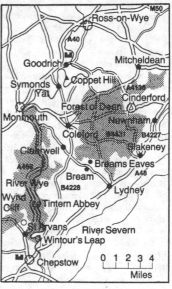

Forest of Dean: a historic tract of forest enhanced by the outstanding scenic splendours of the Wye Valley and studded with the relics of a powerful and fascinating past

River. Symonds Yat with its dramatic view of the Wye Gorge is deservedly famous. Here the river loops round Yat rock in an enormous meander past grassy meadows before plunging through its steeply wooded valley to the sea. A less busy viewpoint can be reached by following a track south from Goodrich and walking along the crest of Coppet Hill for about two miles (3km). This vantage point looks across the Yat rock to the Forest of Dean. The walk can be combined with a visit to Goodrich Castle (AM). Other good viewpoints are, on the Welsh side, Wynd Cliff, just above the main A466 at St Arvans; and, across the river, Wintour's Leap, an unexpected and easily missed spot where the B4228 passes close to the clifftop. Motorists

Lower Middle England

may not notice this owing to a screen of vegetation.

□ Symonds Yat is three miles (5km) S of Goodrich on B4432. Map ref 4B2.

Industrial history. The Romans mined for iron here and there are many clues to the Forest's past importance as a centre for iron working in names such as Foundry Wood, south of Cinderford, and the presence of several hammer ponds. The Scowles, just south-south-east of Bream, is an ancient industrial site where iron was worked for almost 2000 years. It is thought the Romans pioneered the site but today it is a place of deep woodland and dark chasms. Blackpool Bridge, north-west of Blakeney, has a stretch of exposed Roman road which used to connect the iron mines with the great smelting community of Ariconium (see Ross-on-Wye entry) and with the port of Lydney on the Severn. The Clearwell Caves, formerly the Old Ham iron mines, house a museum recording some of the history of mining in the forest. Paths and lighting have been installed so the caves can be easily explored. They are open daily Easter to Sept except Mon and Sat.

□ The caves are on B4321 NW of Lydney. Forestry Commission Offices, Bank St, Coleford, in the heart of the forest just off A4136, will give full details on forest facilities. Map ref 4B2.

391. HIDCOTE MANOR GARDEN
Outdoor 'rooms'

No garden better exemplifies the 20th-century trend towards the division into numerous separate sections, intimately interwoven, yet each distinct in size, shape, character and planting. Here, formal and informal plots are grouped together like a series of rooms with hedges forming the walls. Hidcote owes something to medieval tradition, something to cottage gardening and a great deal to the skill of its creator, Lawrence Johnston, artist and plant lover. When he acquired the land it was bare except for one cedar and two groups of beeches, although the manor house and its farm existed. The garden

and the narrow lanes leading to it tend to be overcrowded at weekends and bank holidays. Open regularly from Apr to Oct. Tel: Mickleton 333.

□ At Hidcote Bartrim, off B4081 near Mickleton. Map ref 5A1.

392. KEYNES PARK
Country park

This is situated in the Cotswold Water Park and has been created from a number of restored gravel pits. Day permits for fishing are available from warden's office, Tel: Cirencester 861459. Private sailboard tuition and hire can be arranged. There is free parking, picnic areas and pleasant lakeside walks. Open at all times.

□ Four miles S of Cirencester. Access from Spratsgate Lane, Somerford Keynes. Map ref 4B2.

393. LECKHAMPTON HILL
Scarp walk

The spa town of Cheltenham, with its splendid Regency terraces, can be the base for a 10 mile (16km) walk along part of the 100 mile (160km) Cotswold Way which runs along the limestone escarpment of the Cotswolds from Chipping Campden to Bath. Start from the foot of Leckhampton Hill.

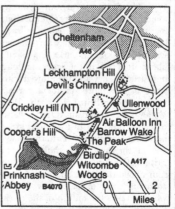

Leckhampton Hill: this makes the start to a memorable walk along part of the limestone escarpment of the Cotswolds

The fortress crowned summit can be reached by several steep paths, or by following a side road which leaves the B4070. Few of southern England's escarpments terminate in cliffs but the Cotswold scarp here is an exception, for creamy oolitic limestones outcrop in the artificially quarried cliffs of the hill, 967ft (294m). The most spectacular feature is the 50ft (15m) pinnacle known as the Devil's Chimney. The route is waymarked via Ullenwood, Crickley Hill country park and Air Balloon Inn to Barrow Wake viewpoint. The Peak, Birdlip, Witcombe Woods and Cooper's Hill (scene of Whit Sunday cheese rolling) lead to Prinknash Abbey and a bus stop for the return journey to Cheltenham. OS map 163 is useful.
□ Cheltenham is six miles (9.6km) NE of Gloucester. Leckhampton Hill is S of Cheltenham on B4070. Map ref 4B1.

394. ROBINSWOOD HILL
Country park

Only 2½ miles (4km) from the centre of Gloucester, this hill, an outlier of the main Cotswold Scarp, has 12½ miles (20km) of footpaths, picnic sites, bridleways, nature trails and a camp site. From it there are fine views across the Vale of Severn and beyond. Parking adjacent to information centre. Tel: Gloucester 413029. This, however, is not always manned. Park is open daily, from dawn to dusk, throughout the year.
□ On the southern edge of Gloucester. Map ref 4B2.

395. SEVERN BORE
Tidal wave

The Bore occurs twice a day on about 130 days of the year but those of any size only occur on about 25 days. A good viewing point is along the eastern edge of the Forest of Dean where the A48 from Lydney to Gloucester runs close to the river at several spots. Other viewpoints are the car park at the north end of Newnham or from the churchyard, and the car park next to the Bird in Hand inn at Minsterworth. Heart of England Tourist Board, PO Box 15, Worcester WR12JT, publishes a free information sheet giving dates on which better-than-usual bores can be expected.
□ Map ref 4B2.

396. THE SLAUGHTERS
Picture postcard villages

Two villages ½ mile (800km) apart which come close to fulfilling the picture postcard image of the Cotswolds. They are situated in the valley of a tributary of the Windrush. This is particularly evident in Lower Slaughter where the river, having passed through a watermill, trickles through the village down the middle of the main street. It is like a smaller and less commercialised Bourton-on-the-Water, but even here crowds can become oppressive in midsummer and at weekends. Upper Slaughter is less obviously a showpiece village and perhaps the more appealing for that. It also has an outstanding Elizabethan manor house with extensive gardens and the remains of a 15th-century priory. The house has a fine Jacobean porch. This is normally open on Fri afternoons only from May to Sept. Tel: Bourton-on-the-Water 20927.
□ Three miles (5km) SW of Stow-on-the-Wold off A436 and A429. Map ref 5A1.

397. SNOWSHILL
Cotswold village

Cotswold stone village, less crowded with visitors than some, on the escarpment overlooking the Vale of Evesham. The quality of the cottages is generally high while Snowshill Manor (NT) is a fine Tudor building with a 17th-century frontage and a terraced garden. The house contains a collection of clocks, toys, bicycles, Japanese armour and musical instruments. It is open daily from May to Sept except Mon and Tues.
□ Three miles (5km) S of Broadway on unclassified roads running between A44 and B4077. Map ref 4B1.

Lower Middle England

398. TEWKESBURY
A town of beauty

Standing at the confluence of the Severn and Avon this is one of the finest half timbered towns in England with spectacular overhanging eaves, a labyrinth of medieval alleys, fascinating old inns and an ancient mill. The Bell was once a monastery guest house. The Hop Pole has a 14th-century fireplace before which Dickens's Mr Pickwick warmed himself. From the tower of the magnificent Abbey Church, with its massive Norman architecture, there is a panoramic view of the Avon and Severn valleys and the Malvern Hills. The Abbey was saved during the Dissolution when the townsfolk bought it from Henry VIII for £453.
☐ On A38 N of Gloucester. Map ref 4B1.

399. ULEY
Hill-fort and long barrow

Two outstanding prehistoric monuments lie immediately north of this village. One can hardly be missed: Uleybury hill-fort, the finest earthwork in the county. It has double ramparts and ditches enclosing an area of 32 acres (13 hectares). From it there are particularly fine views over the surrounding Cotswolds. Less dominating, but also hard to miss, is a chambered long barrow signposted as Uley Tumulus but sometimes known as Hetty Pegler's Tump. Mrs Pegler was apparently the wife of the 17th-century owner of the field in which this grassy mound stands. Those particularly interested in archaelogy can apply for a key to inspect its interior from Crawley Hill Farm in Uley itself.
☐ Uley is five miles (8km) SW of Stroud. Both the village and the prehistoric sites are on or just off the B4066. Map ref 4B2.

400. WESTBURY COURT
Water garden

This seventeenth-century formal water garden had fallen into almost total disrepair until the NT took it over in 1967. The aim is to restore it completely to its original state, since it is the earliest example of such a garden remaining in England. It has a long canal and others forming a rectangle with it. The summer house at the end of the long canal has been restored, as has a gazebo and a small walled garden. Topiary hedges lining the long canal have been replanted and the great wall along it has been rebuilt. Open Apr and Oct on Sat, Sun; from May to Sept daily, except Mon, Tues. Tel: Westbury-on-Severn 461.
☐ At Westbury-on-Severn on A48 SW of Gloucester. Map ref 4B2.

401. WESTONBIRT ARBORETUM
Collection of trees and shrubs

This large 600 acres (252 hectares) arboretum, owned by the Forestry Commission, contains a wide variety of coniferous and broadleaved trees. There is also a surprising amount of natural woodland with many woodland flowers, numerous paths and rides and two recommended walks. Best visited in October when the autumn colours, especially those of the maples, are at their best. Open every day from 10am to sunset, except for the visitor centre which is open from Easter to Nov.
☐ Three miles (4.8km) S of Tetbury on A433. Map ref 4B2.

402. THE WILDFOWL TRUST
Wintering place for wildfowl

Slimbridge, the first Wildfowl Trust centre opened to the public, is on the east bank of the Severn estuary at a place which has always been a wintering ground for wildfowl. It consists of 73 acres (30 hectares) of enclosures, lakes and paddocks where the most varied collection of wildfowl in the world is kept. In winter the graceful yellow and black billed wild Bewick's swans fly all the way from Arctic Russia. Many individual birds return year after year to Slimbridge. Beyond the collection area, hides and

observation towers overlook the salt-marsh known as the Dumbles, where wild duck and wild geese congregate. Here is easy birdwatching with every facility provided. You can see the tame birds close to as you wander through the enclosures, or hire binoculars to observe the wild ones. There is a permanent exhibition, gift shop and restaurant and tea room overlooking a lake. Tel: Cambridge, Glos 333 for entrance fees, hours and membership information. Open daily except 24 and 25 Dec.
□ At Slimbridge. Signposted off the A38, S of Gloucester. Map ref 4B2.

403. WITHINGTON
Village with Roman roots

An attractive village not far from the headwaters of the River Coln. Apart from its appealing domestic buildings in Cotswold stone, and the Roman villa at Chedworth in the next parish, the village is interesting because local historians believe the site to have been continuously occupied and farmed since Roman times.
□ Six miles (9.6km) SE of Cheltenham, S of A40. Map ref 4B2.

Hereford and Worcs.

Here lowland England nudges the mountain land, and the Malverns are its first foothills. The country has the beautiful, fast-running Wye, the orchards of Evesham, the cathedral cities of Hereford and Worcester and Offa's Dyke. Heart of England Tourist Board, Tel: Worcester 29511.

404. AVONCROFT MUSEUM OF BUILDINGS
Buildings of the past

A splendid open-air museum which specialises in rescuing old buildings from destruction and completely restoring them. The buildings which most concern the museum are those which relate to local crafts, or those which modern farming methods have made redundant, for example, the late 18th-century granary from Temple Broughton Farm. There is a small 19th-century counting house which was originally in Bromsgrove's cattle market and which was moved intact to Avoncroft. There is also a 17th-century cruck-framed barn, a fully working windmill and nail and chain workshops. The manufacture of nails and chains was very much a cottage industry of the Black Country. Open daily from 1 Mar to 2 Dec. Tel: Bromsgrove 31363.
□ Redditch Road, Stoke Heath, Bromsgrove. Off M5 at junction 5, and three miles (4.8km) N on to the A4024, just S of Bromsgrove. Map ref 11A4.

405. BEWDLEY
River and railway valley

This town on the River Severn, near the eastern fringes of the Wyre Forest, was a bustling port 500 years ago until it was by-passed by the canal age. As a result it has retained much of its medieval character overlaid with Georgian elegance. The Bewdley Folk Museum is housed in the old market stalls of the 18th-century Shambles. Craftsmen still work there on certain days. The museum is open daily from Mar to Nov. Bewdley is also the headquarters of the Severn Valley Railway. Steam-hauled train rides of up to 12½ miles (20km) as far as Bridgnorth are operated daily during the summer and on weekends at other times. Much of this restored line closely follows the River Severn through one of the most beautiful stretches of its valley - and one which is not generally followed by any road. Riverside walks and picnic areas are available near all the intermediate stations. Tel: Bewdley 403816 or Bridgnorth 4361.
□ Three miles (5km) SW of Kidderminster on A456. Map ref 10B4.

406. BROADHEATH
Elgar's birthplace

Sir Edward Elgar was born here within sight of the Malvern Hills in 1857 in a cottage which was his family's summer home. The cottage in Crown East Lane has a collection of photographs, musical scores and objects associated with the composer. Open daily except Wed.

☐ On B4204 E of Tenbury Wells. Map ref 4B1.

407. BROADWAY TOWER
Country park

This consists of grassland and woods on the Cotswold scarp. It has fine views, a nature trail and Broadway Tower itself, a folly built in 1800 by the Earl of Coventry so that he could see it from his family home 20 miles (32km) away at Worcester.

☐ Nearly two miles (3km) S of Broadway. Map ref 4B1.

408. BROCKHAMPTON
Walking and picnicking

Bringsty Common in the parish of Brockhampton is a hilly area of open heath with splendid views in every direction. Crossed by the main A44 it offers good walking and picnic spots. Lower Brockhampton (NT), two miles (3.2km) east of the old market town of Bromyard, is a small timber-framed moated manor house dating from about 1400. It glories in a fine open-roof Great Hall and has a separate jewel of a gatehouse guarding the moat crossing. Open daily from Feb to Dec, except Tues and Thur.

☐ Off A44 E of Bromyard. Map ref 4B1.

409. CLENT HILLS
Country park

This hilly grassland covers 365 acres (148 hectares) most of which is owned by the NT. The hills range in height from 500ft (152m) to 1000ft (304m) and give magnificent views in all directions. There are also woodlands of larch, pine and mixed hardwoods. The park has picnic areas, bridleways (horses can be hired at Adam's Hill) and footpaths. There are three car parks, refreshment and toilet facilities, a toposcope and information centre. Open daily throughout the year. Explanatory leaflet from Countryside Office, Tel: Worcester 353366, Ext 3553.

☐ Eight miles (13km) W of Birmingham S of Halesowen, ½ mile (800m) NE of Clent village on A491. Map ref 11A4.

410. EVESHAM
Market town

Some market towns grew up around castles, some around abbeys. Evesham is an example of the latter and its role as the market centre for the Vale of Evesham has enabled it to outlive the abbey, of which only a bell-tower and a gateway remain. Nonetheless, these are impressive and the abbey grounds which slope down to the River Avon also contain two churches. Evesham's position close to both the Cotswolds and the forests of Warwickshire, with access to timber and stone, has resulted in an appealing mixture of architectural styles. There are some old stone buildings but the most interesting tend to be half-timbered, such as the Almonry and Booth Hall, or Round House, both from the 14th or 15th centuries.

☐ Six miles (9.6km) NW of Broadway on A44. Map ref 4B1.

411. GOLDEN VALLEY
Remote and peaceful river valley

The placid valley of the River Dore is a place of small villages and farms, narrow country lanes, hills and meadows. A good road runs through it connecting the main villages of Dorstone, Peterchurch, Vowchurch and Abbey Dore. The latter lies at the gateway to Golden Valley and fine examples of Early English architecture can be seen in the great parish church, the red sandstone of its fabric contrasting with the rich green of its setting, which consists of the transepts and chancel of the Cistercian Dore Abbey, founded in 1147. The Abbey was even more richly endowed with estates than Tintern and its properties included 17 granges (outlying farms) of which nine were in the valley. The

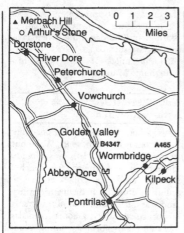

0 1 2 3 Miles

- ▲ Merbach Hill
- ○ Arthur's Stone
- Dorstone
- River Dore
- Peterchurch
- Vowchurch
- Golden Valley
- B4347 A465
- Wormbridge
- Abbey Dore
- Kilpeck
- Pontrilas

Golden Valley and Kilpeck: a gentle river valley steeped in the enduring calm which springs from 800 years of husbandry. Nearby Kilpeck has the most perfect little Norman church in England. Days Out 411, 414

monks were diligent farmers and turned the forest chase into an agricultural estate, laying the foundation of the stock rearing and cultivation upon which Golden Valley depends to this day. The walled and river garden of Abbey Dore Court, specialising in ferns, is open daily. Arthur's Stone on Merbach Hill above Dorstone is a notable chambered tomb dating from Neolithic times.

☐ Valley starts 10 miles (16km) SW of Hereford off A465 on B4347. Map ref 9D1.

412. HAUGH WOOD
Woodland walk

Haugh Wood (Forestry Commission) picnic place is tucked among the oaks and larches. The walk begins at the picnic place and leads through woods of oak and Douglas fir. There are views over Hereford and to the Welsh mountains on walks of 1½ miles (2.4km) and 1 mile (1.6km). Below Haugh Wood the village of Fownhope has an attractive black and white inn, the Green Man, and a church, the Norman tower of which has a broach spire

constructed of 22,000 oak shingles.

☐ Five miles (8km) SE of Hereford on the Mordiford to Woolhope by-road. Map ref 4B1.

413. HEREFORD AND WORCESTER COUNTY MUSEUM
Old farm waggons

The agricultural side of this museum is out of doors and consists of an interesting collection of farm waggons (including the Worcester waggon), gypsy caravans, a bow-fronted Brougham and a Hansom cab. There is also a complete cider press dating from about 1700. Open from Feb to end Nov daily except Fri. Tel: Hartlebury 416.

☐ Hartlebury Castle, Hartlebury, five miles (8km) S of Kidderminster, on A449 from Worcester to Kidderminster road. Map ref 11A4.

414. KILPECK
Norman church

This small village in pleasant, hilly country between the Dore and the Wye possesses England's most perfect little Norman church which stands almost alone in a wholly rural area. It is a masterpiece of sculptural decoration, all in sandstone, marvellously well preserved. The chancel arch has religious figures of exquisite tenderness, but outside the mood is robustly secular, to the point of bawdiness. The gaps among the outside ring of corbels were caused, not by age, but by Victorians shocked at some of the subjects represented.

☐ Ten miles (16km) SW of Hereford off A465. Map ref 9D1.

415. KINGSFORD
Country park

The park comprises 200 acres (81 hectares) of coniferous woodland with some open heathland. During Saxon and Norman times it was at the heart of a great royal forest. It has rich wildlife and there are two waymarked trails, one a nature trail with a small display and interpretative panels along the route. There is also a horse route and a trail for disabled persons; several car parks; picnic areas, a Ranger service and information boards. Leaflets are available from the Countryside Officer, Tel: Worcester 353366, Ext 3553. Open throughout the year.

☐ At Kinver Edge three miles (5km) N of Kidderminster. Map ref 11A4.

416. LEDBURY
Market town

A market town to the west of the Malverns with outstanding black and white timbered buildings. These include houses, inns, and, from the 17th century, the finest half timbered market hall in the country. The church has Norman origins, but is mostly 13th to 14th-century. In the 15th-century Old Grammar School, a restored timber-framed building, a 'Heritage Centre' exhibition tells the story of Ledbury's growth from Anglo-Saxon village to market town (market on Tues). Open weekends from Easter to the Spring Bank Holiday, then daily until Oct. A booklet detailing a 1½ hour tour of the town's most interesting buildings is available at the centre.

☐ Twelve miles (19km) E of Hereford at junction of A438, A449 and A417. Map ref 4B1.

417. LICKEY HILLS
Country park

Wood, heath and meadowland with bridleways, woodland walks, picnic areas and viewpoints on Beacon Hill, Bilberry Hill and Rednal Hill. Within the park there is an 18-hole municipal golf course, bowling green, putting green and tennis courts. At Rose Hill there is a large car park, formal gardens and wildlife pool. The Warren Lane car park gives access to Bilberry Hill and Lickey Warren. Beacon Hill, with its toposcope, is the highest point in the Midlands with views over Birmingham, the Severn Valley, the Malvern Hills and the Black Mountains of Wales. Open daily throughout the year but closes midday on Christmas day. Leaflets and information from Head

Forester, Tel: Birmingham 4533470. Sports facilities also include boating, ski-ing and tobogganing when conditions are suitable.

☐ Eight miles (13km) S of Birmingham. Map ref 11A4.

418. PEMBRIDGE
15th-century inn

This village was on an old coaching road from London to South Wales but the timbered New Inn was already quite old by the time the first coaches called. This fine black-and-white building dates from the 15th century and was once used by wool traders. It also once contained a court room. Its old stables now form the dining room. Opposite the inn is an ancient covered market hall. The church is mainly 14th-century and has a huge detached bell house of pyramidal design. There are also some attractive half-timbered houses in the village.

☐ Seven miles (11km) W of Leominster on A44. Map ref 9D1.

419. ROSS-ON-WYE
Riverside market town

Set on a red sandstone cliff commanding a beautiful stretch of the River Wye, this delightful town attracts many visitors in summer. The parish church dominates the much photographed view of the town from the river. Beyond the church is the Prospect, a walled public garden, which gives fine views of the river's horseshoe bend, Wilton Castle, the town and the Black Mountains. Much of the character of Ross is due to the benefaction of one man, John Kyrle. Alexander Pope extolled the virtues of the Man of Ross in his *Moral Essays*. John Kyrle's home, in the triangular Market Place, is now the office of the *Ross Gazette* and a chemist's. The Market Place is dominated by the massive, 14-arched Market Hall which forms the hub of the town. Panyard Woods lie to the south of Ross and nearby is the site of *Ariconium*, in Roman days an industrial settlement which made arms for the legions. It has been described as the Black Country of Roman Britain. There are good views of the river at Kerne Bridge to the west of Ross.

□ Access via A40 from Gloucester (16 miles, 26km) or M50. Map ref 4B1.

420. SHOBDON
Rococo-Gothic church

The Church of St John the Evangelist is a delicious little ecclesiastical drawing room, created in 1752-6, and now admirably restored in the original colour scheme of white and grey-blue. Great play is made throughout the church with ogee curves, scrolls and pendants. It is marred only by the east window of 1907 and a primitive Norman font which should be moved elsewhere. Arches from an earlier Norman church   all that remains of a former 12th-century priory   have been re-erected in the grounds of the former Shobdon Court.

□ Eight miles (13km) W of Leominster on B4362. Map ref 9D1.

421. STOURPORT
Canal town

The only town entirely created by the canal age. It grew from a single alehouse at the point where the Staffordshire and Worcestershire Canal joined the River Severn and River Stour. Its 18th-century origins have resulted in an appealing marriage between Georgian and canal architecture. Around the canal basin many of the old wharves, warehouses and cottages remain. The basin is used by pleasure craft.

□ Four miles (6.4km) SW of Kidderminster on A451 and A4025. Map ref 10B4.

422. TEME VALLEY
Day out drive

This 50 mile (80km) circuit covers some of the most attractive countryside and delightful towns and villages in the heart of England. It passes hopyards and orchards and is a picture in spring when the fruit blossom is out. The route

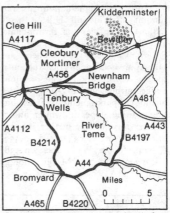

Teme Valley drive: a round trip for motorists, starting from Bromyard

is best followed in an anti-clockwise direction as this reduces the number of awkward right turns. It can, of course, be joined at any point on the circuit. Here we start at Bromyard, a market town with narrow winding streets, following the A44 over Brockhampton's Bringsty Common (see Brockhampton) before turning north on B4197 at Knightsford Bridge. From here the road towards Martley gives good views on both sides and, after Martley, especially from Woodbury Hill. After Great Witley, with its baroque church and ruined Witley Court, the A443 climbs over the Abberley Hills and drops down into the valley of the Teme. At Newnham Bridge the route turns north-east and follows the A456 to the viewpoint of Clows Top, and then north on the B4202 along the edge of Wyre Forest (separate entry) joining the A4117 just before Cleobury Mortimer, a small market town below the Clee Hills. After the hills the route turns south on the B4214 crossing the Teme at Tenbury Wells (Burford House gardens are in a beautiful setting by the river) and returns to Bromyard.

□ Map ref 4B1.

423. WASELEY HILLS
Country park

The park extends over 150 acres (57

hectares). Its highest point is the summit of Windmill Hill at 940ft (286m) giving views of Birmingham and the Black Country to NE and Severn Valley to SW. There are marshy areas and open grassland and a special conservation zone around Sedgebourne Coppice. Other facilities include car parks, picnic areas, ski and tobogganing slopes in winter and a Ranger service. For further information Tel: Worcester 353366, Ext 3553.
□ ½ mile (800m) W of Rubery on A38; just over a mile N of M5, junction 4. Map ref 11A4.

424. WYRE FOREST
Remnant of primeval forest

Wyre Forest lies close to Bewdley and the Severn and, like the Forest of Dean, is a remnant of the primeval forest which once covered England. In the peaceful depths of the forest flora and fauna are relatively undisturbed. In places the Forestry Commission have planted new plantations, established car parks and picnic sites and a series of nature trails and walks. Green Walk, one of three which are waymarked, runs along an escarpment with views over the forest and Clee Hills. Walks start from picnic place by Callow Hill Visitor Centre which tells the story of Wyre Forest with displays of forest crafts, tools and a wildlife exhibit. Hawkbatch picnic place is in oak woodlands within ½ mile (800m) of viewpoint over River Severn and Trimpley reservoir. There are no villages in the 6000 acre (2428 hectares) forest but a few hamlets such as Rock, Pansax, Bliss Gate and Far Forest. Tel: Rock 266302.
□ Callow Hill Visitor Centre is on A456 three miles (4.8km) W of Bewdley. Hawkback picnic place is on B4194 two miles (3.2km) NW of Bewdley. Map ref 10B4.

Hertfordshire

A county of leafy lanes and village greens with old Roman cities (Verulamium) and modern planned ones (Letchworth and Welwyn Garden City). The Icknield Way traverses the top of the county. The Chilterns lie in the west and the Lee Valley in the east. Hertford is the county town. Thames and Chilterns Tourist Board, Tel: Abingdon 22711.

425. ALDENHAM
Country park

The reservoir offers fishing and sailing in a meadow and woodland setting. Fishing requires a daily or season ticket and fishing punts are available for hire. Aldenham Sailing Club has sailing rights on the reservoir but the public can launch dinghies from a special ramp for a small fee. There is ample car parking, picnic tables, toilets, an adventure playground and a horse riding track. Open daily throughout year.
□ 1½ miles (2.4km) W of Elstree and same distance S of Letchmore Heath. Access is between A41 and A411 E of Bushey. Map ref 7A1.

426. ASHWELL
Village since Roman times

A remarkably unspoilt village with some mud-and-timber cottages among a fine collection of domestic buildings from the Tudor period onwards. The village, though, has been occupied since at least Roman times and in the timber-framed early Tudor Town House (AM) there is a museum of village life from prehistoric times to present-day. The church is mainly 14th-century and carved on a wall of its tower is a picture of the old St Paul's Cathedral.
□ Four miles (6.4km) NE of Baldock, between the A1 (the site of the Roman Ermine Street) and the A505 (here following the route of the old Icknield Way). Map ref 6B2.

427. BENCROFT WOOD
Woodland walks

This small but interesting stretch of old coppice woodland has the traditional mix of hornbeam, oak and birch typical of southern Hertfordshire.

There are picnic places within easy reach of the car parks, two forest walks and a route for horse riders. This and nearby Broxbourne Wood are managed by Hertfordshire County Council which publishes leaflets on both. Tel: Hertford County Planning Dept, Hertford 54242, Ext 253.

☐ Four miles (6.4km) S of Hertford on White Stubbs Lane, off by-road forking off B158. Map ref 6B2.

428. NORTHAW GREAT WOOD
Country park

This is a remnant of the extensive forests that covered what are now Hertfordshire and Essex before the Norman Conquest. There are 290 acres (117 hectares) of oak, birch, ash and hornbeam woodland with three coloured waymarked walks: yellow at 2½ miles (4km), blue at 1¼ miles (2km) and red at ¾ mile (1.2km). A horse trail is for use on weekdays only. Wildlife includes badgers, foxes, the small dog-sized muntjac deer which live in dense cover and 70 species of birds, some of which are rare visitors. There is a picnic area but no visitor centre. Open daily throughout the year. Further information from Welwyn Hatfield District Council, Tel: Welwyn Garden 31212.

☐ Five miles (8km) SE of Hatfield on B157. Map ref 6B2.

429. HATFIELD HOUSE
Historic house and garden

The house is an outstanding example of early Jacobean architecture and still looks much as it did in 1612. It was started five years earlier by Robert Cecil, 1st Earl of Salisbury. Adjacent to the present house is a wing of Hatfield Palace where Queen Elizabeth I spent much of her childhood. Inside Hatfield House finely carved woodwork and decorated plaster ceilings still survive. It has many famous paintings, furniture, tapestries and historic armour. Its Georgian kitchen has impressive copperware and huge ovens. The gardens were laid out by the celebrated botanist John Tradescant, although much of today's park was created in the 19th

century. Old and new styles of gardening combine here; an Elizabethan knot garden and modern herbaceous planting in which a parterre, previously used for bedding out plants, is now permanently planted. There are roses old and new, shrubs, trees, including some in fine avenues across the large park. There is a herb garden, a garden of scented plants and a maze. Open daily from Mar to Oct, except Mon, but open on Bank Holiday Mons. Tel: Hatfield 62823.

☐ Off A1 21 miles (33km) N of London. Map ref 6A2.

430. KNEBWORTH
Mansion and country park

The extravagant 19th-century exterior of Knebworth House – turrets, domes and gargoyles – conceals a red brick house dating to Tudor times. The home of the Lytton family since 1492, it was substantially rebuilt in the middle of the last century with the intention of making it into a Gothic palace. Its most famous room is the banqueting hall, with ornately carved oak screen and minstrel's gallery. There is a fine collection of Elizabethan portraits, 17th and 18th-century furniture, and books and manuscripts. In the wooded parklands round the house there is a narrow gauge railway, a railway museum, an adventure playground, a skatepark, a crazy golf course, a deer park with herds of red and fallow deer, and riding stables with horses for hire. The house and park are open daily from Apr to end Sept. Tel: Stevenage 812661.

☐ 1½ miles (2.5km) SW of Stevenage off A1(M). Map ref 6A2.

431. ROYAL NATIONAL ROSE SOCIETY
Rose gardens

New roses are tested over a period of three years and established roses are grown in a well designed display garden. There are also collections of shrub roses, rose species and roses of historic and botanical interest, as well as several model rose gardens. Open daily from mid-June to end Sept but afternoon only on Sun. Closed Aug Bank Holiday. Tel: St Albans 50461. ☐ Chiswell Green Lane, St Albans. Map ref 6A2.

432. ST ALBANS
Remains of a Roman city

Although there are some fine medieval and Georgian buildings in this city, ranging from the cathedral to the Fighting Cock inn, from almshouses to a water-mill, its greatest days far preceded them. On its western outskirts are the remains of one of the largest Roman cities, *Verulamium*, where a Roman theatre, including a colonnaded stage, and a fine stretch of city wall can still be seen. There is also a museum with exhibits discovered during the excavations. Yet these are not the oldest surviving antiquities in the landscape. In Prae Wood, just above the Roman remains, are the banks and ditches of a prehistoric settlement that was a capital of the Belgae, one of the chief tribes of southern Britain in the Iron Age.
☐ Verulamium is one mile (1.6km) W of St Albans' city centre off the A414. Map ref 6A2.

433. THERFIELD HEATH
Barrows and burial mounds

Here, in a region somewhat barren of the relics of prehistory, is a Neolithic long barrow (the only notable one in eastern England) and Five Knolls (not to be confused with the Five Knolls in Bedfordshire), a group of Bronze Age burial mounds. This concentration of antiquities is almost certainly related to the area's proximity to the prehistoric Icknield Way.
☐ One mile (1.6km) W of Royston, a town at the junction of the Icknield Way and the Roman Ermine Street. Map ref 6B2.

Northamptonshire

An undulating countryside of farms and woods with the industrial towns of Corby, Kettering and Welling-borough in the north. Northampton is the county town. East Midlands Tourist Board, Tel: Lincoln 31521.

434. BARNWELL
Country park

The restored sand and gravel pits on the east bank of the River Nene offer a variety of habitats – woodland, meadow, marsh, open water – for the many plants and animals which have colonised them. Barnwell is best known for its birds – 32 species regularly nest in the parkland and many more visit during the year. Facilities include picnic meadows, waterside walks, day fishing (permits available), fishing facilities for disabled persons and a warden service, Tel: Oundle 3435. Open daily throughout the year.
☐ Just over ½ mile (1km) S of Oundle on Barnwell road A605 leading to Thrapston. Map ref 6A1.

435. BOUGHTON HOUSE
Great English house

One of the least known of great English houses and only recently opened to the public, it grew in layers from the Middle Ages until the early 18th century. The medieval and Elizabethan house rambled gently around a series of peaceful courtyards. In the 1690s the Francophile Duke of Montague, who had been ambassador in Paris, redecorated the medieval hall and turned one end of the house into a formal French château. The contents are superb and fascinating throughout, from the very best French furniture to the only surviving country-house shovel board – on which upper servants used to play a grand version of shove-halfpenny. The house and garden are usually open daily from Aug to end Sept except Fri; also on limited days of the week up to late Oct and at Easter and Spring Bank Holidays. Teas are served in the original kitchen amongst gleaming copper. Tel: Kettering 82248.
☐ Off A43, three miles (5km) N of Kettering, on Geddington to Grafton Underwood road. Map ref 6A1.

436. IRCHESTER
Country park

This is undulating reafforested land with a nature trail. Until 1940 the area was mined for ironstone and afterwards planted with pine and larch. The hill-and-dale topography of dry slopes and damp bottoms gives a good variety of habitats and there is a waymarked nature trail which covers them. There are goldcrests, blue tits, great tits, willow tits, long-tailed tits, squirrels and rabbits in the woodland. There are extensive picnic meadows, car parks, facilities for disabled persons, guided walks and a permanent warden and information services. Guide from the warden's office. Open daily throughout the year. Tel: Wellingborough 76866.

☐ Nearly three miles (4km) SE of Wellingborough on road to E of A509. Map ref 5B1.

437. KIRBY HALL
Elizabethan house

One of the most evocative and beautiful of Elizabethan houses, made all the more poignant by the fact that all except the great hall and one corner is a ruin. Originally built by Sir Humphrey Stafford in 1570–5, it was sold soon afterwards to Elizabeth's favourite, Sir Christopher Hatton. It has a courtyard surrounded by great windows and rich Renaissance carving, a long line of curved gables and chimney stacks surveying the restored Elizabethan garden and, round one corner, a pair of enormous bow windows, like the sterns of two Elizabethan galleons moored side by side. The entrance range was remodelled in the time of Inigo Jones, and shows his influence. The hall is open standard DoE hours.

☐ Four miles (6.4km) NE of Corby off A43. Map ref 6A1.

438. KNIGHTLEY WAY
Country path walk

The section from Badby to Preston Capes covers the first four miles (6km) of the Knightley Way. This path passes through Badby Wood, a mixed woodland with wild cherry, ferns and rich bird life. Further on, Fawsley Park has lakes, meadows and woods. There was once a village at Fawsley Park but the tenants were evicted at the end of the 15th century and all that remains now is the church. The village itself lies under lakes created by 'Capability' Brown in the 18th century. Leaflet from Northamptonshire Leisure and Library Services. Tel: Northampton 34833.

☐ Badby is two miles (3.2km) S of Daventry just off E side of A361. Map ref 5A1.

439. LAMPORT HALL
Historic house

This was the home of the Isham family for over 400 years, but is now owned by Lamport Hall Trust. The present house dates mainly from the 17th and 18th centuries. Its south-west front is a rare example of the work of John Webb and was built in 1665 with wings added between 1732 and 1740. The house is set in attractive wooded gardens and parkland and has a fine collection of paintings, furniture and china. Open Sun and Bank Holidays from Easter to end Sept. Also from mid-July to end Aug on Wed, Thur and Fri afternoons. Tel: Maidwell 272.

☐ Eight miles (12.8km) N of Northampton on A508. Map ref 11B4.

440. OUNDLE
County town

The finest among many old buildings in this small market town on the River Nene is an inn – The Talbot, built in 1626 on the site of a monastic hospice. It has three storeys with mullioned windows reaching from ground level to the gables. A central archway leads to the yard. The river has made Oundle into a popular boating centre. Cotterstock Hall, a stone manor house to the north of the town, is where Dryden wrote his *Fables*. The house and gardens are not open to the public.

☐ Eleven miles (18km) SW of Peter-

Lower Middle England

borough at junction of A605 and A427. Map ref 6A1.

441. STANFORD-ON-AVON
Coloured stone church

Easy of access yet very little known. A village church of singular charm, especially recommended to lovers of colour. The stonework is a blend of fawn, pink and grey; the interior unusually rich in medieval glass. Good monuments, and, what is unhappily rare in England, an organ which is a joy to behold.

□ Six miles (9.6km) NE of Rugby and four miles (6.4km) SE of intersection 20 on M1 off B5414. Map ref 11B4.

442. STOKE BRUERNE
Canal centre

This small village on the Grand Union Canal has become something of a mecca for canal enthusiasts. In the village there is a typical canal bridge and lock, a fine example of a canal pub in the Boat Inn, and an excellent Waterways Museum in a former corn mill. Tel: Northampton 862229 for the opening times. There are also regular boat trips in season as far as the Blisworth tunnel, at 3000 yards (2775m) the second longest navigable canal tunnel in Britain.

Stoke Bruerne can also be the starting-point of a drive (with periodic towpath walks) to see several other examples of the scenery and architecture which canals brought to the relatively high and riverless plateau of the Midlands. Along the unclassified road north from Stoke Bruerne to Blisworth are the ventilation shafts of the canal tunnel below. At Braunston there are the old wharves which indicate its former commercial importance as the junction of the old Oxford canal and the Grand Union. At Little Braunston there is a beautiful old toll office and four locks, with Braunston tunnel a none-too-easy walk down the towpath. There are also several old canalside pubs in this area.

□ Stoke Bruerne is three miles (5km) E of Towcester off A508. Map ref 5B1.

The county has both the Chilterns and the Cotswolds. Oxford and its colleges are outstanding attractions and its rivers are the Thames and the Cherwell. Thames and Chilterns Tourist Board, Tel: Abingdon 22711.

443. BANBURY
Europe's biggest cattle market

The town has Saxon origins, but few buildings survive from before the 17th century. Even the Banbury Cross of nursery rhyme fame is a replica erected in the 19th century. The original was destroyed in 1602. Who the 'fine lady on the white horse' was is unclear, although she appears on the town's coat of arms. Banbury's Thursday market is the largest and most important cattle-market in Europe.

□ 22 miles (35km) N of Oxford. Map ref 5A1.

444. BLENHEIM PALACE
Home of the Marlboroughs

This, the birthplace of Sir Winston Churchill, is one of the finest examples of English baroque set in one of the greatest gardens in the country: 2000 acres (809 hectares) of parkland, over 60 acres (24 hectares) of pleasure gardens and eight acres (3.2 hectares) of kitchen gardens alone. The house was the gift of Queen Anne to the 1st Duke of Marlborough for his victory over the French and Bavarians at Blenheim in 1704. It was built by Sir John Vanbrugh between 1705 and 1722 and has magnificent state rooms with tapestries, paintings, sculpture and fine furniture. Outstanding features are the painted ceiling in the Great Hall and the Long Library containing over 10,000 volumes in a room 183ft (55.7m) long. An exhibition of Churchilliana includes his curls at the age of five and some of his paintings and letters. Churchill's burial place is next to his parents in the graveyard on the hill by the little parish church of Bladon to the south of the park. The park and gardens at Blenheim were landscaped by 'Capability' Brown. When he wanted to create a lake as the centrepiece he dammed the River Glyme to produce what Churchill's father, Lord Randolph, told his wife Jennie, was 'the finest view in England'. Open daily from mid-Mar to end Oct.

☐ At Woodstock on A34 eight miles (12.8km) N of Oxford. Map ref 5A2.

445. COGGES MANOR FARM
Farm museum

A 13th-century manor house and an Edwardian farmhouse are part of this 11 acre (4.5 hectares) site where many traditional farm skills, such as hurdle-making and sheep-shearing, can be seen. Quantities of tools, waggons and horse-drawn vehicles show how, a century ago, farmers worked and raised their livestock. Visitors can follow a historic trail marking the moated manor, deserted village earthworks and field systems of medieval times. Picnicking in orchard. There is a tourist information centre for the area at the farm. Open daily from Easter to Sept. Tel: Woodstock 811456.

☐ Off A40, just S of Witney. Access by B4022. Map ref 5A2.

446. COTSWOLD WILDLIFE PARK
Animals in 'natural' surroundings

The park is set out using ditches rather than fences so there is an overall sense of space rather than captivity. There are animals, birds, reptiles and exotic fish from all over the world. The Butterfly House has the largest butterfly flight cage in Britain. Open all year except Christmas Day. Tel: Burford 3006.

☐ Two miles (3.2km) S of Burford on A361. Map ref 5A2.

447. GREAT TEW
Crumbling village

This Cotswold village is one of many acclaimed at one time or another as 'the prettiest in England'. It has become dilapidated now, and some buildings have decayed totally. But it is still possible to admire the 16th and 17th-century thatched cottages set on the slopes of a wooded valley. Part of the charm of this village stems from landscaping of the estate carried out in the early 19th century. Its importance in the 1980s may be as a demonstration of what can happen to the most handsome of villages – and part of our national heritage – if people are not vigilant in their protection.

☐ Five miles (8km) E of Chipping Norton off B4022. Map ref 5A1.

448. MAPLEDURHAM
Country park

This is part of a designated AONB with meadows giving a long frontage to the Thames. It features a restored watermill which was mentioned in Domesday Book and is the oldest surviving mill on the Thames. The park covers five acres (2 hectares) of riverside meadows with picnic area. Mapledurham House is an Elizabethan mansion built in 1588. It contains many paintings – family portraits from the 16th to 18th centuries – oak staircases, moulded ceilings and Elizabethan white plasterwork. The house did much to inspire the work of the poet Alexander Pope. Both house and mill are open in summer at weekends and on Bank Holidays. They also open weekdays for special parties by

arrangement. Tel: Kidmore End 3350.
☐ Four miles (6.4km) NW of the centre of Reading off the Caversham to Woodcote road A4074. Map ref 5A2.

449. ROLLRIGHT STONES
Prehistoric stone circle

A group of three prehistoric monuments all dating from the Bronze Age. A standing circle of nearly 70 somewhat gnarled stones is the largest of these monuments. It must once have been impressive but its state of preservation cannot have been helped by its site alongside an old drovers' road following the route of the prehistoric Jurassic Way. Just across this now-metalled road is the solitary King Stone.
☐ Three miles (5km) NW of Chipping Norton on and just off an unclassified road running between A34 and A44. Map ref 5A1.

450. SINODUN HILLS
Thames valley viewpoint

Where the Thames meanders lazily through the clay vale south of Abingdon, a tree-crowned chalk knoll, sometimes called the Wittenham Clumps, provides a spectacular isolated viewpoint and a breezy escape from the sleepy river valley below. A gentle stroll eastwards across Day's Lock and the river meadows brings you to the ancient Roman town of Dorchester with its massive Norman Abbey and ancient earthworks. Less than three miles (5km) north, past the attractive thatched villages of Little and Long Wittenham, is the Thames-side village of Clifton Hampden.
☐ Near Abingdon, Oxfordshire. A415 E out of Abingdon to Dorchester (Oxon). Map ref 5A2.

451. UFFINGTON
Vale of the White Horse

A small town in the valley beneath the hill crowned by the Iron Age hill-fort of Uffington Castle and the prehistoric outline of the Uffington White Horse. The latter is an extraordinary legacy from the Iron Age – the only prehistoric white horse of the many in the country – and can only really be appreciated from the valley below: from the B4508 road or the modern village of Uffington. The church tower is another good vantage point. The fame of the White Horse and the marvellous views mean the hill can become crowded and the cark park full at weekends. The crowds can usually be left behind, however, by following the route of the ancient Ridgeway track which passes Uffington Castle. About two miles (3.2km) south-west along this path is a chambered long barrow.
☐ Uffington is eight miles (13km) NE of Swindon off B4507. The White Horse and Uffington Castle lie one mile (1.6km) to the S and are reached by a clearly marked road also off B4507. Map ref 5A2.

452. THE WINDRUSH VALLEY
Rural river valley

The gently gliding waters of the Windrush burrow through the Cotswolds in North Oxfordshire, past picturesque villages of mellow grey and yellow limestone. Burford is an ancient market town, with an impressive sloping High Street, leading down to a stone bridge over the river. Upstream and down the water meadows, willows and the surrounding stone-walled farmlands have remained virtually unchanged for centuries, and evoke the atmosphere of agrarian England in the Middle Ages, a time when Burford's wealth was based on sheep and wool.
☐ Near Burford. Access via minor roads off the A40. Map ref 5A2.

Warwickshire

The Shakespeare country and Stratford-upon-Avon are set in a county of farmland and woods. The foothills of the Cotswolds spill over the northern boundary. There is industry at Rugby and the finest of great medieval castles at Warwick, which is also the county town. Heart of England Tourist Board, Tel: Worcester 29511.

453. BURTON DASSETT HILLS
Country park

This park consists of 100 acres (40.5 hectares) of rugged hill countryside situated on a spur which thrusts out into a relatively flat plain. There are good views across the site of the Battle of Edge Hill. Old worked-out quarries, the Church of All Saints and the Beacon Tower (AM) are additional features. There are public footpaths and bridleways and a new viewpoint on Magpie Hill. The park is open daily throughout the year.
□ Just off A41, 10 miles (16km) SE of Warwick and eight miles (12.8km) NW of Banbury. Map ref 5A1.

454. CHESTERTON
Windmill of distinction

An unusual stone windmill stands here on high ground. It was built in 1632 with arches beneath a striking domed roof. Originally a viewing tower for a local nobleman, it is now a scheduled national monument. A superb restoration won a top award in the 1975 European Architectural Heritage Year. It is not normally open to the public, but its exterior is in any case its chief glory. Details of very occasional open days from Warwickshire County Council's Architects Dept. Tel: Warwick 43431.
□ Five miles (8km) SE of Leamington Spa off A41. Map ref 5A1.

455. CHARLECOTE PARK
Mansion and deer park

The young Will Shakespeare is reputed to have poached in the deer park of this mellow, red brick mansion. He was arraigned before Sir Thomas Lucy, Charlecote's owner, in the Great Hall and subsequently fined. Afterwards he is said to have given vent to his irritation by writing ribald verses on the gatehouse wall. The gate house, a gem of its kind, is still there but not the graffiti. But there is still a deer park in which descendants of Shakespeare's poached deer graze. The house has been extensively altered since Sir Thomas built it on the site of an older building in about 1558. It has a fine collection of early 17th century books and family portraits spanning 350 years. Open Apr and Oct on Sat and Sun, and every day in the week following Easter; May to end Sept every day except Mon, but open Bank Holiday Mon. Further information NT regional office, Tel: Tewkesbury 292427.
□ Five miles (8km) E of Stratford-upon-Avon on B4086 Banbury road. Map ref 5A1.

456. COOMBE ABBEY
Country park

Facilities in this woodland park include lake boating and fishing, nature trail, bridleways and the Abbey garden.
□ Four miles (6.5km) E of Coventry on A4114. Map ref 11B4.

457. EDGE HILL
Historic viewpoint

If you are interested in the landscape of the English heartland, where yeoman farmers tilled the red soils of the Midland Plain, few better viewpoints exist than Edge Hill (705ft, 211m) on the Cotswold escarpment, reached from the A422. You can look over the Civil War battlefield of Edge Hill (1642) or visit the nearby village of Cropredy to the east, to recapture the atmosphere of another Civil War battle, when King Charles was almost captured as his army crossed the River Cherwell (1644). Nearby, is the village of Edgcote, the site of a battle in the Wars of the Roses (1469).
□ About seven miles (11.3km) NW of Banbury, off the A422. Map ref 5A1.

458. HARTSHILL HAYES
Country park

This small park lies on a ridge overlooking the Anker Valley and consists of a small woodland area and an open hilltop with views as far as the peaks of Derbyshire on a clear day. There are attractive walks through the woodland and the hilltop is ideal for picnics. Adjoining the park is another woodland area owned by the Forestry Commission and the footpaths through this can be used by the public. The park is open daily throughout the year.

□ Four miles (6.4km) NW of Nuneaton off A47 road to Birmingham. Map ref 11A4.

459. KINGSBURY
Country park

This park consists of 450 acres (182 hectares) of land and water lying in the flat valley of the River Tame. The lakes, formed as a result of gravel extraction, are the main attraction, with lakeside walks, footpaths and nature trails. Other facilities include picnic areas, an adventure playground, a pitch and putt course and wildlife observation points. Activities include fishing, sailing and hydroplaning. There is a display centre, Tel: Tamworth 872660. Open throughout the year except Christmas Day.

□ 10 miles (16km) NE of Birmingham, five miles (8km) S of Tamworth, just E of A51.
Map ref 11A4.

460. PACKWOOD HOUSE
Yew garden

The house is 16th-century with later additions, and is a prime example of domestic Tudor architecture. While its timbers and brickwork make a satisfactory picture, its great glory is the Yew Garden, where clipped yews represent the Sermon on the Mount. A tall yew at its centre depicts Jesus while other yews are cut to represent the multitude. The apostles, in the shape of 12 more yews, are found on a raised walk. A colourful Carolean formal garden contrasts with the deep green of the yews. Open frequently throughout the year. Tel: Lapworth 2024.

□ At Hockley Heath off A34 and B4439 SE of Birmingham. Map ref 11A4.

East Anglia

461. DEDHAM VALE
Area of Outstanding Natural Beauty

Small but delectable tract of low-lying, leafy water-meadow country beside the River Stour immortalised by the paintings of John Constable (1776–1837). Here the Stour divides Essex and Suffolk at the loveliest part of its valley. Area 28 sq miles (72 sq km).
☐ In both Suffolk and Essex. Map ref 6C2.

462. LINCOLNSHIRE WOLDS
Area of Outstanding Natural Beauty

A quietly beautiful 40 mile (64km) expanse of low, rolling chalk country rising between Lincoln and the North Sea coast. It is a landscape of sheep runs and farmland, with few people and many empty roads. The highest point in the area is Normanby le Wold, 552ft (168m). Area 218 sq miles (560 sq km).
☐ In Lincolnshire. Map ref 12B3.

463. NORFOLK COAST
Area of Outstanding Natural Beauty

The main area lies between Snettisham and Mundesley, a magical world of creeks and salt marsh, shingle spits, sea lavender and tidal flats that echo to the cries of gulls, terns, redshank and curlew. The AONB also includes two small outlying areas, one on the coast at Horsey, the other between Royal Sandringham and the Wash. Area 175 sq miles (450 sq km).
☐ North Norfolk. Map ref 13A4.

464. SUFFOLK COAST AND HEATHS
Area of Outstanding Natural Beauty

Covers the coast and heaths from Kessingland down to the Deben estuary, which it follows inland as far as Woodbridge. Best explored from Walberswick, Southwold, Aldeburgh and Orford. At Dunwich the sea is gradually eating away at the crumbling cliffs. Elsewhere, there are lonely marshes and estuaries. Area 152 sq miles (390 sq km).
☐ In Suffolk. Map ref 6D2.

Cambridgeshire

In the north and east are flat fenlands while the south has gently rolling chalk hills. Cambridge enriches the county with its old college buildings, standing in mellow and enduring perfection against water-meadow and stream. Ely Cathedral is a landmark in the flat

East Anglia

landscapes. There is a castle at Kimbolton, the Cromwell Museum at Huntingdon and a famous Botanic Garden in Cambridge itself. East Anglia Tourist Board, Tel: Ipswich 214211.

465. ANGLESEY ABBEY
Herbaceous garden and house

Magnificent herbaceous garden and sweeping lawns, rare trees, avenues and vistas. In spring there are hyacinths, daffodils and cowslips in profusion. The house dates from the 12th century and is a mix of medieval, Elizabethan and early 20th century architecture, with works of art from all over the world. Open daily from Apr to Oct in afternoons but house closed Mon and Fri. Tel: Cambridge 811200 or 811175.
□ Off B1102, near village of Lode, six miles (9.6km) NE of Cambridge. Map ref 6B1.

466. AVERSLEY WOOD
Old established wood

The south part of this wood has recently been acquired by the Woodland Trust and opened to the public. Primary woodland (an area which has always been tree-covered) is rare in East Anglia. Bluebells, wood anemones and dog's mercury carpet the ground and there are several examples of the beautiful wild service tree, now an uncommon species. This quiet attractive wood provides a good alternative to the over-visited Monkswood Reserve not far away. The rest of the wood is private but there is a public footpath which skirts the edge of the whole wood in addition to a 4½ mile (7.2km) walk in the Woodland Trust section.
□ S of Sawtry off A1. Map ref 6A1.

467. BEDFORD LEVELS
Fen drains

The Romans began the process of reclamation in the Fens with the Car Dyke (see Day Out 490) but the Bedford Levels represent the first large-scale attempt to tackle the problem of periodic flooding in this area of potentially rich farmland. The work was carried out at the request of the owner, the Duke of Bedford, by the Dutch engineer Cornelius Vermuyden in the first half of the 17th century. He constructed two artificial channels, the Old and New Bedford Levels, to run side by side for more than 20 miles (32km) from Delph to Denver. In between was a pastureland – the Wetlands (see Day Out 472) – which served to absorb more water in times of severe flooding. Unlike the Car Dyke the Bedford Levels remain a prominent feature of the Fenland landscape today.
□ Good places to see the Levels are from the A1101 road between Wisbech and Ely near Welney, or the A142 road near Mepal between Ely and Chatteris. Map ref 6B1.

468. FERRY MEADOWS
Country park

Ferry Meadows is a stretch of arable and grassland which runs for 10 miles (16km) along the Nene river valley. The park covers 500 acres (202 hectares) and much of it has been created from reclaimed gravel pits. There are some small wooded areas and a number of lakes which support a variety of bird life. One of the lakes is accessible by boat from the River Nene, although power boats are not encouraged. Other facilities include a nature trail, a bridleway, windsurfing and sailing lessons, camping and caravan sites, two cafés and an information centre which displays a history of the park and local craft work which is for sale. Tel: Peterborough 234443.
□ Three miles (4.8km) W of Peterborough on A605 and A47. Map ref 6A1.

469. GRAFHAM WATER
Reservoir recreation

This man-made reservoir has facilities for fishing and sailing. It is also one of the best places to watch water-birds in

England. The beautiful pintail, tufted duck, pochard and Bewick's swans frequent its 2½ sq miles (6.4 sq km). There are public footpaths running around much of the reserve and to places on the south bank (off the B661 at West Perry, north bank (east and west from Hill Farm and Grafham) and round to the south-west corner where the path runs by the water.
□ Five miles (8km) SW of Huntingdon off B661. Map ref 6A1.

---

470. HEMINGFORD
Twin villages

The twin villages of Hemingford Grey and Hemingford Abbots are situated on the River Ouse in a strikingly attractive setting. The former has a moated, stone-built manor house of 12th-century origins, sometimes claimed to be the oldest inhabited house in England. It is not open to the public but remains a considerable attraction in twin riverside villages which also have a fine church on the bend of the river, a watermill, and several thatched roofs, brick and timber-framed cottages. Hemingford Abbots has a thatched inn, the Axe and Compass.
□ Three miles (5km) SE of Huntingdon between A604 and A1123. Map ref 6B1.

---

471. MARCH
Church of the angels

St Wendreda is not the parish church of March; it stands outside in comparative isolation. With its spire and, on the side facing the town, rich battlements, the exterior is a pleasure. The interior, though, is a thrill! This is because of the double hammer-beam roof, which is absolutely aflutter with angels: 78 of them on the wing, and another 40 at rest on the cornices.
□ St Wendreda is one mile (1.6km) S of March. Map ref 6B1.

---

472. OUSE WASH RESERVES
Water-meadows and wildfowl

The Ouse Washes are the water-meadows which lie between the Old and New Bedford Levels. They are regularly flooded in winter providing lush summer grazing for cattle and an attractive breeding habitat for waterfowl. Since the Washes are on the southward migration route from Russia and Scandinavia huge flocks of wildfowl winter on them. The Royal Society for the Protection of Birds, the Wildfowl Trust and other bodies have acquired properties extending along 9½ miles (15km) of the Washes. The RSPB reserve can be reached from the car park at Welches Dam. Public hides are open all year. The Wildfowl Trust's refuge is at Welney. It is important to follow signs and walk below the banks to minimise disturbance to the birds.
□ Welches Dam is E of Chatteris. Access via B1098 or B1093 and then minor road from Manea. Welney is 12 miles (19km) SE of Wisbech on A1101. Map ref 6B1.

---

473. SWAFFHAM PRIOR
Twin churches

There are some attractive thatched cottages here and 16th-century half-timbered buildings, but the village is perhaps most unusual for its two churches sharing a single churchyard. This dates from the time when the village was divided into two parishes, although each shared the same burial ground. Both churches are 12th-century but only one, St Mary's, is still used.
□ Eight miles (13km) NE of Cambridge on B1102. Map ref 6B1.

---

474. WANSFORD
Steam railway

The Great North Road crosses the River Nene here. It first did so by a 16th-century bridge with 12 fine arches but the latterday A1 uses a more modern construction. The town's position on this prime coaching route north from London was important in the history of the Haycock Inn. During the 17th century, as traffic on the roads began to increase, so did the need for post-houses. To meet this demand ale houses or farms were sometimes rebuilt as inns. The Haycock was built round existing courtyards where the old brewhouse can still be seen. One yard had an open gallery (now enclosed to form a passage) of a kind often associated with Elizabethan taverns in towns. The coming of the railway reduced the volume of horse traffic and the inn became a farm. The advent of the motor-car enabled it to re-open as an inn after a break of 40 years. Now it is by-passed by the modern A1. Wansford is now the headquarters of a partially-restored Nene Valley Steam Railway with some steam passenger services to and from Orton Mere during the summer. Tel: Stamford 782854 or 782021.

□ Wansford is six miles (9.6km) W of Peterborough at junction of A1 and A47. Map ref 6A1.

---

475. WICKEN FEN
Relic fen

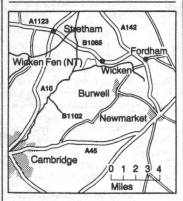

Wicken Fen: what true Fenland looked like before man drained it

Few people realise what the true Fenland looked like before centuries of artificial draining and reclamation. Here is an opportunity to see a 730 acre (295 hectares) remnant of the former 2500 sq miles (6475 sq km) of marshes which once existed in this part of eastern England. Scientifically it is one of the most important 'wetland' nature reserves in western Europe with a range of insect, plant and bird life not found anywhere else. Carefully managed by the NT, who sell informative pamphlets on the great variety of wildlife, which includes such birds as the marsh and Montague harrier, bittern, heron, shoveller, smew and goosander. There is a 1½ mile (2.4km) nature trail open throughout the year except Thur. It begins at the keeper's house (Grid ref TL 564705). Rubber boots are advisable. Tel: Ely 720274. The windpump, which maintains the correct water level in the fen, has been restored as an old Fenland windmill.

□ S of A1123 at Wicken village and 3 miles (4.8km) W of Soham (A142), 17 miles (27.3km) NE of Cambridge via A10. Map ref 6B1.

Essex

Essex has three faces. In the south it is urban and industrial. In the east its ragged coast is a mixture of sea-marsh and estuary while 'upland' Essex to the west and north is farm and orchard country. Chelmsord is the county town and Colchester is one of Britain's oldest towns. East Anglia Tourist Board, Tel: Ipswich 214211.

---

476. ABBERTON RESERVOIR
Easy birdwatching

Abberton's four sq miles (10.3 sq km) attract large numbers of wildfowl. Wigeon, pintail, shoveler, goldeneye, goosander, smew, Bewick's swan, gadwall, scaup, grebes and divers regularly visit the reservoir. Much can be seen from roads which cross it: B1026 and a minor road running south from Layer Breton.

□ Four miles (6.4km) S of Colchester between B1025 and B1026. Map ref 6C2.

---

477. AUDLEY END HOUSE
Jacobean mansion

It is hard to believe that this splendid house with its imposing façade is merely part of the original building. Vanbrugh demolished some of it when he was invited to remodel it in the 18th century. More disappeared later in the century. Robert Adam was responsible for some of its later decoration and 'Capability' Brown landscaped the park. Open daily Apr to Oct except Mon. Tel: Saffron Walden 22399.

□ One mile (1.6km) W of Saffron Walden on A11. Map ref 6B2.

---

478. BLACKWATER ESTUARY
Sea wall and marshes

Between Maldon and Mersea Island, on the north shore of the River Blackwater, there lies a sweep of country which has some of the loneliest, unspoiled landscapes in Essex. Tiny, unobtrusive lanes lead to expanses of sea marsh and sea walls which stretch to the horizon. It is a land of incredible skyscapes where skylarks sing in the shimmering heat hazes that hang over the marshes in summer. In winter, when a wild north-easter is blowing, the cold bites to the bone but the discomfort is forgotten at the spectacle of a sky filled with clouds of geese and other wildfowl. It is a unique part of England, an acquired taste perhaps, and it calls for solid sea wall walking to appreciate it fully. Some of its highlights are:

Heybridge Basin. Here the Chelmer and Blackwater Navigation ends in a sea-lock. The canal basin is full of boats and can be unbelievably busy when the tide is high and the lock is functioning.

There are two pubs within hailing distances of each other and a length of concrete wall on which to sit with a pint and watch the boating world go by.

Goldhanger. The village high street ends at a farm gate and the local football field. Behind the far goalposts is Goldhanger Creek with miles of sea wall snaking away to the east and open sea.

Salcott-cum-Virley. These twin hamlets used to lie on opposite sides of a tidal creek. The creek was blocked off long ago by a new sea wall and its old course is now covered with grass. The lane which runs the length of Salcott ends at a field gate. A short walk on the other side of it leads on to the great swathe of Old Hall marshes and a maze of creeks.

The Strood. This is the causeway on to Mersea Island. To the left the marshes stretch away to the River Colne. To the right they are the Blackwater's domain. The Peldon Rose, old, low-ceilinged, a cosy refuge on a wild night, stands on the 'mainland' nearby. Motorists should exercise caution as high tides sometimes cover the causeway.

West Mersea. Oyster fishery (you can eat them in a hut on the edge of the saltings if you have a mind to) and popular yachting centre, its coast road ends at Old City, a jumble of small weatherboard cottages.

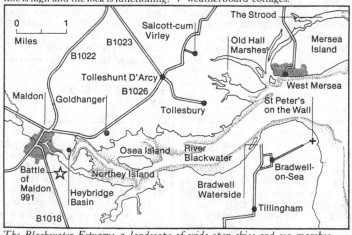

The Blackwater Estuary: a landscape of wide open skies and sea-marshes

East Anglia

□ All the places mentioned can be reached via B1026 from Maldon and the minor road off it which passes through Great Wigborough and Peldon to join the B1025 for West Mersea. Map ref 6C2.

479. BRADWELL-ON-SEA
Romans, Anglo-Saxons and sea walls

The village is not on the sea but Bradwell Waterside is. The creek here is full of moorings sheltered by marshy Pewet Island. The low-lying coast is dominated by the massive outline of the nuclear power station. This obtrusive monument to modern technology rears up in a landscape which has much older landmarks to show. Follow the sea wall from Bradwell Waterside eastwards for a couple of miles (3.2km) towards what looks, from a distance, like an old barn. In fact it is one of the oldest of all England's churches, St Peter's-on-the-Wall, built on the wall of the old Roman fort of Othona by the Anglo-Saxon priest St Cedd in about AD 650. Much of the brickwork from the old Roman fort, one of a chain of romantically named 'Forts of the Saxon Shore', was used in the building of the church. There is an alternative route to it via the lane by the church in Bradwell-on-Sea. Follow it eastwards (it is on the line of the old Roman road) until you come to the farm buildings at the end. From here St Peter's is a short walk away. Southwards from St Peter's is one of the loneliest coasts in East Anglia, the sea wall running almost in a straight line past Dengie Flats and Tillingham Marshes, past outfalls and decoy ponds and the tidal flats of Ray Sands to Holliwell Point and the mouth of the River Crouch. From here it turns westwards to the popular sailing resort of Burnham-on-Crouch with its quay, broad high street and Victorian clock tower. It is a fair day's walk, 12 or 13 miles (19 to 21km), in which sea air and sea birds are dominant.

□ Bradwell-on-Sea is reached via B1018 and unclassified roads from Maldon. Map ref 6C2.

480. CASTLE HEDINGHAM
Norman castle

The town is dominated by the castle keep built about 1140 and set high on a hill overlooking the River Colne. It was from here that the de Vere family, Earls of Oxford, exercised their power and influence for 500 years as lords of the manor. The keep is sufficiently intact to be one of the best preserved examples of an early Norman castle in England. Together with the slightly later Norman church, the castle provided the nucleus around which the medieval town grew but it lacked the economic base to develop into a fully fledged town and today it is more village than urban centre. It has some attractive old houses from Georgian and earlier times.

□ Three miles (4.8km) NW of Halstead off A604 or B1058. Map ref 6C2.

481. DANBURY
Country park

Here there is a variety of interest – woodland walks, a string of lakes for coarse fishing, a walled garden and open parkland with picnic tables. Fishing day-tickets are available from the warden. The park is open from 7am to sunset. Tel: Brentwood 216297. Danbury, one of the highest villages in Essex, also has Danbury and Lingwood Commons (NT) with a mixture of woodland and heath.

□ Danbury is four miles (6.4km) E of Chelmsford on A414. Map ref 6C2.

482. GREENSTED-JUXTA-ONGAR
Saxon church

In this small hamlet is one of the most unusual churches in Britain. St Andrews has a nave wall consisting of vertical, split trunks of oak standing on a wooden sill. (The latter is a Victorian replacement.) It is the only surviving example of a Saxon wooden church and as such is a unique architectural treasure. The chancel was added at the beginning of the 16th century and the nave roof in the mid-19th century when the church was restored. The body of King Edmund rested here on its way from London to Bury St Edmunds.

□ One mile (1.6km) W of Chipping Ongar off A128. Map ref 6B2.

483. HATFIELD FOREST
Remnant of a royal forest

This 1000 acres (405 hectares) of Essex woodland is preserved almost as it was in the days of the Norman kings. It is a benign and open forest full of light and space, its coppices crossed by sunny rides. There are park-like tracts of magnificent pollarded hornbeams, acres of open pasture scattered with islands of hawthorn and, at the centre, a lake (boating and fishing) and a marsh (now a nature reserve) where wild orchids bloom. A nature trail of 1½ miles (2.4km) begins at the Shell House nearby. This was built in 1757. Its walls are decorated with flints, shells and fragments of glass. It was originally used for lakeside picnics. Once much of England looked like Hatfield. The practice of combining pasture with woodland is very old and may go back to the Bronze Age and beyond. It is owned by the NT and is designated as a Country Park. Cars can be driven into the forest to the Shell House where an information room is open summer weekends and Bank Holiday Mon.

□ Four miles (6.4km) E of Bishop's Stortford on minor road S of A120 leading to Bush End. Map ref 6B2.

484. MALDON
Ships and sea salt

Maldon, a picturesque little port at the head of the Blackwater estuary, is much taken up with the manufacture of sea salt, building boats and repairing and restoring old East Coast sailing barges. The Hythe Quay is full of them, berthed alongside each other, presenting the sort of spectacle which was common in the little marshland ports of Essex in their trading heyday. There are two pubs where you can sit outside and watch the steady pace of waterside

life – the Jolly Sailor and the Queen's Head. Upstream from Hythe Quay is Fullbridge Quay where small coasters lie alongside. It is possible to walk between the two by back road and footpath passing the Maldon Crystal Salt Company's sheds on the way. From Fullbridge climb steep Market Hill, past some fine old bay-windowed houses, into Maldon High Street. All Saint's Church has a triangular tower, the only one of its kind in England. Maldon is one of the oldest charter towns, granted in 1171 by Henry II.

The site of the Battle of Maldon, subject of the epic Anglo-Saxon poem which tells of that fierce and bloody encounter with the Danes, is south of the town on a minor road east of B1018.

□ Maldon is at the end of A414 E of Chelmsford. Map ref 6C2.

485. THE NAZE
Fossil hunting

The Naze is a promontory which juts out into the North Sea south of Harwich. There is a tower on the cliff top from which there are excellent views over the saltings and creeks of the Walton Backwaters and the Stour estuary. It is here that the usual London Clay which covers much of Essex gives way to a shelly sand deposit called 'crag' which is rich in fossils – everything from shark's teeth to elephant bones. The beach and cliffs are the best places to search. A nature trail which includes the crag deposits runs through the area which is also rich in plant, bird and insect life. Hamford Water, which lies in the backwaters behind the Naze, is the place which inspired some of Arthur Ransome's children's books.

□ N of Walton-on-the-Naze. Map ref 6D2.

486. ONE TREE HILL
Country park

This park is situated on high land with extensive views to the south over the Thames Estuary. Within its 130 acres (52.6 hectares) there are two important ancient woodlands, scrubland and some meadows and pastures. The name comes from a single large ash tree which once stood at the top of the hill. There is a horse ride around the park perimeter. Open 7am to sunset. Tel: Brentwood 216297.

☐ One mile (1.6km) W along unclassified road off A176 SE of Basildon. Map ref 7B1.

487. WEALD PARK
Country park

Wood, meadow and parkland with a lake for fishing. There are bridleways, walks and picnic spots. The present park consists of the Deer Park and woodlands of a much larger estate held by the Tower family since 1752. Open 7am to sunset.

☐ Two miles (3.2km) NW of Brentwood off A128. Map ref 7B1.

488. WIVENHOE
River village

This quayside town on the River Colne is still involved in boat-building as it has been for centuries. A walk along the river leads to Alresford Creek which winds some three miles (4.8km) inland. Look out for herons feeding. On the opposite side of the river, where thousands of Brent geese winter on the saltings, is one of the three nature reserves on the estuary.

☐ Wivenhoe is SE of Colchester off A133 and B1027. Fingringhoe is S of Colchester off B1025. Map ref 6C2.

Lincolnshire

To the south-east lies the flat, fertile Fenland with Spalding and its bulb fields. Further north the gentle Wolds harbour fine houses such as Harrington Hall and towns such as Alford. Lincoln's hill-top cathedral dominates the surrounding countryside. East Midlands Tourist Board, Tel: Lincoln 31521.

489. BOSTON
Old wool port

This was a great seaport of the medieval wool trade with Flanders and the prime reminder of its past importance is the 15th-century Church of St Botolph, one of the largest parish churches in the British Isles. Its tower, known as the Boston Stump, is 272ft (85m) high and a landmark for many miles around. Like King's Lynn, its great rival as a wool port on the further shore of the Wash, Boston is rich in old warehouses and enticing streets. Now the port, on the tidal River Witham, which not so long ago was in decline, is enjoying a new lease of life from trade within the Common Market.

☐ 15 miles (24km) NE of Spalding. Map ref 12B4.

490. BOURNE
Canal the Romans built

There are some good Georgian houses in this market town and a few Tudor cottages, but the historically-minded are drawn here by even earlier features. Half a mile (800m) to the east of the town (and running north, roughly parallel with the A15 and B1177) is one of the few traceable stretches of the Roman-built Car Dyke. This canal started the long process of reclamation in the Fens but for most of its length, from just north of Peterborough to the River Witham, it has disappeared from view on the ground. In Bourne itself the old castle, now no more than some mounds and a moat, is believed to have occupied the site of the home of Hereward the Wake, the last of the Saxon nobles to resist William the Conqueror.

☐ 10 miles (16km) NE of Stamford at junction of A15 and A151. Map ref 12B4.

491. BRANT BROUGHTON
Limestone church

The Church of St Helen in this village on the River Brant dates back to the 13th century. Built of the finest Ancaster limestone, the exterior is lavish. The grand parapeted tower is crowned by a lovely spire visible for miles. The interior is notable for something all too scarce: really sensitive Victorian restoration. But best of all is the cambered nave roof with angels.

☐ 12 miles (19km) S of Lincoln or six miles (9.6km) E of Newark off A17. Map ref 12A3.

492. BURGHLEY HOUSE
Great English house

One of England's greatest Elizabethan houses. It was built by William Cecil, Treasurer to Queen Elizabeth I, between 1546 and 1587. The site he chose was originally a monastery which perished as a result of the Dissolution measures of Henry VIII. The grounds belong to a different period, being laid out by 'Capability' Brown in the 18th century. The house is normally open Apr to Oct every day except Mon and Fri but afternoons only on Sun. It is sometimes closed during the Burghley Horse Trials which take place in the grounds in early Sept. Tel: Stamford 52451. Burghley stands on the south-eastern side of Stamford, one of the finest medieval towns in the country, which also has particularly outstanding 17th and 18th-century architecture. Part of its importance has been due to its position on major routeways, first the Roman Ermine Street and later the Great North Road.

☐ Burghley House is just over one mile (1.6km) SE of Stamford off B1443. Stamford is 10 miles (16km) NW of Peterborough. Map ref 6A1.

493. CHURCH FARM MUSEUM
Lincolnshire farm life

The house and farm buildings show aspects of farming in East Lincolnshire. Stables contain a blacksmith and wheelwright's workshop and displays of equipment used in connection with pigs and poultry, while the farmyard itself contains larger items of machinery. Other stables house a saddler's shop and veterinary equipment. The main part of the farmhouse was built about 1760, and added to at various times during the Victorian period. Visitors should see the wash-house with its original copper and an early example of a washing machine. Other interesting rooms include the scullery, living room, pantry, parlour and bedrooms. Open daily May to Oct. Tel: Skegness 66658. A few miles inland, on A158 at Burgh-le-Marsh, is the Windmill Museum. The mill, built in 1833, is working (free-wheeling) and open all year. Tel: Skegness 810281.

☐ Church Road South, Skegness. Off A52 Wainfleet Road, Skegness. Map ref 12B3.

494. GIBRALTAR POINT
Sand spit and bird reserve

This sand spit at the mouth of the River Steeping has a 1200 acre (486 hectares) nature reserve and field station. The terrain covers sand hills, marshes, rough grazing and beach. In spring there are thousands of larks singing over the dunes. Occasionally you can see kestrels and short-eared owls but its importance is as a key migration point for birds. Sea lavender grows here and seals can sometimes be seen basking off the sandbanks. There is a car park and many tracks through the dunes for visitors.

☐ S of Skegness at end of minor road off A52. Map ref 12B3.

495. GRANTHAM
Coaching inn and chained library

Grantham has a number of fine old coaching inns of which the most outstanding is, perhaps, The Angel and Royal Hotel which dates from the 13th century, though the present front is mainly 15th-century. It is one of the few remaining inns established for travellers by the Knights Templars. The State Room, above the central archway, was used by Richard III in 1483. In the 18th century the hotel became an important coaching inn on the Great North Road. The modern A1 now by-passes the town, which the fine cathedral-like church of St Wulfram's dominates. Its 14th-century spire, 281ft (85.6m), is a landmark for miles around. The church has a chained library with 83 books with the original chains still fastened to them. Isaac Newton went to school in Grantham and a statue of him stands in front of the Guildhall.

☐ 12 miles (19km) SE of Newark off the A1. Map ref 12A4.

496. HARTSHOLME
Country park

Created out of the grounds of Hartsholme Hall the park has a 23 acre (9.3 hectares) lake surrounded by open parkland. There are pleasant walks, a nature trail and facilities for picnicking, fishing, bird watching and caravanning. The old stable block is now a cafeteria and information centre. Information on guided wild life walks from warden, Tel: Lincoln 686264. Open daily throughout the year.

☐ 3½ miles (5.5km) SW of Lincoln following A1180. The park is on the Skellingthorpe road. Map ref 12A3.

497. HONINGTON
Lowland hill-fort

Hill-forts are almost non-existent amid the flatness of Lincolnshire, and Honington Camp is only raised on a slight plateau. But 'hill' fort it technically is since the Camp has the ramparts and ditches characteristic of

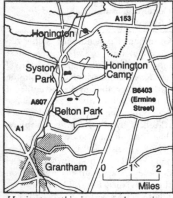

Honington: this is not as dramatic as the Iron Age hill forts of highland Britain but it is virtually the only one in the flatlands of Lincolnshire

these Iron Age settlements. The hill-fort's appearance is quite striking, however, because it is now marooned as an island of uncultivated land amidst farmland.

☐ Honington is five miles (8km) N of Grantham between A607 and A153. The Camp is one mile (1.6km) SE of the village and is reached by a track or footpath leading off A153. Grid ref SK 943432; OS map 130. Map ref 12A4.

498. KESTEVEN
Woodland wildlife

Woodlands scattered in area between Stamford, Grantham and Bourne have Forestry Commission facilities including picnic places and woodland walks. **Morkery Wood** has a picnic place in a small abandoned limestone quarry. A short walk follows a series of old fallow deer trails, used by badgers and foxes.

☐ On Castle Bytham Road 10 miles (16km) N of Stamford.

Ropsley Rise Wood has picnic place and trail where badgers, foxes and long-eared owls may be seen.

☐ One mile (1.6km) NE of Old Somerby off B1176.

Twyford Wood Walk is planted on a World War Two airfield.

☐ Half a mile (800m) E of junction with A1 at Colsterworth.

Clipsham Yew Tree Avenue picnic place adjoins a magnificent avenue of clipped yews about 200 years old.

☐ Eight miles (12.8km) N of Stamford on Stretton to Little Bytham road. Map ref 12A4.

499. LOUTH
Market town

There are a few remains of a 12th-century Cistercian abbey in Louth Park but essentially it is an 18th-century face which this market town presents to the world. Westgate Street probably has the best examples of houses from around this time with many featuring the red brick and tiles characteristic of local buildings. But one building not so constructed is the Church of St James which is considered by some to be a masterpiece of the late medieval Gothic era and which is crowned by a magnificent 295ft (91m) spire. Louth is still a busy market centre with a cattle market on Fri.

□ 26 miles (42km) NE of Lincoln on A157 and A16. Map ref 12B3.

500. MUSEUM OF LINCOLNSHIRE LIFE
Rural life museum

The agricultural, industrial and social history of Lincolnshire, with emphasis on agriculture as the most important factor. There is an extensive collection of large farm equipment and also a small section devoted to the Lincolnshire Poacher which contains animal and mantraps. Open throughout the year (except Dec and Jan) daily Mon to Sat and Sun afternoons. Tel: Lincoln 28448.

□ Burton Road, Lincoln. Map ref 12A3.

501. OLD BOLINGBROKE
Henry IV's birthplace

This is one of a large number of failed towns which dot the English countryside. It is now no more than a single-street village (albeit with a 14th-century church and some 18th-century houses) in a seemingly completely rural area, close to both the chalk wolds and the open marshland country. Yet at one end of this single street is a huge mound, the site of a former castle that obviously once gave hope of better things. It was here that Henry IV was born in 1367.

□ Six miles (9.6km) SE of Horncastle off A1115. Map ref 12B3.

502. SPALDING
Spring bulb field drives

A visit to the dazzling bulb fields of the Fens is a must in early April when the daffodils are out, or the last two weeks in April and first week in May when the tulips are normally in bloom. The local Tourist Information Office at Ayscoughfee Hall, Churchgate, Spalding supplies an excellent map containing signposted routes, called Rural Rides.

These routes, up to 25 miles (40km) long, are updated each year. The information office will tell you the best fields to visit. This is because tulip heads are cut off when they have been in bloom for a few days in order to benefit the growth of the bulb. The trick is to see the fields before this happens. Tel: Tourist Information Office at Spalding 5468 for further details and the date of the local Flower Parade which takes place in May. Spring flowers can always be seen at their best at Springfields Gardens on the A151, near Whaplode on the outskirts of the town. Apart from spring flowers there are 25 acres (10 hectares) of rose gardens with 12,500 bushes on display throughout the summer. Open Apr to Sept. Tel: Spalding 4843.

□ Spalding is N of Peterborough at junction of A16, A151 and A1073. Map ref 12B4.

503. THE WOLDS
Escarpment journey

Escape to Tennyson's 'Calm and deep

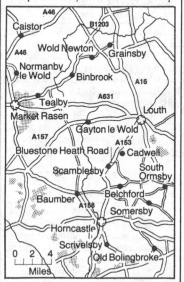

The Lincolnshire Wolds: rolling chalk country of 'calm and deep peace'. Days Out 462, 503

peace on this high wold' by following the lanes which run along the crestline of the chalk escarpment, especially the Bluestone Heath Road between Somersby, Tennyson's birthplace, north via Kelstern and over the county border to Wold Newton. The rolling hills with their vast flocks of sheep, the beechwoods in the hidden valleys, the tiny dreaming villages, belie the turmoil of the towns and main roads on the plains beneath.

□ Somersby is six miles (9.6km) NE of Horncastle off the A158. Map ref 12B3.

Norfolk

Norfolk has three distinctive landscape features: Broadland with its lakes and rivers, the forest and heaths of Breckland and the Cromer Ridge in the north-east. Reed-thatch and flint make appealing village architecture. Other attractions include King's Lynn, Swaffham and Norwich with its castle and cathedral. East Anglia Tourist Board, Tel: 214211.

504. BACTON WOOD
Forest near the sea

Picnic tables set on a grassy area with scattered clumps of pine, only 10 minutes' drive from the sandy beach at Bacton. The forest trail is gently undulating and winds through mainly pine woodland mixed with about 30 different tree species including oak, beech, maple and wild cherry.

□ On by-road running S from B1150 2½ miles (4km) NE of North Walsham. Map ref 13B4.

505. BLAKENEY POINT
Sand spit for birds

The sand dunes and mudflats of Blakeney, and the six mile (9.6km) long shingle beach running out to the point have long been famous for birds and flowers. Altogether 256 different species of bird have been recorded here. The 'swallows of the sea' – common terns and little terns – regularly breed on the point, and oystercatchers and other waders raise their young along the creeks and saltings. In late summer the flats are clothed in the pale lilac haze of flowering sea lavender and the silver-grey foliage of the other sea plants. The Point is reached by walking down the beach from Cley, or by boat from Morston and Blakeney. Tel: NT Warden at Cley 740480.

□ Access is from the A149 north Norfolk coast road. Map ref 13A4.

506. BLICKLING HALL
Country house and gardens

A large garden made over a period of more than three centuries with formal parterres, simplified in the 20th century, and herbaceous plants in place of bedding out. There is woodland intersected by allées in the French manner, a temple, an orangery, fine trees and shrubs and a large landscape lake.

The hall is a memorable building in mellow red brick (about 1620) and has much Jacobean work including the ornate Long Gallery ceiling. House open daily from Apr to mid Oct, except for Mon and Fri (but open Bank Holiday Mons). Early and late in season open afternoons only. Gardens open as above but also Mon and Fri from mid May to end of Sept. Tel: Aylsham 347.

□ On B1354 NW of Aylsham on A140. Map ref 13B4.

507. BRECKLAND
History, heaths and forest

The barren heathlands of Breckland are one of the most arid areas in the country. Glacial sands left after the Ice Age have contributed to the making of a vast tract of poor, open country many acres of which have now been planted by the Forestry Commission to create England's largest lowland forest. During the Middle Ages 'sandblows' made the area even more desert-like and arid, with up to 30 villages being abandoned, although there is plenty of evidence of farming and settlement in Breckland long before this. Grimes Graves (see Day Out 514) are located here. But while farming was difficult in late medieval times the land did support rabbits. Parts of Breckland are still known as Warrens with fortified lodges where gamekeepers lived. The 15th-century Thetford Warren Lodge, near the B1107 Thetford to Brandon road, is open standard DoE hours.

Thetford. This small, ancient market town was once the cathedral city of East Anglia and boasted 20 churches and several monasteries. Only three churches remain but there are other fine buildings which reflect its past importance. Ancient House Museum exhibits Breckland life and history.

Thetford Forest. Picnic sites and forest walks are available at several locations – Bridgham Lane, Devil's Punchbowl, Hockham, Lynford, Two Mile Bottom. St Helen's picnic place, signposted from the road half a mile (800m) north of Santon Downham is by the bank of a small river. There is a church (13th-century) and the site of a moated manor house nearby. A two mile (3.3km) nature trail across woodland, heath and meres is open most days during summer at East Wretham Heath, north-east of Thetford.

☐ Thetford is on main Cambridge to Norwich road A11. Santon Downham forest information point is on minor road running N from B1107, 4¾ miles (7.6km) NW of Thetford. Open working hours weekdays. Map ref 6C1.

508. BRESSINGHAM
Gardens and steam museum

An unusual combination of colourful informal gardens, nurseries and one of the most comprehensive collections of steam engines, both road and rail, which makes Bressingham the largest live steam museum in Europe. There are over 40 of them plus a steam driven roundabout. Different railways take visitors on steam trips through the grounds. There are six acres (2.4 hectares) of gardens stocked with 5000 species of hardy plants. Open afternoons, Sun and Thur May to Sept and Wed in August. Also Bank Holiday Mons. Tel: Bressingham 386.

☐ 2½ miles (4km) W of Diss on A1066 Diss to Thetford road. Map ref 6C1.

509. BROADLAND CONSERVATION CENTRE
Floating exhibition

A nature trail of just over ¾ mile (1.2km) leads over paths and catwalks through marshy alder thicket to the Broadland Centre, a thatched building floating on pontoons between Malthouse and Ranworth Broads. The centre has an exhibition which shows the natural life of the Broads and demonstrates the urgent need for conservation. From the gallery upstairs, visitors have superb views over the surrounding Broadland. Cars should be left in the car park located opposite the Maltsters public house at Ranworth. Tel: South Walsham 479.

☐ Ranworth Broad is 9 miles (14.5km) NE of Norwich along B1140 turning off at the village of South Walsham. Map ref 13B4.

510. THE BROADS
Unique waterways

There are more than 30 Broads, or lakes, and with the many rivers and interconnecting channels in the area, they amount to over 200 miles (320km) of navigable water. The scale of the Broads meant that they were long assumed to be natural features. In the 1950s scientific research revealed their man-made origins as old peat diggings which were flooded by a rise in sea level in the 13th century. The best way to see the Broads is by boat which can be hired in centres such as Wroxham and Horning, by the hour, day or week. There are organised boat trips too, but remember that the Broads are among the most congested waterways in the British Isles. In the summer especially boats may be booked up months in advance and visitors may have to content themselves *watching* other people messing about in boats. Many villages have fine churches and waterside pubs (although the latter, at least, get crowded) and places worth a detour include Broadlands Conservation Centre at Ranworth Broad (see previous entry), the ruins of St Benet's Abbey (south of Horning), and the

East Anglia

windmills at Horsey Mere (NT nature reserve) and Thurne. A water tour in association with the Naturalists' Trust operates daily throughout the summer from the dyke adjacent to the Pleasure Boat Inn, Hickling. Tel: Norwich 25540 for details of other nature reserves in the Broads which are worth visiting.

□ The Broads are contained in a roughly triangular area between Lowestoft, Norwich and Sea Palling. OS map 134 gives the best cover. Map ref 13B4.

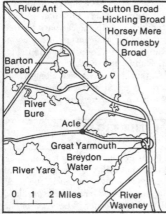

The Norfolk Broads: a scenic network of 200 miles (320km) of navigable waterways

511. CASTLE ACRE
Town on Peddars Way

Tucked away in the lanes north of Swaffham is one of the few towns on the line of the Peddars Way, a Roman and before that a prehistoric trackway which crosses the county. It is a small place now, but boasts military and monastic remains unlike anything else in East Anglia. At one end of Castle Acre is a massive Norman castle mound. Only fragments of the flint walls, a 13th-century gateway and two towers remain but the size of the site – some 15 acres (6 hectares) – indicates its former importance. And at the other end of the town are impressive remains of an 11th-century Cluniac priory (open standard DoE hours). Peddars

Way itself is now mainly a 'green road' and as such it offers good walking, especially south past Great Palgrave and North Pickenham.

□ Castle Acre is four miles (6.4km) N of Swaffham, off A1065. Map ref 13A4.

512. COUNTRYSIDE COLLECTION
Martham farm museum

Rural life of the late 19th century is portrayed here in the traditional Norfolk flint buildings of the area. Harnesses, historical agricultural equipment and tools of the local craftsmen are on show. Open throughout the year seven days a week. Tel: Great Yarmouth 740223.

□ Between Martham and Somerton about nine miles N of Great Yarmouth. Access via A149 and B1152. Map ref 13B4.

513. CROMER RIDGE
Norfolk's 'mountain' range

This stretch of high land, over 300ft (91m) in places, runs from near Cromer in a westerly direction behind Sheringham towards Holt and Salthouse and eastwards towards Mundesley. It is about five miles (8km) wide. In an area of gentle, undramatic topography its wooded slopes and heights produce unexpected and impressive scenery. It rises sharply from the lower country near the coast but its slopes are gentler on its landward side. Much of it is covered by heather and bracken which is a sure sign of its sandy, gravelly nature. It is also made up of much chalk and rocks from as far away as Scandinavia, Scotland and the north of England which were carried there by glaciers. The ridge itself is a moraine which was left by the glaciers. By its nature it provides interesting country for walks and many viewpoints – Franklin Hill, Roman Camp, the highest point in Norfolk, Pretty Corner, Upper Sheringham. Perhaps the most romantic way of enjoying this small, unusual piece of country is to take a steam train from Sheringham's old station to Weybourne. Trains

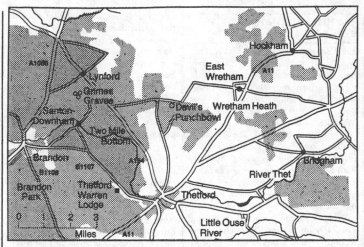

Breckland and Grimes Graves: one of the great man-made forests of lowland England was once sandy waste and heath. Grimes Graves is the site of the most important flint mine in prehistoric Britain. Days Out 507, 514, 525

operate daily from Easter to Oct. Tel: Sheringham 822045.

There are good cliff walks along the coast to Cromer which is a pleasant seaside resort. The cliffs between West Runton and Trimingham have peaty beds at their base which can sometimes be seen where not hidden by cliff falls. These are believed to have formed in a warm inter-glacial period under lake and estuary conditions. In these have been found the remains of elephant, rhinoceros, sabre-toothed tiger, bear and hippopotamus (first appearance in the country). Cromer Museum (open daily) exhibits the geology and natural history of the area.

Gastronomic note: for 20 miles (32km) along this coast clinker-built boats launched from the beach (there are no harbours) fish for crabs. They put down creel pots in strings of 20 to 30 at a time, 100 to 200 pots per boat. Much of the catch is landed at Sheringham and Cromer where it is possible to buy direct from fishermen. The crab fishing is at its best in May and June with lobsters mainly in July and Aug.

☐ Cromer and Sheringham are main centres for area. Access via A149, A148 and B1159. Map ref 13B4.

514. GRIMES GRAVES
Prehistoric flint mines

The site of the largest and most important flint mines known to have existed in prehistoric Britain. In all more than 800 shafts have been identified with a labyrinth of galleries leading off the shafts which were up to 40ft (12m) deep. Here, 4000 years ago, Neolithic man hacked flints from the chalk, with primitive antler picks. Between here and Salisbury Plain a trade in flint tools was maintained along the chalk Ridgeway. The site of this axe factory – for that is what it was – is now some 34 acres (12.5 hectares) of humps and hollows. The prehistoric miners themselves contributed to this landscape by filling in exhausted shafts with waste material from new ones. Natural subsidence over the last 2500 years has done the rest. It must rank as one of the earliest examples of industrial dereliction and was produced by the need for axes to clear more forest for cultivation. The site is under the protection of the Department of the Environment and is open during normal DoE hours.

☐ Four miles (6.4km) NW of Thetford off A134. Map ref 6C1.

515. HOUGHTON HALL
Palladian opulence

Like Boughton House (see Day Out 435), this is a great English house that has been opened to the public comparatively recently. The quintessence of Palladian opulence, it was built in the 1720s for Sir Robert Walpole, for 20 years the most powerful man in Britain. The outside is mainly by Colin Campbell, the interiors superbly decorated by William Kent. The rooms are not as large as photographs suggest: like many great English houses, Houghton turns out to be more intimate than one expects. Splendid contents (including Lord Cholmondeley's important collection of 20,000 model soldiers) and peacocks and milk-white deer in the surrounding parklands set off the architecture. Several breeds of shire horses are on view in the stables. The house and grounds are normally open Thur, Sun and Bank Holidays from Easter to end Sept. Tel: East Rudham 247.
□ 13 miles (21km) E of King's Lynn, off A148. Map ref 13A4.

516. HUNSTANTON
Cliffs, boats and birds

This is East Anglia's only west-facing holiday resort. The long sandy beach is backed by cliffs which have been eroded to reveal horizontal stripes of red carstone and white chalk. The cliffs are excellent for autumn and winter bird-watching and the cliff walk, past a ruined chapel and disused lighthouse, now a private house, to Holme-next-the-Sea, is about 1½ miles (2.4km). There are boat trips from Hunstanton to Scoby Island and to the new lighthouse and cliffs. June to Sept daily.
□ On the A149. Map ref 13A4.

517. KING'S LYNN
Historic port and market town

An outstanding market town. Many fine buildings reflect its importance and prosperity from the 12th century onwards. It was Bishop's Lynn before this particular ecclesiastical property passed to the crown in 1204. But by then the town had already acquired not one but two market-places. Saturday Market, as it is known for the obvious reason, arrived first to be followed around 50 years later by Tuesday Market. Many of King's Lynn's oldest and most interesting buildings are grouped around these. Originally each had its own guildhall and church. The town's prosperity was based primarily on its dual role as market centre for the surrounding farmland and as port on the Great Ouse. It was particularly noted as a wool port during the late Middle Ages but unlike places such as Lavenham, it did not remain ossified in the past when the wool trade declined. There are some excellent buildings from the 17th to 19th centuries to testify to its continuing success as a port and market town. It was once a walled city but only the South Gate and a small part of the wall remain. Once, too, it housed many monastic orders but again little remains other than their titles which appear as names of streets or houses. It is the variety as well as the number of fine buildings which is so appealing. They cover many centuries and represent a mixture of private, religious and public buildings, located in ancient streets or by riverside quays. A tourist office is located in the Town Hall and a booklet details its historic buildings. Tel: King's Lynn 61241.
□ 13 miles (21km) NE of Wisbech on A47. Map ref 13A4.

518. NORFOLK RURAL LIFE MUSEUM
Norfolk's rural past

A new museum, housed in what is the only former workhouse open to the public in Norfolk, showing the history of the county for the past 200 years. There is a row of reconstructed craftsman's shops – saddler, basket-maker, bakery, smithy and wheelwright, and a fine collection of steam and internal combustion engines. Open May to end Sept, Tues to Sat daily, Sun afternoons. Tel: Dereham 820563.

☐ Beach House, Gressenhall, East Dereham. Two miles (3.2km) NW of East Dereham on B1146. Map ref 13A4.

519. NORTH ELMHAM
Saxon cathedral

In the upper reaches of the Wensum valley is this little-known jewel in the quiet Norfolk countryside. It was not always quiet. Just north of the village church are the ruins of a Saxon cathedral, built early in the 11th century. A 14th-century manor house was later built in the same moated enclosure but the Saxon elements are clearly recognisable since they were built from a distinctive local flint and deep brown carstone conglomerate. Elmham was the seat of the bishopric from AD 800 (or even earlier) before the latter moved first to Thetford and then to Norwich. The small cathedral survived largely because it was incorporated into the manor house.

☐ Five miles (8km) N of East Dereham near junction of B1145 and B1110. Map ref 13A4.

520. SANDRINGHAM
Royal residence

Sandringham House is the country residence of the Royal Family. Here King George V and King George VI died. More happily it is where the Queen and her family spend their summer holidays. During the summer months, when no member of the Royal Family is present, the house and grounds are often open to the public. Tel: King's Lynn 2675 for details or check with local tourist boards (see appendices). But a country park covering some 300 acres (121 hectares) of the Sandringham estate is open throughout the year. This includes a nature trail through wood and heathland. The parish church of St Mary Magdalene contains many Royal memorials.

☐ Eight miles (13km) NE of King's Lynn off B1440. Map ref 13A4.

521. TITCHWELL RESERVE
Seashore and marsh birds

This RSPB Reserve covers reedmarsh, saltmarsh and sandy shore. The most delicate of terns, the little tern, breeds here. So do oystercatchers and bearded tits. Winter wildfowl include Brent geese, goldeneye, wigeon and sometimes unusually high numbers of eider duck. Access from east sea wall from A149 between Titchwell and Brancaster; or west sea wall from A149 between Thornham and Titchwell. Car park. Information centre. Tel: RSPB, Sandy (Beds) 80551.

☐ Five miles (8km) E of Hunstanton, Norfolk. Map ref 13A4.

522. WALPOLE ST PETER
Limestone church in flint country

Unlike most Norfolk churches, this mostly 14th-century building is built not of flint but of limestone. It has a gorgeous exterior, with ornamental parapets, grand gargoyles and closely spaced ranges of windows, and a noble interior bathed in light, with a raised east end. There is much handsome woodwork, and six more chandeliers, all with attractive wrought-iron suspension rods, have been added to the fine original one of c.1700. Lovingly maintained in a churchyard worthy of it, this is among the most glorious of all village churches.

☐ 10 miles (16km) W of King's Lynn between A17 and A47. Map ref 12B4.

523. WELLS-NEXT-THE-SEA
Old-fashioned port

The delight of this small place is in its old houses, large town green and its creeks, sea marshes, sand dunes and pine woods. The Quay is dominated by a tall granary and has some fine houses and several old inns. Occasionally coasters trade here. Whelks and cockles are fished. Holkham Hall two miles (3.2km) west of the town was the home of Coke of Norfolk, otherwise Thomas William Coke, Earl of Leicester, one of the great farm improvers of the 18th-century Agricultural Revolution. Here he transformed a sandy wasteland into fertile pastures and woodland. The hall itself is a Palladian glory and was designed by William Kent. The interiors are rich and elaborate, especially the marble entrance hall and the saloon. The hall is open Thur May to Sept, plus Mon and Wed in July and Aug and spring and summer Bank Holiday Mons. Tel: Fakenham 710227 for details.

☐ Wells is on A149 north Norfolk coast road. Holkham is off A149. Map ref 13A4.

---

524. WYMONDHAM
Church of conflict

The great abbey church of this attractive market town was shared between monks and parishioners, who were constantly at loggerheads. The monks' part has mostly perished, apart from their tower of 1400, with its graceful octagonal top. Some 50 years later the parish asserted its independence by building the grand west tower, seemingly to overpower the other. The lofty nave survives, crowned by a fine hammer-beam roof with enchanting floral bosses. There are many other fine buildings – from a 17th-century market cross to the Green Dragon inn said to date from the 14th century.

☐ Eight miles (13km) SW of Norwich on A11. Map ref 6C1.

Suffolk

Rich farmland, sandy heaths, seamarshes and forests make England's easternmost county. Constable painted it, Gainsborough was born there (in Sudbury). It is a county of old houses, sleepy villages and towns of character such as Bury St Edmunds and Lavenham. Ipswich is the county town. East Anglia Tourist Board, Tel: Ipswich 214211.

525. BRANDON PARK
Country park

This 30 acre (12 hectares) park comprises the former landscaped grounds of Brandon House and has a fine collection of trees, open lawns and an ornamental lake. It is set in the heart of Thetford Forest with its many woodland tracks and bridleways. The park has picnic areas, an information room and a full-time warden service.

☐ One mile (1.6km) S of Brandon on B1106. Map ref 6C1.

---

526. CLARE CASTLE
Country park

Centred on the ruins of a Norman castle complete with earthworks, 100ft (30.4m) high *motte* and moats, this park also fronts a millstream of the River Stour and includes the disused Clare railway station. It has pleasant walks, a butterfly garden, a wildlife enclosure, parking and picnic facilities, information room and full-time warden service. There is fishing on the river and launching facilities for canoes and non-motorised boats.

☐ In Clare between village and the River Stour off the A1092. Map ref 6C2.

---

527. CONSTABLE COUNTRY
Artist's landscapes

John Constable was one of the greatest of English landscape painters and his work will always be associated with the Stour Valley of Suffolk where he was born and mostly lived. Identifying the places Constable painted as they are today is a popular recreation, especially at the locations listed below. Sometimes, however, he removed a particular building to a different setting for artistic purposes. Dedham Church is the most notable example of this artistic licence. Several of the places become very crowded during summer months, notably Flatford Mill which is approached by a narrow lane. **Dedham.** In addition to the much-painted church, with its 15th-century tower, there are many superb timber-framed cottages, Georgian houses and old inns on and off the high street. Constable attended the local grammar school.

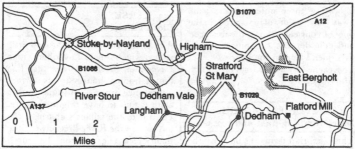

Dedham Vale and the Constable Country: here are the idyllic scenes which inspired England's greatest landscape painter. Days Out 461, 527

East Bergholt. Constable's birthplace and where he married the rector's daughter and painted many of his most famous paintings. Several houses in the village are Elizabethan.

Flatford Mill. This was one of the watermills owned by John Constable's father and is now owned and protected by the NT. Adjoining the mill, with its 15th-century mill-house, is **Willy Lott's Cottage,** the early 17th-century subject of the *Hay Wain* among other paintings.

Stoke-by-Nayland. Yet another village of the Stour valley – Stratford St Mary, Langham and Higham are others – much loved by Constable. The Perpendicular church, with its spire, features in many paintings.

There is no particular order in which these places should be visited. OS maps 155 and 168 will help you to find not only roads between these locations but also footpaths, enabling you to leave the car behind at times. Among them will be paths used by Constable himself, such as that which took him to school at Dedham and which features in *The Corn Field*.

☐ Flatford Mill is on N bank of the River Stour one mile (1.6km) S of East Bergholt off the B1070. Map ref 6C2.

528. DAWS HALL
Wildfowl farm

The farm has a fine collection of waterfowl and pheasants in an extensive garden of rare trees. Open Sun only from Easter to end Sept. Tel: Twinstead 213.

☐ Daws Hall is at Lamarsh two miles (3.2km) NW of Bures on minor road. Map ref 6C2.

529. DEBENHAM
Source of the Deben

A classic linear village stretched along not only the main road but also the River Deben. It has long been a centre of rush weaving and the church dates back to Saxon times. The Elizabethan Crows Hall (not open to the public) is one of Suffolk's many moated manor or farm houses.

☐ 10 miles (16km) N of Ipswich on B1077. Map ref 6C1.

530. DUNWICH
Lost to the sea

Dunwich has a long history but there is little left to show for it: a few ruins, some narrow leafy lanes which were once streets and now and then the bones of the long dead revealed in the crumbling cliffs. The last church of the old town has long since fallen into the sea but its cliff-top graveyard is still under attack. The Dunwich Museum (open from Spring Bank Holiday to end Sept on Sat, Sun, Tues, Thur afternoons) tells the story of the town and its decline, from a flourishing port to what it is now, a handful of houses, an inn and a church. It is a strange place, splendid in its wild isolation (except on a fine summer weekend) with a great curve of stone and shingle beach stretching away northwards past Reedland and Corporation Marshes to Walberswick, a bracing three mile (4.8km) walk away. Take plenty of newspaper in the boot of your car to wrap the fresh cod and flounder you can buy from the fishermen's hut on the beach.

□ Reached by minor road off B1125. Map ref 6D1.

531. EASTON FARM PARK
Dairy farming past and present

This Victorian farm was built by the Duke of Hamilton in about 1870 as a model dairy farm. It now houses a museum of early farm equipment and tools. The Victorian dairy, octagonal in design, has many items which would have been in daily use: butter churns, cream settling pans, a cheese press and a butter worker. Contrasting with this is a modern milking parlour, a part of the working farm, where present day equipment is on show. Traditional livestock such as the Suffolk Punch heavy horse and Suffolk sheep are also kept here. There is also a nature trail. Open daily Apr to Oct. Tel: Wickham Market 746475.

□ Off B1078 three miles (4.8km) NW of Wickham Market. Map ref 6D2.

532. FRAMLINGHAM
Castle town

A market town which, like many others, grew up around a castle. Both town and castle remain impressive. The castle dates from the late 12th century and although it was altered substantially four centuries later its outward appearance was largely unaffected: thirteen towers survive intact and it is possible to walk round nine of them. It is open standard DoE hours plus Sun mornings Apr to Sept. The parish church dates from the 15th century and many delightful cottages and other buildings from the 16th to 19th centuries, notably on Market Hill, Castle Street and Church Street. The focal point is the Market Square, which is more of a triangle than a square. Markets are still held every Sat.

□ Seven miles (11km) W of Saxmundham at junction of B1119 and B1116. Map ref 6D1.

533. KERSEY
Cloth village

A beautiful village, set in a steep little valley, which is near Lavenham. Like Lavenham, Kersey owes its fine timber-framed houses to its former importance in the wool trade. Kersey cloth is said to have originated here. Central to the village's charm is the ford where the River Brett crosses the main street. The view from the church on the hill overlooking the village is delightful.

□ 1½ miles (2.5km) NW of Hadleigh off the A1141. Map ref 6C2.

534. LAVENHAM
Showpiece village

For about 150 years, from the beginning of the 15th century, Lavenham was one of the most prosperous towns in England - and it shows. It rose to riches on the back of the wool trade, the legacy of which is a stunning collection of timber-framed houses, colour-washed and with ornately decorated plasterwork, and a huge parish church with 141ft (43m) spire. Among the many superb buildings are the Swan and the 16th century Guildhall overlooking the Market Square.

□ Six miles (9.6km) SE of Bury St Edmunds on the A1141. Map ref 6C2.

535. LONG MELFORD
Country town

A highly attractive small town with an impressive long main street and green. Around the green are a huge 15th-century church, some 16th-century almshouses and an Elizabethan mansion, Melford Hall, one of the best early Elizabethan houses in the British Isles. It is built in red brick and still has its original panelled banqueting hall and a collection of Chinese porcelain captured from a Spanish galleon. It is open Wed, Thur and Sun afternoons and Bank Holidays from Apr to end Sept. Just north of the church is the moated Kentwell Hall, also 16th-century and approached by a ¾ mile

(1.2km) avenue of limes planted in 1678. This is open daily except Mon and Tues from mid-July to mid-Sept; Sun, Wed, Thur in May, June and end Sept; Sun only and Easter in Mar, Apr and Oct. Tel: Long Melford 207.
□ Three miles (5km) N of Sudbury on A134. Map ref 6C2.

536. MINSMERE
Bird reserve

Minsmere covers 1560 acres (631 hectares) of land with a wide variety of habitat: open water and reedbeds, woods, heathland and scrub. There is general access to part of the reserve from Minsmere Cliff and several public hides are located by the dunes overlooking the 'Scrape' where many wildfowl, wading birds (notably avocets) gulls and terns are seen. The splendid marsh harrier which breeds at Minsmere may often be spotted.
□ Minsmere Cliff is reached by minor road running eastwards off B1125 from Westleton which is E of A12 at Yoxford. Map ref 6D1.

537. MUSEUM OF EAST ANGLIAN LIFE
East Anglian crafts

This mostly open-air museum covers 70 acres (28.3 hectares) where historic buildings, saved from ruin elsewhere, have been reconstructed on site. The 14th-century farmhouse came from Combs, a village near Stowmarket. Its roof is thought to be unique in Suffolk – it is 'aisled' like a church. The 18th-century blacksmith's forge was moved from Grundisburgh in 1972 and the whole of Alton Watermill was moved from Stutton near Ipswich. In 1979, the last remaining windpump from a group on the Minsmere Levels was re-erected here. Open daily from Apr to end Oct. Tel: Stowmarket 2229.
□ Abbots Hall, Crowe Street, Stowmarket. Map ref 6C2.

538. NEWMARKET
Race horses and earthworks

The headquarters of English horse-racing, one of the most famous and oldest courses in the country, is on the south-western outskirts of the town on Newmarket Heath. The town is the home of the National Stud. The heath is also the best place to see what remains of Devil's Dyke, an impressive post-Roman earthwork probably erected in the 6th century AD by the East Anglians against their neighbours the Middle Angles. Devil's Dyke was one of a pair of such earthworks – the other was Fleam Dyke running roughly parallel with Devil's Dyke some 10 miles (16km) further south that seem to have been built to bar access along the Icknield Way which runs through them.
□ Newmarket is 12 miles (19km) E of Cambridge; Devil's Dyke runs NW SE across the Heath from just beyond the point where A45 and A11 meet. Map ref 6B1.

539. OTTER TRUST
Otter watching

On this 23 acre (9.3 hectares) riverside site at Earsham, broadcaster and conservationalist Philip Wayre has set up a reserve principally for otters. The River Waveney runs along the boundary of the reserve and a small stream passes through the otter breeding enclosures. Otters were transferred to Earsham from the Norfolk Wildlife Park in 1975 and since then a number of cubs have been successfully reared. There are not only British otters, but also European, North American and Asian short-clawed otters, not to mention the filmstar otter who played Tarka in the film of Henry Williamson's book. Visitors can go right up to the otter pens to see the animals. The greatest activity takes place at feeding times: noon and mid-afternoon. There is also a collection of water fowl on the lakes and a wood with deer. Facilities include a large car park, pleasant tea room and an interesting and well-stocked gift shop. Open Mar to end Nov daily. Tel: Bungay 3470.
□ Earsham is just SW of Bungay off A143. Map ref 6D1.

East Anglia

540. PARHAM
Moated manor

Parham Hall is an early 16th-century manor house, timber-framed with high gables and still surrounded by a moat. It is one of 500 moated sites in Suffolk alone and probably replaced an earlier moated farmhouse from the 12th or 13th centuries which is when most such dwellings were constructed. The moat provided drainage (on heavy soils) and protection. Parham Hall is not open to the public, but still makes a picturesque sight when viewed from outside.
□ Eight miles (13km) N of Woodbridge on B1116 between Wickham Market and Framlingham. Map ref 6D2.

541. PIN MILL
Sailor's delight

This is an attractive tree-encircled hamlet on the south shore of the Orwell estuary. It has been completely taken over by yachtsmen and barge owners. At the top of the 'hard' is the Butt and Oyster Inn, which is sometimes itself awash at high spring tides. The Orwell is one of several East Coast rivers which are much favoured by cruising yachtsmen in search of a day or two of calm water, good pubs and green grass.
□ SE of Ipswich off B1456 road to Shotley Gate. Map ref 6C2.

542. RAKE FACTORY
Craftsmen working in wood

Here, in a 70-year-old factory, near Sicklesmere, where belts turn and there is the smell of newly worked wood in the air, traditional country tools are still made: rakes, scythe handles, milking stools, platters and household ware. Everything is for sale. The factory is open Mon to Fri. Tel: Cockfield Green 630.
□ Sicklesmere is on A134 S of Bury St Edmunds. Map ref 6C1.

543. RIVER ALDE
Estuary extraordinary

The Alde is the oddest of rivers. At the

point where it could be expected to debouch into the sea it makes a sharp turn and flows parallel to the shore for about nine miles (14.5km). In places it is separated from the waves by no more than a few dozen yards of shingle, and it is of this that the long attenuated spit which stretches southwards from Aldeburgh to Orfordness and beyond is made. The spit, built by the drift of beach material along the coast, has deflected the course of the river. Eventually the Alde joins with Butley River to make the River Ore which flows into the sea at Orford Haven. These rivers and their marshes, the remarkable landform of the spit and the heathlands and forests which lie just behind the coast all combine to make a tract of country unlike any other in the British Isles. Some of its highlights are:

Rendlesham Forest. Here Staverton Park and the Thicks to the west of Butley represent something rare: an area of untouched natural landscape where ancient oaks are descendants of the trees that grew in prehistoric times. There is a picnic place at Butley Corner (FC) and a 2½ mile (4km) forest walk through pinewoods starts from here.

Iken. Beautiful and tranquil, with heathland running down to the Alde, a little beach near Iken Cliff and Iken Church standing by itself on the edge of the estuary.

Orford. Dominated by the great tower which is all that remains of a castle which was once part of a substantial military complex. From the top of it there are fine views over Orford, its quay and the Suffolk coast. Open standard DoE hours.

☐ B1084 from Woodbridge and B1078 from Wickham Market give access to this area. Map ref 6D2.

544. RIVER BLYTH
A river to sail or walk

The Blythe is a curious river and like the Alde behaves in its own unconventional way. Its narrow sea-entrance just south of Southwold is tricky but tow-boaters need not worry because there is easy launching on the Southwold bank. At first the river follows a reasonably straight course upstream – under the Bailey bridge, past Buss Creek (this runs round the back of Southwold virtually making the town into an island) with Tinker's Marshes on the left, Reydon Marshes on the right, and then suddenly opens out into a huge tidal lake much of which is uncovered at low water. At its western end is Blythburgh, its great

The Suffolk Coast: here there is the little which is left of Dunwich lost to the sea, the quiet charms of seaside Walberswick and Southwold, the great tidal waters of the Blyth and the rich birdlife of the Minsmere reserve. Days Out 530, 548, 546, 544 and 536 respectively

church of Holy Trinity rising above the marshes. This is the sailor's way of coming upon the place. The size of the church belongs to a 15th-century Blythburgh, a town with its own mint and jail and quays busy with shipping. But like so many East Coast ports the silting of its river put paid to its prosperity. Today all that is busy is the A12 which crosses the river here. The walker's way of coming upon Blythburgh is out from Southwold, crossing the Bailey bridge that others sail under, then following the track of the old Southwold Railway across Walberswick Common and on through the lovely countryside on the south bank of the estuary into Blythburgh itself.

☐ Southwold is at the end of the A1095. Blythburgh is on the A12 NE of Saxmundham. Map ref 6D1.

545. ROSARIUM
Roses, roses, roses

This garden at the Lime Kiln, Claydon, is dedicated to roses. The rosarium was begun in 1918 and has over 50 varieties of roses including about 20 very rare varieties. The roses grow naturally and most of them are the old-fashioned, scented ones. Open afternoons June to mid-July. For further information during opening months, Tel: Ipswich 830334.

☐ Claydon is on A45 three miles (4.8km) N of Ipswich. Map ref 6C2.

546. SOUTHWOLD
Limestone church

A small seaside town with a truly sumptuous church. Although the Church of St Edmund, King and Martyr, is not quite as magnificent as Long Melford's church externally, this mainly flint building, with flush-work ornamentation in limestone, is of greater appeal within. The great feature of the interior – lofty and very light since the destruction of Victorian glass during the last war – is the screen with its charming, largely original, decoration. The roofs, well restored in 1867, also make a great show. Southwold is an elegant town built on the cliff tops facing the North Sea. Its lighthouse is in the town surrounded by houses. One of its notable characteristics is the open greens between many of its buildings. It was rebuilt in this way following a disastrous fire in the mid-17th century. It was discreetly fashionable as a Victorian and Edwardian bathing resort and still manages to retain something of that atmosphere.

☐ 10 miles (16km) S of Lowestoft on A1095 near the mouth of the River Blyth. Map ref 6D1.

547. STOUR
River estuary

The tidal waters of the rivers Stour and Orwell meet in busy Harwich Harbour before they join the sea. The Stour forms the boundary between Essex and Suffolk and flows in its upper reaches through Constable country. One of the best places to view the Stour is from the sea wall at Wrabness Point. This is reached by turning down a lane off the B1352. This latter road, running parallel with the Stour's south bank, offers attractive views of the estuary and of the countryside of Suffolk beyond it. Upstream from Wrabness is one of the largest swanneries in England at Mistley.

At the mouth of the estuary, on the Felixstowe side, Landguard Point is a favourite spot for searching for semi-precious pebbles among the shingle. A ferry operates from Harwich to Felixstowe Dock and there are cruises on the two rivers from Harwich from Apr to Oct.

☐ The two rivers occupy a triangular stretch of country with Manningtree, Harwich/Felixstowe and Ipswich at its three points. Map ref 6C2.

548. WALBERSWICK
Nature reserve

This village is the location of a national nature reserve which overlooks the estuary of the river Blyth to the north and to the south includes most of the reed beds of Westwood Marshes. There are mudflats, pools, brackish lagoons,

rough grazing and heath, all of which attract a large number and variety of birds. The hen harrier and the great grey shrike are regular winter visitors. So are snow buntings. The rare marsh harrier, short-eared owl, twite and a number of waders may also be seen.

☐ Five miles (8km) E of Blythburgh on B1387. Map ref 6D1.

549. WOLVES WOOD
Nightingales singing

This RSPB reserve consists of 92 acres (37 hectares) of mixed woodland. Follow the signposted path from the large sign at the entrance. In early summer listen especially for warblers and nightingales. Open all year.

☐ Two miles (3.2km) E of Hadleigh off A1071 to Ipswich. Map ref 6C2.

550. WOODBRIDGE
River port and market town

Woodbridge has always earned its living partly from the sea and partly from the land. There has been a tide mill here on the River Deben for 800 years and now, after a major restoration, hopefully it will last for another 800 years – and in working order too!

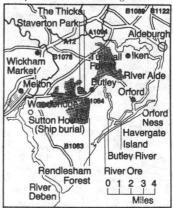

River Alde and Woodbridge: the Alde drains a sweep of country unlike any other in the British Isles.
Another Suffolk river, the Deben, contributes to the special character of this small town. Days Out 543, 550

The mill-pond· is now a miniature marina and the old ferry quay has become a yacht harbour. At the quayside dinghies and motor boats can be hired by the day. It's a popular place for yachting, and sailors and poets have always loved its wide river. Given an hour before and after high water it's possible to sail up river to Melton and Wilford Bridge. This is a romantic and appropriate way to arrive at the latter for the short walk to Sutton Hoo, site of the famous Anglo-Saxon ship burial, 100ft (30m) above the tides on the Deben's eastern shore. Unfortunately the site itself, now filled in, is not accessible, but the countryside here makes for good agreeable walking. And all about is rural, river estuary Suffolk at its best. The best view of Woodbridge is from a boat in the river but the dry land vista from Kyson Hill, a few acres of NT land on the west bank, will do the visitor very well. It was once said Woodbridge had not an ugly building in it, but it does have a mix of styles – 16th-century with Georgian bits and bobs – all of which work together happily. The red brick Shire Hall dominates the market square. The King's Head and the Angel are inns for looking at as well as drinking in. Outside the Bell is an old steelyard which measured Woodbridge's commerce in wool, hay and hides up until the 1880s.

□ Woodbridge is six miles (9.6km) E of Ipswich off A12. The Tide Mill is open daily from mid-July to mid-Sept. Map ref 6D2.

Upper Middle England

551. PEAK DISTRICT
National Park

Covers 542 sq miles (1387 sq km). With motorways (M1, M6, M62) virtually hemming in the park on three sides there is fast access to the Peak from London, the Midlands and the North. Sheffield and Manchester are almost on the Park's doorstep. Half a dozen main roads converge on Buxton and there is a choice of scenic routes across the 'Dark Peak' of the northern park. There are wild walks over peaty moors and the gritstone 'edges' of the north, and gentle strolls through idyllic limestone dales in the south. The famous Pennine Way long-distance footpath begins at Edale. Main park information centre at Market Hall, Bakewell. Open daily in summer; weekends and some weekdays in winter. Tel: Bakewell 3227. Other centres at Hope Valley, Castleton and Edale.
☐ Map ref 11A2.

552. CANNOCK CHASE
Area of Outstanding Natural Beauty

A surprising oasis of wild upland heath and forest on the doorstep of the Black Country. The highest point is Castle Ring, 800ft (240m). There are miles of quiet tracks and forest rides to explore. Foxes, badgers and wild fallow deer roam among the bracken slopes, relic oaks and dark stands of Forestry Commission pines. Cannock Forest Centre, with a forest and deer museum, is open Mon to Fri, and is 1½ miles (2.4km) out of Rugeley on Penkridge Bank Road.
☐ Map ref 11A3.

553. SHROPSHIRE HILLS
Area of Outstanding Natural Beauty

A wild cavalcade of empty hills and rolling ridges, haunted by the past and crowned by prehistoric hill-forts such as Caer Caradoc. To the west the hills spill over the Welsh Border at Offa's Dyke to encompass the lonely uplands of Clun Forest. To the north a long arm of the AONB reaches out to include the unmistakable pyramidal silhouette of the Wrekin. Church Stretton is the best centre for walkers wishing to explore the Long Mynd and Stiperstones; historic Ludlow is a good base for the Clee Hills. Near Craven Arms is Stokesay Castle, the finest medieval fortified manor house in England, open daily Mar to Oct, except Tues.
☐ Map ref 8D2.

Cheshire

Cheshire is where the landscape pauses for breath between the Pennine Hills and the uplands of North Wales: a low-lying plain of green fields, peaceful meres and magpie-patterned buildings, as exemplified by Little Moreton Hall and the historic streets of Chester, the county town. North-West Tourist Board, Tel: Bolton 591511.

554. ALDERLEY EDGE
Village and scarp

On the south-eastern fringes of this commuter village for Manchester is a stretch of wooded sandstone escarpment, the scene of copper mining from possibly pre-Roman times to the last century. Now it is used strictly for leisure purposes with hardly any visible evidence of its industrial past. At nearby Nether Alderley a 15th-century corn mill with wooden watermill has been restored to full working order by the NT and is open daily, afternoons (except non-Bank Holiday Mons) July to Sept and on Wed, Sun and Bank Holiday Mons from Apr to June and Oct. Tel: Wilmslow 528961.
□ Alderley Edge village is five miles (8km) NW of Macclesfield on A34 and A535; Alderley Edge escarpment is one mile (1.6km) SE of the village astride B5087. Map ref 11A2.

555. ARLEY HALL GARDENS
Famous gardens

Vintage herbaceous borders (among the first to be established in England), roses, topiary, walled gardens and remarkable avenues of pleached limes and clipped holm-oaks. Open Tues to Sat and Bank Holiday Mons, Mar to Oct. Tel: Arley 353 and 284.
□ Six miles (9km) W of Knutsford and five miles (8km) from M6, Junction 19 or 20. Map ref 10B2.

556. ASTBURY
Old church

The Church of St Mary is sensational:

the King's College Chapel of parish churches. It is mainly gritstone, a far tougher material than the Triassic sandstone that is general in Cheshire. The lofty, light interior is most distinguished, with glorious wood-work, in a county famous for its woodcarving: roofs and screen of just before 1500; seating and pulpit Jacobean.
□ One mile (1.6km) SW of Congleton off A34. Map ref 11A3.

557. CHOLMONDELEY CASTLE GARDENS
Rare farm breeds

A farm with a collection of rare breeds of farm animals is one of the attractions in the grounds of the Marquess of Cholmondeley. The castle is not open to the public, but the farm and gardens with lakeside picnic area are open Apr to Sept, Sun and Bank Holidays. Tel: Cholmondeley 203.
□ Six miles (9.6km) N of Whitchurch, off A49. Map ref 10B3.

558. DELAMERE FOREST
Forest walks

Waymarked walks through pine woods linking with the 14 mile (22.5km) Cheshire Sandstone Trail which passes through the forest. They vary in length from half to three miles (800m to 4.8km). There is also an easy forest trail through Scots and Corsican pinewoods with views of Blakemere Moss, 1½ miles (2.4km). All start from visitor centre half a mile (800m) W of Delamere Station.
□ Access from B5152 near Delamere Station. Map ref 10B2.

559. ECCLESTON
Riverside hamlet

This hamlet grew up around the gates of Eaton Hall, a family home of the Dukes of Westminster, and adjoins a picturesque stretch of the River Dee. It is close to nearby Chester but visited by few tourists. You can drive there along the characteristically straight route of an old Roman road. Or better still, walk along the southern banks of the Dee through the meadowland that extends from Eccleston virtually into the city itself.

☐ Two miles (3.2km) S of Chester on signposted minor road. Map ref 8D1.

560. LITTLE BUDWORTH COMMON
Country park

Little Budworth Common, on which the country park is based, is an ancient landscape, a rare relic of the great forests of Mara and Mondrem that covered most of Cheshire in the Middle Ages. It is a place with a slightly untamed atmosphere, for it was never built upon, never farmed nor planted with trees. A secluded backwater, ideal for walking and nature study; a network of sandy tracks leads through the park. Horse riding is allowed on the west side of the Coach Road. There are two free car parks, toilets and facilities for the disabled. Information boards and Ranger service. The park is open throughout the year; enquiries to Assistant Countryside Officer, Tel: Northwich 3874.

☐ The park lies very close to Oulton Park Motor Racing Circuit, just off the A54 Kelsall to Winsford road. Map ref 10B3.

561. LITTLE MORETON HALL
Historic house

The pinnacle of black-and-white timbered building, this 16th-century moated manor house (NT) is built on three sides of a quadrangle with an open view on the fourth over a well laid out garden. A feature of the house, as medieval Gothic merged with English Renaissance, is the intricately carved gables. Usually open every afternoon except Tues and Good Fri, Apr to Oct. Also open weekend afternoons in Mar. Tel: Congleton 2018.

☐ Four miles (6.4km) SW of Congleton off A34. Map ref 11A3.

562. LOWER PEOVER
Historic inn

This village has a 16th-century timbered church but the inn, the Bells of Peover, is even older. Ironically, it was founded in 1369 for the priests of an earlier church. Mainly rebuilt, it later became the Warren de Tabley Arms and in 1895 was given its present name after a licensee named Bell whose grave is in the adjoining churchyard. During the Second World War the inn served as a billeting place for officers of the American Army who were based nearby.

☐ Three miles (5km) S of Knutsford on B5081. Map ref 10B2.

563. LYME PARK
Country park and historic house

The extensive grounds of Lyme Park, which rise on the borders of Derbyshire and Cheshire, offer breathtaking views of the Peak District, the rugged foothills of the Pennines, and the Cheshire Plain. The park, with its famous herd of red deer, is steeped in history. Lyme Hall was for 600 years the seat of the Legh family and is the centrepiece of the park. Adjacent to the hall are the Orangery and the intricate formal gardens – a sharp contrast to the wild moorland on which the deer roam. Recreation facilities in the park include a pitch and putt course, a children's playground, a nature trail, an orienteering course, cycle hire and a cafeteria. Special events are organised during the year and the annual Lyme Sheepdog Trials are always popular. The park is open throughout the year and the hall Mar to Oct. Cars must use the car park near the hall. Tel: Disley 2023.

☐ Main entrance is on the A6 Manchester to Buxton road, half a mile (800m) W of Disley village. Map ref 11A2.

564. MARBURY PARK
Country park

This delightful country park still retains the air of peaceful gentility it had during its days as a country estate. There are woodlands and pastureland bordering Budworth Mere. There is a network of level waymarked footpaths;

picnic and barbecue areas; facilities for bird-watching and nature studies; a waymarked horse ride and jumping area; a bird hide; and a private swimming pool (permits available). There is an information caravan, with display and guides and checklists for sale, and a Ranger service. The park is open daily throughout the year and there is a free car park. Tel: Northwich 77111 or 3874.

□ The park is on the outskirts of Comberbach, two miles (3.2km) N of Northwich. There are directional signs on approach roads. Map ref 10B2.

565. MOW COP
Moorland viewpoint

This straggling moorland village, perched on the impossibly steep slopes of a gritstone crag, provides one of middle England's finest viewpoints. From its 1100ft (330m) summit, with its gritstone pinnacles and 18th-century folly, the panorama includes the far-spreading Cheshire Plain, the Pennine moors and the headwaters of the Trent. Walk northwards along the narrow, rocky scarp of Congleton Edge, three miles (4.8km), or follow the steeply plunging lanes three miles W to Little Moreton Hall (see Day Out 561). Mow Cop is also the starting-point for the Staffordshire Way – a waymarked long-distance footpath in three sections: Mow Cop to Rocester, Rocester to Cannock Chase, and Cannock Chase to Kinver Edge. Total distance: 90 miles (144km).

□ Near Biddulph, on Cheshire-Staffordshire border, W of Biddulph on minor road off A527 or A34. Map ref 11A3.

566. PECKFORTON HILLS
Scenic landscapes

Among the rich farmlands of the Cheshire plain, these steep sandstone ridges of heath and pine forest give a startling scenic contrast. Red cliffs, gorse and woodland glades abound. Black-and-white cottages crouch beneath prehistoric hill-forts and a variety of castles, ancient and modern. At the northern end of the range of hills stand Beeston Castle ruins (AM), open daily, standard DoE hours, and Sun, Apr to Sept. There is a good drive from Bulkeley on the A534 to Beeston, with paths up the hills at Peckforton.

□ At Peckforton, on minor road off A49, four miles (6km) S of Tarporley. Map ref 10B3.

567. STYAL
Industrial archaeology

An unusual combination of natural beauty, industrial building and historic interest. Quarry Bank Cotton Mill was erected here by Samuel Greg in 1784, to be followed shortly by some well designed workers' cottages that together comprise an unusually complete industrial community. But there is also a fine half-timbered farmhouse and the setting of the wooded Bollin valley remains attractively rural despite bordering Manchester's Ringway airport. The old mill, now restored, houses a textile museum and is open to the public every day except Mon. Also weekends in Jan and Feb. Tel: Wilmslow 527468.

□ Two miles (3.2km) N of Wilmslow. Map ref 10B2.

568. TATTON PARK
Country park and historic house

A thousand years of history are crammed into Tatton's spacious grounds. Here is a 15th-century manor house, surrounded by traces of an ancient village and fields, an elegant mansion with fine gardens and park – the former country home of the Egerton family. In the park are a herd of deer, ornamental sheep and wildlife waterfowl on the mere. There are two waymarked trails (details in a leaflet). Permits are available for fishing, riding and sailing; there is swimming on the east bank of Tatton Mere, where the sandy shore drops away; picnicking throughout the parklands; a restaurant in the converted stable block; a park shop; full-time Ranger service. Tatton Park is owned by the NT and run by Cheshire County Council. The park is open throughout the year (not open Mon except Bank Holidays). Tel:

Knutsford 3155.

□ Tatton Park is just off M6 at junction 19 and M56 at junction 7. Map ref 10B2.

569. TEGG'S NOSE
Country park

Wood, heath, moors, nature trail.
□ Two miles (3km) E of Macclesfield off A537. Map ref 11A2.

Derbyshire

The best of Derbyshire lies within the Peak District National Park, where the peat bogs and gritstone edges of the Pennine moors provide a striking contrast with the limestone scenery of the incomparable Derbyshire Dales. Buxton, Bakewell, Matlock and Castleton make good bases for days out. East Midlands Tourist Board, Tel: Lincoln 31521; North-West Tourist Board, Tel: Bolton 591511.

570. ARBOR LOW
Prehistoric monument

This is the greatest 'henge' monument of northern England. The ring bank encompassing the stones is still 6ft (1.85m) high and some 250ft (77m) in diameter. About 50 stones (or their fragments) now lie prone on the ground. Close by is Gib Hill, a large Bronze Age tumulus standing on an earlier Neolithic cairn.
□ 10 miles (16km) SE of Buxton, one

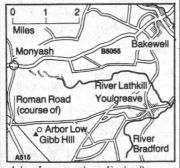

Arbor Low: northern England's greatest 'henge' monument lies 10 miles (16km) south east of Buxton

mile (1.6km) E of A515 road. Grid ref SK 161636; OS map 119. Map ref 11A3.

571. ASHBOURNE
Market town

This spacious market town on the edge of the Peak District has some fine buildings. St Oswald's Church, with its 212ft (65m) spire, was thought by the novelist George Eliot to be the handsomest in all England. Another writer who knew the town well was Dr Johnson who, with James Boswell, stayed many times at The Green Man and Black's Head. This 17th-century inn was enlarged in the following century to cater for coach traffic. Outside it a remarkable old gallows sign still spans the street. A town trail leaflet is available from the tourist information office just off Ashbourne's large triangular Market Place. (Market days Thur and Sat). Tel: Ashbourne 3666. The town is an ideal base for exploring the limestone dales of the Southern Peak, notably Dovedale (NT), with its clear waters, limestone crags, stepping stones, footpaths and hanging woods.
□ 11 miles (18km) NW of Derby at junction of A52 and A515. Map ref 11A3.

572. BAKEWELL
Market town

Popular small touring centre for the Derbyshire Dales. The 13th-century bridge over the River Wye is one of the oldest in England. Other notable buildings include the handsome parish church of All Saints with its lofty spire, and the 17th-century Bath House, still fed by warm springs known in Roman times. The Peak Park information centre is in the 17th-century Market Hall, Bridge Street. Tel: Bakewell 3227.
□ Midway between Buxton and Matlock on A6. Map ref 11A2.

573. BOLSOVER CASTLE
Historic building

In 1612, Sir Charles Cavendish,

younger son of the formidable Bess of Hardwick, built himself a small mock castle on the site of a genuine Norman one, on the brow of a steep escarpment above a valley. His son, the Duke of Newcastle, added a long range of state rooms in which to entertain Charles I for an afternoon's visit, and a huge riding school in which to indulge his passion for *Haute Ecole*. The mysterious vaulted rooms and carved alabaster chimney pieces of the castle, the crazily eccentric façade of the ruined state rooms, the cavernous riding school complete with a little room, like a royal box at the opera, from which the Duke looked down on his horses, combine with the surrounding coal mines to produce a group of buildings as memorable as it is strange. Now a historic monument, it is open standard DoE hours plus Sun mornings, Apr to Sept.

☐ Bolsover is six miles (9.6km) E of Chesterfield on A632. Map ref 11B2.

574. CASTLETON
Limestone caverns

This busy village is an excellent centre for a part of the Peak District National Park that is full of fascinating things to see and do. (Further information from Park information centre in Castle Street, open daily, summer only. Tel: Hope Valley 20671.) You could start with the ruins of Peveril Castle (AM), the Norman keep featured in Sir Walter Scott's *Peveril of the Peak*. It is open standard DoE hours, plus Sun mornings, Apr to Sept. The castle overlooks the entrance to the great labyrinth of the Peak Cavern, open daily, Easter to mid-Sept. Tel: Hope Valley 20285. The area has long been associated with lead mining and the extraction of Blue John, a beautiful translucent fluorspar which is made into jewellery and ornaments. Blue John Cavern is also open daily. Tel: Hope Valley 20638. Alternatively, you could take a mile long (1.6km) boat trip – *underground* – in the Speedwell Cavern – to see the Bottomless Pit and its sinister water. Tel: Hope Valley 20512. Or visit Treak Cliff Cavern.

Tel: Hope Valley 20571. Other places of interest are the Winnats Pass, a dramatic gorge through which the main road used to wind, and 1½ miles (2.4km) to the east, Mam Tor, the 'Shivering Mountain', with its precipitous slopes of unstable shales.

☐ 12 miles (19km) SW of Sheffield on A625. Map ref 11A2.

575. CHATSWORTH
Stately home and garden

One of the greatest English country houses, the so-called 'Palace of the Peak', built in 1707 for the 1st Duke of Devonshire and incorporating an earlier house. Every room is filled with fabulous treasures. The very large and magnificent garden reveals the changing style of three centuries of garden-making. The huge water-staircase, or cascade, and fountains were made in the 17th century. There is an 18th-century landscape by 'Capability' Brown, dramatic rockwork by Sir Joseph Paxton, an arboretum and pinetum planted in the 19th century, and the very latest in suspended glasshouses – completed in 1971. House and gardens open daily Apr to Nov (house closed Mon.) Tel: Baslow 2204. Nearby is the 'model' village of Edensor, constructed by the 6th Duke of Devonshire on a site where it could not be seen from Chatsworth House. The original Edensor was razed to the ground on the Duke's orders because it spoilt the view! Sir Gilbert Scott rebuilt the church, which contains many Cavendish family monuments.

☐ Four miles (6.4km) NE of Bakewell on B6012 via A619. Map ref 11A2.

576. CHEE DALE
Limestone landscape

An exceptionally fine scenic stretch of the valley of the River Wye overhung by limestone pinnacles and the cliffs of Chee Tor. Footpaths follow the river. Downstream the Wye leads into Miller's Dale, then Monsal Dale and the pretty village of Ashford-in-the-Water.

☐ Five miles (8km) E of Buxton via A6 to Blackwell, then B6049. Map ref 11A2.

577. CHELMORTON
Old field patterns

This street or linear village, comprised mainly of farmhouses, provides a striking illustration of field enclosure patterns in upland Britain. Close to the village, on either side of the street, the fields are narrow and rectangular. They look like the old strip farming, albeit enclosed within the drystone walls that form the field boundaries. And, indeed, they were laid out in the old open fields that once surrounded the village – fields still possibly being farmed in the traditional 'strip' manner as late as the mid-17th century. Higher up on the moors – the village itself is more than 1000ft (300m) above sea level – a different pattern of enclosure is revealed. Here the fields are square shaped: the result of parlimentary enclosure acts on former open common land.
□ Five miles (8km) SE of Buxton off A5270. Map ref 11A2.

578. CRESWELL CRAGS
Limestone caves

The grey cliffs of this narrow gorge contain caves which were once the home of Stone Age hunters. Many important paleolithic remains have been found here. There is now a picnic site and visitor centre with interpretative exhibits, and footpaths through the crags. Open Tues, Sat and Sun, May to Sept; Tues, Fri, Sat and Sun, Mar, Apr and Oct. Also Nov to Feb, Sun only. Tel: Worksop 720378.
□ Off A60 Worksop-Mansfield road. Map ref 11B2.

579. CROMFORD
Industrial archaeology

The small village on the River Derwent where in 1771 Richard Arkwright built not only his pioneering water-powered cotton mill but also a model village of workers' houses. North Street is its best surviving example. There was also a chapel where Arkwright was buried. A fine 15th-century bridge crosses the Derwent whose rushing waters – for a few decades before the steam revolution – turned this picturesque valley into a considerable industrial centre. Cromford is also the starting point for an 11 mile (17.6km) 'motorised trail' around such transport landmarks as the Cromford Canal, the High Peak Railway and Crich village (with its tramway museum). A leaflet is available locally or write to the Arkwright Society, Tawney House, Matlock, Derbyshire. A horse-drawn canal boat offers trips on summer weekends to Lea Wood Pump House from Cromford Wharf.
□ Two miles (3.2km) S of Matlock on A6. Map ref 11A3.

580. ELVASTON CASTLE
Country park

This lovely country estate, formerly owned by the Earl of Harrington, has long straight avenues, a serpentine lake, topiary gardens, specimen trees, woodlands, a Moorish Temple and several grottoes. The castle is closed for repairs at the time of going to press, but old craft workshops and a gardener's cottage have been turned into a Working Estate Museum, giving visitors a picture of the life and work of a self-sufficient estate community at the turn of the century. A new information, exhibition and field study centre will open in 1981. Other facilities include a riding school, caravan and camp site (open Apr to Oct), picnic areas and a nature trail. The park is open daily throughout the year. Tel: Derby 71342.
□ The park is four miles (6.4km) E of Derby on the B5010 Borrowash to Thulston road, which can be approached from the A52, the A6005 or the A6 – all approaches are signposted. Map ref 11B3.

581. GOYT VALLEY
Pennine walks

A delightful wooded valley with a tumbling stream set among the wild Pennine moorlands of the Peak District National Park. Numerous contrasting walks and viewpoints have made this a popular picnic spot but no cars are allowed. A large car park allows visitors to stroll through the valley but a minibus service helps the less active to reach the remoter spots.

☐ Off A5002, three miles (5km) NW of Buxton. Map ref 11.A2.

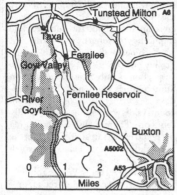

Goyt Valley: a popular beauty spot for picnics and walks in the Peak District National Park

582. HADDON HALL
Historic house

This incredibly romantic medieval stone manor with beautiful terraced rose gardens in the valley of the Wye is the home of the Duke of Rutland. Below the gardens the Wye is spanned by a packhorse bridge. The Hall itself has splendid rooms, a medieval banqueting hall dating from 1370, Mortlake tapestries and dark, rambling kitchens. Open daily (except Sun and Mon), Apr to Sept. Also Bank Holidays. Tel: Bakewell 2855.

☐ Two miles (3.2km) SE of Bakewell on A6. Map ref 11A2.

583. HARDWICK HALL
Country park and historic house

'Hardwick Hall, more glass than wall' is the epithet that has for nearly four centuries so aptly described this great symmetrical building with its six turrets and huge windows, set on its magnificent hilltop site. It remains almost as it was left in 1608 by its builder, Bess of Hardwick, Countess of Shrewsbury. The gardens provide lakeside car parking and picnic areas; fishing (daily charge), boating and canoeing on the broad Millers' Pond; an information room; and a nature trail (leaflet available describing the park's historical and wildlife interests). The park and house are managed by the NT, which also owns two rare breeds, Longhorn cattle and White-faced woodland sheep, both grazing in the park. The house is open afternoons, Apr to end Oct (except Mon and Tues); the gardens are open every afternoon.

☐ Situated four miles (6.4km) NW of Mansfield, E of M1 between junctions 28 and 29. Map ref 11B3.

584. KEDLESTON HALL
Stately home

Not open to the public very often, but worth every effort to see. A great Palladian house decorated and altered by Robert Adam at the height of his career. The huge hall lined with alabaster columns leads to a circular saloon modelled on the Roman Pantheon. Adam's state bed and drawing-room furniture have never been excelled. Usually open only Bank Holiday and Sun afternoons, Apr to Sept. Tel: Derby 840396.

☐ Four miles (6.4km) NW of Derby between A52 and B5023. Map ref 11A3.

585. LADYBOWER AND UPPER DERWENT VALLEY RESERVOIRS
Man-made lakes

This staircase of large reservoirs was created by damming the Derwent's headwaters to form the Howden Reservoir in 1912 and the Derwent Reservoir in 1916, and finally the Ashop Brook and lesser tributaries to form the vast Ladybower Reservoir (completed 1943), which helps to supply Sheffield, Derby, Nottingham and Leicester. Its construction drowned the two villages of Derwent and Ashopton, whose ruins are occasionally exposed during summer droughts.

Much of the surrounding moorland is owned by the NT, and a maze of footpaths enables ramblers to obtain splendid views of these cradled lakes. Starting at Easter 1981, a new 'Park and Ride' scheme will operate from Fairholmes to King's Tree. Leaflets from Park information centres or from Fairholmes.

☐ Ten miles (15km) W of Sheffield on A57. Map ref 11A2.

586. MELBOURNE HALL
Stately home and garden

Stately home of Queen Victoria's first Prime Minister, the great Lord Melbourne. The splendid formal garden has remained largely unaltered since it was laid out by Wise, in the style of Le Nôtre, at the end of the 17th century. There are allées, water basins, fountains, statues, urns and a wonderful wrought-iron pavilion, the 'Iron Arbour' or 'Birdcage', which was made by Robert Bakewell, the 18th-century ironsmith. Open regularly, Easter to end Sept. Tel: Melbourne 2502.

☐ Melbourne, on A514 S of Derby. Map ref 11A3.

587. MIDDLETON
Rail trail

One of the landmarks of the former Cromford and High Peak Railway has now become a focal point of an enjoyable day out. The railway, one of the first in Britain, opened in 1819 to carry minerals and owed more to the concepts of the canal age. A series of stationary engines hauled trucks up steep inclines which were linked by moving engines operating on the level stretches. The line reached a height greater than 1000ft (308m) over the Peak plateau, but travel was a slow business. When a passenger service was introduced in the mid-19th century a traveller could expect to take up to six hours to cover just 20 miles (32km). Yet the last stretch of the line closed as recently as 1967.

With the closure of the line, however, the track has been made into a fine upland footpath and bridleway

known as the High Peak Trail. This runs from Cromford to Buxton – a distance of 37 miles (59km) – linking with the Tissington Trail at Parsley Hay. It is readily accessible at Middleton Top where another attraction is one of the original stationary steam winding engines built in 1829 by the Butterly Company to haul waggons up the Middleton incline. The engine, now restored by the Derbyshire Archaeological Society, is on public display in an 1825 engine house. Inspection is only possible at certain limited times (Sun and Bank Holidays). Further information from countryside warden based at Middleton Top. There is also a picnic area here, and leaflets are available from the information centre. Tel: Wirksworth 3204.

☐ 1½ miles (2.4km) SW of Cromford (signposted locally). Map ref 11A3.

588. RIBER CASTLE FAUNA RESERVE AND WILD LIFE PARK
Rare farm breeds

Apart from its quota of zoo inmates, Riber Castle has been developing its collection of rare domestic breeds of livestock. Ten breeds of cattle and twenty breeds of sheep now jostle with the most comprehensive specialist collection of lynxes in the world. Open daily throughout the year. Tel: Matlock 2073.

☐ Riber Castle, Matlock, off B6014 on Matlock-Tansley road. Map ref 11A3.

589. SHARDLOW
Canal port

Shardlow was in existence before the Canal Age, but the town owed its greatest prosperity to the nearby junction between the Trent and Mersey canal with the River Trent. For a time Shardlow became an important inland port and many old wharves and warehouses remain from these years in the late 18th and early 19th centuries.

☐ Eight miles (12.8km) SE of Derby on A6. Map ref 11B3.

590. SHIPLEY
Country park

Shipley Park consists mainly of the estate of the former Shipley Hall, which had been disfigured by extensive coal mining since the early 18th century. In conjunction with the National Coal Board the area has been opencast, reclaimed and landscaped to form a new country park. Features include Mapperley Reservoir Nature Reserve and Shipley Hill, where a history trail tells the story of the development of the house, gardens and estate, though there is little evidence today of the splendour of the former Shipley Estate. There is fishing and boating, with permits available, and a miniature railway; car parking is free. The park is open daily throughout the year. Tel: Langley Mill 69961; Park Rangers, Tel: Langley Mill 5480.

□ Shipley Park is less than three miles (4.8km) from the M1. Main car park is signposted off the A608 Heanor to Derby road. Map ref 11B3.

591. TISSINGTON
Country trail

Tissington is an attractive village with

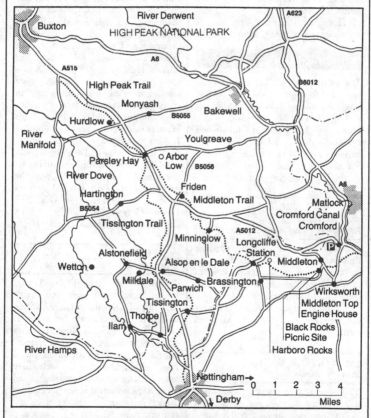

Middleton Trail: the track of the old Cromford and High Peak Railway is now an upland footpath and bridleway accessible at Middleton. Day Out 587. From Tissington there is access to a trail for horse-riders, walkers and cyclists which runs from Ashbourne to Parsley Hay. Day Out 591

a Norman church, wide grass verges and a colourful tradition of well-dressing going back to the 14th century. The village has given its name to a 13 mile (21km) stretch of disused railway line known as the Tissington Trail. It runs from Ashbourne to Parsley Hay where it joins a similar trail known as the High Peak Trail. The old rail route is now a fully developed trail for walkers, horse-riders and cyclists, with car parking facilities at the former stations. An illustrated leaflet describing the route (and covering facilities such as bike hire) is available from the Information Section, Peak National Park, Bakewell, Derbyshire.

☐ Tissington is four miles (6.4km) N of Ashbourne, off A515. Map ref 11A3.

Leicestershire

The countryside of Leicestershire is typical of the hunting shires of middle England: low undulating fieldscapes with quickthorn hedges, spinneys and beckoning church spires. Charnwood Forest adds a wilder dimension. Belvoir Castle imparts a fine flourish of feudal history. East Midlands Tourist Board, Tel: Lincoln 31521.

592. BATTLEFIELD OF BOSWORTH
Battlefield and country park

Where Richard III was defeated in the final battle of the Wars of the Roses, in 1485. It is now a country park set in farmland and woodland with visitor centre and battle trail.

☐ 11 miles (17km) W of Leicester between A444 and A447. Map ref 11B4.

593. BELVOIR CASTLE
Stately home

This large, romantic castle riding upon a lofty ridge overlooking the Vale of Belvoir has been the ancestral home of the Dukes of Rutland since the reign of Henry VIII, though most of the existing building is 19th-century. Paintings, tapestries, beautiful water

garden. Open Apr to Oct, Wed, Thur, weekends and Bank Holidays. Tel: Knipton 262.

☐ Six miles (9.6km) W of Grantham on minor roads between A52 and A607. Map ref 12A4.

594. CHARNWOOD FOREST.
Scenic landscapes

The southern fringe of Charnwood Forest is reached through Anstey on the B5327 out of Leicester. Little is left of the ancient woods which once covered this landscape of heathlands, boulder-strewn hillocks and pre-Cambrian rocks rising above the rich farmlands of the plain, though new plantations flourish. Stand on Beacon Hill, 818ft (242m) across the road from Broombriggs Farm (with farm trail) at Woodhouse Eaves, off B591 – or Bardon Hill, 912ft (274m) off A50 – and you can see the curious rock formations of the surrounding hills, all carved from part of England's prim-eval floor uncovered from beneath the much newer rock strata. Neighbouring Bradgate Park, a medieval hunting park, is a wilderness of moorland paths and lakes with fallow deer roaming by the ruins of a Tudor Mansion, once the home of Lady Jane Grey. Open all year; ruins open Apr to Oct. Tel: Leicester 871313.

☐ NW of Leicester. Map ref 11B3.

595. FOXTON
Canal architecture

A 'staircase' of 10 locks lifts the Grand Union Canal more than 75ft (23m) near this village with its church dating back to the 13th century. Set in a rural countryside between Leicester and Market Harborough, Foxton epitom-ises the engineering skills of the Canal Age. For in addition to the locks there are the overgrown remains of an inclined plane or lift that operated for about 10 years at the turn of the century. Now, with its shops, café and summer boat trips, Foxton has become a popular place for a day out.

☐ Three miles (5km) NW of Market Harborough off A6. Map ref 11B4.

596. GREAT CASTERTON
Archaeological site

This small village of pleasant stone-built houses on the old Great North Road was once a larger settlement. Here stood a Roman town on the line of Ermine Street which at this point the Great North Road (now known as the A1) follows. Remnants of the Roman defences can still be seen in the form of mounds, hollows and ditches. The village also has a large 13th-century church with 15th-century tower.

☐ Two miles (3.2km) NW of Stamford near junction of A1 and B1081. Map ref 12A4.

597. HALLATON
Folklore village

An attractive village with an unusual conical Buttercross standing on the small green. The green is surrounded by fine 17th to 19th-century stone-built cottages and houses, some thatched. In a house off the High Street is a tiny museum with local farm implements. Open weekends May to Oct. Tel: Hallaton 295. On Easter Monday the village is the scene of the Hare Pie Scramble, a bizarre folk custom acted out each year.

☐ Six miles (9.6km) SW of Uppingham between A47 and B664. Map ref 11B4.

598. INGARSBY
Deserted village

One of 67 deserted medieval villages in Leicestershire and still visible in the form of grassy mounds (where houses stood), and faint green hollows which were once lanes or fish-ponds. The village was destroyed as a living community in 1469 when the owners of the manor, Ingarsby Abbey, decided to turn all the land (including that on which the village stood) into sheep pastures.

☐ Five miles (8km) E of Leicester off minor road, ¾ mile (1.2km) N of Houghton-on-the-Hill on A47. Grid ref SK687053; OS map 140. Map ref 11B4.

599. OAKHAM
Market town

Once the county town of Rutland, England's smallest county, which lost its struggle for survival in the local government reorganisation of 1974. Oakham remains a busy market centre, with general markets on Wed and Sat, and cattle on Fri. In the market square is an old Buttercross, complete with stocks. Oakham Castle, in Market Street, has a lofty banqueting hall and a famous collection of ornamental horseshoes. The castle is open throughout the year, but opening times vary. Tel: Oakham 3654. The Rutland County Museum in Catmos Street contains a mixture of farm implements and craft tools and a display of Rutland wagons painted their original bright orange.

☐ On A606, SE of Melton Mowbray. Map ref 12A4.

600. RUTLAND WATER
Fishing and bird-watching

A reservoir created in 1970 of enormous dimensions: walk round it and you will have covered 24 miles (38km). It is many things for many people. For anglers it is the largest man-made fishing water in the country – stocked with half a million trout. (Fishing permits are available from Whitwell Lodge – well signposted locally.) For naturalists there is an extensive nature reserve at its western end. Part of the reserve known as Lyndon Hill is open to the public on afternoons at weekends and Bank Holidays; other parts, with facilities for bird-watching etc, require special permits (see below). But even without a special hobby to pursue, the footpaths along the reservoir's landscaped shores make pleasant walking, with attractive villages such as Empingham and Exton either on or near the Water. For further information about permits for the nature reserve or any other activity at Rutland Water, Tel: Empingham 321.

☐ Immediately SW of Oakham between A606 and A6003. Map ref 6A1.

Upper Middle England

601. STAUNTON HAROLD
Fine church

An estate church, with only the Georgian-fronted mansion for company. Not at all Puritan, yet all built, almost unbelievably, during the Commonwealth. Apart from the lovely setting, the special features are the finely proportioned tower, the pretty little organ high up in the west gallery, the wealth of 17th-century woodwork and the magnificent wrought-iron screen of *c.*1715, which is probably by Robert Bakewell, the greatest English smith.

□ Four miles (6.4km) NE of Ashby-de-la-Zouch off B587. Map ref 11A3.

Nottinghamshire

Contains the relic oaks of Sherwood Forest, the spacious parklands of the Dukeries, and the broad vale of the Trent, which flows through Nottingham, the county town. Newark Castle, Southwell Minster and Newstead Abbey are important attractions. East Midlands Tourist Board, Tel: Lincoln 31521.

602. BURNTSTUMP
Country park

A small country park with nature trail through woodland and a selection of country walks. There are two car parks, several picnic areas, toilet facilities and a restaurant on the edge of the park, in Forest Lodge. There is no visitor centre. Open daily throughout the year.

□ Burntstump lies outside Arnold, seven miles (11.2km) N of Nottingham between A60 to Mansfield and A614 to Doncaster. Map ref 11B3.

603. CLUMBER PARK
Country park

Large park landscaped out of the heathland bordering Sherwood Forest by 'Capability' Brown and developed by the first Duke of Newcastle in the 18th century. The old mansion has long since disappeared but the Doric-style 'Temple' still stands just inside the Boat House Plantation, and the stables and chapel are still intact. The park, with its veteran oaks, fine avenues of limes and long serpentine lakes, offers excellent walks and glimpses of a wide variety of wildlife: great crested grebe, mute swan, Canada goose, mallard, coot, moorhen and tufted duck much in evidence. Facilities include: fishing in the lake, (permits available from Water Bailiff); cycles for hire; horse riding; nature walks (leaflets at shop); orienteering by arrangement. The park is open all year and is managed by the NT. Information from the Administrator, Clumber Estate Office, Tel: Worksop 476592 or 476653.

□ Clumber Park is situated four miles (6.4km) SE of Worksop. Map ref 11B2.

604. HOLME PIERREPONT
Country park

Restored gravel pits offering fishing, riverside walk, water sports.

□ Five miles (8km) SE of Nottingham. Map ref 11B3.

605. LAXTON
Medieval field systems

A classic site in the evolution of the English landscape where a medieval open-field system has escaped the enclosure movement. Systems of farming have changed but one can still appreciate the spaciousness of the hedgeless arable land that once surrounded every medieval village. (Under the traditional system of open-field farming arable land was divided into three parts and farmed on a three-year cycle; one-third was left fallow and two-thirds farmed each year.)

□ Four miles (6.4km) E of Ollerton, two miles (3.2km) S of A6075. Map ref 11B2.

606. NEWSTEAD ABBEY
Historic house and garden

Ancestral home of Lord Byron, containing many treasures of the Byron family. The original 12th-century abbey was built by Henry II to atone for the murder of Thomas à Becket. Today it is owned by Nottingham City Council, together with its extensive gardens and lakes. Open daily, afternoons only, Apr to Sept. Tel: Blidworth 3557.

□ Near Linby, off A60, eight miles (12.8km) N of Nottingham. Map ref 11B3.

607. RUFFORD
Country park and historic house

Timbered medieval manor with wood and park, lake, mill.

□ 15 miles (24km) N of Nottingham on A614 near Ollerton. Map ref 11B2.

608. SHERWOOD FOREST
Country park

Few English forests have such fame as that of Sherwood and its popular folk hero, Robin Hood. Most of the mighty oaks have been felled over the centuries, but enough survive here to give a flavour of the medieval forest which provided a perfect refuge for the legendary outlaw and his merry men. Edwinstowe Church is where Robin is said to have married Maid Marian, and the Major Oak (his hideout) is one mile (1.6km) N of the village. The Visitor Centre explains the economic and natural history of the Forest. Park and Visitor Centre open all year. Tel: Mansfield 823202.

□ Off B6034 near Edwinstowe, two miles (3.2km) W of Ollerton. Map ref 11B2.

609. WOLLATON HALL
Museum and nature trail

This fine Elizabethan hall houses the City of Nottingham Natural History Museum. It has collections of botany, zoology and geology and a new insect gallery. Outside are formal gardens, a deer park and lake. The nature trail leads around the lake. Fallow and red deer roam in the park. Open every day except Christmas Day. For opening times, Tel: Nottingham 281333.

□ Three miles (5km) W of Nottingham city centre, off A609. Map ref 11B3.

Shropshire (Salop)

The River Severn divides this historic Border county, where ridge upon ridge of wild hills roll westward into Wales, and Ludlow Castle still broods above the Teme. Shrewsbury, the county town, has many fine half-timbered buildings. Heart of England Tourist Board, Tel: Worcester 29511.

610. ACTON SCOTT WORKING FARM MUSEUM
Rural life

Life on a Shropshire upland farm before mechanisation, with many animals of the period rarely seen nowadays. It also demonstrates 19th-century arable techniques with displays of butter-making and other traditional crafts. Open daily in afternoons, Apr to 1 Nov; afternoons only on Mon to Sat in Apr, May, Sept and Oct. All day Sun, Bank Holidays. Tel: Marshbrook 306 or 307.

□ Wenlock Lodge, Acton Scott, three miles (5km) S of Church Stretton. Off A49 between Ludlow and Church Stretton. Map ref 10B4.

611. BRIDGNORTH
Market town

An ancient market town by the River Severn. Low Town and High Town are linked by a bridge and the Castle Hill railway which has a 2 in 3 gradient. Only a tower remains of the Norman castle which used to stand here, but it is a memorable one since it is leaning at an angle of 17 degrees – three times greater than that of the leaning tower of Pisa. Other interesting buildings include a 17th-century half-timbered hall, the upper part of which served as a barn before being re-erected on the original structure's arches; Bishop Percy's House, built in 1580; the medieval North Gate (now a museum); some 18th-century houses in East Castle Street; and the Church of St Magdalene built by Thomas Telford.

□ 14 miles (22km) W of Wolverhampton. Map ref 10B4.

Upper Middle England

612. BURFORD HOUSE GARDENS
Riverside garden

Clever use of herbaceous perennials and shrubs, in a beautiful setting by the River Teme, makes a fine garden created by John Treasure, containing many unusual plants and specimen trees and shrubs. The house and garden are open afternoons Apr to Oct. Tel: Tenbury Wells 810777.
☐ Tenbury Wells, off A456 Worcester to Ludlow road. Map ref 10B4.

613. CLEE CLUN RIDGEWAY
Drovers' road drive

A prehistoric track running along the watershed crest separating the Clun and Teme valleys in the Welsh borderlands. The route was first used for trade with Ireland but later became a well used drovers' route. Today it can make a picturesque upland drive.
☐ From Newtown head E on A489 to Kerry. Turn right via minor road to B4368 and follow this SE to climb onto the ridge beyond the Anchor Inn. Map ref 9D1.

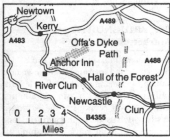

Clee Clun Ridgeway: this prehistoric track in the Welsh Borderlands runs along the crest between the Clun and Teme valleys

614. ELLESMERE
Little lakeland

Locally termed Shropshire's 'Lake District', Ellesmere's nine meres or lakes, all accessible, are waterfilled hollows created when buried ice blocks melted at the close of the Ice Age. Today these placid lakes are the haunt of moorhen, heron, kingfisher, grebe and many other birds. They are also used for angling, sailing and swimming. Boats are for hire throughout the summer months. Colemere Country Park is just over three miles (5km) south-east of Ellesmere and to the north of Colemere village.
☐ Seven miles (11km) NE of Oswestry on A495. Map ref 8D2.

615. HODNET HALL GARDENS
Lakeside gardens

Well-planted lakeside gardens which extend over 60 acres (24 hectares), contain magnificent forest trees, sweeping lawns and ornamental lakes, including a chain of pools fed by underwater springs which attract waterfowl. Open Apr to Sept daily, afternoons only. The house itself is not open to the public. Tel: Hodnet 202.
☐ Near Market Drayton, just off A442. Map ref 10B3.

616. IRONBRIDGE
Industrial archaeology

The very name is the epitome of the Industrial Revolution but the area around Ironbridge has an undeniable place in a book on the British countryside. First, because the Severn Gorge and the valleys that join it, such as Coalbrookdale, have largely reverted to their natural form: steep, tree-lined and attractive. Second, because many of the developments which so altered the landscape were pioneered here, and third, because there is a series of outstanding museums where this long-neglected area's past can be explored and celebrated.

The award-winning Ironbridge Gorge Museum Trust runs a series of museums on different sites (see map). The Blists Hill Open Air Museum, for instance, would provide a stimulating day out in itself. It has a stretch of canal, the Hay inclined plane linking canal and river, a Telford-designed tollhouse, mine works, mills, footpaths and even a special leaflet on the plants and wildlife to be seen.

Leaflets are available on each of the

various museums. The Trust's shop, next to the great iron bridge itself (erected in 1779 and now pedestrianised), also sells pamphlets on walks in the area – both nature and industrial heritage trails. The museums can be visited in any order, but the Trust believes the best starting point is the Coalbrookdale Museum and Furnace Site where Abraham Darby first used coke to smelt iron in 1709. One ticket covers all museums. They are open throughout the year, but opening times vary. Tel: Ironbridge 3522.

□ Four miles (6.4km) SW of Telford on A4160. OS map 127. Map ref 10B4.

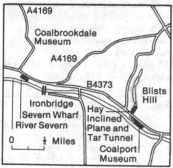

The Ironbridge Gorge Museum Trust sites in Coalbrookdale

617. LONG MYND
Scenic hills

Wild ridge of heathery uplands (NT) with marvellous walks and views. An ancient track, the Port Way, runs the entire length of the 10 mile (16km) long hill crest.

□ W of Church Stretton, off B4370 13 miles (23km) S of Shrewsbury. Map ref 8B1.

618. LUDLOW
Historic country town

A perfect example of the planned medieval castle-town – and one of the more successful of those established near the Welsh border. The castle, on a wooded bluff above the River Teme, was under construction by 1085 at much the same time as the Norman architects were laying out the streets of the new town in a rectangular pattern that largely survives today. Notable features of the town are the 15th-century church of St Lawrence, the 16th-century Feathers Hotel, the extensive town wall and the streets of timber-framed and Georgian brick buildings.

□ Midway between Hereford and Shrewsbury on A49. Map ref 10B4.

619. MERRINGTON GREEN NATURE TRAIL
Wildlife

This trail shows the once-grazed common land of Merrington Green in the process of changing to scrubby woodland. It lies on heavy clay soil (take boots on wet days) and takes one to two hours to walk. There are birds and plants of scrub in plenty, damp parts with rushes and marsh thistle, and splendid views. There are fish in a deep pool, once a marl pit (from which coarse lime-rich clay was extracted to improve the fertility of poor soils) and other swampy pools rich in aquatic life: water plantain, marsh horsetail, dragonflies and damsel-flies. Information leaflet from Shropshire Conservation Trust, Tel: Shrewsbury 56511.

□ Five miles (9km) N of Shrewsbury off B5067 (on by-road). Map ref 10B3.

620. OFFA'S DYKE
Historic earthwork

This linear earthwork can be seen as clearly as anywhere along its 168 mile (268km) length from the neighbouring Llanfair and Spoad Hills. The dyke was constructed by King Offa in the last quarter of the 8th century to define the western limits of the Saxon kingdom of Mercia. Details of walks along the Dyke are available from the Offa's Dyke Association, Knighton, Powys (enclose SAE). Tel: Knighton 528752.

□ Llanfair and Spoad Hills are three miles (5km) W of Clun, S of B4368. Grid ref SO 254805; OS map 137. Map ref 9D1.

Upper Middle England

621. OLD OSWESTRY
Prehistoric hill-fort

This is an outstanding hill-fort from Iron Age times built on a glacial mound just north of the modern town. Its elaborate ramparts and ditches were built at several different times; the western gateway is particularly intricate. The site covers some 68 acres (27 hectares) and, like most hill-forts, is an interesting place for exploration and picnics with fine views over the surrounding countryside.
□ One mile (1.6km) N of Oswestry between B4579 and A483. Grid ref SJ 295304; OS map 126. Map ref 8D2.

622. PRESTON MONTFORD NATURE TRAIL
Wildlife

Ferns, flowers and birdlife abound in this Shropshire Conservation Trust reserve on the banks of the Severn, in a wilderness known as Preston Rough. The trail is short (about 1km) but has ten stops (marked by an alder leaf symbol) pointing out different habitats. Contact the warden at the Field Centre for permission to use the trail and bird-watching hide. A booklet lists wildlife species (including sand martins, moisture-loving plants such as golden saxifrage, and goat willow – an important source of artists' charcoal). Tel: Preston Montford Field Centre: Montford Bridge 380.
□ Montford Bridge is four miles (7km) NW of Shrewsbury. Map ref 8D2.

623. STIPERSTONES
Moorland hills

In the moorland hills of south Shropshire the 1700ft (510m) Stiperstones offer a contrasting scene to that of the more famous Long Mynd and Wrekin. Their long, bouldery ridge is punctuated by jagged tors of white quartzite rock. Approached easily on foot from the car park, these crags offer a delightful, breezy viewpoint and a jumbled frost-shattered wilderness of rocks and heather above the surrounding wooded valleys and farmlands where ancient Roman lead mines once flourished. The tiny village of Snailbeach is surrounded by the remains of a lead mine, once the richest in England. Derelict surface buildings still stand. Explore with care as there are a number of open shafts.
□ Minor road on E of A488 at Ploxgreen leads to the Bog. Car parking. Map ref 8D2.

624. STOKESAY CASTLE
Fortified manor house

A romantic, well preserved manor house dating from the 13th century. It is moated and fortified, with two stone towers, splendid gabled banqueting hall and picturesque half-timbered gatehouse. Open daily Mar to Oct, except Tues.
□ Approx ¾ mile (1km) S of Craven Arms on A49. Map ref 9D1.

625. WENLOCK EDGE
Limestone escarpment

This remarkably straight escarpment of ancient limestone is a well known landmark to the north-west of the attractive market town of Much Wenlock. Good viewpoints of Apedale and the Church Stretton hills can be found at intervals along its narrow wooded crest. Explore the peaceful villages of neighbouring Hope Dale or the lovely Elizabethan mansion of Wilderhope (NT), off the B4271, built from Wenlock limestone. Open Apr to Sept on Wed, and Sat afternoons, Oct to Mar. Note the vertical limestone rock of Major's Leap, north of the B4371 about 2½ miles (4km) from Much Wenlock, with its legend of Civil War heroism. Much Wenlock Museum in the High Street has geological, social and local history exhibits. Open Apr to Sept. Tel: Much Wenlock 727773. Also visit the striking Guildhall in the Square, dating from 1577, open Apr to Sept, and Wenlock Priory (AM) and abbey ruins, open standard DoE hours.
□ From Much Wenlock access is via B4371 or B4378. Map ref 10B4.

626. THE WREKIN
Beacon hilltop

This isolated hill affords commanding views over the Vale of the Upper Severn so it is little wonder that it should have been crowned with extensive ramparts to strengthen the position still further. It was an important hill-fort of Iron Age Britain. Its height is 1334ft (411m), and so clearly does it stand above the surrounding land that in later generations it served as a beacon hill. Even today it is still crowned with a warning light to aircraft.

☐ Two miles (3.2km) SW of Wellington off A5. Map ref 10B4.

627. WROXETER
Roman site

In the 2nd century AD this was the site of the fourth largest city of Roman Britain. But, like Silchester, *Viroconium* did not become the location of a major settlement in later times: the small present-day village of Wroxeter developed a little distance away from the Roman site. At least this means that some of the Roman remains are still visible on the ground, notably earthworks which were once the city ramparts and the stone foundations of the baths and a colonnade. In Wroxeter itself the Norman church probably incorporates stone from the old Roman city. The Roman site and museum are open standard DoE hours plus Sun mornings, Apr to Sept.

☐ Five miles (8km) SE of Shrewsbury off B4380. Grid ref SJ 565087; OS map 126. Map ref 10B4.

Staffordshire

Staffordshire has some lovely countryside to compensate for the industrial areas of the Black Country and the Potteries. It offers the wild uplands of Cannock Chase, the millstone grit hills known as the Roaches, near Leek, and shares the beautiful limestone scenery of Dovedale (protected by the National Trust) with Derbyshire. Architectural splendours include triple-towered Lichfield Cathedral. Heart of England Tourist Board, Tel: Worcester 29511.

628. ALTON TOWERS
Landscape gardens

Do not be put off by the fact that Alton Towers has become a fun-fair and amusement park for the Potteries. The enormous and mostly gutted house, partly designed by Pugin, provides a backcloth of towers and gables for one of England's most extraordinary and elaborate gardens. It was made early in the 19th century in a bare valley. It is now magnificently planted with trees and shrubs and ornamented with many strange buildings including a Chinese pagoda which is also a fountain, a Roman colonnade, a Gothic tower, a Druid stone circle and an elaborate conservatory. The Gothic mansion is now sadly a ruin. Open daily, Easter to Oct. Tel: Oakamoor 702449.

☐ At Alton, off B5032 four miles (6.5km) E of Cheadle. Map ref 11A3.

629. BLITHFIELD RESERVOIR
Bird-watching

One of the best places in this part of England to watch birds in winter. Species likely to be seen include pintail, and goldeneye, Bewick's swan and jack snipe.

☐ Eight miles (13km) E of Stafford, off B5013. Map ref 11A3.

Upper Middle England

630. CHEDDLETON
Watermills

Two watermills have been preserved here beside the Caldon Canal in the beautiful wooded valley of the River Churnet. Both contain much of the original machinery (including the two waterwheels) and are open on weekend afternoons throughout the year. One mill was formerly used to grind corn; the other stands as a memorial to the many which once ground flint for the local pottery industry.
☐ Three miles (5km) S of Leek on A520. Map ref 11A3.

631. CHURNET VALLEY
River walk and industrial archaeology

The Churnet is at its most attractive in the steep and largely wooded stretch between Oakamoor and Alton. A minor road follows the valley here but better still is a nature walk along the route of the old Churnet Valley Railway – no leaflets but there is a picnic area at Oakamoor. Near Alton it is possible to see remnants of the old Caldon Canal while in Dimmings Dale (west of the minor road at an old smelting mill) former hammer ponds add to the beauty of what is now an unspoilt rural area.
☐ Oakamoor is three miles (4.8km) NE of Cheadle on B5417; railway walk begins off minor road S from Oakamoor to Alton. OS map 119. Map ref 11A3.

632. COOMBES VALLEY
Bird-watching

This RSPB reserve lies in a wooded valley and covers 261 acres (106 hectares). It provides a refuge for a large number of woodland birds including sparrowhawk and pied flycatcher. By the stream watch out for dipper and kingfisher. Report to the information centre on arrival. For car park charges and opening times, Tel: RSPB Reserves Dept, Sandy (Beds) 80551.
☐ Leek. Map ref 11A3.

633. GREENWAY BANK
Country park

Wooded valley at head of River Trent with lake, arboreta and sandstone outcrops.
☐ Four miles (6.4km) N of Stoke-on-Trent off A527. Map ref 11A3.

634. HAWKSMOOR NATURE RESERVE TRAIL
Wildlife

Bracken and heather moorland and some woodland, this nature reserve and bird sanctuary slopes down to the river Churnet. Birds you may see include curlew and lapwing, redstart, nightjar and warblers. Nature trail and four recommended walks also cover farmland, river, railway and disused canal. Open all year. Limited parking, six cars only.
☐ Two miles (3km) NE of Cheadle on B5417. Map ref 11A3.

635. HIGHGATE COMMON
Country park

Heath, wood, bridleways.
☐ Two miles (3km) W of Kingswinford. Map ref 11A4.

636. INGESTRE
Parish church

The Church of St Mary is one of the best 17th-century churches in England outside London. Probably by Wren himself, it was built between 1673 and 1676. The interior is notable for its fine proportions and admirable craftsmanship in wood and stucco. Look particularly at the pulpit, reredos and imposing screen bearing a splendid Royal Arms. This stately classical church has no need of stained glass, and that in the nave, at least, should be removed.
☐ Five miles (8km) E of Stafford off A51. Map ref 11A3.

637. MANIFOLD VALLEY
Limestone dale

Start from the picturesque village of

Upper Middle England

Ilam with its Saxon church and ancient ridge and furrow field patterns, and stroll northwards along the beautiful wooded limestone gorge where the Manifold River, a tributary of the Dove, disappears underground in dry weather through its rocky bed of porous limestone. Ilam was rebuilt as a model village in the 19th century, with estate cottages clustered around a tall Gothic cross. Ilam Nature Walk (NT) is set in the grounds of Ilam Hall, 1½ miles (2.4km) from the car park. The Hall itself is a Youth Hostel and not open to the general public. Alternatively, drive down the steep lane from Wetton, three miles (4.8km) further up the valley to Wetton Mill, or walk south-west from Wetton along the track of the old Manifold Valley Light Railway, now a footpath, to Beeston Tor.

☐ Ilam is reached by minor road, four miles (6.4km) NW of Ashbourne. Map ref 11A3.

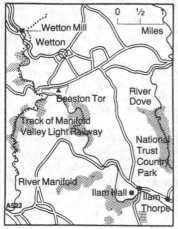

Manifold Valley: a beautiful wooded limestone gorge which is well footpathed

638. PARK HALL
Country park

Park Hall Country Park is situated on the south-eastern fringes of the city of Stoke-on-Trent. It lies astride a major ridge line which gives extensive views to the west across the city and to the east across rolling farmland towards the Peak District. Much of the park is heath and grassland with enclosures provided by a series of canyons and coniferous woodland. Dramatic cliffs and canyons remain from the award-winning reclamation on sand and gravel quarries. Informal recreation includes picnicking, walking and nature study; there are barbecue facilities, an events area and horse riding by permit. Several free car parks. The visitor centre is open Sun afternoons, Easter to end Sept, Tel: Stoke-on-Trent 331889. The park opens daily throughout the year.

☐ Between Weston Coyney and Hulme on W side of A520, three miles (4.8km) SE of Hanley. Map ref 11A3.

639. STAFFORDSHIRE COUNTY MUSEUM
Farm museum

Agricultural history is on show in what was designed in the 19th century as a home farm to the estate, but in 1975 was taken over and turned into an agricultural museum. The farm is also a breeding centre for rare local livestock. A fine collection of horse-drawn vehicles, all with strong Staffordshire connections, is in the coach-house. Open end Mar to mid-Oct, Tues to Fri. Also weekend afternoons. Closed Mon except Bank Holidays. Tel: Little Haywood 881388.

☐ Shugborough, Stafford. On A513, 5½ miles SE of Stafford. Map ref 11A3.

640. TUTBURY
Castle and church

Ruined 14th-century stronghold where Mary Queen of Scots was twice imprisoned. Open daily except Christmas and Boxing Day. Tutbury itself is an attractive village beside the River Dove with a fine Norman church. There is also a tannery housed in the old mills with 18th-century twin waterwheels and corn chutes. Open Tues to Sat. Tel: Burton on Trent 813300.

☐ Four miles (6km) NW of Burton on A50. Map ref 11A3.

Northern England

641. LAKE DISTRICT
National park

Easy access by road off M6 motorway, which skirts the eastern edge. Within the park, roads run through the major dales and along the lake shores to converge on Ambleside and also at Keswick. Here every road is a scenic drive – traffic jams permitting – to which the Lakeland passes, Kirkstone, Whinlatter, Honister, Hardknott and Wrynose, add the drama of far-ranging vistas.

If you can leave your car and walk there are endless possibilities in this, the largest national park in England and Wales. Serious climbers head for spots such as Wasdale and the crags of Great Gable and Scafell Pike, whose 3206ft (997m) summit is England's highest. Yet these brooding fell tops can also be reached by walkers, provided you are reasonably fit, well shod and clad for the hills. Ambleside, Borrowdale, Coniston and Patterdale (for Helvellyn) are favourite walking centres. There are park information centres at Ambleside, Bowness, Brockhole, Coniston, Glenridding, Hawkshead, Keswick, Pooley Bridge and Waterhead. These all close for varying periods during the winter months, but the Cumbria Tourist Board provides a year-round service. Tel: Windermere 4444. There is also a weather service for lakeland. Tel: Windermere 5151. As uncertain as the weather for 1981 is the fate of some mobile information centres: spending cuts may cause these to be reduced or axed altogether.

For sightseeing, the lakes, hills and dales steal most of the glory, but there is also a fine stretch of sea coast at Ravenglass. In the Cumbrian section we feature some Lakeland areas which remain relatively uncrowded on even the busiest Bank Holiday.
☐ Map ref 14B2.

642. NORTHUMBERLAND
National park

Few roads pierce this remote and splendid park, wedged between the Roman Wall and the Scottish Border, with the Border Forest Park on its western flanks. Indeed, there is only one main road, the A68, running through Redesdale on its lonely way from Otterburn to Carter Bar. Otherwise this is a walkers' park, offering superlative fell walks in the Simonside and Cheviot Hills. The finest of all is the Pennine Way long-distance footpath, which also takes in a spectacular length of the Roman Wall before swinging north towards High Cheviot, 2674ft (815m), the park's loftiest summit. Another well known route is the old

Salters' Road, heading for the Border via Bleakhope, Nagshead Knowe and Davidsons Linn. The one major obstacle regarding access in the park is the presence of military firing ranges between Redesdale and the River Coquet. The park covers 398 sq miles (1031 sq km). Park information centres at Byrness, Ingram, Once Brewed and Rothbury are open from Easter to Sept. (As with all national parks dates of close-down vary.) Otherwise, contact Northumbria Tourist Board. Tel: Newcastle-upon-Tyne 817744.

□ Map ref 17C1.

643. NORTH YORK MOORS
National park

One of the better parks for motorists. Viewpoints with or close to car parking include Sutton Bank on the scarp of the Hambleton Hills, Robin Hood's Bay on the Yorkshire coast, Danby Beacon and Newgate Bank. The park covers 553 sq miles (1432 sq km). For walkers, a huge variety of cliff paths, forest trails and moorland treks beckon. Best known are the 90 mile (144km) Cleveland Way long-distance footpath, the 40 mile (64km) Lyke Wake Walk over the moors, and Wade's Causeway, one of the best preserved Roman roads in Britain. Information centres at Danby Lodge, Pickering and Sutton Bank are open daily Easter to Sept or Oct, weekends in winter. Also park offices at Helmsley. Tel: Helmsley 70657 (weekdays only).

□ Map ref 15B2.

644. YORKSHIRE DALES
National park

Most roads follow the line of the dales, but sometimes climb over the fells to give glorious panoramic views. Notable viewpoints (with or near car parks) include Buttertubs, Dodd Fell and Newby Head. For walkers there are old Roman roads, a marvellous stretch of the Pennine Way long-distance footpath which takes in the dramatic limestone landscapes of Malham and the ascent of Pen-y-ghent, 2273ft (693m), as well as

innumerable gentler walks in the dales from Kettlewell and other villages – a perfect counterpoint to the wild fell tops. Swaledale, Wensleydale, Wharfedale and Ribblesdale are the four major dales, but there are others, Dentdale and Littondale among them, which are every inch as delectable. National park centres at Aysgarth Falls, Clapham, Grassington, Hawes, Malham and Sedbergh are open daily from Apr to Sept or Oct – dates of close-down vary. Further information from park offices at Leyburn. Tel: Wensleydale 50456. The park covers 680 sq miles (1761 sq km). See map on page 213.

□ Map ref 15A2.

645. ARNSIDE AND SILVERDALE
Area of Outstanding Natural Beauty

A small but serene tract of coastline on the Lancashire–Cumbria border at the northern end of Morecambe Bay, beside the estuary of the River Kent. Total area 47 sq miles (75 sq km). Much of it is owned by the NT, including Arnside Knott, 522ft (159m), a favourite viewpoint and the site of a nature trail featuring such characteristic limestone plants as rockrose, columbine and burnet rose. Leaflet from local shops. Another attraction is the 18th-century waterpowered Heron corn mill, at Beetham. Open daily except Mon, Apr to Sept. Tel: Carnforth 4858.

□ Arnside Knott is one mile (1.6km) SW of Arnside. Map ref 14B2.

646. FOREST OF BOWLAND
Area of Outstanding Natural Beauty

This wild collision of moorland fells on the Yorkshire border is Lancashire at its loneliest, a far cry from the industrial conurbations of Liverpool and Manchester. Highest points are Ward's Stone, 1836ft (560m), near the infant River Wyre, and Pendle Hill, 1831ft (558m), once the haunt of the notorious 'Lancashire Witches'.

Northern England

Minor roads penetrate the Hodder Valley and the wild pass known as the Trough of Bowland. There is a country park at Beacon Fell (north-west of Longridge) and several picnic sites in the north-west, including Weatheroak Hill, Birk Bank, Bull Beck and Crook o'Lune. Total area: 502 sq miles (803 sq km).
□ Map ref 14B3.

647. NORTHUMBERLAND COAST
Area of Outstanding Natural Beauty

A gloriously uncluttered Heritage Coast stretched between two classic salmon rivers, Tweed and Coquet. It keeps a low profile for the most part, but the Whin Sill breaches the bays and sandhills in places, forming dolerite crags surmounted by hoary sea-castles at Bamburgh and Dunstanburgh. Sturdy Northumbrian fishing cobles put out from village harbours such as Boulmer and Beadnell. Craster is renowned for oak-smoked kippers; Seahouses for boat trips to see the grey seals and seabird colonies of the Farne Islands (NT). The most romantic spot on the entire coast is Lindisfarne. Total area: 80 sq miles (129 sq km).
□ Map ref 17D1.

648. SOLWAY COAST
Area of Outstanding Natural Beauty

Apart from a small gap around Silloth, this includes the whole of the sandy southern shores of the Solway Firth between Maryport and the mouth of the River Lyne just below Gretna on the Scottish Border, with splendid views across the Firth to the hog-backed Scottish hill of Criffel. Total area: 67 sq miles (107 sq km).
□ Map ref 17B2.

Cleveland

A small county dominated by Teeside but including stretches of coast and the North York Moors. Northumbria Tourist Board, Tel: Newcastle 817744.

649. GUISBOROUGH
Monastic remains

An attractive little town in the shadow of the Cleveland Hills. It grew around a 12th-century Augustinian priory, parts of which can still be seen. The ruins, which include a gatehouse, dovecote and the priory's east end, are open standard DoE hours. Close to the ruins is a restored 15th-century church. Guisborough is conveniently sited for exploring both sea and moors.
□ Seven miles (11km) SE of Middlesbrough on A171. Map ref 15B1.

650. NEWHAM GRANGE
Farm museum

An agricultural museum is incorporated into the running of a farm stocked with rare breeds of animals, especially pigs and poultry. There is also a 19th-century veterinary surgery and a late 19th-century saddler's shop, complete with tools and equipment of the period. Open daily during summer, Sun only during winter. Tel: Middlesbrough 245432 ext 3831.
□ S of Middlesbrough at Coulby Newham near junction of A174 and B1365. Map ref 15B1.

Cumbria

The county has a long coastline but it is the beauty of the Lake District which draws most visitors; Windermere is the largest lake in England. The northern fells and Pennine areas are less crowded, however. Other attractions include Carlisle, Kendal, Keswick and Penrith. Cumbria Tourist Board, Tel: Windermere 4444.

651. ALSTON
Market town and an unexpected industrial landscape

Said to be England's highest market town, at 1000ft (305m) above sea level. By 1982 enthusiasts of the South Tynedale Railway hope that a narrow gauge railway will be operating from the old railway station; at present the station houses only a tourist inform-

A glossary of some common placenames with Saxon or Norse origins

MODERN FORM	MEANING
Barrow-; Bar-; berry; -burgh	Hill, mound, tumulus
Barton	Corn farm, outlying grange
Beck	Stream
Brock-; Brough-; brook; -broke	Brook, stream
Brough; -burgh; -bury; -borough	Fortified place
-bourne; -borne	Stream, spring
-by	Village, settlement, farm
Cleve-; Clif-; cliff; -ley	Cliff, bank
Coate; Coton; -cot; -cote	Cottage
Deane; Den-; -dean; -den	Valley
Dun-; den; -don; -ton	Down, hill
Ea-; E-; ey; -eau	Stream, river, island
Frith	Woodland
Hale; Hal-; -all; -hall	Nook, narrow valley
-ham	Village, manor, homestead, meadow, enclosure
-hampton	Home farm
-hanger	Slope
-hay; -hey	Fence, enclosure
Had-; Hat-; Hed-; Heath-	Heath, heather
Holt-; -hurst	Wood
Lea-; -leigh; -ley; -low	Forest, wood, glade, clearing
Med-; mede	Meadow
-mond; -mont	Mount, hill
-stead; -sted	Place, religious site
Stret-; Sturt-; Stred-; Strat-	Street
Thwaite-; -thwaite	Clearing or meadow
-ton; -tone	Enclosure, farmstead, village
Wick-; Wig-; wich; -wick	Dwelling, farm
-worth; -worthy	Enclosure

ation office. Open all year, Tel: Alston 696. Market day is Sat.

The surrounding Alston Moor seems as 'unspoilt' as it is possible to be, yet it has been the scene of lead mining since Roman times. One of the most important developments was around Nenthead, five miles (8km) south-east of Alston on A689. In the early 18th century, the London Lead Company launched a major develop-ment of the area's potential. Now only the cottages and chapels remain, with the former lead works itself crying out for restoration.

□ 18 miles (29km) NE of Penrith on A686. Map ref 17C2.

652. BIRDOSWALD
Hadrian's Wall

Only a limited excavation has so far

been undertaken at this fort (*Cambo-glanna*) but it is on one of the most dramatic stretches of Hadrian's Wall in Cumbria. Two well preserved gates and a tower have been uncovered and the *vallum* can be seen on the edge of the escarpment with room for only the southern mound. Access to these remains and this stretch of the wall is available at reasonable hours of the day via the nearby farmhouse. A Roman road headed north-west from this point – grid ref NY 615663 – to the outlying fort at Bewcastle. West of Birdoswald the wall became a turf construction apart from its forts and milecastles. See also Day Out 723.

□ Six miles (9.6km) NW of Halt-whistle off B6318. Map ref 17C2.

653. BOWNESS-ON-SOLWAY
Fishing village and nature reserve

The little fishing village stands on the narrowest part of the Solway Firth with fine views over to Scotland just two miles (3.2km) away. It was the westerly end of Hadrian's Wall and the site of a Roman fort. Part of the road from Carlisle follows the line of the wall across a sometimes dangerous, boggy area but little remains of the wall or fort around Bowness other than the ditch of the old *vallum*. Bowness is an interesting village with a fortified farm to remind us of a more turbulent past and cottages whose charm has withstood sometimes excessively fussy 'restoration'. To the south is Glasson Moss, an NCC nature reserve with a public right of way available to anyone interested in rare mosses. This is also a good place to see flocks of greylag geese.

□ 12 miles (19km) W of Carlisle off B5307. Map ref 17B2.

654. CASTLERIGG
Prehistoric stone circle

The finest stone circle in the Lake District, a region that has few spectacular prehistoric remains. Thirty-nine stones are still standing in a circle 100ft (30m) across which is also known as the Keswick Carles. It has a

magnificent setting amid the surrounding mountains. Little is known about the history of the site, but that does not diminish its grandeur.

□ One mile (1.6km) E of Keswick via a lane off A591. Grid ref NY 292237; OS map 90. Map ref 14B1.

655. DUDDON VALLEY
Uncrowded Lakeland

One of the least known Lake District valleys. Lacking in lakes but abounding with quiet, wooded tracts, flowing streams and tantalising views of the high fells. Take either the west bank or east bank roads to the north from Duddon Bridge. There narrow and twisting lanes provide many picnic spots and viewpoints, especially the path to the stepping stones of the Low Crag gorge to the west. The road climbs ultimately to the bleak and windswept fells at Cockley Beck farm where you can choose between spectacular climbs west to Hardknott Pass (see Day Out 660) or east via Wrynose Pass to Langdale and Ambleside. Duddon Valley itself has two 'hidden' lakes which can be approached only on foot: Seathwaite Tarn, two miles (3.2km) north-east of the village, and Devoke Water (via the minor road which runs north-west off the main Duddon Valley road at Ulpha). OS map 96 details the paths to the lakes.

□ N from Duddon Bridge off A595. OS map 96. Map ref 14A2.

656. EDEN VALLEY
Unexplored river valley

This is not in the Lake District National Park but it is nonetheless an attractive and uncrowded river valley. The valley is lush yet remains relatively unexplored despite its proximity to the M6. Start at Armathwaite and work south taking in Nunnery Walks (a garden), Kirkoswald (castle), Long Meg and Her Daughters (stone circle), Milburn (village green) and end at Appleby. Or vice versa.

□ Armathwaite is nine miles (14km) SE of Carlisle off A6; Appleby is 12

miles (19km) SE of Penrith on A66.
Map ref 14B1.

657. ENNERDALE
Uncrowded Lakeland forests

Ennerdale Water is the most isolated
lake, without a road on either side. It is
the only lake with this distinction and
distinction it is now that parts of the
Lake District are so often clogged with
cars. The lake has been threatened by a
controversial water authority scheme
to raise its natural level. But it is still
marvellous walking country here and
in the valley beyond both for sturdy
fell-walkers and for the less ambitious
attracted by Forestry Commission
trails and picnic areas in Ennerdale.
Broadmoor. Picnic place in young
hardwoods at side of River Ehen and
starting point for seven mile (11km)
walk round lake. Approach from
Ennerdale Bridge on road signposted
to Ennerdale Lake.
Bowness Knott. Picnic place beside
larches with views over Ennerdale
Water to Angler's Crag. From Croas-
dale take road to Raughton for one
mile (1.6km). At end of public road
take forest road to car park.
Nine Becks walk. Over rough and
steep ground through woods and over
becks into heart of Ennerdale. Great
Gable and Pillar tower above route.
Many fine views. Nine miles (14.5km).
Starts from Bowness Knott car park.
Smithy Beck trail. Along edge of
Ennerdale Water climbing into forest
and past site of medieval settlement
and former iron bloomery. Two miles
(3.2km) with shortcut back to lakeside
after one mile (1.6km). Also starts from
Bowness Knott car park. Leaflets
available from FC centres at Grizedale
or Whinlatter (see Day Out 672).
□ Four miles (6.4km) E of Cleator
Moor via minor roads to Ennerdale
Bridge. Map ref 14A1.

658. FURNESS
Isolated peninsula with abbey

The peninsula is, as its name implies,
the 'fur-ness' or the far peninsula
almost marooned by the sandy reaches
of Morecambe Bay. There is still a sense
of isolation as well as beauty here – two
qualities associated with the Cistercian
monks who took over a Sauvignac
house here in 1147. The considerable
remains of the monastery – only
Fountains was wealthier – are in a
sheltered wooded valley to the north of
Barrow and are open standard DoE
hours.

On Piel Island, three miles (4.8km)
south of Barrow, are the ruins of a
Norman motte-and-bailey castle
which served as a defence and
warehouse for the monks. The castle
and island can be visited by boat from
Roa Island, a promontory rather than
island linked to the mainland south-
east of Barrow by a causeway.

The largest of the offshore islands is
Walney, immediately opposite Barrow
to which it is linked by the A590. A
three mile (4.8km) nature trail starts
from West Shore Road along the sand
dunes of Walney Island, which forms a
natural breakwater for the shipbuild-
ing town of Barrow. (The nature
reserve at Haws Bed, at the southern tip
of Walney, is not open to the public.)

Other places worth a visit on – or
near – Furness are the market town of
Ulverston (market day is Thursday);
the Millom Folk Museum, which
recalls a century of prosperity which
followed the discovery of the great iron
ore deposits of the Hodbarrow Mine
(open Easter to Sept); Dalton with its
14th-century pele tower; Bardsea
country park two miles (3.2km) south
of Ulverston with views over the bay;
and the village of Cartmel with its 12th-
century priory church and some
delightful secular architecture.
□ Barrow-in-Furness is 25 miles
(40km) SW of Windermere on A590.
Map ref 14A2.

659. GRIZEDALE
Forest trails and theatre

Millwood forest trail, one mile
(1.6km), starts from a Forestry
Commission visitor centre in the heart
of Grizedale Forest. The centre is open
all year. Tel: Satterthwaite 272 or 273.
It is also the starting point for the

circular 9½ mile (15.2km) Silurian Way over rough ground and steep gradients traversing plantations of oak, larch, spruce and pine with excellent views over forest and lakes. Leaflets for these and other walks are available at the visitor centre. The forest has the usual picnic areas but there is also a theatre which stages musical and other performances. Tel: Satterthwaite 291. Trout fishing is possible in Grizedale Beck; tickets from shop at camp site, Easter to Sept.
□ The visitor centre is three miles (4.8km) S of Hawkshead on minor road to Satterthwaite. Map ref 14B2.

660. HARDKNOTT PASS
Roman fort

Near the summit of Hardknott Pass, nearly 1300ft (400m) above sea level, stands a stone wall and earth embankment of a Roman fort dating from the 2nd century. It is in a magnificent position, though whether the soldiers of Rome relished this posting is somewhat doubtful.
□ 10 miles (16km) W of Ambleside on minor unclassified road via Eskdale to Ravenglass. Grid ref NY 218015; OS map 90. Map ref 14A2.

661. HAWESWATER
Lakeland drive

The eastern side of Lakeland has fewer large lakes than the west but that of Haweswater is well worth a visit, notwithstanding its artificiality and its major dam. The minor road climbs from Bampton village into the woodlands of Haweswater Beck before skirting the lakeshores for four miles (6.4km). There are many interesting views of the high fells to the west and if you are tempted to walk to the high corries there is a choice of paths where the road ends at the southern tip of the reservoir. But take care on these and other upland paths in the Lake District: boots, anoraks and, often, experience are essential on the higher and tougher stretches.
□ Five miles (8km) by minor road W of Shap. OS map 90. Map ref 14B1.

662. JOHNNY'S WOOD
Nature trails

Some lovely walks over fell and forest with short diversions to see attractive waterfalls. There are superb views over Borrowdale, Seathwaite and the fells. The oak woodland is full of birdlife, flowers, mosses and ferns, excellently described in the Woodland Walk leaflet produced jointly by the NT and the Cumbria Naturalists' Trust and available locally or from NT information centres. Tel: Ambleside 3003. Walks of 2 to 2½ miles (3 to 4km) start from the car park at Seatoller on B5289. Stout footwear is advisable.
□ Seven miles (11km) S of Keswick on B5289. Map ref 14A1.

663. LANERCOST PRIORY
Abbey church

A former priory of Austin Canons, beautifully situated in the Irthing Valley. It is partly ruined, but the nave is now the parish church. It is pink sandstone without, grey limestone within: both taken from the Roman Wall less than a mile away to the north. The west front forms a singularly chaste composition in lancets, while the lofty interior is chiefly memorable for its gorgeous clerestory, with exceptionally bold ornamentation.
□ 12 miles (19km) NE of Carlisle off A69. Map ref 17B2.

664. LANGDALE PIKES
Mountains and archaeology

A characteristic example of the bare rugged landscapes of the highest parts of the Lake District. But what makes this area particularly interesting is that the apron of scree beneath the Pike of Stickle was the site of a prehistoric 'axe factory' (grid ref NY 273073; OS map 90) whose products were traded widely in Britain. The road from Ambleside follows the Great Langdale Beck. A path continues up the valley for just over one mile (1.8km) from where the road ends to beneath the axe factory, before continuing up the fells. OS map 90 shows paths in the area. The nearest museum in which to see examples of Langdale axes is the Museum of Lakeland Life in Kendal. Tel: Kendal 22464.

☐ Six miles (9.6km) W of Ambleside off B5343. Map ref 14A2.

665. LONGSLEDDALE
Uncrowded Lakeland

A dead-end valley which like Kentmere, its neighbour to the west, is often missed by people on the crowded route between Keswick and Windermere. Yet it is very accessible, being near the southern gateway to the lakes, very attractive and very isolated. A minor road follows the valley for about five miles (8km) north-west from Watchgate.

☐ Off A6 at Watchgate four miles (6.4km) N of Kendal. Map ref 14B2.

666. NORTHERN FELLS
Undiscovered Lakeland

A broad area located, as the name indicates, at the northern end of the Lake District. It is much less crowded than the south with miles of unfenced roads heading across the fells where cars are rare, let alone traffic jams. It is also, of course, great fell-walking and riding country – see OS map 90. Villages which are either attractive in themselves or good bases for exploring these fells are Caldbeck (birth and burial place of John Peel), Hesket Newmarket, Ireby, Mosedale, Mungrisdale, Orthwaite and Uldale.

☐ S of B5299 and B5305 from 12 miles (19km) SW of Carlisle. Map ref 14B1.

667. RAVENGLASS
Castle and railway

Its position at the mouth of three rivers once made it a port but tourism is its main industry now. Access to the Ravenglass Nature Reserve, the largest breeding colony of black-headed gulls in Europe, is by permit only; apply to the County Land Agent and Valuer, 1 Alfred Street North, Carlisle. But there is a nature trail in the grounds of Muncaster, a 13th-century fortress with a 14th-century pele tower built on the site of the Roman fort of *Glannaventa*. There are fine views from the castle over the Esk estuary, and renowned rhododendron gardens among other attractions; the grounds are open daily Easter to early Oct, the castle Tues, Wed, Thur and Sun afternoons during the same period. Tel: Ravenglass 614. Remains of a Roman bath-house can also be seen. Ravenglass is the western terminus of a narrow gauge railway which runs seven miles (11km) up to Dalegarth in Eskdale with daily steam services in summer and more limited operations in winter. Tel: Ravenglass 226. The line, which was built to haul iron ore from Eskdale to the coast, also has a small museum at the Ravenglass terminus. Near the Dalegarth terminus at Boot is Eskdale Mill, a restored corn mill, dating from the 16th century, with an exhibition on the history and technique of milling. Open Easter to Sept except non-Bank Holiday Sats; Tel: Eskdale 335.

☐ 12 miles (19km) NW of Millom on A595. Map ref 14A2.

668. ST BEES HEAD
A walk along the cliffs

The red sandstone cliffs at this headland rise to over 300ft (91m) and are a breeding ground for guillemot and puffin. There are magnificent views over Solway Firth from the clifftops where a lighthouse is open to the public. Tel: Whitehaven 2635. A path leads down to the beach. The village of St Bees, which grew up around a priory, is the western terminus for an as yet unofficial long-distance footpath linking the Irish and North Seas. A fine circular seven mile (11km) walk can use part of this route by heading west from St Bees seawall (see map overleaf). Head towards Fleswick Bay – a tremendous rift in the coast where an alternative to the clifftop path is the descent to and ascent from the pebble beach: shorter but steep. After Fleswick Bay continue north past the lighthouse. At an old quarry crater turn south by passing

Northern England

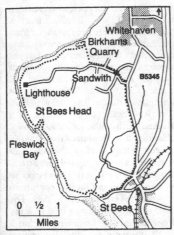

St Bees: the starting-point of a seven-mile (11km) walk

between two cottages into a red sandstone-flagged lane. Return by this lane and a private road (open to walkers) to St Bees via Sandwith.

☐ Four miles (6.4km) SW of Whitehaven off B5345. OS map 89. Map ref 14A1.

---

669. SCAFELL PIKE
The easiest way up England's highest mountain: 3206ft (989m)

The ascent of Scafell Pike from any direction is serious hill-walking. Its topography – along with that of the neighbouring peak, 3162ft (975m) Scafell – is complex, and the crags plunging within range of its summit are among the biggest in Britain. In mist there is always danger here, and even the 'easy' route suggested here is only safe when fine weather is forecast and everyone is well prepared.

Wasdale Head offers the easiest approach – from the camp site at the head of Wastwater (see map). Follow the path past Brackenclose climbing hut in the trees, and cross Lingmell Beck by the footbridge just beyond. Turn immediately right along the beckside until the left branch of Lingmell Ghyll is crossed by boulder-hopping. The path now climbs between the two streams via heavily eroded footsteps.

Keep to the track that carries on at the top rather than the one which veers to the right (the climber's path to Hollow Stones amphitheatre and the Scafell crags directly above it). The Scafell Pike route, however, swings off to the left and curves around the 'safe' side of the mountain and into the col between it and Lingmell. A well blazoned track continues right up towards the summit: a huge stone dome with a massive cairn. It is safest to return the same way. All the other descents hold one threat or another (as does most certainly the ascent of the twin mountain, Scafell) to anyone save experienced hill-walkers and mountaineers. For this type of hill-walking the 1:25,000 OS maps are greatly preferable to the standard 1:50,000 series. NB: There is no direct route for walkers between Scafell Pike and Scafell via Broad Stand.

☐ Wasdale Head is 10 miles (16km) NE of Ravenglass via A595 and minor roads to Wastwater. Map ref 14A2.

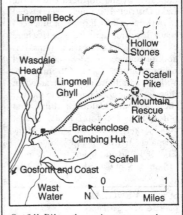

Scafell Pike: the easiest way to the peak of England's highest mountain

---

670. STAVELEY
Unexpected industrial landscape

The water resources of the Lake District were used to generate power from the 13th century onwards, but this exploitation was at its peak in the mid-19th century. The most concentrated area of industrial development – in what now seems a most unlikely region for any such history – was Kentdale on the south-eastern fringes of the Lake District. Here bobbin, textile, paper and snuff mills were once strung out along the River Kent and its tributaries like a string of beads, with Staveley the main centre of activity. Most mills have long since closed, but many relics remain of an unexpected past for a valley which now forms part of the Lake District national park.

☐ Five miles (8km) NW of Kendal. Map ref 14B2.

671. TALKIN TARN
Country park

The woodlands and open pastureland around the Tarn now form a country park set in undulating countryside with pleasant views of the hills to the south. The accent is very much on active leisure pursuits such as boating (fees vary depending on season and period of use), fishing (no charge), sub-aqua diving (no charge, but subject to prior appointment), rowing and sailing. There is also a camp site. The park is open daily throughout the year, Tel: Brampton 3129. Further details from County Land Agent and Valuer, Tel: Carlisle 23456.

☐ Two miles (3.2km) S of Brampton off A69. Map ref 17B2.

672. THORNTHWAITE FOREST
Forest walks and views

A Forestry Commission visitor centre on Whinlatter Pass tells the story of man's impact on the Fells and also provides leaflets and maps detailing a number of walks or trails. The centre is open daily from Easter to Oct. Tel: Braithwaite 469. It is the starting point of Comb Forest Trail, a 1½ mile (2.4km) waymarked circuit with good views of Derwentwater and Bassenthwaite lake. One mile (1.6km) east of the visitor centre is Noble Knott picnic place overlooking Bassenthwaite. Walks of varying length and steepness start from here through old oak woods,

young silver firs, Douglas fir. larch, spruce and sycamore. Details of a permanent orienteering course can be obtained from the visitor centre.

☐ Visitor centre is two miles (3.2km) W of Braithwaite on B5292. Map ref 14A1.

673. ULLSWATER
Uncrowded Lakeland

Uncrowded Ullswater can be found simply by driving down the minor road along its eastern shore (see map). Most visitors stick to the busy A592 which runs along the western shore. Leave the A592 at the northern end of the lake, where the Dunmallet hill-fort dominates the hamlet of Pooley Bridge, and follow the minor road south via Howtown to Martindale. You are away from the lake as well as the crowds by now and there is a choice of routes up into the Fells. Hallin Fell just north of Martindale village is an outstanding viewpoint over Ullswater. For the more ambitious a marvellous circular walk goes up Boardale over to Patterdale and back to Martindale along the roadless southern shore of Ullswater, approx seven miles (11km) in length but often rugged walking with tremendous views over the lake towards Helvellyn's corries. Roads also

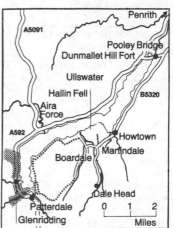

Ullswater: the paths and roads of the quieter southern shore

lead from Martindale village some of the way up Boardale as well as to isolated Dale Head facing the cul-de-sac valleys of Bannerdale and Rampsgill.

☐ Martindale is five miles (8km) SW of Pooley Bridge. Map ref 14B1.

674. WASTWATER
Nature trails in uncrowded Lakeland

Uncrowded because like Ennerdale you have to work your way around the west coast to get into it. A dramatic valley with the deepest lake in England. The lake is followed by a minor road on its northern shore with numerous parking bays. It is popular with climbers since Wasdale Head provides a good, if arduous, way up to Great Gable and Scafell. Far less rigorous are two trails of about $1\frac{1}{2}$ miles (2.4km) each laid out by the Cumbria Naturalists' Trust. Walks vary to include lakeside, mixed woodland, rough fell, a small tarn and riverside, pasture, bog and magnificent views. Leaflet available from national park information offices. The trails start at Nether Wasdale from cattle grid just north of Wasdale Hall six miles (9.6km) east of Gosforth.

☐ The lake is five miles (8km) NE of A595. Map ref 14A2.

675. WORDSWORTH'S LAKES
Lakes and houses

There were other Lake poets Coleridge and Southey – but nobody was more closely identified with the Lake District than William Wordsworth (1770–1850). Three of the houses in which he lived are open to the public. The house at Cockermouth, where he was born and which features in *The Prelude*, is open daily except Thur, Apr to Sept (NT). Tel: Cockermouth 824805. Dove Cottage at Grasmere, where he lived from 1799 1808 is open Mon to Sat, Mar to Oct. Tel: Grasmere 418. And $2\frac{1}{4}$ miles (4km) south of Dove Cottage at Rydal Mount, where he lived from 1813 until his death, the house is open Mar to Dec.

Tel: Ambleside 3002.

Rydal Mount and Dove Cottage each contain some of the poet's personal belongings and are particularly vulnerable to crowding at weekends. The Lakes, of course, were a source of inspiration to Wordsworth as well as his home. **Aira Force** waterfall, the source of the legend in 'The Somnambulist', can be approached by a footpath from a car park close to the junction of A592 and A5091 on the northern shore of Ullswater. **Gowbarrow Park** close to Aira Force is where in 1804 the poet saw his 'host of golden daffodils'. They still grow wild there.

☐ Dove Cottage is at Grasmere which is four miles (6.4km) NW of Ambleside; Wordsworth House at Cockermouth is in the main street of the town which is eight miles (13km) E of Workington. Map ref 14B2.

Durham

Coal mining and industry predominate in the east but to the west are the moors and valleys of the Pennines. Upper Teesdale and Weardale are scenic but the city of Durham, with its cathedral, castle and university, is the prime attraction. Northumbria Tourist Board, Tel: Newcastle-upon-Tyne 817744.

676. BARNARD CASTLE
Market town with a castle and museum

A market town at a crossing point of the River Tees which not only grew around a castle but took its name from it: the present castle was built by one Bernard Balliol. But if the town is now dominated by anything it is not the ruined castle which takes the eye but the Bowes Museum. This was built on the edge of the town in the 19th century in French Renaissance style and houses one of the most important art collections in the country. The museum is open daily all year – afternoons only on Sun – except for a week or so around Christmas and the New Year. Tel: Teesdale 37139.

In the town itself there is a three-tiered octagonal market hall from the 18th century (although livestock markets on Wed are now held in Vine Road) and an even earlier stone bridge across the Tees by the castle. The castle is open standard DoE hours plus Sun mornings Apr to Sept.

Other places worth a visit and only a short distance away include, to the south-east, the ruins of 12th-century Egglestone Abbey and the attractive Greta Bridge where the Greta joins the Tees; to the north-west, Bowes, with the village bisected by the line of a Roman road and a Norman castle set within the old Roman fort; to the north-east Staindrop with yet another medieval castle, Raby Castle; and to the north-west the magnificent waterfalls of Upper Teesdale (see Day Out 683).

☐ 16 miles (26km) W of Darlington on A688. Map ref 15A1.

677. BEAMISH
Farm and industrial museum

A home farm forms part of the 200 acre (494 hectare) North of England Open Air Museum, most of which is concerned with an excellent reconstruction of a northern colliery. There are also tram cars and steam engines. The farmstead itself is mostly as it was in the 1790s with a few Victorian additions, plus geese, cattle and chickens. Open daily Apr to Sept; daily except Mon, Oct to Mar. Tel: Stanley 31811.

☐ Three miles (4.8km) W of Chester-le-Street on A693. Map ref 17D2.

678. BRANCEPETH
Gothic church

The Church of St Brandon is situated in the park of the mainly 19th-century castle, one of Britain's biggest white elephants. This church, Gothic of various dates, is memorable for a remarkably complete set of 17th-century woodwork, partly of 1638 and partly post-Restoration, but all associated with Bishop Cosin of Durham who had been Rector here. The interior is thus exceptionally harmonious.

☐ Four miles (6.4km) SW of Durham on A690. Map ref 15A1.

679. DERWENT WALK
Nature trail along an old railway line

A nature trail through woods and parkland known as the Derwent Walk has been created along the route of a disused railway line. In all the route from Blackhill, near Consett, to Swalwell covers some 10½ miles (17km). It forms the axis of a country park in the Lower Derwent Valley; further areas of woodland are being acquired to extend the park. Throughout its length the Walk passes through a wide variety of trees, shrubs and wild flowers. Horse-riders and cyclists can also use the Walk which is accessible from several points so that shorter stretches can be undertaken. Picnic areas have been established at the sites of several former stations — one at Ebchester is alongside an old signal cabin which during summer weekends is used as an information centre. Trail leaflets are available from the planning departments of Durham County Council and Tyne and Wear Council.

☐ Blackhill is 1½ miles (2.4km) NW of Consett. Map ref 17D2.

680. HAMSTERLEY
Forest drive and walks

A forest drive (toll) leads through 4½ miles (7.2km) of mixed woodland beside the winding Bedburn and Spurlswood Becks. There are several picnic places and six waymarked walks ranging from 1½ miles (2.4km) to an eight mile (13km) trek through the forest to High Acton Moor. A Forestry Commission visitor centre near Bedburn one mile (1.6km) west of Hamsterley has leaflets on the walks as well as displays about the forest. Open weekdays and some summer weekends. Tel: Witton-le-Weas 312. Access to the forest via either Hamsterley west of A68 or Wolsingham off A689.

☐ 10 miles (16km) W of Bishop Auckland. Map ref 15A1.

681. HARDWICK HALL
Country park

This country park is part of what was a landscape garden set in a landscape park. The gardens of Hardwick Hall were created around a 20-acre (8 hectare) lake, which was said to be 'the finest sheet of water in the north of England'. Many features of the gardens have now disappeared, although a $\frac{1}{2}$ mile (0.8km) long lake survives. But by using the map of 18th-century Hardwick, which appears in the information leaflet, you can have hours of fun searching for clues of how it once must have looked here. There is now a nature trail, picnic areas, bird hides, children's play area, a wealth of wildlife in and around the lake and the woodlands, two miles (3.2km) of footpaths and an information centre, with permanent warden service. Tel: Sedgefield 20745. Open daily throughout the year.

☐ Hardwick Hall is situated alongside the A177 Durham to Stockton road, $\frac{3}{4}$ mile (1.2km) W of Sedgefield and $2\frac{1}{2}$ miles from the A1(M) Bradbury interchange. Map ref 15A1.

682. TAN HILL
Highest inn in England

Tan Hill Inn is claimed to be the highest inn in England at 1732ft (534m) above sea level. It is certainly one of the loneliest. It stands at a junction of minor moorland roads which link the A66 following the old Roman route through the Stainmore Gap to the B6270 along Upper Swaledale. The inn has survived in this bleak setting for centuries. In its time it has served colliers from the now deserted mines south-east of the inn, and the 'packmen' who used the inn as a staging post along drovers' roads such as Jagger Lane which goes east and west of Tan Hill. Now the inn caters for motorists touring the Dales and for walkers along the Pennine Way; it is one of very few inns actually on the route of this long-distance footpath.

☐ $3\frac{1}{2}$ miles N of Keld off B6270. Map ref 15A1.

683. UPPER TEESDALE
Waterfalls and river valley

One of England's loveliest valleys. It can be enjoyed by car along the B6277 which heads up the valley from Middleton, once an important lead mining centre. But it can also be walked, following the Pennine Way for some of the route (see map). Head west from Middleton on the southern bank of the Tees along the waymarked Pennine Way. The flat valley floor with its green fields, woods and swinging meanders is soon replaced by gorges and cataracts as the limestone valley walls close in. Three miles (4.8km) upstream is Low Force waterfall; another two miles (3.2km) on is High Force, 70ft (21m) and claimed by many to be England's finest waterfall. It is caused by a very hard band of igneous rock – the Whin Sill – which has invaded the limestone and withstood the river's down cutting. From here the Pennine Way continues steeply across dark moorlands for four miles (6.4km) to Caldron Snout, England's highest fall, cascading down 200 feet (60m) into a formidable gorge. Stout footwear and anoraks are essential for this walk. For those prepared for a longer walk, the Pennine Way continues westwards across the narrow neck of the hills to the hanging valley of High Cup Nick – one of the most spectacular viewpoints in the whole of Britain and accessible only on foot.

But for those disinclined to walk these long distances, Caldron Snout can be approached part of the way by car via the B6277 and a side road at Langdon Beck which leads to a picnic site at Cow Green Reservoir. Here a nature trail allows rare Alpine plants to be examined – but *not* picked; a path leads to Caldron Snout.

☐ Middleton is eight miles (13km) NW of Barnard Castle on B6267. OS map 91. Map ref 15A1.

Greater Manchester

An overwhelmingly urban county despite embracing fringes of the

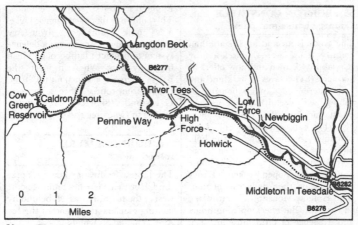

Upper Teesdale: one of England's most spectacular river valleys. Day Out 683

Pennines and Cheshire Plain. North-West Tourist Board, Tel: Bolton 591511.

684. ETHEROW
Country park

This park covers 160 acres (65 hectares) of woodland, marsh and water areas through which the River Etherow flows. There are two nature trails (guide and work books are available) featuring many wild flowers, birds, woodland and game birds, and facilities for sailing, angling and model boats with picnic areas throughout the park and guided tours on request. The park is open daily from dawn till dusk and there is a permanent Warden service. Tel: 061 427 6937.
□ The park is situated at Compstall, off the B6104 three miles (4.8km) E of Stockport. Map ref 11A2

685. HAIGH HALL
Country park

The largest country park in the Greater Manchester area with 370 acres (150 hectares) of wood and heathland offering scope for a multitude of interests including a nature trail, fishing and an arboretum.
□ Two miles (3.2km) NE of Wigan. Map ref 14B3.

Humberside

The area is divided into two by the Humber, with the northern sector having the finest scenery – the Wolds. Other attractions include Burton Agnes Hall, Beverley Minster, the North Sea coastline, and Skipsea Castle. Hull is the major city. Yorkshire and Humberside Tourist Board, Tel: York 707961.

686. BEVERLEY
Market town and agricultural museum in an old windmill

A lively market town which was formerly the county town of the old East Riding. Only one 15th-century gateway survives from the original five. The 13th-century Minster is the outstanding single building but there are many others from later periods. The 18th century for instance contributed the guildhall, an ornate market cross and many fine Georgian houses and shops. Market day is Sat. Four miles (6.4km) south of the town a 19th-century windmill houses an agricultural museum. It is usually open May to Sept, details from Beverley council, Tel: Hull 882255.
□ Nine miles (14km) N of Hull on A1079. Map ref 12B2.

Northern England

687. BURTON CONSTABLE
Country house and park

The grounds around an Elizabethan country house were landscaped by 'Capability' Brown and now offers its 200 acres (81 hectares) of parkland and lake where you can go boating or fishing (with permit). The Yorkshire Farm Machinery Preservation Society also has an exhibition of farm machinery in the stables of the hall, although it is looking for a more permanent home of its own. The house and grounds are open weekends Easter to late May, then daily except non-Bank Holiday Mons and Thur until the end of Sept. But check opening hours and existence of farm museum. Tel: Skirlaugh 62400.

☐ 7½ miles (12km) NE of Hull off B1238. Map ref 12B2.

688. ELSHAM HALL
Country Park and craft centre

A craft shop sometimes has craftsmen at work (pottery, copper, silver, etc) while outdoor attractions in this country park include pony-trekking (by the hour), fishing, a bird sanctuary and guided nature trails on summer Suns or by appointment. Open daily throughout the year but opening hours vary according to season or day. Tel: Barnetby 698.

☐ Four miles (6.4km) NE of Brigg off A15. Map ref 12B2.

689. FLAMBOROUGH HEAD
Clifftop views and nature trail

Reputedly named from the flaming beacon which burned here prior to the construction of the lighthouse, the headland is a grass-covered plateau from which there are fine coastal views. The 150ft (46m) chalk cliffs, the termination of the Yorkshire Wolds at the coast, are riddled with caves and sea stacks such as the King and Queen, Adam and Eve and the outermost High Stacks. Arches can be seen near North Sea Landing and Kindle Scar. There are splendid clifftop walks northwards to Bempton Cliffs, which have one of England's largest seabird colonies. This clifftop walk covers Danes' Dyke, a 2½ mile (4km) long Iron Age embankment constructed as a defence system to protect Flamborough Head from invasion. Where it meets the B1255 there is a short nature trail. Leaflet from tourist office.

☐ Five miles (8km) NE of Bridlington on B1259. Map ref 12B1.

690. HORNSEA MERE
Inland lake

The largest freshwater lake in Yorkshire, Hornsea Mere lies ½ mile (800m) west of the town. It was left behind by melting glaciers at the end of the Ice Age. The lake, which is two miles (3.2km) long and about one mile (1.6km) wide, has good walks around the southern side. Although the public is not allowed access to the RSPB nature reserve it is still possible to see wildfowl and swans. Another legacy of the Ice Age around Hornsea is the clay deposited by retreating ice sheets. This now forms cliffs along the coast which are being eroded more rapidly than any other coastline in Europe if not the world. Take, for instance, the parish church at Mappleton, south of Hornsea. In 1786 the church was 633 yards (579m) from the sea; in 1912 it was 418 yards (382m); and in 1979 only 170 yards (155m).

☐ E of Hornsea off B1244 or B1242. Map ref 12B2.

691. MILLINGTON
One-day walk on the Wolds

This village, on the western edge of the Wolds, can be the base for an excellent day's walk of some 12 miles (19km) along stretches of an unofficial long-distance footpath known as the Wolds Way. The route, which takes the walker through some wonderful chalk valleys, is best started in an eastern direction from Millington towards Warren Farm. OS map 106.

Waymarks then lead north to the end of Greenwick Plantation. Return along track and path to Huggate via Glebe Farm, then along the road

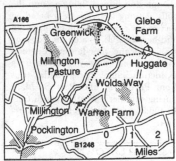

Millington: a seven-mile (11km) walk along part of the Wolds Way

leading south. Walk westwards along a bridle road to Millington Pastures. a well-known local beauty spot. From here the Wolds Way can be retraced via Warren Farm to Millington.

☐ 14 miles (22km) E of York off B1246 and 2½ miles (4km) NE of Pocklington. OS map 106. Map ref 12A2.

---

692. NORMANBY HALL
Regency house and country park

The gardens and grounds around the house have been developed as a country park covering 168 acres (68 hectares) of wooded parkland. Part of this ground is a deer park and there are also museums, a nature trail and bridleways as well as facilities for sports such as fishing and archery. Open Apr to Oct daily except Tues; Nov to Mar daily except Sat. Tel: Scunthorpe 720215.

☐ Four miles (6.4km) N of Scunthorpe on B1430, E of Normanby village. Map ref 12A2.

---

693. PATRINGTON
Decorated church

Remote and little visited, Patrington has the finest Decorated village church in the country, although the spire, soaring aloft through an exquisite pinnacled diadem, was a Perpendicular addition, as was the big east window. As well as the nave, the transepts also have aisles, allowing for some unusual cross-vistas. The pro-

fusion of carved detail is another delight.

☐ 15 miles (24km) SE of Hull on A1033. Map ref 12B2.

---

694. RUDSTON
Standing stone

The tallest standing stone in the country towers over the village church at a height of 25ft 9in (7.8m). It may once have been even larger   not only because its present top appears to be slightly damaged but because of the name it gave to the village which grew around it. *Rood* is an Old English word for 'cross' and *stan* means 'stone'. The monolith is believed to date from the Bronze Age and was probably some kind of pagan symbol. If so the site now represents an example of the quite common practice for Christian churches to adopt pagan holy sites and thereby somehow sanctify them. The stone itself is composed of gritstone which does not occur here naturally; its nearest source is at least 10 miles (16km) away from Rudston.

☐ Five miles (8km) W of Bridlington on B1253. Map ref 12B1.

---

695. SPURN HEAD
Sand spit and nature reserve

A three mile (4.8km) long sand spit in places only 150ft (45m) wide. Its shape has changed many times over the centuries as a result of coast erosion, sometimes being obliterated altogether and taking with it lost towns such as one called Ravenspur where Henry Bolingbroke landed in July 1399. A month later he forced Richard II to abdicate and himself founded the Lancastrian dynasty. Now artificial groynes help to preserve Spurn Head but it is still breached by exceptional seas. Its isolation has made it a good place for bird watching. The Yorkshire Naturalists' Trust has a nature reserve and bird sanctuary here, access and parking is limited. Tel: York 59570. No dogs.

☐ 25 miles (40km) SE of Hull on private road at end of B1445. Map ref 12B2.

Northern England

A partly independent holiday isle, with varied scenery and a mild climate. Attractions include Tynwald parliament at Douglas, Snaefell mountain railway and Peel Castle. Isle of Man Tourist Board, Tel: Douglas 4323.

696. THE AYRES
Sandy beaches and Ice Age legacy

A wilderness of flat heathland behind miles of deserted sandy beaches at the northern tip of the island. There are picnic sites and car parks at Ballaghennie and Point of Ayre where the old and new lighthouses are notable landmarks – the one in current use is open to the public. Tel: Douglas 88238. There are miles of walks over the heather-covered shingle ridges of the ancient storm beaches, behind which is the bewildering hummocky terrain of a gigantic terminal moraine of a former ice-sheet – termed the Bride Moraine, from Bride village. To the north of the A3 Sulby to Ballaugh road is the Curraghs Wild Life Park, open Easter to Sept. Tel: Sulby 7323. In Ramsey itself the Grove Rural Life Museum recreates the household of a Victorian businessman with a horse-driven threshing mill among the agricultural equipment on show. Open daily except Sat from mid-May to Sept but afternoons only Sun. Tel: Ramsey 5522.

□ Seven miles (14km) N of Ramsey off A16. Map ref 8A1.

697. CALF OF MAN
Nature reserve and bird-watching

This small island with its steep cliffs and pebbly beaches – off the south-west tip of the Isle of Man – is one of the most exciting spring and autumn migration points in the British Isles; 233 species of bird have been recorded here. Its 620 acres (250 hectares) are owned by the Manx National Trust and managed as a reserve. Before even reaching the islet, visitors are likely to spot shag, chough and fulmar flying around the cliffs. Among the 37 regular breeding species are razorbill, guillemot, puffin and herring gull. Watch also for grey seals and the four-horned Loghton sheep – only narrowly saved from extinction. There are regular day-trips from Port Erin and Port St Mary during summer – weather permitting.

□ Off SW tip of Isle of Man. Map ref 8A1.

698. CASTLETOWN
Nature trail

Just outside this old capital of the island – with its fine 14th-century fortress of Castle Rushen – is the Scarlett nature trail of geological as well as natural history interest. Limestone (rare on this island of slate) and the only volcanic rocks on the Isle of Man are both magnificently exposed along the waymarked trail which in its shortest version is 1¼ miles (2km) long. There is also a wealth of plant and bird life, with thyme, birdsfoot trefoil and stonecrop on the clifftops, excellent seaweed zonation on the rocky low-tide shores, an interesting array of lichens and a seabird colony on the columnar basalt rocks known as the Stack. This is a favourite haunt for gulls, auks, shag and cormorant. Among passage migrants are whimbrel, whinchat, yellow wagtail and golden plover. Details of this and other trails on the island from local bookshops or the Manx tourist centre in Douglas.

□ The nature trail is ½ mile (0.8km) SW of Castletown. Leave Castletown Square by Queen Street and follow the road which leads round the bay. There is car parking space at Scarlett Quarry – Stop 1 of the trail. Map ref 8A1.

699. CREGNEASH
Coastal scenery and a 'living museum' village

The village is sited on a peninsula at the extreme south-western tip of the island which offers coastal scenery as spectacular as anything in south-west England or Pembrokeshire. There are the dramatic cliffs and savage tidal currents of Calf Sound between the mainland and the islet of Calf of Man (see Day Out 697). Coastal walks include the narrow gorges called the Chasms north-east of Spanish Head or the western cliffs which rise northwards beyond Port Erin to the 700ft (210m) precipices of Bradda Head. From the latter there can be excellent views as far as the mountains of Mourne and Snowdonia.

In Cregneash itself is the Manx Folk Museum with many examples of traditional crafts such as a smithy, weaver's shed and a crofter-fisherman's cottage. The cottages have been restored with great care and sensitivity. The thatching, for instance, has been redone in the comparatively rare Southside Manx style, using wheat straw. A small flock of the rare Manx Loghton sheep complete the picture of Cregneash as a 'living museum'. The village is worth visiting at any time but the folk museum as such is open daily May to Sept but afternoons only on Sun. Tel: Douglas 5522.
☐ Five miles (8km) W of Castletown on A31. Map ref 8A1.

700. GLEN MONA
Mountain and coastal walks

A good centre from which to explore some of the island's most beautiful scenery. Footpaths lead to the foothills of 2036ft (621m) Snaefell or to the head of lonely Glen Cornaa. Seawards, there are walks down the beautiful wooded Glen Mona or Ballaglass Glen to the enchanting hidden bay of Port Cornaa. Two miles (3.2km) south is the picturesque Dhoon Glen with its waterfalls, rapids and hanging wood-lands, whilst to the north are the rocky coastal cliffs of Maughold Head and its lighthouse (open every afternoon except Sun). For the archaeologically-minded, just over ½ mile (800m) east of Glen Mona there is the excellent example of a Neolithic gallery grave or long cairn at Cashtal-yn-Ard, grid ref SC 462892; OS map 95.
☐ 4½ miles (7.2km) S of Ramsey on A2. Map ref 8A1.

701. LAXEY
Mountain railway and the world's largest waterwheel

The A18 road passes close to the summit of 2036ft (621m) Snaefell, the island's highest (and only) mountain. The electric railway which starts from Laxey goes right to the top. Also here is picturesque Laxey Glen but the old harbour town is dominated by the world's largest surviving waterwheel – the Lady Isabella. The huge wheel, which is 72ft (22m) in diameter, was already out of date when it began service in 1854. Its function was to pump water out of the lead mines and it did so by using the free-running waters draining off the eastern slopes of Snaefell. On the English mainland, where coal was plentiful, similar wheels which had existed in mining areas such as the Pennines and Cornwall were then being abandoned in favour of steam pumps. The Laxey mines closed in 1919 but if the wheel had a limited life in the mining industry, it has since served the island's tourist industry well. The wheel is open daily from approx Easter to Sept. Occasionally it has to close for repairs, so it might be best to check, especially early in the season. Tel: Douglas 26262.
☐ Seven miles (11km) NW of Douglas off A11. Map ref 8A1.

Lancashire

A varied county with moors, plain and vast sandy beaches plus heavy industry in the south. Attractions include Lancaster and seaside resorts for all tastes. North-West Tourist Board, Tel: Bolton 591511.

702. BLACKSTONE EDGE
Britain's finest surviving Roman road

The finest exposed piece of original Roman road in the country – so fine that a few experts have doubted that its paving stones and kerb stones may owe more to packhorse days than Roman. Most historians, however, are con-vinced of its Roman origins. It is on the

Northern England

line of the Roman road between the forts at Manchester (*Mamucium*) and Ilkley (*Olicana*) and is exposed as it climbs the Pennines near Littleborough. The road surface is 16ft (5m) wide with a central channel and ditches on either side.

□ One mile (1.6km) E of Littleborough on A58, then by signposted footpath. Grid ref SD 975170; OS map 109. Map ref 15A3.

703. FORMBY HILLS
Sand dunes and nature trails

By 1910 the ancient fishing village of Formby was buried under the dunes and a new town has now grown up two miles (3.2km) from the coast. Dunes have been building up here for thousands of years from glacial deposits offshore. Take care when swimming as tides are swift along this coast. There is a 1¾ mile (2.8km) nature trail on Formby Point where you may see birds such as oyster catcher or sanderling and animals such as red squirrels or natterjack toads. The trail is open all year and a leaflet is available from the NT hut at the trail start in the car park at the end of Victoria Road (past Freshfield Station, Formby). Or, out of season, contact the Lancashire Naturalists' Trust; Tel: Slaidburn 294. Always open. Three miles (4.8km) to the north near Ainsdale is an NCC reserve consisting of 1216 acres (492 hectares) of dunes, marshes and pinewoods. There is a three mile (4.8km) nature trail through an area which contains some 380 species of flowering plants and many species of birds and butterflies. Reserve is ½ mile (0.8km) from Freshfield Station: cross the railway line and then the golf course (via Montagu Road). Reserve is on the coastal strip.

□ W of Formby which is six miles SW of Southport on A565. Map ref 14B3.

704. HEALEY DELL
Walks in a moorland clough

A beautiful Lancashire clough (deep valley) just two miles (3.2km) from Rochdale town centre with woods,

waterfalls, a so-called 'Fairy Chapel' of curious waterworn rocks and a history going back to Saxon times. The nature trail reveals a disused railway, flourishing rookery, and a profusion of plants: rushes, ferns, mosses, orchids and moorland grasses. A comprehensive reserve booklet published by Lancashire Naturalists' Trust is available at reserve entrance. Tel: Slaidburn 294.

□ Two miles (3.2km) NW of Rochdale off A671 at junction of Market Street and Shawclough Road. Map ref 15A3.

705. HOGHTON TOWER
Elizabethan house and gardens

A fortified 16th-century hilltop house, restored during the 19th century but containing 17th-century panelling. Inside is an exhibition of dolls' houses; outside are walled gardens and an old rose garden. Open Easter except Good Fri, Sun late Apr to Oct plus Sat July to Aug, afternoons only. Tel: Hoghton 2986.

□ Five miles (8km) SE of Preston on A675. Map ref 14B3.

706. LYTHAM ST ANNES
Nature reserve

This reserve consists of sand dunes and damp dune slacks, all that remains of a much more extensive dune system. In the past this site suffered considerable human disturbance. Today the reserve shows recolonisation by characteristic dune plants such as marram grass and sea buckthorn. A booklet produced by the Lancashire Naturalists' Trust, and available at the reserve, details a walk through the reserve. Tel: Slaidburn 294. Open all year.

□ Lytham St Annes is six miles (9.6km) S of Blackpool on A584; the nature reserve is E of the town off Clifton Drive North. Map ref 14B3.

707. MORECAMBE BAY
Sandy bay and bird-watching

At low tide almost 50 sq miles (38,850 hectares) of sand or mud are exposed in this vast bay which straddles the

Lancashire-Cumbria boundary. But it can be treacherous – listen for siren warning that the tide is coming in and do not attempt to walk over the sand to Furness ('Fur-Ness' – the far peninsula) without a guide. Once, though, there were daily coach services across the sands from Hest Bank, just north of Morecambe, to Kent's Bank, just south of Grange-over-Sands: a distance of seven miles (11km).

Good viewpoints over the bay are Arnside Knott (see Day Out 645); Hampsfell Hospice, two miles (3.2km) north of Grange-over-Sands where there is also a woodland nature trail; and Humphrey Head, south of Kent's Bank. The bay is an excellent area for bird-watching, especially in winter with large flocks of ducks, waders, geese and seabirds. At Leighton Moss, between the villages of Silverdale and Yealand Redmayne, is an important RSPB reserve.

This reserve is one of the few places in the British Isles where you are likely to see otters. Dense reedbeds around the meres shelter Britain's most northerly breeding bitterns and many other species. Rarities include migrant ospreys and marsh harriers. Also frogs, dragonflies, sticklebacks and eels. The reserve is open during the summer. Permits and leaflets are available from its reception centre; further information from RSPB Reserves Dept. Tel: Sandy 80551.
□ Map ref 14B2.

708. RIBCHESTER
Roman fort

Sited on the north bank of the River Ribble where the Roman road from Manchester to Carlisle crossed it from Ilkley to the Fylde, it was the headquarters for some of Rome's toughest soldiers – the Sarmatian heavy cavalry. Parts of the fort, *Bremetennacum,* are visible and finds from the site are displayed in the adjoining museum. Open afternoons except Fri, Feb to Nov; Sat afternoons only, Dec to Jan. Tel: Ribchester 261.
□ Nine miles (14km) NE of Preston on B6245. Map ref 14B3.

709. RUFFORD
Medieval Hall and folk museum

The Old Hall, owned by the NT, is a medieval timber-framed manor house with an outstanding hammerbeam roof. The hall is late 15th-century with wings added in the 17th and 19th centuries. One wing contains the Philip Ashcroft Folk Museum, a collection of ancient farm implements and domestic relics from Lancastrian life. Open afternoons daily Apr to Sept, daily except Mon and Wed in Mar and from Oct to Christmas. Closed late Dec to Feb. Tel: Rufford 821254.
□ Seven miles (11km) N of Ormskirk on A59. Map ref 14B3.

710. WYCOLLER
Country park

A 352 acre (147 hectares) country park of heath, grassland and open moorland near the historic village of Wycoller. In the village is a picturesque packhorse bridge and a number of fascinating old stone buildings. The park has extensive views over the surrounding countryside, picnic areas, nature walks and bridleways on the slopes of the Pennines. The car park is ⅓ mile (500m) from the village and the country park. Open daily throughout the year. Further information from Countryside Officer of Lancashire County Council; Tel: Preston 54733.
□ The park lies three miles (4.8km) E of Colne. From Colne centre take A6068 for ¾ mile then B6250 towards Trawden for ¼ mile (400m). Wycoller is signposted through Winewall. Map ref 15A3.

Merseyside

Dominated by Liverpool – its main attraction – and the River Mersey. Also containing Southport. North-West Tourist Board, Tel: Bolton 591511.

711. THE WIRRAL
River estuary and country parks

The Wirral peninsula has become part

Northern England

of the Merseyside conurbation. It is a sandy rimmed peninsula with the River Dee on one side and the Mersey on the other. Since the Dee silted up the Mersey has taken over as the major shipping channel. The tide in the Dee estuary comes in very quickly and it is possible to get marooned. The area is noted for its bird life, particularly in autumn. One of the small islets at the mouth of the estuary is a bird observatory. It can be reached at low tide from West Kirby or Hoylake but permits are required. From Thurstaston Hill there is a fine view of the estuary while just south of Thurstaston village on the Dee estuary there is an excellent visitor centre for the Wirral Country Park – the first country park to be opened. It stretches between West Kirby and Parkgate, an interesting shrimping village, along the route of a disused railway line. In all, the park covers 43 acres (17 hectares) and includes three nature trails. Leaflets are available from the visitor centre, which is open all year except Christmas Day although opening hours vary according to season. Tel: 051 648 4371. From the centre there are fine walks along the cliffs or along the sandy beach. Some old railway stations have been turned into picnic areas. On the Mersey side of the Wirral is another country park at Eastham Woods, six miles (9.6km) SE of Birkenhead, off the A41, with a nature trail and river views.

□ Thurstaston visitor centre is signposted SW off A540 six miles (9.6km) SW of Birkenhead. Map ref 8D1.

Northumberland

England's most northerly county and quintessential Border country – it boasts the Roman Hadrian's Wall and many fine Norman castles. Towns include Berwick-on-Tweed and Alnwick. Outstanding scenery inland (Northumberland national park) and on the coast (AONB). A new attraction soon will be the Kielder reservoir, now in its final stages. Northumbria Tourist Board, Tel: Newcastle-upon-Tyne 817744.

712. BAMBURGH
Castle on the coast

The village and dune-sheltered beach are dominated by a majestic castle – one of the most dramatic in England. The present building dates largely from the 19th century but even the original Norman castle (of which the keep remains) was not the first fortress to occupy this rocky crag of igneous basalt called the Whin Sill which runs the width of the Northumberland national park. For 300 years before the Norman Conquest this was the capital of the kingdom of Northumbria. The castle is open afternoons daily, Mar to Oct. Tel: Bamburgh 208. Also in Bamburgh is the Grace Darling Museum in honour of the heroic daughter of the keeper of the Longstone lighthouse (see Day Out 722) who in 1838 saved the lives of eight ship-wrecked travellers. Open Apr to mid-Oct.

□ 17 miles (27km) S of Berwick-on-Tweed on B1340. Map ref 17D1.

713. BLANCHLAND
'Model' village and ancient inn

This 'model' village in the Derwent Valley has been well restored in recent years; a ban on car-parking in the village square helps as it would in many other traffic-congested villages and market towns. Blanchland, as it now stands, dates mainly from the 18th century, but it was built around the site of an abbey founded seven centuries earlier by an order known as the Premonstratensians. The 13th-century church incorporates what remains of the old abbey church. Otherwise the village's most distinguished building is probably the inn, the Lord Crewe Arms. It was formerly a manor house and also includes some of the old abbey buildings, notably the Abbot's Lodging, the Guest House and the abbey kitchen and food store, while the old cloisters now form the inn's garden. One of the bedrooms is reputed to be haunted, but that is another story.

□ Nine miles (14.4km) S of Hexham on B6306. Map ref 17C2.

714. BOLAM LAKE
Country park

Over 90 acres (37 hectares) of lake and woodland here comprise a country park offering fishing, bird-watching, forest walks and boating (inflatables and canoes only). The park is open daily throughout the year and entry is free. Picnic areas are conveniently situated throughout the park, close to the car parks. There is a small visitor centre, which opens at irregular hours. If the centre is not manned, information and leaflets are provided at the park signboards.

□ The park lies 16 miles (26km) NE of Newcastle via A696 to Belsay and is signposted from three miles (4.8km) outside Belsay. Map ref 17D2

715. BORDER FOREST PARK
Forest drives, walks and lake

The park extends over 145,000 acres (58,700 hectares) along the Cheviots and neighbouring hills. Between them and beyond the few main roads forest roads lead to hill tracks linking the dales. Peel Fell at 1975ft (602m) is the park's highest point and stands right on the Border. There are views from its summit across northern England and southern Scotland from the North Sea to the Solway Firth. The area is rich in history with hill-forts, Roman camps, fortified farmsteads and castles.

A Forestry Commission Visitor Centre is open late May to Sept at Kielder Castle which was built as a shooting lodge in the 18th century for the Duke of Northumberland. This is 17 miles (27km) north-west of Bellingham on the C200 road which runs for approx 25 miles (40km) from Bellingham on the B6320 to Saughtree on B6357. Opening hours of the visitor centre vary from weekdays to weekends. Tel: Kielder 50209. Facilities in different parts of the Park include Wark Forest (Day Out 732) and the following:
Kielder Forest: a drive along 12 miles (19km) of forest roads starting from either Kielder Castle (see above) or Blakeshopeburnhaugh, two miles

(3.2km) SE of Byrness on A68. Short walks and picnic places along the drive for which a toll is charged. Kielder Castle will be at the northern tip of the vast new Kielder reservoir now being formed in Northumberland and due to be completed in 1982. Between Kielder Castle and Falstone along or off the minor road to Bellingham described above there are a number of picnic places. One of these is at Ferny Knowe, near Falstone, where there is also an information centre with an exhibition on the Kielder reservoir scheme. Open Easter to Oct. Leaflets available from the Tower Knowe visitor centre. Open Easter to Oct.
Duchess Drive: circular waymarked paths lead up the Kielder Burn and round Castle Hill. Three loops of 1½ miles (2.4km), two miles (3.2km) or five miles (8km) start from Kielder Castle visitor centre (as above).
Redesdale Forest: Blakeshopeburnhaugh picnic place is in a glade of a spruce forest by the River Rede. Short riverside walk. Located two miles SE of Byrness off A68. Cottonshopeburn picnic place is in a small attractive side valley of the River Rede 1¼ miles (2km) SE of Byrness. Day permit trout fishing on about one mile (1.6km) of the river is available.

□ Map ref 17C1.

716. CAMBO
Village and country house

The village was part of a 13,000 acre (5263 hectares) estate which in 1942 was given along with 16 farms and 17th to 18th-century Wallington Hall to the NT. Much of the land on the Wallington estate lies beyond the 1000ft (305m) contour so that the farms represented a similar brand of pioneering to that introduced to Exmoor by the Knight family (see Day Out 122). Wallington Hall itself is open afternoons except Tues, Apr to Sept, then Wed, Sat and Sun afternoons in Oct. The grounds, which include a lake and a walled flower garden are open daily all year. Tel: Scots Gap 283.

□ 12 miles (19km) W of Morpeth off B6342. Map ref 17C2.

Northern England

717. CHEVIOT HILLS
Mountain drive and walk

For one of the loneliest roads in the Border country, drive into the uppermost reaches of Coquetdale by taking the lane which leads west from Alwinton. Follow the tortuous windings of the Coquet past lonely farmsteads deep into the hills, with nothing to break the solitude except the moorland sheep. Continue on the tarmac road steeply up to the last hill farm at Makendon and walk the remaining mile (1.6km) to what must have been one of the loneliest Roman fortresses in Britain or, for the more energetic, reach the highest of the Cheviot Hills – Windy Gyle (2036ft, 619m) – by taking a track which leaves the road going north-west towards the summit via Hindside Knowe. This follows the spur known as the Street and strikes the summit ridge near Mozie Law. A one mile (1.6km) walk eastward along the Pennine Way gives striking views of the Cheviot (2676ft, 810m) and glimpses into the deeply incised Scottish valleys beneath. Complete a memorable seven mile (11.2km) walk by returning southwards via Little Ward Law and the farm at Trows – but look out for the warning flags of the artillery ranges. Boots, anoraks and experience of hill-walking required for the longer walks.
☐ Alwinton is 10 miles (16km) NW of Rothbury off B6341 on minor roads. OS map 80. Map ref 17C1.

718. CHILLINGHAM
Rare animals

The Chillingham Wild White Cattle are probably the last herd of horned white cattle which remains in Britain today. Cattle such as these, descendents of prehistoric wild oxen, have grazed the foothills of the Cheviots for over 700 years. They now roam the 300 acres of parkland which surrounds Chillingham Castle. Open Apr to Oct except Tues. Tel: Chatton 213 (office) or 250 (park warden).
☐ Four miles (6.4km) SE of Wooler off B6348. Map ref 17D1.

719. CRAGSIDE
Country house and park

Cragside was built between 1869 and 1896, mainly to the designs of Norman Shaw. The client was Lord Armstrong, millionaire inventor and manufacturer of hydraulic machinery and armaments. Hidden at the heart of 900 acres (364 hectares) of park is a romantic medley of towers, chimney stacks and half-timbered gables which climb up a hillside so steep that the second floor is below ground level at the back of the house. Inside, inglenooks, stained glass, winding corridors and staircases, pre-Raphaelite pictures, boudoir, billiard-room and gun-room vividly recreate the mixture of fantasy and practicality that made up the habitat of a Victorian tycoon. The house (now NT) is open afternoons (except Mon other than Bank Holidays) mid-Apr to Sept and then on weekend and Wed afternoons in Oct. The grounds, which are noted for their rhododendrons, now also form a country park with waterfalls, lakes and streams. Four waymarked walks lead from the three main car parks; details of these walks are shown on information boards at the car parks. The country park is open daily Apr to Oct, then weekends only Nov to Mar. Tel: Rothbury 20333.
☐ Near Rothbury 13 miles (21km) SW of Alnwick on B6341. Map ref 17C1.

720. CRASTER
Walks, kippers and castle

Famous for its kippers – the oak-curing kipper sheds can be visited – but outstanding also for its scenery, part of the Northumberland Coast AONB. A coastal path leads north for $1\frac{1}{2}$ miles (2.4km) to Dunstanburgh Castle, a ruined 14th-century castle standing on cliffs 100ft (30m) above the sea. Beneath the walls of the castle – open standard DoE hours plus Sun mornings Apr to Sept – is a chasm called Egyn Cleugh and a derelict harbour.
This is part of a rewarding three mile (4.8km) coastal walk from Craster car

park to Low Newton which passes a wide range of dune plants and colonies of kittiwake, fulmar and ringed plover. Leaflets are available from the NT caravan in Craster car park Apr to Oct, from the hide at Newton Pool (see below); or NT regional office (Tel: Scots Gap 234). At Newton Pool, just south of Low Newton, is an NT nature reserve with an observation hide always open. Tel: Embleton 365 or Scots Gap 234.

□ Six miles (9.6km) NE of Alnwick off B1339. Map ref 17D1.

721. ELSDON
Border village

This has one of the biggest greens, some seven acres (2.8 hectares), among the many 'green' villages of Northumberland's 'Border Country'. Elsdon was the former territorial capital of Redesdale and still has the remains of a Norman motte-and-bailey style castle. In peaceful times its large green served as a market-place for sheep driven across the Pennines through a complex network of drovers' roads; in less peaceful times it offered security for the village livestock as the village defended itself by stockading all the gaps between the houses set around the green. Another reminder of its turbulent days as a frontier settlement is the 14th-century pele tower house, a fortified parsonage generally regarded as the finest of such buildings surviving in Northumberland. The church itself is in the middle of the green (also for security) while at the edge of the green is a stone cattle pound or pinfold.

□ 27 miles (43km) NW of Newcastle-upon-Tyne on B6341 off A696. Map ref 17C1.

722. FARNE ISLANDS
Nature reserve and trails

There are 28 outcrops in the sea of the volcanic rock known as the Whin Sill which covers much of Northumberland. They lie between two to five miles (3 to 8km) off the shore but only three islands can be visited by the public: the Inner Farne, Staple Island and Longstone. Boat trips operate from Seahouses (weather permitting). The NT charges a landing fee; no dogs are allowed. The Inner Farne has a 14th-century chapel and a pele or fortified tower, plus the famous Longstone lighthouse (see also Day Out 712). But the islands are best known as breeding grounds for seals and seabirds.

This NT reserve is one of the most important in the country and access may be restricted during the breeding season – mid-May to mid-July. Among the birds which breed here are puffin, guillemot, razorbill, shag, up to 1000 eider duck and three species of tern (arctic, common and roseate). There are nature trails on Inner Farne and Staple Island – get trail leaflets and information about boat services available from NT and tourist information office at Seahouses, Tel: Seahouses 720424 or NT Northumberland regional office, Tel: Scots Gap 234.

□ Off coast from Seahouses which is 15 miles (24km) N of Alnwick on B1339. Map ref 17D1.

723–726. HADRIAN'S WALL
Roman frontier wall

The most dramatic Roman monument in the landscape of Britain, originally stretching 73 miles (117km) from Wallsend-on-Tyne (Tyne and Wear) in the east through Northumberland to Bowness-on-Solway on the Cumbrian coast. It was built of stone up to 20ft (6m) high in the east and turf 12ft (3.7m) high in the west and used every natural advantage offered by the contours of the land. Dotted along its length were forts, milecastles – smaller forts between the larger ones – signal stations and a supporting infrastructure of roads, depots and military outposts.

An integral part of the defences was a system of ditches and earthworks – see illustration indicating their original dimensions. The road running between wall and *vallum* was known as the Military Way, but should not be confused with the Military Road built parallel with the wall after the Jacobite rebellion of 1745. This much later road

Northern England

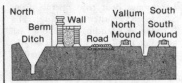

Cross-section of the Roman Wall in its heyday. The vallum was not always this close to the wall, since it ran on a straight course while the wall took advantage of the contours of the land in order to maximise its defensive strength

actually robbed the wall of many stones, but enough remains to convey a dramatic echo of life in Roman Britain. Even today it can seem a wild, if beautiful, place and it does not need a vivid imagination to comprehend what a posting on the wall must have been like for the Roman legionnaires.

Today, however, the people who walk along the wall do so for pleasure. And in places they do so in sufficient numbers to threaten the foundations which have lasted since AD 122–130 when the wall was first built. Large sections of the wall can still be followed, particularly in its central sector, either on foot or by car. But because roads leading to the forts can be crowded in high season there is a special bus service operated by the Northumberland national park authorities from their Once Brewed Information Centre on the Military Road (B6318) 2½ miles (4km) west of Housesteads. Open mid-Apr to late Oct. Tel: Barden Mill 396.

OS maps 85–88 in the 1:50,000 series cover the entire length of the wall – numbers 86 and 87 feature the most visited sections. But the OS also publishes a special two inch to the mile (roughly 1:31,680) devoted solely to Hadrian's Wall. Detailed guidebooks on the history of the wall or suggesting walks can be obtained locally.

A number of forts, camps or milecastles along the wall have been excavated and can now be visited   see map. Birdoswald is described in Day Out 652. Listed below are some of the most interesting Northumberland sites – all of which, with their accompanying museums, are open standard DoE hours plus Sun mornings Apr to Sept.

723. Housesteads

A garrison fort (*Vercovicium*) covering three acres (1.2 hectares) of moorland and the only one to have been completely excavated. In fact, excavations are still under way and will probably reveal traces of the buildings that preceded the largely 4th-century remains that are visible. The complex building history of this site is well explained in a site museum. An important element in the appeal of this fort is its position on a notably dramatic section of the wall with fine views over Crag Lough. A little to the south-west of Housesteads is Chesterholm or *Vindolanda*, the site of another fort, where a turret and length of wall have been reconstructed in their original form and size. Considerable archaeological finds have been made here recently. *Vindolanda* lies midway between the Military Road and Barden Mill.

☐ 10 miles (16km) NW of Hexham off B6318. Map ref 17C2.

724. Chesters

Another fort (*Cilurnum*) in a specta-

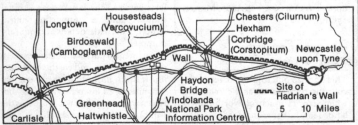

Hadrian's Wall, the northwest frontier of the Roman world, spanned the neck of England from coast to coast, a distance of 73 miles (117km)

cular position. It was the headquarters of a cavalry unit and visitors can see gateways, a barrack block and, among other remains, a complete bath house close to the River Tyne. It was here that the wall crossed the Tyne and the remains of the bridge are still visible.
☐ Four miles (6.4km) N of Hexham off B6318. Map ref 17C2.

725. Corbridge
This is a short distance south of the wall but worth a detour for here was the great supply base of *Corstopitum* for the Roman soldiers manning the wall two or three miles (3 to 5km) to the north. Workshops as well as temples have been found here. Good site museum.
☐ Three miles (5km) E of Hexham on western edge of Corbridge off A68. Map ref 17C2.

726. A walk along the wall
Many walks can be done along the wall. This one also incorporates part of the Pennine Way and totals 20 miles (32km) but it can easily be broken into shorter walks. Start from the village of Greenhead three miles (4.8km) northwest of Haltwhistle at the junction of A69 and B6318, the 'Military Road'. Half a mile (0.85km) north of Greenhead the Pennine Way crosses the B6318. Follow Pennine Way signs since from here to the Steel Rigg viewpoint and car park the long-distance footpath follows the route of the wall itself. Immediately south of Steel Riggs is the Once Brewed youth hostel and national park information centre (see above for details). Follow the wall then as far as Housesteads and ascend Sewingshield summit before heading back to Greenhead. You can, of course, start from several other places en route and similarly return without completing the full 20 mile (32km) distance. OS map 86 details this and other paths so that circular routes can be devised if you would prefer to avoid retracing your steps.
☐ Map ref 17C2.

727. HEATHERSLAW MILL
Mill and farm museum
The mill stands on the banks of the River Till midway between the villages of Ford and Etal. A massive 19th-century stone building, it occupies a site used by a water-driven corn mill since the 13th century. For the last 50 years of its working life this was primarily a pearl barley mill, and few such mills can still be seen in working order; leaflets and exhibits within the mill explain the distinctive nature of barley milling. Until recently the mill and its outbuildings also housed an agricultural museum but flooding has now jeopardised the continued existence of the museum on this site. As this book went to press the museum exhibits were housed in an old drying kiln opposite the mill, but its owners are looking for a new home. The mill is open daily, Apr to Oct. Tel: Crookham 338.
☐ On B6354 between Ford and Etal 11 miles (17.6km) SW of Berwick-on-Tweed. Map ref 17C1.

728. HEXHAM
Market town with Saxon crypt
There was a Saxon bishopric established here in the 7th century and although the town, then known as Hagulstad, was largely destroyed by the Norsemen, a Saxon crypt survives in the priory church. In the south transept is a large Roman memorial stone showing a Roman standard-bearer riding roughshod over an ancient Briton. Although this otherwise mostly 13th-century church is probably the most distinguished individual building in the town there are many others of note, including the 15th-century Moot Hall and a 14th-century prison known euphemistically as the Manor Office and now housing a museum devoted to Border history and a tourist information office. Open daily and Sun afternoons in summer; closed Sun in winter. Tel: Hexham 605225. There is also a 13th-century bridge over Halgut Burn which joins the River Tyne at Hexham. The town still serves as an agricultural centre for the surrounding Northumberland countryside. Market day: Tues.
☐ 23 miles (37km) W of Newcastle-upon-Tyne on A69. Map ref 17C2.

729. LINDISFARNE
Island priory, castle and nature reserve

The approach to the island is dramatic – across a causeway from Beal which is uncovered at low tides. You can save yourself a wasted journey by checking the tides in advance; Tel: Northumbria Tourist Board, Newcastle 817744. Once on the island, there is much to see.

The buildings include an 11th-century priory (open standard DoE hours plus Sun mornings Apr to Sept), a 12th to 13th-century church, and Lindisfarne Castle, a small 16th-century fort (NT) which earlier this century was turned into a holiday home for Edward Hudson, founder of *Country Life*. The Edwardian maestro Sir Edward Lutyens was responsible for the work which was romantic, inventive – and uncomfortable. Features are stone vaults, massive arches, winding stairs and superb views over the island with its limestone cliffs and sand dunes. Open daily except Fri mid-Apr to Sept, Wed, Sat and Sun early Apr; and weekend afternoons only in Oct. Tel: NT regional office, Scots Gap 234.

The wildlife of the island is equally famous, although the national nature reserve is best seen out of season when there are fewer visitors and more birds, including huge numbers of geese, duck (up to 25,000 wigeon), arctic swans and flocks of waders. Lindisfarne is the only place where pale-bellied Brent geese from Spitzbergen winter regularly. Dunes, saltmarsh and mudflats combine to create a magical expanse of wild coast. Seals are often seen, and many interesting plants grow in the dune slacks, including grass of Parnassus and northern marsh orchids. Tel: reserve office, Belford 386.
□ Five miles (8km) E of Beal. Map ref 17D1.

730. STOCKSFIELD
Farm museum

This farm museum is centred around its unique display of vintage tractors, although there are many other items depicting farm life and machinery over the centuries. These include a working waterwheel and mill, a 13th-century wishing well, a farmhouse kitchen and an animal enclosure. A short length of narrow gauge railway is due to open soon. Open daily throughout year, except over Christmas, although opening hours are shorter during winter. Tel: Stocksfield 2553.
□ W of Corbridge on A69 near junction with A68. Map ref 17C2.

731. WANSBECK
Reclaimed riverside country park

The park takes its name from the river which runs through its 143 acres (58 hectares) of grass and woodland. A weir has been built where the river joins the sea to maintain the water at a high level. This has two advantages: one is that it permanently covers some rather unsightly mudflats and the other is the creation of a tide-free sheltered lagoon for canoeing and sailing. For landlubbers this 2½ mile (4km) long 'lake' offers waterside walks, picnic areas, camping and a one mile (1.6km) nature trail. Leaflets are available from either Wansbeck council offices in Ashington – Tel: Ashington 814444 – or the warden who is based at the park's caravan site throughout the year. What makes the park especially admirable is the fact that in 1970 this now attractive and popular site was a derelict and virtually inaccessible stretch of riverside.
□ ½ mile (800m) S of Ashington. Car park, picnic area and trail start are via Wellhead Dene Road which is E off A1068 between Ashington and Guide Post. Map ref 17D1.

732. WARK FOREST
Forest walks

Warksburn picnic place is beside a stream in an open glade in tall spruce forest at Stonehaugh. The Warksburn Trail and three other waymarked forest walks start from here; leaflets are available from an honesty box at car park by picnic site. Access from

Chollerford on B6320 to Nunwick where there is a left turn signposted Stonehaugh. (See also Day Out 715.)
□ NW of Hexham. Map ref 17C2.

733. WARKWORTH
Norman castle

This small town within a loop of the River Coquet was laid out in the 12th century. It has all the features of a Norman planned settlement plus the characteristic of a border town – even the bridge across the river is fortified. The main street, connecting church and castle, served as the market-place. Much of the medieval street layout remains and a great deal of Norman work survives in the large 12th-century church. There are also impressive remains of the castle – a setting for part of Shakespeare's *Henry IV* since it was the birthplace of Henry Percy (Hotspur). The castle is open standard DoE hours plus Sun mornings Apr to Sept.

Half a mile (800m) from the castle is a 14th-century hermitage and chapel set into the cliff (AM); it is reached by boat and is open standard DoE hours plus Sun mornings Apr to Sept.
□ Seven miles (11km) SE of Alnwick on A1068. Map ref 17D1.

North Yorkshire

A large county containing two national parks covering the Dales and the North York Moors. Other attractions include York itself with its Minster, walls etc; Harrogate; Pickering; Ripon Cathedral; Whitby; and Settle. Yorkshire and Humberside Tourist Board, Tel: York 707961.

734. BRIDESTONES MOOR
Nature reserve, trail and a forest drive

The Bridestones Moor Nature Reserve is approached by a Forestry Commission drive through Dalby Forest. This 10 mile (16km) toll drive leads to walks and picnic places as well as the nature reserve; it starts either near Low Dalby on minor road to Whitby from Thornton Dale east of Pickering on A170 or from minor road from Hackness 3¾ miles (6km) west of Scarborough. The nature reserve, owned by the NT and managed jointly with the Yorkshire Naturalists' Trust, is within the North York Moors National Park on the edge of Dalby Forest.

A four-mile (6.4km) NT circular nature trail leads through the typical habitat of the moors: oakwood with a gill; paths through heather and lichen covered moor; and the Bridestones themselves. These are large and impressive weathered outcrops of sandstone known as millstone grit – a good view of the area can be seen from Low Bridestone, about ½ mile (800m) uphill from the reserve entrance. The nature trail continues down a steep-sided valley to the marshy area of Dovedale Beck path. A trail leaflet describing the varied wildlife is available.

Other facilities include walks from one to three miles (1.6 to 4.8km) in length and picnic places. Staindale Lake, halfway through the forest, is frequented by waterfowl. The FC visitor centre at Low Dalby is the main source of information about the forest and can provide leaflets for the various walks and trails. Usually open daily Easter to Oct. Tel: Pickering 60295. Check, too, with the visitor centre about permits for trout fishing in Dalby Beck. (In case of difficulty in obtaining the nature trail leaflet, contact the NT or Yorkshire Naturalists' Trust. Tel: York 29621 or York 59570 respectively.)
□ Seven miles NE of Pickering. Map ref 12A1.

735. CASTLE HOWARD
Country house and early landscape gardens

Not a castle but so named because it was erected for the Howard family on the site of an old castle called Henderskelfe. The house was designed by Sir John Vanbrugh and built at the beginning of the 18th century. It is surrounded by gardens to match the grandeur of the house: one of the most important and earliest landscape gardens in the country with lakes, bridges and temples. A more formal garden and two rose gardens have been added in succeeding centuries. House and grounds are open daily Easter to Oct. Tel: Coneysthorpe 333.

☐ Six miles (9.6km) W of Malton on minor road to Coneysthorpe off A64. Map ref 15B2.

736. CROPTON FOREST
Forest walks

Three walks wind through a mixed coniferous forest in spectacular Newtondale, a valley which was cut by torrents of glacial meltwater at a late stage of the Ice Age. But it is only in the last 50 years that the slopes have been forested. Before that they were bare sheep pasture. A more recent change has been the closing of a toll drive which used to operate through the forest. Now to see the valley or to try the walks, you should travel by the steam trains of the North York Moors Railway.

Services operate from mid-Apr to late Oct between Pickering in the south and Grosmont in the north; at Grosmont the line links up with British Rail. Tel: Pickering 72508. A new halt called Newtondale has now been built along the line and it is from here that the three forest walks begin.

The shortest leads down the valley to Rapers Farm picnic site; it uses good tracks, avoids steep climbs and can be walked at a leisurely pace in about an hour. The medium-length walk ascends to Needle Point, a superb viewpoint, and is about three .miles (4.8km) in length and involves a steep climb. Both these walks return to Newtondale halt. The third walk is six miles (9.6km) long and intended for more experienced walkers. It also climbs to Needle Point but then continues down the valley to Levisham where there is another station. Picnic tables are dotted along the routes of all three walks and wildlife in summer can include sparrow hawk, green and great spotted woodpeckers, heron, siskin and roe deer.

Trail leaflets were being prepared as this book went to press. Ask about their availability at FC visitor centre in Low Dalby (see Day Out 734) or local national park information centres. However, a mapboard at Newtondale halt shows the starting points for the three walks which are all waymarked in different colours.

☐ N of Pickering. Map ref 12A1.

737. FAIRBURN INGS
Bird-watching

A large flooded area created by coalmining subsidence constitutes this RSPB reserve which is well known for its wildfowl. In spring there are good numbers of garganey and summer brings a number of breeding duck. Late summer and autumn sees huge numbers of sandmartins and swallows. Both Bewick's and whooper swans come to the lakes in winter. Access all year from the public footpath from Fairburn. Two public hides. Tel: RSPB Reserves Dept, Sandy 80551.

☐ Two miles (3.2km) N of Ferrybridge off A1. Map ref 15B3.

738. FALLING FOSS
Waterfalls and walks

Falling Foss forest walk starts from a picnic place and car park near the waterfalls of Little Beck passing through mainly broad-leaved woodland to the Hermitage, a cell carved out of the rock in the 18th century, and to the waterfall viewpoint. The Forestry Commission waymarked walk is three miles (4.8km) long, although short cuts can be taken. It can also be started at the May Beck car park. The latter is also the starting point for the four mile (6.4km) waymarked May Beck farm trail which shows different forms of land use: agriculture, forestry, game conservation and recreation. FC trail leaflet from Low Dalby information centre (see Day Out 734) or regional office; Tel: Pickering 72771. May Beck leaflet from national park offices, Tel: Helmsley 70657 (weekdays only).

☐ Five miles (8km) S of Whitby off B1416. Map ref 12A1.

739. FOUNTAINS ABBEY
Monastic ruins in a landscaped valley

The dramatic ruins of this large Cistercian Abbey, founded in 1133, provide a vivid picture of the impact of this order upon remote parts of the country. The Cistercians deliberately chose places such as the site of Fountains which was described in the 12th century as 'a place remote from all the world, uninhabited, set with thorns, fit more for the dens of wild beasts than for the uses of mankind'. The monks contributed much to the taming of the landscape – but not everything, for the abbey ruins now form part of the garden known as Studley Royal.

Here, in this wooded valley known as Skelldale, the history of the 18th-century landscape revolution can be traced from the first tentative steps in placing formal pools and classical temples in a completely informal setting, to the final romantic triumph which took in the ruins of Fountains Abbey as the garden's culminating feature, and provided them with a setting which appears completely natural.

The abbey and grounds are open all year. The abbey is floodlit during Aug and Sept. Tel: Sawley 639.
□ Four miles (6.4km) SW of Ripon off B6265. Map ref 15A2.

740. GILLING CASTLE
Elizabethan house

This castle, beloved of Elizabethan enthusiasts, is in the village of Gilling East between the attractive Hambleton and Howardian Hills. It contains the most richly decorated Elizabethan great chamber in England, a sumptuous concoction of pendentive-scattered plaster ceiling, painted frieze, elaborate panelling and armorial stained glass, all bought by Randolph Hearst, the American millionaire. He never looked at it, and the room spent several decades in packing cases before being reinstated in recent years. Approach by a handsome entrance front and baroque hall added on in the early 18th century, possibly to the designs of James Gibbs. Now it is a school, so there is little in the way of furniture. The hall and great chamber of the house are open throughout the year except Sun; the grounds June to Sept only. Tel: Ampleforth 238.
□ Four miles (6.4km) S of Helmsley on B1363. Map ref 15B2.

741. GOATHLAND
Moorland walks and glacial gorge

An attractive stone-built village straggling across a spur of the Esk valley below lovely stretches of the North York Moors. A good base for walking: south-west to the Roman road (see Wheeldale Moor, Day Out 759) past deep becks and foaming waters to Forestry Commission plantations; south-east to the high open moorlands of Goathland or Fylingdales where standing stones and earthworks testify to the area's importance 3000 years or so before the construction of the three globes of the early warning radar station (also visible from A169 Whitby to Pickering road). South of Goathland is the impressive gorge of Newtondale, followed by the North York Moors Railway but not by roads. The gorge was torn out largely by waters overflowing from an ice-impounded lake complex which formed in the northern dales of the moors when the last major ice sheet invaded this area from the north. (See also Day Out 736.)
□ Seven miles (11km) SW of Whitby off A169. Map ref 12A1.

742. HELMSLEY
Market town

As with many market towns, Helmsley grew around a castle, a 12th-century one now largely in ruins but with some fine earth ramparts; open standard DoE hours plus Sun mornings Apr to Sept. The market square still forms the heart of the town – market day is Fri – for Helmsley was an important centre for moorland sheep farmers. The Black

Swan inn in the market square was originally a 16th-century packhorse inn for the sheep drovers. Later it became a coaching inn and a Georgian frontage was added. Still more recently a Georgian house and former vicarage were added to the inn. Helmsley is a starting point for the long-distance Cleveland Way and, for the less ambitious, a three mile (4.8km) walk to Rievaulx abbey. The North York Moors National Park has an office in the town; open weekdays only. Tel: Helmsley 70657.

□ 14 miles (22km) NW of Malton on A170 and B1257. Map ref 15B2.

743. HORTON-IN-RIBBLESDALE
Hill-walking

This moorland village is on the route of the Pennine Way and can be used as the base for a seven mile (11km) circular walk incorporating part of this most famous of long-distance footpaths (see map). Start in the village by taking the vicarage lane until it ends and becomes the Pennine Way path* to Hull Pot (one of many well known pot-holes in the area). Then turn right to begin the steep climb up the Penyghent mountain (2273ft, 694m) that dominates the village below like a crouching lion. In fact, if you think of it as a lion you climb its flanks and mane by cart track and

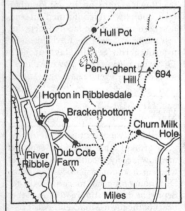

Horton-in-Ribblesdale: the base for the ascent to Pen-y-ghent

summit ridge and descend via its 'nose' (*keeping the wall on your right*) to Churn Milk Hole. You return to Horton via Long Lane, Dub Cote Farm path and Brackenbottom road.

*There are alternative routes of the Pennine Way around Horton-in-Ribblesdale, one of which does *not* ascend Penyghent. To be absolutely sure of following the correct route, use OS map 98.

□ Five miles (8km) N of Settle on B6479. Map ref 14B2.

744. HUTTON-LE-HOLE
Showpiece village and dale of the daffodils

So pretty – with a beck running through the middle and sheep grazing on the stream's grassy banks – that tourism is becoming its prime occupation. The village has a long history, possibly going back to prehistoric times, but certainly it is of Domesday vintage. Some of its past is recalled in the Rydale Folk Museum which occupies 18th-century farm buildings. Several crafts are displayed here as well as old farm implements and reconstructed buildings; the museum is open daily July to Sept, afternoons only Apr to June and in Oct. Tel: Lastingham 367.

North of the village is Farndale, known as the dale of the daffodils. Here in a nature reserve wild daffodils can be seen each spring in an abundance once common in Britain. Short and long walks along the River Dove begin at car parks at Lowna, just over one mile (1.6km) north-west of the village, and Low Mill, four miles (6.4km) to the north. A leaflet is available from a national park information caravan at Low Mill car park at weekends during daffodil season or from NP information centres at Pickering, Sutton Bank or Danby Lodge. Open daily in summer, weekends in winter. Or NP offices in Helmsley (weekdays only), Tel: Helmsley 70657.

NB: *it is an offence to pick or damage any flowers in the Farndale nature reserve.*

□ Nine miles (14km) NE of Helmsley off A170. Map ref 15B2.

745. INGLEBOROUGH
Cave and hill-fort

Ingleborough Show Cave is almost $\frac{1}{3}$ mile (500m) long. It is reached either by a one mile (1.6km) nature trail from the Yorkshire Dales national park information centre at Clapham – open Apr to Sept, Tel: Clapham 419 – or via Clapdale Lane north of Clapham. The cave is open daily Mar to Oct, Thurs and weekends for rest of year. Tel: Clapham 242. A footpath continues past the cave through Trow Gill Gorge to Gaping Gill, the largest limestone cave in Britain.

Ingleborough Cave is at the foot of Ingleborough Mountain, a 2373ft (712m) peak crowned by an Iron Age hill-fort which is a superb viewpoint. The easiest way up the mountain is from Hill Inn, north-east of Ingleborough on B6225. The geologically-minded should note the water-eroded limestone terraces on the ascent up Ingleborough Mountain and the South Craven fault which, passing ·through Ingleton, Clapham and Settle, has created the great cliff of Giggleswick Scar alongside the A65 north-west of Settle.

□ Just over one mile (1.6km) N of Clapham off A65/B6480. Map ref 14B2.

746. KETTLENESS
Lost village and clifftop views

This headland at the east end of Runswick Bay was the site of a village at the foot of the cliffs which was carried into the sea by a landslide in 1829. You can still see walls belonging to the houses at the foot of the cliffs. Good views from the cliffs and the remains of a Roman lighthouse. You can walk along the Cleveland Way footpath to Runswick Bay, down a steep hill. The old village of Runswick met a similar fate in 1682 when it too slipped into the sea. Nearby Staithes is an attractive old fishing village, also with fine cliffs. Care should be taken when walking on these cliffs.

□ 16 miles (26km) SE of Redcar by footpath off A176. Map ref 15B1.

747. MALHAM
Spectacular limestone scenery and drovers' roads

This hamlet is at the heart of some quite extraordinary scenery all of which is essentially the consequence of the effect of water on limestone. The results around Malham are so dramatic that the area can become very crowded, especially during summer weekends.

It is not therefore a place for the touring motorist at these times; indeed, the most remarkable features can be seen only on foot – see map. There is an information centre at Malham and here, too, is one of the few car parks in an area more notable for parking restrictions. In summer months it would be worth enquiring about the special railway excursion trains run at weekends to nearby Settle for ramblers. Tel: Settle 3617 or Airton 363. Main attractions of the area are:

Malham Cove. An almost sheer cliff 300ft (92m) high. It was formed by massive faulting in the limestone blocks which here slipped vertically away from one another. The plateau above it is extremely porous, so any water that falls disappears into 'swallow holes' and does not see daylight again until it has travelled through many miles of underground caverns. In the Ice Age, however, the fissures became filled with ice and massive waterfalls created the horseshoe-shaped cove which at the time must have seemed as dramatic as Niagara does today.

Limestone Pavement. Between the

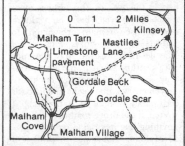

Malham and its attractions, including Malham Tarn, Gordale Scar, Malham Cove and Mastiles Lane

Cove and Malham Tarn the limestone has been exposed at the surface and divided into a series of fissured blocks which the dissolving action of rainfall is continually widening. The fissures are known as 'grikes'.

Malham Tarn. An outcrop of impervious Silurian slates preserved by faulting has enabled the Tarn or lake to develop in a hollow. It is a renowned centre for the wildlife and landforms associated with limestone. Much of the area is now owned by the NT and the local Field Studies Centre has an information centre about the tarn and surrounding area. A small stream flows south from the Tarn but disappears into swallow holes.

Gordale Scar. Water still falls over this cliff (formed from the same vertical faulting as Malham Cove) because surface clays have clogged the fissures in the limestone along the route followed by the tumbling Gordale Beck.

Mastiles Lane. A man-made phenomenon after the natural ones. The 1300ft (400m) moors above Malham were the scene of a great autumn fair when thousands of cattle and sheep changed hands. The drovers converged on Malham along drove roads from all parts of the north. The most famous of these roads was Mastiles Lane which was initially established in the 13th century as a monastic route from the sheep and cattle granges of Fountains Abbey near Ripon to the Lake District; bases of old monastic crosses survive in places. Many 'green roads' have been metalled for use by cars in the 20th century, but a three mile (4.8km) stretch between Malham and Kilnsey remains restricted to walkers and horse-riders. This part of Mastiles Lane was walled in the mid-18th century when traffic was probably at its peak and the enclosure movement was making its first inroads on upland Britain. It is the longest stretch of the drove road to survive in anything like its original condition.

□ Malham is four miles (6.4km) E of Settle; OS map 98 covers all the locations described here, including the clearly marked Mastiles Lane heading NE to Kilnsey. Map ref 15A2.

748. NEWBY HALL
Country house and gardens

Both house and grounds have been developed at different times over the last 300 years. In the 18th century Robert Adam added rooms to the original 17th-century structure; in the 19th century a church was among the additions; and in the 20th century the grounds were laid out with 25 acres (10 hectares) of trees, shrubs and herbaceous perennials stretching down to the River Ure. Grounds open daily Easter to Sept; house afternoons daily except non-Bank Holiday Mons June to Sept, otherwise Wed, Thurs, weekend, and Bank Holiday afternoons in Apr, May and Sept. Tel: Boroughbridge 2583.

□ Three miles (4.8km) SE of Ripon on B6265. Map ref 15A2.

749. NIDDERDALE
River valley and country park

The River Nidd falls from Great Whernside (2310ft, 693m) through Gouthwaite Reservoir (one of the finest bird sanctuaries in the area), past Pateley Bridge and Knaresborough (a picturesque market town dominated by the remains of a 14th-century castle) to join the River Ouse at Nun Monckton. At the head of Nidderdale, on a minor road north of Lofthouse, is How Stean Gorge, a spectacular limestone valley sometimes known as Yorkshire's 'Little Switzerland'. Other things to see in or near Nidderdale are Foster Beck Mill, one mile (1.6km) north of Pateley Bridge; Stump Cross Caverns at Greenhow Hill five miles (8km) west of Pateley Bridge on B6265 (open daily Easter to Oct), and Brimham Rocks (NT), $2\frac{1}{4}$ miles (3.6km) east of Pateley Bridge.

The latter are weird blocks of sandstone sculpted by wind and rain on heathery moorland. They now form the centrepiece of a country park. Leaflets and maps of paths are available from an information centre open Apr to Oct in Brimham House. Details from NT regional office. Tel: York 29621. See map.

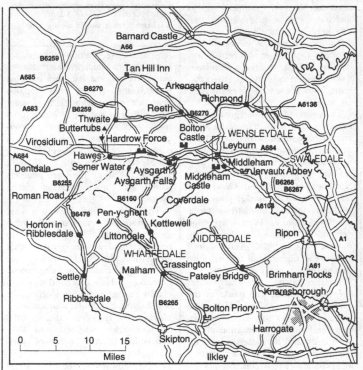

The Dales: Swaledale, Wensleydale and Wharfedale are the best-known dales in this national park but there are many others worth discovering in what is the heart of 'Herriot's Yorkshire'. Days Out 644, 749, 756, 757, 758

□ Pateley Bridge is 10 miles (16km) SW of Ripon on B6265. Map ref 15A2.

750. RAVENSCAR
Geological trail

The waymarked Ravenscar Geological Trail is divided into two sections, the first covers nearly 2½ miles (4km) inland to the Quarry, the second follows the path to the shore covering a further two miles (3.2km) with a steep climb. The rocks exposed in the quarry and on the coast belong to the Jurassic period, the grey shale contains alum, important in leather curing, hence the quarries. There is a major geological fault in the rocks at this point which has helped expose its geological history. Many museums throughout the country have fossils which were found

in Ravenscar. An excellent explanatory booklet is available from the North York Moors National Park information centres; for telephone numbers etc. see Day Out 643.

□ Trail starts outside Wildlife Centre on minor road off A171 into Ravenscar eight miles (13km) N of Scarborough. Map ref 12A1.

751. RICHMOND
Market town and Norman castle

One of the most attractive market towns in the north of England. It grew around a castle set on a bluff of rock high over a loop of the beautiful River Swale. The importance of this position commanding the entrance to Swaledale was soon recognised by the Normans: their castle was built soon

213

after the Norman Conquest and as such it is one of the earliest in England. The keep in particular has survived splendidly. It can be visited during standard DoE hours plus Sun mornings Apr to Sept. Also recommended is a walk around the outside of the 11th-century walls: the views over the river are superb.

The town of Richmond grew on the hill which sloped down from the castle and it developed around a huge cobbled market-place that must be one of the largest in Britain. For centuries it was the largest corn-market in the North and markets are still held there on Sat. Around the market-place, and leading off from it along narrow streets or alleys known as 'Wynds' are some delightful old houses including a tiny theatre built in 1788. A town trail leaflet is available from tourist office (see below).

Another particularly attractive and easy walk is along the banks of the Swale to the ruins of Easby Abbey one mile (1.6km) to the south-east. In summer the tourist information office is open daily and Sun afternoons, Tel: Richmond 3525. In winter contact local council, Tel: Richmond 4221.
□ 13 miles (21km) SW of Darlington on A6108. Map ref 15A2.

752. RIEVAULX ABBEY
Monastic ruins

Architecturally this is England's finest ecclesiastical ruin. Fountains is better preserved, but Rievaulx is much more poetic. The choir is Early English at its most exquisite, and comparable with Lincoln Cathedral. The church is very unusual in running north-south, because of the narrowness of the valley. No one should fail to visit the Rievaulx Terrace on the hill above, laid out in the 1750s. Abbey open standard DoE hours plus Sun mornings Apr to Sept; Terrace open daily Apr to Oct except Good Friday. Rievaulx is a pleasant three mile (4.8km) walk from Helmsley and is near the route of the long-distance Cleveland Way.
□ Three miles (4.8km) NW of Helmsley off B1257. Map ref 15B2.

753. ROBIN HOOD'S BAY
Village and a walk along the cliffs

An attractive fishing village set between cliffs which are important to geologists (since a fault has revealed their history dating back 300,000 years) or simply dramatic to laymen. The cliffs overlook a bay which has a rocky reef running in strange concentric patterns which are the result of constant coast erosion. Boggle Hole is a pebble cove at the mouth of Mill Beck and on the shore itself are boulders which are the remains of glacial deposits.

The path around the bay is way-marked since it forms part of the long-distance Cleveland Way. From here to Scarborough is a 16 mile (26km) walk along beautiful coastal scenery (see map). Start out along the shore, ascend from Boggle Hole and continue south via Ravenscar (where a hotel on the site of a Roman lighthouse is prominent); Hayburn Wyke (a dell with a waterfall on the beach); and Cloughton Wyke four miles (6.4km) north of Scarborough.
□ Five miles (8km) SE of Whitby off A171. OS maps 94 and 101. Map ref 15B2.

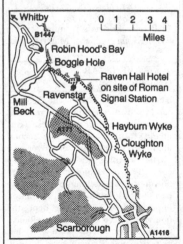

Robin Hood's Bay: a clifftop walk along part of the Cleveland Way

754. SKIPTON
Castle and canal

Skipton is surrounded by moors near the head of Airedale. Its strategic position was marked in the 11th century by the construction of a castle (although most of the present building dates from the 13th and 14th centuries) and in the 19th century by a canal. The 130 mile (208km) Leeds-Liverpool canal reaches its most northerly point near Skipton. Even many stretches of the canal in Lower Airedale, near the Leeds conurbation, offer surprisingly tranquil cruising and towpath walking, while its technical accomplishments include not only the crossing of the Pennines themselves but the staircase of locks known as the Bingley 5-rise just north of Bingley. Boats can be hired at Skipton and other places in Airedale for cruises on the canal details from the Yorkshire and Humberside Tourist Board. Other attractions of Skipton include the Craven Museum, with its exhibitions on local geology and natural history. Tel: Skipton 4079. And, of course, there is the castle itself, open daily throughout the year (except Christmas Day and Good Friday) but on afternoons only on Sun. Tel: Skipton 2442.

☐ Eight miles (13km) NW of Keighley on A6. Map ref 15A3.

755. SUTTON BANK
Walks and views

The highest point reached by the A170 as it climbs from Thirsk over the Hambleton Hills on the western fringes of the North York Moors. Many people park their cars and simply admire the view. At the car park is a national park information centre which is open daily Easter to Sept and weekends in winter. Tel: Thirsk 597426. This can also be the starting point for several different walks with outstanding views. These include:

Garbutt Wood Nature Trail. 2½ miles (4km) heading north of A170. The cliffs of the hills are jurassic rock cut away by glacial meltwater. On the bank top different rocks are signalled by changes in vegetation – heather on poor soil and a richer flora including the yellow-flowered rockrose on alkaline soils. There are many microhabitats in the fissures of fallen rocks. The old birch woods hold many ferns as well as flowers, fungi, an aspen grove, sycamore, oaks and conifers. A leaflet is available from information centre or Yorkshire Naturalists' Trust. Tel: York 59570.

Kilburn White Horse Walk. Walk begins along minor road south of A170 near Sutton Bank and signposted Yorkshire Gliding Club and then continues on paths to the Kilburn White Horse carved in 1857 on the limestone hillside. The actual Walk is 1½ miles (2.4km) but add another half mile (800m) if walking from Sutton Bank. NB: do not walk on the white horse itself. Leaflet available from information centre.

☐ Four miles (6.4km) E of Thirsk on A170. Map ref 15B2.

756. SWALEDALE
River valley and moors

Less well known than Wensleydale to the south, heather-covered Swaledale is perhaps less crowded and the more charming because of this. Richmond Castle (see Day Out 751) guards the eastern entrance to the valley which is followed at first by the A6108 and then the B6270 (see map on page 213). But explore, too, the side valleys and minor roads which follow them such as Arkengarthdale north-west of Reeth; the old 'high road' from Reeth to Richmond; West Stone Dale north of Keld and leading to Tan Hill Inn (see Day Out 682); and the roads south towards Wensleydale. One of these – south from Thwaite – is named after a pair of well known pot or swallow holes – the Buttertubs.

For walkers the Pennine Way crosses Swaledale near Keld and heads north up West Stone Dale. Shorter walks can be made to several waterfalls (called forces in the Dales). Less obvious, but still visible, are the relics of the lead mining which was once an important industry here. Villages to see include

Keld and Muker but Reeth is probably the best centre for exploring upper Swaledale; there is also a folk museum in the village.

The valley of the Swale becomes progressively more wooded as it heads towards Richmond while to the west the B6270 heads over the Pennines towards the Lakes and Penrith. No one map covers Swaledale neatly; the best OS coverage is on sheets 92 and 98. National park centres are at Hawes (open Apr to Sept, Tel: Hawes 450) and at Aysgarth Falls (open Apr to Oct, Tel: Aysgarth 424) in Wensley-dale (see below).

□ W of Richmond. Map ref 15A2.

---

757. WENSLEYDALE
River valley and moors

The beautiful River Ure, having left the wild moors of the high Pennines, flows eastwards along a valley known as Wensleydale which is popular with both walkers and motorists. See map on page 213. OS map 98 covers most of Wensleydale. There are national park centres at Aysgarth Falls and Hawes (see previous entry) and also at Askrigg. The latter is open May to Sept. Tel: Wensleydale 50441.

Drives. The A684 runs the length of Wensleydale from Leyburn in the east to Moorcock Inn west of Hawes where it divides, with the B6259 following the Eden Valley to the north and the A684 running down Garsdale towards Kendal and the Lake District. But don't miss some of the smaller valleys such as Coverdale and Walden Beck or the minor roads heading over the moors to Swaledale or Wharfedale for dramatic upland drives.

Walking. The Pennine Way crosses Wensleydale at Hawes and is the prime route for serious ramblers or hill-walkers. But shorter walks can be undertaken such as the one mile (1.6km) stretch of the Pennine Way from Hawes to Hardrow Force (see below); the wooded walks along a disused railway line from Aysgarth to the falls of Aysgarth Force, and two miles (3.2km) along the River Bain from Bainbridge to the lake of Semer

Water. There is also a stretch of Roman road running south-west from Bainbridge where the site of their fort, *Virosidium* on Brough Hill, still dominates the village.

Waterfalls. Hardrow Force one mile (1.6km) north of Hawes is the highest waterfall in Yorkshire. Somewhat oddly it is located behind a public house, the Green Dragon. A small charge is made to walk through the pub garden to a dell where the water falls over a limestone ledge into a pool 100ft (300m) below. You can actually walk behind the waterfall. Aysgarth Force is an attractive series of waterfalls and rapids near the village of Aysgarth where the Ure plunges through a wooded gorge. Other smaller water-falls can be seen along the side of the valley.

Villages. Askrigg, Aysgarth and Bainbridge are all attractive villages but Hawes is the only one which approaches the status of a town. Markets are still held in its cobbled streets and market square on Tues (livestock) and Wed. Other features of Hawes are the Upper Dales Folk Museum and demonstrations of Wensleydale cheese-making – details of both from the national park information centre in Hawes, open daily Apr to Sept, Tel: Hawes 450.

Buildings. Near Leyburn, and guarding the eastern entrance to Wensley-dale, is Middleham Castle. This still has an excellent 12th-century keep and was said to have been the favourite fortress of Richard III if that can be a recommendation; open standard DoE hours. Bolton Castle, a 14th-century fortress near Redmire, which once held Mary Queen of Scots captive, is open daily all year except non-Bank Holiday Mons. Tel: Leyburn 23408. Jervaulx Abbey, a ruined Cistercian abbey near Middleham, is also open all year. Constable Burton is an 18th-century Palladian mansion near Leyburn surrounded by an extensive garden; the gardens are open daily Easter to July, but the precise opening times of the house were undecided when this book went to press. Tel: Bedale 50428.

□ Map ref 15A2.

758. WHARFEDALE
River valley and moors

Whereas Swaledale and Wensleydale head east-west, Wharfedale runs from north to south and offers perhaps a greater variety of scenery than its more northerly neighbours. Upper Wharfedale is bare and lonely country with tiny hamlets such as Hubberholme that are not much more than pub and church. Lower down the scenery is lusher and villages become larger – Grassington is almost a town with its neat cobbled square. Most of Wharfedale forms part of the Dales National Park and offers magnificient upland walking. It is also easily accessible to motorists since the B6160 follows the valley from just north of Ilkley until it heads over the moors into Wensleydale. Heading off this main valley and its sometimes crowded road are some unspoilt and less well known smaller dales of great charm, notably Littondale (with its lovely village of Arncliffe) and Langstrothdale at the very head of Wharfedale. Places to see include 12th-century Bolton Priory at Bolton Abbey; the narrow gorge of the Strid, reached by riverside walks of about two miles (3.2km) north of Bolton Abbey; the nature reserve of Grass Wood and also Bastow Wood near Grassington; and Ilkley itself at the southern end of Wharfedale, with its brooding Cow and Calf Rocks as well as its much sung-about moors. OS map 98 covers the northern stretches of Wharfedale; 104 the southern half. National park centres at Grassington and Malham are open Apr to Oct. Tel: Grassington 752748 or Airton 363 respectively. See map on page 213.
□ Map ref 15A2.

759. WHEELDALE MOOR
Roman road

One of the best stretches of Roman road still visible. The surface stones have eroded away – or have been taken away for other uses – but the 16ft (5m) wide foundations and occasional kerbstones and culverts remain for up to 1½ miles (2.4km) across the North York Moors. This was part of a Roman road from Malton to Whitby that is also known, for reasons unknown, as Wade's Causeway. Roman camp-sites are visible (more clearly in winter when vegetable is less) along the route of the road south of Stape at Crawthorn.
□ Three miles (5km) SW of Goathland. Follow the narrow minor road to the hamlet of Hunt House from where a, signposted path leads to the uncovered Roman road. Grid ref SE 805975; OS map 94. Map ref 12A1.

South Yorkshire

A Metropolitan county covering a little of the Pennines but mostly industrial areas around Sheffield where Abbeydale Industrial Hamlet is a major attraction. Yorkshire and Humberside Tourist Board, Tel: York 707961.

760. BARNSLEY
Country parks and watermill

Known for its coal mining and beer rather than any rural delights, but two country parks are close by. One at Worsbrough, two miles (3.2km) to the south on A61, is set around a waterpowered corn-mill, but there is also a nature trail and fishing in a reservoir in nearly 100 acres (38.5 hectares) of wood and farmland. Cannon Hall Park, 4½ miles (7km) north-west of Barnsley, also has fishing plus gardens in parkland surrounding a 17th to 18th-century mansion.
□ Two miles (3.2km) E of junction 37 on M1. Map ref 15A4.

761. CONISBROUGH
Norman castle

There is some Norman work in the church of this small town on the Don but nothing so impressive as in the castle which boasts the earliest circular keep in England. It dates from the mid-12th century and is still 90ft (27m) high. Before Conisbrough, which was built around 1165, keeps had been rectangular (as with the Tower of

London's White Tower). Inside the keep there is a hall on the first floor with a chapel above it. The chapel, too, is an unusual shape: basically hexagonal but squeezed into an elongated shape by one of the six buttresses which support the walls of the keep. Some earthworks are all that remain of the outer bailey but much of the stone wall that surrounded the inner bailey still survives. The castle site is open standard DoE hours plus Sun mornings Apr to Sept.

☐ Five miles (8km) SW of Doncaster on A630. Map ref 11B2.

762. RINGINGLOW
Moorland views

Barely five miles (8km) from Sheffield city centre yet wild and apparently remote moorland within the Peak District National Park. Ringinglow is not much more than a bog, a pub and some cottages, but it has given its name to a road which offers a stunning drive across the Hallam Moors. Plenty of places to stop for views, picnics or walks. Rock climbers will head for Stanage Edge, a rocky outcrop revered among climbers. Among good routes for walkers is one along the top of Stanage and then via the line of an old Roman road, known as the Long Causeway, to the Redmires Reservoirs. Other paths lead towards the Ladybower Reservoir, in the Derwent Valley.

☐ The Ringinglow road runs north of A625 between Hathersage and Bamford in the W and Sheffield in the E. OS map 110. Map ref 11A2.

763. ROCHE ABBEY
Monastic remains

The most southerly of the great Cistercian houses of Yorkshire. The valley of the River Ryton in which it stands now seems less remote than it may have been in the 12th century when the abbey was founded, but it is still a beautiful setting. The gothic transepts and gateway to the old abbey church are the prime remains, although the outline of other buildings is

clearly visible. The setting was landscaped in the 18th century by 'Capability' Brown as part of the design for the grounds of Sandbeck Hall. The abbey remains are open standard DoE hours plus Sun mornings Apr to Sept.

☐ Two miles (3.2km) SE of Maltby off A634. OS map 111. Map ref 11B2.

Tyne and Wear

Metropolitan county centred on Newcastle-upon-Tyne and Sunderland. Northumbria Tourist Board, Tel: Newcastle 817744.

764. WASHINGTON
The American Connection

Washington Waterfowl Park on the eastern outskirts of the new town is managed by the Wildfowl Trust and the Washington Development Corporation, and consists of 110 acres (45 hectares) of land, pools and pens on the north bank of the River Wear. The wildfowl enclosures are landscaped into the hillsides while in the valley lies the Wild Refuge which includes a wader lake and several ponds where visitors can watch wild birds from screened hides. In the Hawthorn Wood, which borders the refuge, there is a nature trail and bird feeding stations overlooked by a large hide. Migrant birds are to be seen in early spring or autumn. Later on the wintering wildfowl gather for the coldest months. The breeding season for the wildfowl is at its height between April and June. Open daily throughout the year except over Christmas. Tel: Washington 465454.

There is a special emphasis on American birds in the Park since the town has taken its name from what was the ancestral home of George Washington. Washington Old Hall, the family home from 1183 to 1613, is open afternoons daily, except Tues, Mar to Oct and weekends Nov to Feb. Tel: Washington 466879.

☐ Five miles (8km) W of Sunderland. Map ref 17D2.

West Yorkshire

Metropolitan county with some moorland but more industry around Leeds and Bradford. Harewood House is top attraction. Yorkshire and Humberside Tourist Board, Tel: York 707961.

---

765. BRAMHAM PARK
French-style gardens

Large garden in the style of Versailles with allées through dense woodland, formal pools, statues, urns, temples and other decoration. New planting of exotic trees and shrubs has been introduced in the gardens and grounds around a Queen Anne mansion. Open Easter to Sept on Tues, Wed, Thur and Sun afternoons. Tel: Boston Spa 844265.
□ Five miles (8km) S of Wetherby on A1. Map ref 15B3.

---

766. BRONTË COUNTRY
Literary shrine on the moors

The Brontës will always be associated with the somewhat bleak village of Haworth on the Yorkshire moors. And Emily's *Wuthering Heights* will always be the quintessential novel of these moors. Old cottages are set around a cobbled main street that climbs steeply from the valley to the church (and parsonage) at the top of the hill. A bypass has been siphoned off the traffic to leave this street free for pedestrians and not even the crowds and souvenir shops can totally dispel the atmosphere of Haworth as it must have been when the Brontë family lived here in the first half of the 19th century. This is due as much to the proximity of the moors as to the survival of so many old buildings. The moors still begin close to the parsonage where the sisters lived and wrote.

This house is now a Brontë museum and, along with the adjacent church, the most obvious attraction for visitors. But even the pub, the Black Bull, claims its link with the legend by reminding visitors that it was there that Branwell Brontë spent so much of his time. The museum is open daily except the last three weeks of Dec. Tel: Haworth 42323. The village itself can become crowded at times during the summer but it is usually easy to leave most of the crowds behind – and to recapture even more of the Brontë atmosphere – by heading for the moors themselves.

The sisters' favourite walk was reputedly the two miles (3.2km) to a small waterfall now known as Brontë Falls – the route is signposted from West Lane at the top of the village (see

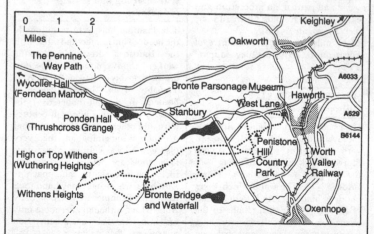

Brontë country: the village of Haworth and the moorland features linked by fact and legend to the Brontës

map). Literary pilgrims may wish to walk one mile (1.6km) further to a ruined farmhouse called High or Top Withens, allegedly the setting for *Wuthering Heights* itself. Other buildings claimed by Brontë devotees to be models for places featured in the novels are Ponden Hall, a 17th-century farmhouse near the neighbouring hamlet of Stanbury (Thrushcross Grange of *Wuthering Heights*) and slightly further afield, Wycoller Hall (Ferndean Manor of *Jane Eyre*).

The final evocation of the 19th century can be attained through the steam railway which runs through Haworth from Keighley and Oxenhope; services at weekends and Bank Holidays all year, daily July to Aug. Tel: Haworth 43629.

□ Four miles (6.4km) SW of Keighley on A6033. Map ref 15A3.

767. HARLOW CAR GARDENS
Gardening in a cool climate

The 60 acres (24 hectares) of Harlow Car Gardens have been laid out by the Northern Horticultural Society to demonstrate the possibilities, and to discover the limitations, of gardening in the north of England. Features include a rose garden, herbaceous borders, rock gardens, water gardens, a woodland garden, an arboretum and extensive trial grounds. Open all year, Tel: Harrogate 65418.

□ 1½ miles (2.4km) from centre of Harrogate off B6162 to Otley. Map ref 15A3.

768. HEPTONSTALL
Hilltop nature trail

Up a steep lane from Hebden Bridge is the lovely hilltop village of Heptonstall with its ancient weavers' cottages. Slurring Rock nature trail starts from the car park at the Lodge at Horse Bridge (NT). The walk, which takes about 1½ hours, descends to the banks of Hebden Water then climbs to the escarpment above the woods — a favourite haunt of woodland birds and a number of red squirrels. A booklet is available from a tourist information

centre in Hebden Bridge, Tel: Hebden Bridge 3831.

□ One mile (1.6km) N from Hebden Bridge. Map ref 15A3.

769. KIRKSTALL ABBEY
Monastic ruins and folk museum

The Cistercians are generally renowned for their agricultural impact upon the remote landscapes in which their monasteries were sited. But here, alongside the River Aire, they also pioneered the exploitation of iron ore in an area now dominated by industry. The abbey was built in 1152 by monks from Fountains Abbey. Although falling masonry has restricted public access temporarily, the grounds are still open and extensive remains of the abbey, particularly its walls, can still be seen. The monks here were also noted for craft skills such as spinning, weaving and pottery so it is quite appropriate that the former gatehouse is now a folk and craft museum. Open daily but afternoons only on Sun. Tel: Leeds 755821.

□ Three miles (5km) NW of Leeds off A65. Map ref 15A3.

770. SHIBDEN HALL
Hill farming and cottage industry

The Pennine hills were traditionally the home of hill farmers and later, with the Industrial Revolution, textile workers, the two occupations becoming inextricably intertwined. The West Yorkshire Folk Museum, which is housed in a half-timbered 15th-century hall, with a fine 17th-century barn and other farm buildings around it, shows something of this very distinctive local culture. Most of its farm tools are housed in the barn, including an early threshing machine with horsewheel and many hand tools from the Pennine area. Open daily Mar to Oct, although afternoons only on Sun. In Feb open only Sun afternoons. Tel: Halifax 54823.

□ ¼ mile (400m) SE of Halifax on A58. Map ref 15A3.

Scotland

771. BEN NEVIS, GLEN COE AND BLACK MOUNT
National Park Direction Area

Covers Scotland's highest mountain and most famous glen. The summit of Ben Nevis, 4406ft (1343m), can be reached by a rough five mile (8km) track from Glen Nevis, but great care should be taken. The brooding pass of Glen Coe, where Campbells murdered MacDonalds in the notorious clan massacre in 1692, attracts large numbers of visitors but is still enormously impressive. Total area: 610 sq miles (976 sq km).
☐ Map ref 20B4.

772. CAIRNGORMS
National Park Direction Area

Magnificent mountain wilderness dominated by sub-arctic summits of Braeriach, Ben Macdui, Cairn Toul and Cairn Gorm itself, all over 4000ft (1218m). Below the peaks lie the resinous pinewoods of Rothiemurchus and the Glenmore National Forest Park, idyllic Loch Morlich and the Spey Valley. The Aviemore Centre, a Spey Valley sport and leisure complex, offers skiing in the winter; walking, pony-trekking, canoeing and fishing. Total area: 180 sq miles (288 sq km).
☐ Map ref 21A4.

773. GLEN AFFRIC, GLEN CANNICH AND STRATHFARRAR
National Park Direction Area

A trio of wild glens thrusting deep into the North-west Highlands. Cannich and Struy are the gateways. To make a scenic circular drive from Inverness, take the A82 beside Loch Ness, then A831 through Glen Urquhart, returning by the A9 along the Beauly Firth. There is glorious loch scenery in Glen Affric, where relic pines of the ancient Caledonian Forest survive. Golden eagles patrol the surrounding hills, and red deer are common. Total area: 260 sq miles (416 sq km).
☐ Map ref 20B3.

774. LOCH LOMOND AND THE TROSSACHS
National Park Direction Area

Romantic mingling of lochs, birchwoods, glens and mountains with the tourist village of Aberfoyle as its main centre. Loch Lomond is the largest loch, 23 miles (37km) long, and studded with 30 islets. The Rob Roy country of the Trossachs surrounds the lochs of Katrine (for steamer cruises), Achray and Venachar. Total area: 320 sq miles (512 sq km).
☐ Map ref 18D2.

Scotland

775. LOCHS TORRIDON, MAREE AND LITTLE LOCH BROOM
National Park Direction Area

A wild and remote tangle of glens and sea lochs in the North-west Highlands, lorded over by the red sandstone walls of the Torridon mountains and the looming peaks of Slioch and An Tealach, all well over 3000ft (914m). The whole area is a stronghold for Highland wildlife (pine marten, wild cat, golden eagle). The Beinn Eighe National Nature Reserve protects more than 10,000 acres of mountain and pine forest, as well as providing picnic sites and nature trails starting from Loch Maree. The NTS Visitor Centre is at junction of A896 and Diabaig Road. Total area: 500 sq miles (800 sq km).
□ Map ref 20B3.

NTS RANGER/NATURALIST GUIDED WALKS

Several of the Days Out listed under Scotland refer to the Ranger/Naturalist Service operated by the National Trust for Scotland. The service was established in 1969 and now consists of 10 full-time and 6 seasonal Rangers, all qualified naturalists with extensive local knowledge. A small charge is levied at the NTS properties to help defray the costs of running the Ranger Service. The Service operates at 15 NTS properties, including Balmacara, Ben Lawers, Blair Atholl, Glen Coe, Grey Mare's Tail, Inverewe, Morvich and Torridon.

For the guided walks, which you are warmly invited to join, binoculars are useful and a packed lunch should be carried on full-day excursions (which are unlikely to exceed 12 miles, 19km). Walkers should be physically fit and should have had some experience of hill-walking. Stout footwear and proper clothing are essential. If you come inadequately equipped you will be turned away. Walks may be cancelled at short notice in the event of bad weather.

□ Further details from Mr Douglas Bremner, Chief Ranger, The National Trust for Scotland, Suntrap, 43 Gogarbank, Edinburgh EH12 9BY. Tel: Edinburgh 8212.

Borders

The salmon rivers of the Tweed and Teviot cross this region of rolling hills and ruined abbeys. Melrose, Selkirk, Jedburgh, Kelso and Peebles are among its main towns and attractions. Border Tourism Division, Tel: St Boswells 3301.

776. DAWYCK GARDENS
Riverside forest garden

Forest garden with exotic trees and shrubs by River Tweed. Arboretum. Open daily, Good Fri to Sept. Tel: Edinburgh 552 7171.
□ At Stobo, six miles (9.6km) SW of Peebles on B712. Map ref 17B1.

777. JEDBURGH
Border abbey/Roman road

Extensive ruins of what is perhaps the noblest of the four great 12th-century Border abbeys founded by David I. The town of Jedburgh is an ancient Royal Burgh. Queen Mary's House, where Mary Queen of Scots once stayed, is now a museum. Walkers can follow the line of Dere Street – the Roman road built by Agricola. What is now the broad green highway of this route is particularly well preserved in a stretch south from Jedfoot, where the A698 crosses Jed Water some two miles (3.2km) N of Jedburgh.
□ 10 miles (16km) SW of Kelso. OS map 80. Map ref 17C1.

778. KELSO
Old market town

A charming market town still centred on its wide cobbled square and 18th-century Court House. Little remains of the once-great 12th-century abbey, but John Rennie's graceful bridge over the Tweed still stands, giving excellent view of Floor Castle, the splendid

Borders mansion built by. William Adam in 1721 (but much altered a century later). The castle is open afternoons, May to Sept; Tel: Kelso 3333.

Other places of interest within easy reach of Kelso include the 16th-century Smailholm Tower, seven miles (11km) west, off B6404, in a romantic setting on a rocky outcrop above Eden Water. It is open standard DoE hours, but if locked, apply for the key at nearby Sandyknowe Farm.

☐ Kelso is 20 miles (32km) SW of Berwick-on-Tweed, on A698. Map ref 17C1.

779. MELROSE
Border Abbey

The site of one of the five great Border abbeys – the others are Dryburgh, Jedburgh, Kelso, and Sweetheart Abbey in Dumfriesshire. Like the remains at Dryburgh these are set in the green pastures of the Tweed Valley. Melrose was founded as a Cistercian monastery in 1136. Under its patronage the nearby village of Fordel blossomed into the present market town of Melrose. The abbey suffered severely during the Border wars but considerable restoration work was commenced in the 19th century. Much of this work was inspired by Sir Walter Scott whose house near Abbotsford is nearby (see Day Out 781). The abbey is open standard DoE hours.

☐ Four miles (6.4km) SE of Galashiels on A6091. OS map 73. Map ref 17B1.

780. ST ABB'S
Fishing village

This small village attracts some tourists, but it remains largely the fishing community it has always been. The cottages are grouped around the tiny harbour which is formed here in an otherwise inhospitably rugged coast. The cliffs to the north of the village rise to a height of more than 300ft (92m) forming a wild and dramatic promontory at nearby St Abb's Head.

☐ 12 miles (19km) NW of Berwick off A1107. Map ref 16C2.

Some common Scottish place-names and their English meanings

Modern form	Meaning
Allt	Knoll
Beg	Little
Blair	Plain
Clach	Stone
Coire	Mountain hollow
Craig	Cliff
Drum	Ridge
Eccle	Church
Eilean	Island
Gart	Enclosure
Inch	Island
Inver	Rivermouth
Kyle	Strait
Mairns	Home Farm
Mor	Big
Mull	Headland
Strath	Wide Valley

781. THE SCOTT COUNTRY

Sir Walter Scott was born in Edinburgh in 1771. He continued to maintain close links with the capital and his use of the Trossachs in general and Loch Katrine in particular as settings for *The Lady of the Lake* and *Rob Roy* helped enormously to establish the popularity of these places. However, he is . most closely associated with the Borders. It was in the rolling hills drained by the Tweed that Scott lived most of his later years and where he died. Few Border towns of any size do not have some link with Scott – local tourist information offices can provide details of his association with such places as Kelso, Melrose and Selkirk. Other places to see must begin with the home which he built and where he lived for 20 years until his death there in 1832.

Scotland

Abbotsford. This was the highly personal off-shoot of the fortune Scott made from his novels. The outside (mostly designed by William Atkinson in 1822 to 1824) is of interest to historians as a pioneer of the 'Scottish Baronial' style, but it is the inside which really makes the house worth a visit. Dark brown woodwork, stained glass, Gothic fireplaces, books, armour, antlers, and curiosities of all kinds, are crowded together to epitomize all Scott's enthusiasm for the past. His own study is still much as he left it, and personal relics and portraits of his many beloved dogs abound. Abbotsford house is situated off A7 three miles (5km) west of Melrose and is open daily, late Mar to Oct and on Sun afternoons.

Scott's View. This name has been given to a dramatic viewpoint on Bemersyde Hill overlooking a tight meander of the Tweed and beyond to the Eildon Hills. Legend has it that Scott so loved this view that the horses taking his hearse to Dryburgh Abbey stopped here out of habit. Three miles (5km) south of Earlston on B6356 and clearly indicated by parking lay-bys etc.

Dryburgh Abbey. Scott's burial place and one of the great Border abbeys. Here the beauty of the ruins is enhanced by their setting in a loop of the salmon-filled waters of the Tweed. Three miles (5km) SE of Melrose off B6356.
□ Map ref 17B1.

782. TRAQUAIR HOUSE
Historic house

Few houses are more sympathetically redolent of lost causes. The Stuarts of Traquair were the leading Jacobite and Catholic family in the Scottish Lowlands, and political and religious persecution left them without the means to spoil their house by restoration in the 19th century. The old castle grew gradually upwards as well as outwards and the result is like something in a fairy story. Charming panelled and painted rooms inside, with Stuart and Jacobite relics of all varieties, it is absolutely unlike anything in England. Open afternoons, mid Apr and early Oct, also mornings, July and Aug. Tel: Innerleithen 830323.
□ Near Innerleithen, six miles (9.6km) SE of Peebles near junction of B709 and B7062. Map ref 17B1.

783. WALKERBURN
Museum of rural life

The Scottish Museum of Wool Textiles at Walkerburn tells a story which has its origins in the time when textiles were very much a cottage industry and when a man would raise and shear his own sheep leaving his wife to take the raw wool and do the rest. Visitors can see her spinning wheel, the plants she might have used to make her dyes and the finished article such as the Shepherd's Plaid of 1875. Other displays show the tools of the trade and the processes of textile manufacture. Open daily and weekends by arrangement, Easter to end Sept. Tel: Walkerburn 281.
□ Tweedvale Mill, Walkerburn on A72 E of Innerleithen. Map ref 17B1.

Central

This small region covers part of Loch Lomond and the Trossachs – that wild tangle of mountains, lochs and birch forested glens whose Gaelic name

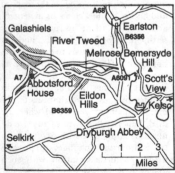

Scott's Country: most towns of any size in the Scottish Borders have some form of association with Sir Walter Scott

means 'the bristly country'. Other worthwhile attractions include Stirling Castle, the fine view from the nearby Wallace Monument, and the Borestone (NTS visitor centre, rotunda and statue of Robert the Bruce) on the site of the Battle of Bannockburn. Central Regional Council. Tel: Stirling 3111.

784. ANTONINE WALL
Roman Britain

Little now remains of a wall that for a time marked the northern frontier of not only Roman Britain but the Roman Empire itself. But it is still the most important Roman work to survive in any form in Scotland. It was built around AD 142 with the intention of superseding Hadrian's Wall but was finally abandoned. This new frontier consisted of a turf rampart on a stone base with a ditch to the north and a military way or road running parallel to the wall on its southern side. There were forts every two miles (3.2km) or so of its 37 mile (57km) length from the Forth to Clyde estuaries. The proximity of the forts to one another was far greater than at Hadrian's Wall and an indication of the resistance expected – and encountered.

Within 20 years the fortifications were abandoned and although they were reoccupied temporarily they were abandoned again, and finally, before the end of the 2nd century. The concentration of population in subsequent centuries in this part of Scotland has taken its toll of the Roman remains, the military way being scarcely visible at all and the ditch generally surviving better than the ramparts.

By far the best preserved fragment of the Antonine Wall is at **Rough Castle** near Bonnybridge where ditch, rampart, military way and a former Roman fort can be seen. The site can be visited at any reasonable time without charge.
☐ Rough Castle is at grid ref NS 853799 which is one mile (1.6km) E of Bonnybridge; OS map 64. Map ref 16A2.

785–6. QUEEN ELIZABETH FOREST
Forest park

Covers 65 sq miles (167 sq km) of one of the most scenic areas in Central Scotland. It extends from the Trossachs, 26 miles (41.85km) north of Glasgow, westwards to Loch Lomond, along the southern fringe of the Highlands. Included are the summits of Ben Lomond and Ben Venue, and six beautiful lochs: Lomond, Chon, Ard, Vennacher, Achray and Drunkie. There are 170 miles (273.5km) of forest roads open to the public on foot. Facilities in the separate forests of the park include:

785. Achray Forest. The David Marshall Lodge picnic and information centre is open daily mid-Mar to mid-Oct. Off A821 one mile (1.6km) north of Aberfoyle. A waterfall trail starts from lodge car park. Achray forest drive is a seven mile (11.2km) long Forestry Commission road, open summer, except Tues. Starts off A821 1½ miles (3.2km) north of lodge. There are many other forest walks and trails.
☐ Map ref 18D1.

786. Loch Ard Forest. The Silver Ring scenic walk leads through forest and by lochan and riverside for six miles (9.6km), starting from Aberfoyle. Loch Chon picnic place is at forest edge beside loch. Access via B829 seven miles (11.2km) west of Aberfoyle.
☐ Map ref 18D1.

787. ROWARDENNAN
Lochside walk

The hamlet of Rowardennan is a popular base for the ascent of Ben Lomond, 3192ft (984m). It is also the starting point for a splendid walk along the eastern shores of Loch Lomond. The route is part of the West Highland Way, which runs for 92 miles (148km) from Milngavie to Fort William. From Rowardennan pier head north to Ptarmigan Lodge, then via forestry road to footpath alongside Loch Lomond by Rowchoish and Inversnaid Hotel to Rob Roy's Cave. Total distance to the cave and back is about 10 miles (16km).

Rowardennan can be reached by road or by ferries which operate on Loch Lomond from Balloch and Inverbeg.

◻ 10 miles (16km) NW of Drymen at end of road (at first B837, then unclassified) on E shore of Loch Lomond. Map ref 18D2.

788. THE TROSSACHS
Mountains and loch

The wooded hills of the Trossachs and in particular Loch Katrine were used by Scott as the setting for *The Lady of the Lake*. Ellen's Isle in the loch is named after Ellen Douglas, the actual Lady of the Lake, but the 'Silver Strand' of the poem is now submerged. The loch also figured in another of Scott's works, *Rob Roy*, since Rob Roy MacGregor was born at Glengyle at the head of Loch Katrine, or Loch Cateran as Scott called it. Scott's descriptions of the Trossachs – Gaelic for 'Thorny Place' and referring to the narrow pass between Lochs Katrine and Achray – did much to open up this previously little-known area to tourism. The debt is acknowledged in the name of the steamer which in the summer plies up and down Loch Katrine. It is called the *Sir Walter Scott* and, since no road follows the shores of this steep-sided loch, is the best way of enjoying its beauty other than, perhaps, by foot or pony-trekking. Boats operate mid-May to Sept; details from Callander tourist office, Tel: Callander 30624. The area, with Loch Lomond, forms one of Scotland's five National Park Direction Areas and also contains part of Queen Elizabeth Forest Park (see Day Out 785).

◻ Map ref 18D1.

Dumfries and Galloway

Attractions include the coast of the Solway Firth, towns such as Dumfries and Kircudbright and several castles. Dumfries and Galloway Tourist Association, Tel: Newton Stewart 2549.

789. BURNS COUNTRY
Poet's corners

Robert Burns was born in 1759, a son of the land: a small and basically unsuccessful farmer like his father before him. It is hardly surprising therefore that his poems should reflect both the nature of his daily work and also the area in which he lived. South-western Scotland is thus rich in associations with a self-styled 'plough-man poet' whose work reached an infinitely wider public than could happily cope with its Ayrshire dialect. The Scottish Tourist Board would be the first to agree that 'A Man's a Man for A'That' and has devised an

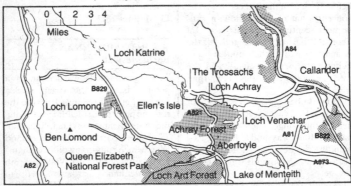

The Trossachs: Sir Walter Scott used the wooded hills and the waters of Loch Katrine for the settings of The Lady of the Lake *and* Rob Roy – *one reason for the locality's popularity*

elaborate Burns Heritage Trail to take visitors to places linked with Robert Burns. Free maps and leaflets about this trail are available from the Board (address in appendix) and it is marked by signs along the way. The Burns Country falls into two parts and, very briefly, these are the highlights of each part.

Ayrshire

Ayr. A statue, the 17th-century church where Burns was baptised, a narrow footpath known as the Auld Brig and featured in 'The Twa Brigs' and the Tam o'Shanter inn, so-called not just through commercial opportunism but because Douglas Graham of Shanter Farm (the model for Tam o'Shanter) really did supply the old brewhouse with malted grain.

Alloway. The birthplace of Robert Burns. The cottage in which he was born is open throughout the year (although closed Sun Nov to Apr) but it is no longer the only building with a Burns connection in or around Alloway. There is also a museum, a 'Land 'o Burns' Interpretation Centre, a monument, the Auld Brig o'Doon over the river and, 1½ miles (2.5km) to the south-east, Mount Oliphant to where the Burns family moved in 1766.

Tarbolton. The Burns family moved to Lochlea Farm near here in 1777 and in a 17th-century house now owned by the NTS Burns formed the Bachelors' Club with his friends. Open Apr to Sept, otherwise by appointment. Tel: Tarbolton 424. Lochlea Farm is about one mile (1.6km) north of Tarbolton on the B744 to Mauchline.

Mauchline. After the death of his father Burns moved yet again – to Mossgiel Farm near here and briefly to Castle Street at a house now named after him. He met and married Jean Armour in Mauchline where a local town trail takes visitors around the other Burns connections.

Irvine. While living at Lochlea Farm Burns grew flax and he went to Irvine to learn the trade of flax dressing. A plaque now marks the house in Glasgow Vennel where he lodged.

Kirkoswald. Souter Johnnie's Cottage was built in 1785 as the home of John Davidson, the cobbler Souter Johnnie of 'Tam o'Shanter'. It is now a museum with furniture of the time and the working tools of a village cobbler. Davidson and Douglas Graham (the prototype of Tam o'Shanter himself) are buried in the churchyard along with Hugh Rodger whose school Burns attended to learn mathematics and land surveying in 1775.

Galloway

Burns moved to Galloway in 1788. By then the first or 'Kilmarnock' edition of his poems had been published. But at first he remained a farmer.

Ellisland. Burns took over a farm here in 1788 and built a new farmhouse. He also tried to introduce new farming methods, but they were not a success. Here he began to work as an exciseman but, more lastingly, wrote 'Tam o'Shanter', 'Auld Lang Syne' and other poems. Ellisland is seven miles (11km) north of Dumfries on A76; an exhibition in the Granary explains his agricultural innovations while plaques around the farm indicate inspirations of various poems.

Dumfries. He moved here in 1791, after the failure of his farm at Ellisland, to work full-time as an exciseman. He lived first in a flat in the Wee Vennel (now Bank Street) and finally in a house in Mill Vennel. Both the house and the street of this latter home now bear his name. There is a museum in the house and some scratched verses and other mementoes can also be seen in the Globe Inn which he described as his favourite house. He died in 1796 and was buried in St Michael's churchyard. In 1815, however, his remains were moved to a mausoleum erected to his memory.

His years in Galloway also took him to some other villages and towns in this extreme south-western corner of Scotland. He regularly visited the quays of Kingholm and Glencaple (south of Dumfries via B725) in his duties as an exciseman trying to combat smuggling. But his connections with Gatehouse of Fleet (see also Day Out 796) and Kirkcudbright are poetic. At the former, in the Murray Arms Hotel, he wrote 'Scots Wha Ha'e' and at the

Scotland

latter, in the Selkirk Arms Hotel, he wrote 'Selkirk Grace'.
□ Map ref 19D1.

790. CAERLAVEROCK
Winter wildfowl refuge

A large nature reserve extends along six miles (9.6km) of coastline here between the River Nith and the Lochar Water on the Scottish shore of the Solway Firth. The saltmarsh (called merse locally) is a great attraction for winter wildfowl. In particular it is one of the principle haunts of barnacle geese in Britain. In October they begin to arrive, building up to a winter peak of over 8000. Pinkfeet and greylag geese also winter on the reserve and peregrine, hen harrier, merlin and sparrowhawk may be seen. Contact the warden of the Nature Conservancy Council (Tel: Glencaple 275) first if you wish to explore the mudflats. For easy bird-watching make your way to East Park to enjoy the facilities of the Wildfowl Refuge, including an observatory and decoy pond. Tel: Refuge Manager, Glencaple 200, for admission times and charges.
□ Seven miles (11.2km) SE of Dumfries off B725. Map ref 17A2.

791. CLATTERINGSHAWS
Deer Museum

The Galloway Deer Museum is situated beside Clatteringshaws Loch with a picnic place and car park nearby. It has many wildlife exhibits, including a collection of antlers. Book here for observation hides in the Red Deer Range where red deer can be seen in their natural surroundings.
□ Seven miles (11.2km) W of New Galloway on A712. The Red Deer Range is further down the A712, about eight miles (12.8km) NE of Newton Stewart. Map ref 19D2.

792. DRUMLANRIG CASTLE
Turrets and trails

The first Duke of Queensberry, who rebuilt Drumlanrig from 1679 onwards, was a feudal chieftain by inheritance, and a powerful contemporary statesman by achievement. His house is semi-baronial, semi-baroque, a sensational mixture of turreted towers and lush Baroque carving, built on a ducal scale in glowing pink stone, and splendidly sited at the centre of a surrounding amphitheatre of hills. A dramatic horseshoe staircase leads to the entrance, which is in a tower capped by a dome carved in the form of an enormous ducal coronet. Inside are carved and panelled rooms, and superb pictures, furniture and contents of many dates. There are nature trails and a children's adventure play area in the grounds. House open afternoons late Apr to Aug; also over Easter. Tel: Thornhill 30248.
□ Three miles (5km) N of Thornhill off A76. Map ref 17A1.

793–795. GALLOWAY FOREST PARK
Forest walks and picnics

The park covers 240 sq miles (615 sq km) of scenic forests and hills and it contains 16 lochs, and much of the Rhinns of Kells. There are six hill walks and picnic places: information leaflet from Forestry Commission, 231 Corstophine Road, Edinburgh. Tel: Edinburgh 0303. The A712 scenic tourist route (the Queen's Way) from New Galloway to Newton Stewart passes through the park. Forest facilities include:

793. Bennan Forest. Raiders Road forest drive (7 miles, 11.2km) winds from Stroan Loch along the picturesque Blackwater of Dee. Forest walks from Stroan Loch car park are ¾ mile (1.2km) and 1¼ miles (2km) long. Enter the toll drive from A762 four miles (6.4km) south of New Galloway.
□ Map ref 17A2.

794. Carrick Forest. Cornish Hill walk, on high craggy country with long distance views, is three to four miles (4.8 to 6.4km). Stinchar Falls walk runs six miles (9.6km) along riverbanks and forest roads with panoramic views. The waterfalls are at their best after rain. Both walks start from Stinchar car park eight miles (12.8km) south of

B741 on Straiton to Glentrool unclassi-fied road. Fly fishing is permitted for brown trout in some lochs and for trout and salmon in River Stinchar east of Pinvalley. Permits and bookings from Forest Office at Barr.
☐ Map ref 19D1.

795. Kirroughtree Forest. Forest garden with over 60 different species of broadleaved and coniferous trees. Signposted on A75 ½ mile (800m) south of Palnure. A wild goat park, in which feral goats can be seen in their natural habitat, is on A712 seven miles (11.2km) NE of Newton Stewart.
☐ Map ref 19D2.

796. GATEHOUSE OF FLEET
Planned burgh

The symmetry of the pleasant stone-built houses set along and off the main road through Galloway to Stranraer is a clue to this burgh's planned origins. It was laid out in the late 18th century as a cotton milling town beside the Water of Fleet. The mill has gone but a slight urban air remains. The main road, of which the wide main street of Gatehouse forms a part, is one of the most attractive in Scotland with fine views both to the sea and inland. Near Gatehouse – 'Kippletringan' in Scott's *Guy Mannering* – are two 15th-century castles – the ruined strongholds of Ruso and Cardoness.
☐ 12 miles (19km) SW of Castle Douglas on A75. Map ref 19D2.

797. GREY MARE'S TAIL
Waterfall

High in the wild grassy fells north-east of Moffat, this spectacular 200ft (60m) waterfall is formed by the Tail Burn plunging from Loch Skeen. Wild flowers and a herd of feral goats are to be seen. Visitors are advised to keep to the paths. A ranger/naturalist service runs guided tours from the car park information point between July and Aug. For details, Tel: Chief Ranger, NTS Edinburgh 8212. This part of Scotland also boasts another great natural spectacle: the huge grassy hollow at the head of Annandale

known as the Devil's Beeftub (north of Moffat, just off A701). Border raiders hid their stolen cattle here.
☐ 10 miles (16km) NE of Moffat on A708. Map ref 17B1.

798. LOCHINCH AND CASTLE KENNEDY GARDENS
Trees and rhododendrons

In the early 17th century a formal garden with grassed terraces was created between two large natural lakes and around the ruined Castle Kennedy. More than a hundred years later a collection of exotic trees and shrubs, including araucarias and rhododendrons, was planted in this setting. It has grown to great size and beauty. Open daily, except Sat, Apr to Sept. Tel: Stranraer 2024.
☐ On A75 three miles (5km) E of Stranraer. Map ref 19C2.

799. THREAVE
Gardens, wildfowl, castle

Peat, rock and water gardens, and a splendid display of daffodils in Apr and May. The estate includes the NTS school of practical gardening, a visitor centre and a shop. The bird refuge is a roosting and feeding place for wild geese and duck, Nov to Mar. Threave Castle (14th-century) is on an island in the River Dee. Tel: Castle Douglas 2575.
☐ Off A75, one mile (1.6km) W of Castle Douglas. Map ref 17A2.

800. WHITHORN PRIORY
Early Christian site and walks

Here in the 4th century St Ninian founded the first Christian church in Scotland. No trace of the original building remains. The present priory ruins date from the 12th century, but the adjoining museum (open standard DoE hours) contains much older crosses and tombstones, including Scotland's oldest Christian memorial – the 5th-century Latinus Stone. Two moorland walks, each one a round trip of about eight miles (13km), lead to St Ninian's Cave, at Port Castle Bay on

Scotland

the west coast, and the isle of Whithorn to the south-east, with its 13th-century ruined chapel.

☐ 10 miles (16km) S of Wigtown on A746. Map ref 19D2.

Fife

The peninsula between the Firths of Tay and Forth. Attractions include Falkland Palace, St Andrews, Dunfermline Abbey. Fife Tourist Authority, Tel: Glenrothes 75441.

801. CULROSS
Town and palace

This remarkable small town of steep cobbled streets and picturesque houses with white, crow-stepped gables and red pantiled roofs, has been superbly restored and cared for by the NTS. It is a perfect example of an almost unaltered burgh town of the 16th and 17th centuries. Culross Palace, with its beautiful painted ceilings, was the home of Sir George Bruce, who developed the sea-going trade in salt and coal from Culross at the beginning of the 17th century. The palace is open standard DoE hours.

☐ Six miles (9.6km) W of Dunfermline on B9037 off A985. Map ref 16A2.

802. EAST NEUK
Village architecture

On the northern shore of this peninsula is St Andrews, one of Scotland's most ancient and historic towns with its ruined cathedral (founded 1160), castle (1200) and university (1412), whose students still wear red gowns. But it is best known for the famous golf course and club, the Royal and Ancient (1754) – the premier club in the world and the ruling authority on the game. Southwards along the coast are a string of small towns whose status as Royal Burghs reflects the area's importance as trade expanded to Scandinavia and the Low Countries during the 16th and 17th centuries. These burghs contain some of the most attractive examples of traditional cottage styles from these centuries to be

found in Scotland. These well preserved 'little houses' date from the years when the burghs were being established. Approaching from the west, these are the most interesting places.

Dysart. Not technically on the peninsula and now almost swallowed up by the mostly industrial Kirkcaldy but still with enough fine old houses to make it worth a stop.

Pittenweem. Here the 'little houses' are grouped around a harbour. Five miles (8km) offshore is the Isle of May, a national nature reserve. Enquire locally about trips to the island.

Anstruther. Anstruther Easter and Anstruther Wester are two Royal Burghs on either side of the harbour. The village was an important herring port and a fisheries museum is housed in a group of buildings from various periods which enclose a courtyard adjoining the harbour.

Crail. Oldest of the Royal Burghs, with crow-stepped, red-tiled houses clustered around the fishing harbour.

☐ East Neuk lies between the firths of Forth and Tay. The distance is approx 25 miles (40km) between Dysart and Crail. Map ref 16B1.

803. FIFE FOLK MUSEUM
Rural bygones

Situated in a restored 17th-century Weigh House and some adjoining cottages of a later date, this collection of tools is associated with a variety of regional trades. It includes those of stone mason, saddler, cartwright, reed-thatcher and claypipe maker. Special to this part of Scotland are the exhibits connected with hand-weaving and the spinning of flax. Open daily (except Tues), afternoons only, Apr to Oct. Tel: Glenrothes 75441.

☐ Ceres, off A916, three miles (4.8km) S of Cupar. Map ref 16B1.

Grampian

A large region with Aberdeen as its principal city. Exceptionally rich in castles of which the most notable are Balmoral (near Ballater) and Brae-

mar. The mountains attract climbers while the salmon rivers of the Dee, Findhorn and Spey draw anglers.
Grampian Regional Council, Tel: Aberdeen 23401.

804. CRAIGIEVAR CASTLE
Romantic castle

The castles built in and around Aberdeenshire in the late 16th and early 17th centuries are amongst the most romantic and unusual buildings in the British Isles. Craigievar is possibly even more exciting than its neighbours at Crathes and Castle Fraser. From a small ground plan it shoots up seven floors, and at the top swells out into a frenzied skyline of towers and turrets, all built in pink granite. Inside, winding stone stairs and a great hall with rich Elizabethan-style plasterwork. Now owned by the NTS, the castle is open May to Sept, 2 to 7 daily (not Fri). Grounds open all year. Tel: Lumphanan 635.
□ Six miles (9.6km) S of Alford on A980. Map ref 21B3.

805. CRATHES CASTLE
Castle garden

An ancient Scottish mansion (NTS) with old yew hedges and aadern garden made in a series of enclosures, each with a distinctive decorative treatment. It has a fine collection of herbaceous plants and shrubs, many of them rare. The castle contains a unique painted ceiling and 16th-century relics. Open all year. Tel: Crathes 525.
□ Three miles (5km) E of Banchory off A93. Map ref 21B4.

806. CULBIN FOREST
Pines and dunes

This vast coniferous forest on the shores of the Moray Firth has been planted to stabilise the shifting dunes of the Culbin Sands. The Forestry Commission started reclaiming this Scottish Sahara in the 1920s, and Culbin Forest is proof of their success. Today the FC runs conducted tours through the forest and sands from Elgin and Nairn during the summer season. Various stages of reclamation can be seen, including 'thatching' the sand with birch wood so that trees can be planted on stable ground. The forest is the home of nightjar, crested tit and capercaillie. Further details from FC Conservancy Office, Tel: Inverness 32811. The Falconer Museum at Forres has archaeological and geological exhibits relating to the Culbin Sands. Open May to Sept. Tel: Forres 2938. Also to be seen in Forres is Sheno's Stone, thought to commemorate a Viking victory. Across Findhorn Bay - a good place for bird-watching in winter and sailing in summer – is the fishing village of Findhorn. It is the third such village to be founded on this site, its predecessors having been destroyed first by a sandstorm and then by a flood.
□ Off A96 to Dyke or forest road from Nairn to Kintessack. Map ref 21A3.

807. CULLEN BAY
Sands and crags

Nearly two miles (3.2km) of white sands, cradled between the craggy headlands of Scar Nose and Logie Head. This lovely bay, overlooked by Cullen, has a series of isolated rocks: the Three Kings, the Bow Fiddle, Boar Crag and Red Crag. The sands here are known to sing or whistle but not as well as the sands at Sunnyside, east of Logie Head. A good walk to Sunnyside from Cullen runs along a clifftop path, and on to the 15th-century ruins of Findlater Castle perched high above the sea.
□ 13 miles (21km) W of Banff off A98. Map ref 21B3.

808. CULSH
Prehistoric site

Probably the only day out in this book for which you will need a torch. At Culsh is one of the best preserved and most accessible of several 'earth houses' in Scotland. And unlike most other Scottish examples the roof of the Culsh earth house is still intact. You can walk several yards along a curving pitch-black passageway.

Its original function is unclear. It could have been a dwelling but it might also have been a hiding place or simply storage room. Open to visitors at all reasonable times, but if locked apply for key at adjoining Culsh Farm.

☐ 1½ miles (2.5km) NE of Tarland beside B9119. Grid ref NJ 505055; OS map 37. Map ref 21B4.

809. DUNOTTAR CASTLE
Historic sea castle and clifftop walks

Spectacular ruined clifftop fortress approached down a cleft in the rock called St Ninian's Den, where the headland has split from the main cliff. The castle stands on a rocky promontory surrounded on three sides by the sea, 160ft (48m) below. The oldest surviving part of the castle is the 14th-century keep. Other outstanding features of this remarkable castle are the gatehouse, the large well and the horrific Whig's Vault, used as a prison in 1685, where many people died. Open to the public all year except Sat in winter. Tel: Stonehaven 62173.

There is a clifftop path to Crawton, three miles (4.8km) to the south, where the sandstone cliffs are breeding grounds for fulmar, razorbill, guillemot and kittiwake. Catterline, a little further south, is a picturesque village, loved by artists, clinging to almost vertical cliffs. There is an RSPB reserve here (Fowlsheugh, open all year).

☐ Two miles (3.2km) S of Stonehaven off A92. Map ref 21B4.

810. ELGIN
Market town

This market town and Royal Burgh stands beside the River Lossie six miles (9.6km) from the sea. Little remains of the castle but despite substantial plundering the ruined 13th-century cathedral is still considered to be one of the finest church buildings in Scotland. Also ruined but still impressive is Duffus Castle, three miles (5km) northwest of Elgin. A 14th-century tower crowns the Norman *motte* but what makes the ruin particularly striking is that the keep is still surrounded by a water-filled moat.

☐ 22 miles (35km) E of Nairn on A96. Map ref 21A3.

811. MUCHALLS
Cliffs/village/castle

This tiny, privately-owned, 17th-century castle overlooks the sea and has ornate plasterwork ceilings, fine fireplaces, a secret staircase – and a ghost! Open May to Sept, Tues and Sun. Tel: Newtonhill 217. To the north of the castle and village of Muchalls is a fine stretch of cliff scenery. Between the Burn of Elsick and the Burn of Muchalls are two great rock arches, called Grim Brigs. The nearby village of Stanathro was entirely rebuilt in the 19th century as a 'model village' for fishermen but the growth of Aberdeen's fishing industry lured many of them away.

☐ Four miles (6.4km) N of Stonehaven off A92. Map ref 21B4.

812. PITMEDDEN HOUSE
Historic garden

The Great Garden of Pitmedden was first made about 1675 and reconstructed in the 1950s. It is a large rectangular parterre, enclosed by a high stone wall and terraces. It has many beds, elaborately patterned with clipped box and filled in summer with annuals, many of which would not have been available in the 17th century. Open all year. Tel: Udny 445.

☐ 14 miles (22km) N of Aberdeen near junction of A920 and B999. Map ref 21B3.

813. SANDS OF FORVIE
Dunes and birds

The Sands of Forvie are the least disturbed dune system in Scotland. The NCC has a reserve here with the largest breeding colony of eider duck in Britain, as well as waders and duck in winter, and four species of tern. The area around Newburgh Bar is closed to the public during the breeding season

(Apr to July). Huge parabolic dunes, some rising to 200ft (60m) cover what was once fertile land and villages. The remains of Forvie Church can still be seen and there is evidence of Iron Age settlements. Visitors are requested to keep to the footpaths when visiting this reserve.

☐ 14 miles (22km) N of Aberdeen N of Ythan estuary, stretching some four miles (6.4km) N to Collieston. Map ref 21B3.

814. SLAINS CASTLE
Sea castle on the cliffs

Extensive 17th-century ruins sprawl over the clifftop, north of Cruden Bay. This is the second Slains Castle – the first one, with only a ruined tower still standing, is on a promontory, six miles (9.6km) south, near Collieston. Open to the public at all reasonable times. To the north of the castle is the Bullers of Buchan, an awesome natural amphitheatre in the cliffs. Dr Johnson, who was rowed into the chasm, called it a 'monstrous cauldron', as the sea rushes through a natural arch in rough weather.

☐ Seven miles (11km) S of Peterhead, on A975. Map ref 21B3.

815. TOMINTOUL
Highland village

An altitude of 1160ft (358m) makes this the highest village in the Highlands, although not, surprisingly, in Scotland (see Day Out 886). Its foundation in such an apparently hostile environment was the work of the 4th Duke of Gordon who was anxious to try his hand at settlement planning. The village thus established in the late 18th century is very much alive today – as a holiday centre for anglers or coach parties touring the Highlands. Some fine mountain roads radiate from here. Nearby Glenlivet is famous both for its whisky distillery and as the site of a bloody battle in 1594 between the armies of the Earl of Huntly and the Earl of Argyll.

☐ 13 miles (21km) SE of Grantown-on-Spey. Map ref 21A3.

Highland

Vast in area but small in population, this region covers not only the mountainous mainland of northern Scotland but also islands such as Skye and Lewis plus many smaller ones. Inverness is its largest town. Highlands and Islands Tourism Council, Tel: Grantown-on-Spey 2650 or 2773.

816. ACHARACLE
Walk/loch cruise

A little town on a little road to the Western Isles situated at the southwestern tip of Loch Shiel. Acharacle is popular with anglers and in the summer boat trips operate along the loch, enabling ramblers to combine a day's walk of some 20 miles (32km) with a restful cruise. Enquire locally about cruise timetables in order to complete the round trip.

Start near Acharacle's Loch Shiel Hotel along a track heading east across the base of the mountain slopes to Achnanellen and Polloch, then along a forestry road running on Loch Shiel's eastern shore. Callop river bridge at the loch head leads to A830 – the Road to the Isles between Fort William and Mallaig – and Glenfinnan for the boat journey back down the loch. It was at Glenfinnan that Bonnie Prince Charlie raised his father's standard in 1745. A monument marks the spot in a magnificent setting where the River Finnan enters the head of the Loch.

☐ Acharacle is between 35 and 40 miles (56 to 64km) SW of Fort William via either A830/A861 or A82/A861. OS map 40. Map ref 20B4.

817. AFFRIC FOREST
Historic pine forest

This is a classical highland glen: fine mountain, loch and forest scenery, with an important remnant of old Caledonian pine forest and good chance of seeing golden eagles. There are four car parks and picnic places by loch and river. Four waymarked forest walks vary from ¾ mile (400m) to a 2½

Scotland

mile (4km) circuit. Several longer walks round Loch Affric and Loch Benevean run through a pine reserve and to Dornie, Glen Cannich and Guisachan.

☐ Access via A831 from Beauly or Drumnadrochit to Cannich and follow road to Fasnakyle power station. Map ref 20B3.

818: APPLECROSS PENINSULA
Highland seascapes

It is now possible to drive round this remote peninsula on a recently opened road, which has opened up spectacular seascapes formerly seen by very few.

Applecross Peninsula: a new road circuits this remote peninsula. Parts of it rate as the most spectacular coast road in Britain

Start at the pretty village of Shieldaig on its sea loch and turn west for the coastal village of Kenmore. The coast road runs across trackless moorland past abandoned crofts, always with magnificent views across the sea to the islands of Raasay and Skye. The road from Applecross village to Kishorn is said to be one of the most spectacular in Britain, climbing to the 2054ft (616m) Bealach-na-Ba – the Pass of the Cattle – before zig-zagging steeply down to Loch Kishorn and the Rassal Nature Reserve, the most northerly ash forest in Britain.

☐ Shieldaig is 28 miles (45km) N of Kyle of Lochalsh on A896. Map ref 20B3.

819. ARDNAMURCHAN LIGHTHOUSE
Scotland's Land's End

If you want to stand on the westernmost point of the British mainland don't go to Land's End – the tip of Ardnamurchan is 23 miles (37km) further west. A twisting road follows the south coast of the Ardnamurchan peninsula across barren moorlands which cover the worn-down wreck of an enormous volcano, active here 60 million years ago. The lighthouse provides excellent views of the islands of Coll, Tiree, Rhum, Eigg and Muck and is open to the public at the discretion of the keeper, Tel: Kilchoan 210. At Sanna Bay to the north are magnificent white sands and dunes.

☐ Off B8007, five miles (8km) NW of Kilchoan. Map ref 20B4.

820. ARNOL, ISLE OF LEWIS
Crofting village

It would have surprised the original residents of house No 42 that it is now scheduled as an historic monument. It has been preserved as an excellent example of a traditional Hebridean 'black house'. The name correctly implies the bleak existence which must have been led by those first inhabitants. Built without mortar and roofed with thatch on a timber framework this 'black house' also has the typical central peat fire in the centre of the kitchen but no chimney. Other black houses even lacked windows and were sometimes shared with the family's livestock. These low hovels were still being built in the 19th century. Ruined examples can be seen in many parts of the Hebrides but the house at Arnol retains many of its original furnishings, such as they were. Open standard DoE hours except Sun.

☐ Arnol is 15 miles (24km) NW of Stornoway. OS map 8. Map ref 20A2.

821. BEINN EIGHE NATIONAL NATURE RESERVE
Highland wildlife

The principal feature of the Beinn Eighe Reserve is the natural pinewood which extends along the shore of Loch Maree, one of the few remaining fragments of the great Caledonian forest. The Glas Leitre nature trail starts at the Loch Maree picnic site and takes a circular route of about one mile (1.6km). With binoculars you may see golden eagles, and red or roe deer. The trail is at times steep and rough. Tel: Nature Conservancy Council, Inverness 39431.

☐ The nature trail is on the S side of Loch Maree on A832, but the nature reserve itself also extends W of A896 at junction with A832 at Kinlochewe. Map ref 20B3.

822. BEN NEVIS
The easiest way up Scotland's highest mountain: 4406ft (1343m)

Even its easiest path is a serious affair - especially as the name 'Tourist Route' lures many up it unprepared. It was after all a pony track made for the former Observatory (1883–1904) on the summit. Yet cloud can cap the mountain when the rest of the sky is clear and it averages only two hours of bright sunshine a day. There is an annual rainfall of nearly 160 inches. Snow may fall up here at any time of year. And it is on the summit and easy slopes where many have died because of sudden changes in weather.

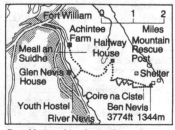

Ben Nevis: this shows the easiest route up Scotland's highest and most regularly climbed mountain

The Tourist Route begins from Glen Nevis, that tremendous glen around the mountain's western and southern flanks. Cross the River Nevis by bridge and follow the road to Achintee Farm on the east bank 2½ miles (4km) from Fort William. The well worn pony track starts here and rises diagonally round the steep flanks of Meall an Suidhe until it reaches the ruins of Halfway House to continue up in rocky zig-zags to the lip of Coire na Ciste before turning right for the summit. This ascent of five miles (8km) takes four to five hours plus another three for descent. Fine weather is vital. And be careful on the summit plateau where lingering snow forms huge cornices overhanging space at the edges of the mountain.

☐ Map ref 20B4.

823. CAIRNGORMS
Mountain walks

Glenmore Forest Park on the lower slopes of the Cairngorm mountain range (access via A951 from Aviemore) covers 4000 acres (1620 hectares) of pine forest surrounding Loch Morlich. There are facilities for sailing, canoeing, fishing, car parks and picnic areas, and Glenmore Forest treks for energetic walkers, three to six miles (4.8 to 9.6km) long. Information centre on access road.

But for an even more rugged walk, an exhilarating high-level five mile (8km) circuit known as the Northern Corries of Cairn Gorm is popular among experienced hill-walkers. *Good weather, hill-walking equipment, including stout footwear, and experience are necessary for this walk.*

From the summit of Cairn Gorm descend to the right to the Fiacall Ridge summit (no marked footpath on this stretch). Then follow a track along the edge, marked with cairns or stones, and dropping slightly for ½ mile (0.8km). Ascend Coire an t-Sneachda, staying along the edge before descending into a col. Climb 500ft (154m) to the Cairn Lochan summit. Continue around corrie edge and down to flat grassy area, then more steeply to corrie

Scotland

base. Now follow cairned footpath via Jean's Hut back to Coire Cas car park above Aviemore. OS map 36 in the 1:50,000 series is necessary for this walk, and OS map 36 in the 1:25,000 desirable. The main touring centre for the Cairngorm region is the Speyside village of Aviemore. The Aviemore Centre, a year-round, multi-million pound leisure complex, provides facilities for all kinds of outdoor activities, including skiing, fishing, canoeing and hill-walking.

☐ Aviemore is on the A9 to Inverness. Map ref 21A4.

Cairngorms: the rugged walk, known as the Northern Corries of Cairn Gorm circuit, is for experienced hill-walkers only

824. CALEDONIAN CANAL
Highland canal

There are 60 miles (96km) of waterway but only 22 miles (35km) of canal, as the remaining sections run through natural lochs in the Great Glen. Great problems were encountered during its construction so that although the route was surveyed by Telford in 1801 and building begun under his direction two years later, the canal was not completed until 1847. The most impressive section is Telford's series of eight locks near Banavie, known as Neptune's Staircase. An exciting inland waterway for the inexperienced, with motor cruisers for hire, although they get booked months in advance for high season. The lochs are also popular with yachtsmen who trail their craft behind their cars.

☐ Banavie – the site of Neptune's Staircase – is three miles (5km) N of Fort William and close to the south-western end of the canal. It then flows through Lochs Lochy, Oich and Ness between other canalised sections before reaching the North Sea at Clacnaharry, a suburb of Inverness. Map ref 20B4.

825. CALLANISH, ISLE OF LEWIS
Prehistoric monument

The Stonehenge of northern Britain. This magnificent and complex prehistoric monument has a central burial chamber and tall thin monoliths up to 16ft (5m) high. There is also an avenue of standing stones which points to the distant skyline of the mountains of Harris. The scale of the monument, with its stone circle nearly 40ft (12m) in diameter, has been known for fewer than 100 years: the stones were buried beneath layers of peat when excavations began towards the end of the 19th century. This, and its isolated situation, enabled the monument to avoid destruction as well as erosion. Many prehistoric monuments in Scotland disappeared after the Reformation, as the Protestant churches regarded them as pagan places, perfectly suitable for quarrying or for plundering for building materials.

☐ 13 miles (21km) W of Stornoway, well signposted from the village of Callanish on A858. Grid ref NB 213331; OS map 13. Map ref 20A2.

826. CAPE WRATH
Giant sea cliffs

Cape Wrath is the north-westernmost corner of the Scottish mainland, a wild, desolate and forbidding reach of empty hills and boggy moors which end abruptly in dramatic cliffs. The cliffs of Clo Mor, three miles (4.8km) south-east of Cape Wrath, are the highest sea cliffs on the mainland of Britain, towering 921ft (280km) above the waves. To visit this remote coast you must follow the A838 to Durness, cross the Kyle of Durness by ferry and continue by minibus for the last 11 miles (18km) to Cape Wrath lighthouse (open to the public). Tel: Durness 244. Ferry and bus operate only between May and Sept.

About 1½ miles (2.4km) east of Durness at Leirinmore, is Smoo Cave, a giant cavern in the limestone cliffs, which visitors can enter on foot.
□ Map ref 20B2.

827. CORRIESHALLOCH GORGE
Gorge and waterfall

Here the thunderous Falls of Measach crash 200ft (60m) into the long wooded gorge of Corrieshalloch four miles (6.4km) south of Loch Broom. Park by A835, and take the path leading to the spectacular suspension bridge viewpoint.
□ On A835 about 12 miles (19km) SE of Ullapool. Map ref 20B3.

828. THE CUILLINS, ISLE OF SKYE
Mountain scenery

The so-called 'Black Cuillins' of Skye are a range of savage rocky peaks forming the most impressive mountain landscape in the British Isles. The highest peak is Sgurr Alasdair, at 3309ft (1099m), but these mysterious, brooding mountains possess a majesty far greater than their height, with savage pinnacles and awesome ridges to challenge experienced mountain walkers and climbers. The Cuillins are a rock-climber's paradise, but the beauty of their wild skylines can also be enjoyed by motorists and walkers. There are marvellous views from Elgol, Sligachan and Glen Brittle. There are paths from Sligachan into Glen Sligachan, and boat trips operate from Elgol to lonely Loch Coruisk. Details from Isle of Skye Tourist Organisation, Portree. Tel: Portree 2137 or Broadford 361 or 463.
□ W of Broadford. Map ref 20B3.

829. CULLODEN
Highland battlefield

The best-preserved crofting farmhouse in Scotland is probably Old Leanach, around which the Battle of Culloden raged on 16 April, 1746. It not only survived the battle (the last on British soil), but has been restored to its original thatched state. The farmhouse stands near a huge memorial cairn to the dead and a visitor centre which explains the story of Culloden and the defeat of Bonnie Prince Charlie's Highlanders. The moorland site of the battle (now partly forested) and its clan gravestones can be visited throughout the year. The visitor centre and museum are open daily from mid-Mar to mid-Oct.

A battlefield trail follows the battle line of Jacobite and Hanoverian armies past clan and regimental cairns. There is also a Culloden Forest trail running for 2½ miles (4km) through mixed woods and felled areas. Access off B9006 about ½ mile (800m) west of Culloden Visitor Centre.

One mile (1.6km) to the south-east across the River Nairn are the Stones of Clava, an impressive group of Bronze Age standing stones and cairns.
□ Five miles (8km) E of Inverness on B9006. Map ref 21A3.

830. DUNCANSBY HEAD
Geos and sea stacks

These majestic sandstone cliffs, rising to 210ft (63m), have been ravaged by pounding seas to form caves, chasms (known as geos), arches and huge sea stacks. To the west of the lighthouse is Long Geo, a ravine with 200ft (60m) vertical walls running inland from the sea. Further west is the natural bridge known as the Glupe. The lighthouse commands a fine view of Orkney and the Pentland Skerries. Open to visitors, but check first; Tel: John o'Groats 202. There is an easy walk along the cliffs to the south with grand views of the sea stacks and famous tidal race called the Rispies. A steep path leads down to an empty shingle beach where the cliff has been cut into an arch, called Thirle

Scotland

Door. The beach in the Bay of Sannick to the south-west is known for its cowrie-like shells called 'Groatie Buckies', believed to be lucky.

☐ Minor road or cliff path from John o'Groats leads to the lighthouse. Map ref 21B2.

831. DUN CARLOWAY, ISLE OF LEWIS
Archaeological site

A type of building found quite widely in northern Scotland, but nowhere else in the British Isles, are brochs. These are circular buildings dating from late Roman or early Christian times which in effect were highly defensive manor houses or fortified homes. Usually the circular towers had inner and outer walls. One of the best preserved of such brochs is Dun Carloway with walls 11ft (3.4m) thick containing a spiral passageway and still standing up to 30ft (9.25m) high. Open standard DoE hours.

☐ 15 miles (24km) NW of Stornaway off A858. Grid ref NB 190413; OS map 13. Map ref 20A2.

832. DUNNET HEAD
Wild seascape

The road to Dunnet Head and its lighthouse is the most northerly on the British mainland. Although the lighthouse is perched on the cliffs more than 300ft (90m) up, the windows are still sometimes broken by stones hurled up by winter gales. Open to visitors, Tel: Thurso 85272. On a clear day you can see Orkney, the Old Man of Hoy and much of the north coast of Caithness, including Cape Wrath, 60 miles (96km) away. Dunnet Head itself is a great sandstone promontory rising over 400ft (120m) and covered with heather and rare plants, peat bogs and pools. An excellent spot to enjoy the celebrated Caithness sunsets. The cliffs are alive with seabirds. To the south is Dunnet Bay with high white sand dunes offering a complete contrast to the huge cliffs. Access from Dunnet.

☐ From Dunnet on B855. Map ref 21A2.

833. DUNVEGAN CASTLE, ISLE OF SKYE
Historic sea castle

Splendidly hoary castle on a sea-washed rock at the edge of Dunvegan Loch, looking across the water to the curious flat-topped mountains known as Macleod's Tables. Stronghold of the chiefs of the Clan Macleod for at least seven centuries, there is a grim bottle dungeon, paintings, and unique clan treasures like the 'Fairy Flag', Rory Mor's drinking horn, MacCrimmon's pipes, and relics of Bonnie Prince Charlie. Open afternoons, Easter to mid-Oct (all day June to mid-Sept). Closed Sun. Boat trips to seal colony.

☐ On A863 and A850 at head of Loch Dunvegan. Map ref 20A3.

834. FALLS OF GLOMACH
Waterfall

An arduous 1½ hour climb brings you to the Falls of Glomach, hidden in the hills above wild Glen Elchaig. The falls are among the highest in Britain, plunging 370ft (113m). Stout footwear and suitable clothing are essential.

☐ Access from unclassified road off A87 at Ardelve, 18 miles (28km) E of Kyle of Lochalsh, or by a 7 mile (11km) long-distance walkers' path through the hills from Croe Bridge on Loch Duich via Dorusdain. Map ref 20B3.

835. FOREST OF HARRIS, ISLE OF HARRIS
Hebridean wilderness

Here the term 'forest' simply means an unenclosed deer moorland. There are no trees in this trackless wilderness, only hidden lochs, golden eagles, staggeringly beautiful coastlines and magnificent views. Climb the slopes of Clisham, 2622ft (781m), to the north of Tarbert, to see remote St Kilda far to the west. Take the passenger ferry to the Isle of Scarp, off the west coast of the island; arrange a sea-angling trip from Tarbert; watch the spinning of Harris tweed at Ardhasig, on the A959; or tackle the rugged walk through the lonely valley north of Amhuinnsuidhe,

off the B887, to see the most magnificent glacially truncated spur in Britain – the overhanging 1400ft (420m) precipice of Sron Ulladale.
□ Off B887. Map ref 20A2.

836. GLENCOE
Wild Highland glen

A main road, the A82, runs through the brooding Pass of Glencoe, the most famous and perhaps also the finest of all the Highland glens. This is Scotland at its most awe-inspiring, with glowering peaks towering above the winding road. Leave the main road and walk along the old road to a rock platform called the Study for magnificent views of the precipices of Bidean nam Bian, 3766ft (1128m). The NTS Visitor Centre at Clachaig explains the area's geology and the story of the notorious Glencoe Massacre of 1692. Also guided tours are run by the Ranger/Naturalist Service Centre open Apr to Oct. Tel: Ballachulish 307. Near the centre is the start of the Signal Rock Trail, a short (1½ miles, 2.4km) historic trail through woodland and mountain scenery above the site of the Massacre.
□ SE of Fort William near Ballachulish. The A82 runs out of Ballachulish through the Pass of Glencoe. Map ref 20B4.

837. GLEN SHIEL
Scenic drive

One of the most beautiful roads in Scotland is the A87, which runs the length of wild Glen Shiel to the salty tidal waters of Loch Duich and the romantic Eilean Donan Castle on its rocky islet, with the Cuillins of Skye on the western horizon. Soaring above Glen Shiel are the majestic summits known as the Five Sisters of Kintail. The dominant peak, Sgurr Fhuaran, is 3505ft (1052m) above sea level. One of the best viewpoints for the Five Sisters is the Ratagan Pass, reached from Shiel Bridge at the head of Loch Duich by a narrow zig-zag road running over the hills to Glenelg, on the Sound of Sleat.
□ W of Fort Augustus on A87. Map ref 20B4.

838. GLEN ROY
Long-gone lake

High on the mountain side of Glen Roy three grassy terraces stand out against the darker heather. These are the 'Parallel Roads' of Glen Roy. They look artificial, so much so that local legends claim them to be hunting roads built by kings of old. In fact they are the signatures of a long vanished Ice Age lake, the old strand lines which show the lake's different levels as it slowly drained. It was impounded by ice, not only in Glen Roy, but also in neighbouring Glens Gloy and Spean. In Glen Roy the lake stood at a maximum height of about 1150ft (350m). As the ice retreated the water level dropped, first to about 1075ft (320m), then to 850ft (260m). Similar lake beach lines have been found at only one other place in Scotland – Rannoch Moor.
□ Glen Roy is off A86 at Roybridge E of Spean Bridge. Map ref 20B3.

839. GLENURQUHART FOREST
Forest waterfall

The Falls of Divach walk leads ½ mile (800m) through oak woods to falls which are impressive in spate. Access is via Drumnadrochit, turning first right in Lewiston. Reeling Glen has a picnic place and trails in the woodland setting of a miniature glen. Trails are 1¼ miles (2km) and 2½ miles (4km) to the head of the glen. From A9 Inverness to Beauly turn left to Moniack, left over bridge and left again.
□ Access via A82 from Inverness. Map ref 21A3.

840. GOLSPIE
Old coaching inn/castle

The Sutherland Arms was built in 1808 by the Duke of Sutherland as the first coaching inn in the country on the main post-chaise route from Glasgow and Edinburgh to John o'Groats. This fishing and holiday town was the administrative centre for the old county of Sutherland.

Just north-east of the town is

Scotland

Dunrobin Castle, the home of the Dukes of Sutherland for 500 years. The castle (much restored in the 1920s) is surrounded by a great park which includes a fine formal garden. Open May to Sept, weekdays and Sun afternoons; Tel: Golspie 377.
☐ Five miles (8km) SW of Brora on A9. Map ref 21A2.

841. GREY CAIRNS OF CAMSTER
Prehistoric burial chambers

One round cairn and one long cairn have been restored here, both dating from Neolithic times. The round stonecovered chamber is particularly impressive with a diameter of 59ft (18m). The burial chamber within this mound can be reached only by those willing to crawl on hands and knees since the passage is only 3ft (1m) high on average. Access is possible at any reasonable time, as is also the case at the Hill o' Many Stones – around 200 small stones in 22 apparently parallel rows four miles (6.4km) north-east of Lybster off A9.
☐ The Grey Cairns are four miles (6.4km) N of Lybster off minor road to Watten. Map ref 21A2.

842. HALKIRK
Planned village

Massive walls remain from the 14th-century Brawl Castle on the opposite bank of the River Thurso but this village has its origins in the late 18th century. It was one of the planned settlements created by Sir John Sinclair as part of his scheme to improve the lot of tenant farmers, many of whom had been displaced in favour of vast sheep estates. With its grid-iron street plan the village has a somewhat formal appearance.
☐ Six miles (9.6km) S of Thurso off A882. Map ref 21A2.

843. HANDA
Seabird island

This small island with its sandy bays and 400ft (121m) cliffs has been an RSPB reserve since 1962. No permits are needed and boats to Handa are run by local fishermen from Tarbet. Members may stay in the bothy. (Contact Edinburgh office; Tel: Edinburgh 5624.) Summer warden: c/o Mrs A. Munro, Tarbet. Among the main attractions are the Arctic skua and great skua or bonxie, both of which breed here, but the island is also internationally important for its colonies of guillemot, kittiwake, razorbill, fulmar, puffin and shag. Black-throated and red-throated divers frequent the bays. Grey seals, porpoises and even killer whales are occasionally seen. The interior of the island is lochan-studded moorland and peat bog where orchids and bog asphodel grow.
☐ Off the Sutherland coast about one mile (1½km) from Tarbet, three miles (5km) NW of Scourie. Map ref 20B2.

844. INVEREWE
Sub-tropical Highland garden

What was once a barren and windswept peninsula has been converted into a marvellous collection of mainly exotic and sub-tropical plants from many parts of the world. The secret is the windbreak of evergreen trees painstakingly nursed to maturity from 1862 when Osgood Mackenzie decided to make a garden in this damp, stormy, but nearly frost-free place. Open all year. NTS. Tel: Poolewe 200.
☐ At Poolewe A832 between Lochs Maree and Ewe. Map ref 20B3.

845. INVERPOLLY NATIONAL NATURE RESERVE
Highland wildlife

The Knockan Cliff nature trail explores the east end of this second largest reserve in Britain. Start at the NCC Information Centre at Knockan Cliff, (which has pamphlets on local geology, fauna and flora). This is a marvellous viewpoint for the red sandstone monolithic peaks of Stac Polly, Cul Beag and Cul Mor. The variety of wild habitats – cliff, mountain, loch and woodland –

provides a refuge for pine martens, wild cats and golden eagles. Wild flowers to be seen include mountain avens and autumn gentian. You can drive through the Inverpolly reserve by following the A837 beside Loch Assynt to the picturesque fishing village of Lochinver, then heading south on a narrow, tortuous road with stupendous views of Suilven and Stac Polly before meeting the A835. Reserve open May to Sept, daily, Mon to Fri. Tel: Ullapool 2135 or Lochinver 330.

☐ Eight miles (12km) S of Inchnadamph on A835. Map ref 20B2.

---

846. KINGUSSIE
Highland life

The position of this little 'capital of Badenoch' in the Spey Valley between the Monadhliath Mountains and the Cairngorms has made it an ideal centre for outdoor recreation: skiing, angling, pony-trekking, canoeing, sailing (on nearby Loch Insh) and hill-walking. Well worth a visit is the Highland Folk Museum in Duke Street. The farming section has extensive displays illustrating the traditional way of life in the Highlands. A special feature is a tinker encampment. Open daily, Apr to Oct, and weekdays, Nov to March. Tel: Kingussie 307.

☐ On A9, 12 miles (19km) S of Aviemore. Map ref 21A4.

---

847. KINLOCHLEVEN
Military road walk

In the 18th century many so-called 'military roads' were built through the Highlands to link army garrisons and help control the clans. One such road is known as Major Caulfield's Military Road and part of it can be followed today to make a stirring 15 mile (24km) walk over the hills from Kinlochleven to Fort William. Only the final five miles (8km) of this walk are along a metalled surface. Otherwise the 'road', begun in 1724, is a 'green road' ideal for sturdy walking. It zig-zags up the north-facing hillside above Kinlochleven, strikes west above the Allt Nathrach, cuts through a pass and

descends the Allt na Lairige Moire by Lairigmor to Blarmfoldach and Fort William.

☐ Kinlochleven is 23 miles (37km) SE of Fort William on A82. OS map 41. Map ref 20B4.

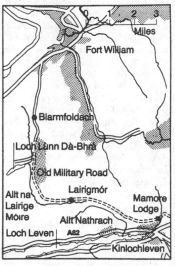

Kinlochleven: this walk follows an old military road over the hills from Kinlochleven to Fort William

848. LOCH GARTEN STATUTORY BIRD SANCTUARY
Osprey eyrie

This small loch in the Abernethy Forest is famous as the Scottish home of the osprey, which returned to breed here after an absence of over half a century and is now increasing. Responsive to the intense public interest in these spectacular fish hawks, the RSPB thoughtfully provided a hide from which the breeding ospreys may be viewed at the eyrie. The observation post is open from about mid-Apr to mid-Aug. It is important to keep strictly to the signposted path. In this pine forest, loch and moorland habitat you may also see capercaillié, crested tit and crossbill.

☐ At Strathspey off B970, four miles (6km) E of Boat of Garten. Map ref 21A3.

Scotland

849. LOCH NESS
Scenic drive

From Inverness to Fort Augustus the A82 follows the western shores of this immense loch lying in the fault-guided Great Glen. The ruined Castle Urquhart, midway along the loch, is a good viewpoint. There are deeper and more spectacular lochs in Scotland, but none so famous as Loch Ness, home of the legendary Loch Ness monster. Controversy still rages over the existence of what some people believe to be a creature akin to the prehistoric plesiosaurs of Jurassic times. There are boat trips and cruises in summer, mostly from Inverness but also from Fort Augustus. For details contact the Tourist Information Office, Tel: Inverness 34353.
□ Map ref 21A3.

850. MALLAIG
Island excursions/sailing

A little herring port with a glorious setting on the Sound of Sleat, looking over the sea to Skye. Mallaig is the western end of the 'Road to the Isles' and a major departure point for car ferries and passenger steamers bound for Skye and other islands of the Hebrides. Armadale, barely six miles (9.6km) away, is the nearest point on Skye served by ferry services. Other ferries call at the smaller islands of Rhum, Eigg, Muck and Canna – the round trip itself is a magnificent voyage on a fine day. For information about ferry services, Tel: Caledonian Mac-Brayne at Mallaig 2403. Places of interest within easy reach of Mallaig include the silver sands of Arisaig, and Loch Morar, whose waters – the deepest known inland water in Europe – are said to harbour a monster similar to that of Loch Ness.
□ Mallaig is 38 miles (61km) W of Fort William on A830. Map ref 20B4.

851. NAVER FOREST
Forest walks/village

Two areas have been opened up to visitors in this most northerly of Forestry Commission forests. At Syre the Rossal Trail offers an interpretative walk around Rossal, a pre-clearance village. This starts on a forest road off B873 just over Naver Bridge at Syre (south-east of Tongue). Also in Naver Forest but almost 15 miles (24km) away to the north are the Borgie Walks short sheltered walks in the north coast's only large woodland area. These are located off A836 at Borgie Bridge five miles (8km) east of Tongue.
□ Map ref 21A2.

852. RHUM
National nature reserve

The mountain summits and cliffs have a specialised alpine flora with plants such as purple saxifrage, moss campion and the rare pennycress. Guillemot, razorbill and fulmar nest on the cliffs and thousands of Manx shearwaters breed in mountain-top burrows. Golden eagles (three or four pairs) breed regularly on Rhum and an attempt is being made to reintroduce the sea eagle. The dunes, marsh, moor, lochans and sea coast support a wide range of wildlife, including seals and otters. Highland cattle, red deer, wild goats and Rhum ponies graze the hill ranges. Tel: Chief Warden, Rhum 26.
□ Access by boat from Mallaig and Arisaig during summer months. Map ref 20A4.

853. SHIN FOREST
Forest waterfalls

There are forest walks on either side of Kyle of Sutherland. The Shin Falls walk of 1½ miles (2.4km) starts at the falls car park off A836 Lairg to Bonar Bridge road. The Drumliah walk through sheltered larch woods, 1¾ miles (2.8km), starts on A836 north of Bonar Bridge. Carbisdale Castle walk starts from the castle grounds, running through woodland to a small loch, 2¼ miles (3.6km) away. From A9 at Ardgay take the Culrain road. Keep right to castle gates, and park inside. Raven rock walk is an exciting 1½ miles (2.4km) through a precipitous river gorge. From A837 Rosehall to Inver-

shin take first left and first left again.
□ S of Lairg. Access via A837 and
A836. Map ref 21A2.

854. STORR FOREST, ISLE OF SKYE
Forest walks

Storr Forest walk gives rewarding
views of the island of Raasay and the
Sound of Raasay. The path continues
to a black rock steeple called Old Man
of Storr via a two mile (3.2km) walk.
□ Seven miles (11km) N of Portree on
A855. Map ref 20B3.

855. TROTTERNISH, ISLE OF SKYE
Skye drive

The wild and lonely Trotternish
peninsula makes a marvellous circular
drive from Portree around this north-
eastern corner of the Isle of Skye.
Splendid views of Hebridean seascapes
can be seen at Kilmaluag and Uig, and
there are many remarkable sights,
including the Quiraing. This extraordinary mass of rocky towers and
pinnacles stands above the A855 at
Digg, overlooking Staffin Bay. A rough
zig-zag path climbs to the natural 120ft
(36m) obelisk called the Needle.
□ N of Portree. Map ref 20B3.

Lothian

Made up mainly of three former
counties: East Lothian, Midlothian
and West Lothian (an ancient kingdom ruled by King Lot), Lothian is
bounded by sea and beautiful hills – the
Lammermuirs, and the Pentlands on
the outskirts of Edinburgh. Edinburgh
is overwhelmingly the chief attraction
of this busy commercial, mining
and farming region. Others include
Hopetoun House. Lothian Regional
Council, Tel: Edinburgh 229 9292.

856. ALMONDELL COUNTRY PARK
Pentland hill walks

A network of paths and bridges
constructed by young people from all
over the world. Nature trails give
access southwards into the scenic and
historic Pentland Hills, stretching 20
miles (32km) westwards from the edge
of Edinburgh Hillend (ski slope).
These offer countless easy hill walks
along signposted routes, between A70
and A702. A favourite starting place is
the pub/restaurant at Flotterstone (off
A702) seven miles (11.2km) south of
Edinburgh. Obtain the Pentland
walks map from Edinburgh bookshops.
□ Park entrance off A71 at East
Calder or Mid Calder, 12 miles (19km)
SW of Edinburgh. Map ref 16A2.

857. BASS ROCK
Island gannetry

Bass Rock is a great sea-washed crag,
the neck of an old volcano. It is about a
mile in circumference and rises to 350ft
(107m) a conspicuous landmark off the
East Lothian coast. The most famous
summer residents are the 7500 pairs of
nesting gannets. Shag, fulmar, puffin,
kittiwake and guillemot also breed
here. The best views of the seabird
colonies may be had from boating
around the island and boats run every
day in summer from North Berwick
weather permitting. Tel: North
Berwick 2373.
□ Near North Berwick. Map ref
16C2.

858. HADDINGTON
Historic country town

A historic and attractive town, with
129 buildings scheduled as of special
architectural or historic interest. This
old county town of East Lothian is still
largely contained within the triangular
medieval pattern laid down in the 12th
century. A town trail takes in the most
interesting buildings (details available
locally) but garden enthusiasts should
make for Haddington House where the
gardens have been restored in 17th-
century style. Three miles (5km) north
of Haddington is an Iron Age hill-fort
known as the Chesters.
□ 17 miles (27km) E of Edinburgh on
A1. Map ref 16B2.

Scotland

859. PRESTON MILL
Working watermill

Preston Mill on the River Tyne is a rare example of a watermill in working order – yet once there were 14 on the Tyne alone. The present building dates from the 17th century, though there has been a mill on this site since the 12th century. Surrounding it is an attractive group of pantiled buildings: a picturesque kiln and former granary and stable out-buildings now used to house an exhibition about the mill. The mill is owned by the NTS and is open all year, Sun afternoons; also weekdays, Apr to Sept. Tel: East Linton 426. Nearby, and also owned by the NTS, is Phantassie Doocot – a medieval dovecote with nesting places for 500 birds.
□ At East Linton, 5½ miles (9km) W of Dunbar off A1. Map ref 16C2.

860. THE ROYAL BOTANIC GARDEN
Rare plants

The largest and best-stocked rock garden in the British Isles is here. The garden also has many exotic trees, shrubs and herbaceous plants both outdoors and under glass. The main rhododendron collection is now grown at Benmore, near Dunoon, Strathclyde, and tender plants from the southern hemisphere, including tree ferns and cabbage palms, are at Logan Botanic Gardens on the Mull of Galloway. Open all year. Tel: Edinburgh 552 7171.
□ Inverleith Row and Arboretum Road, Edinburgh. Map ref 16B2.

861. SOUTH QUEENSFERRY
Forth bridges

A breezy little Royal Burgh on the shore of the Forth, formerly the port for an ancient ferry crossing. It offers magnificent views of the two great bridges now spanning the water – the 1½ mile (2.4km) railway bridge of 1890 is one of the engineering wonders of the world. The neighbouring road bridge was, when completed in 1964, the largest in Europe. The town has a pier, yachts, seaside walks. Buildings include the chapel of a Carmelite friary (1440), and Hawes Inn of *Kidnapped* fame.
□ South Queensferry is nine miles (14.5km) NW of Edinburgh. Map ref 16B2.

862. YELLOWCRAIG NATURE TRAIL
Wood and seashore

The trail begins at the car park attendant's hut. It passes through mature and recent plantations of mixed woodland up to the Yellow Craig itself (part of the core of an ancient volcano) then down to the seashore. The rocks and rock pools have an interesting flora and a number of different seaweeds may be seen when the tide is out. There are also dunes and dune pasture. A nature trail booklet with details of geology, birds and plants (pegs mark out the most interesting flowers) is published by the East Lothian District Council. Tel: North Berwick 2197.
□ At Dirleton. Access road leads from B1345 towards sea. Map ref 16B2.

Orkney and Shetland

Two groups of islands off the north coast of Scotland. Both are rich in prehistoric sites. Lerwick is the main town of Shetland; for tourist information, Tel: Lerwick 3434. Kirkwall, with its superb cathedral, is the main town of Orkney; Tel: Kirkwall 2856, for tourist information on Orkney.

863. COPINSAY, ORKNEY
Bird reserve

This island reserve of 200 acres (80 hectares) is a memorial to the distinguished naturalist James Fisher. The cliffs of old red sandstone give shelter to colonies of breeding seabirds, with especially large numbers of kittiwake and guillemot. Day visits to the island can be arranged from Newark Bay. Tel: Deerness 245.
□ Off Deerness, Mainland, two miles

(3km) SE of the Point of Ayre. Map ref
21B1.

864. JARLSHOF, SHETLAND
Ancient settlement

Continuity of settlement can rarely be
demonstrated more vividly than at this
site close to Sumburgh airport. The
remains of a complex succession of
settlements are visible alongside each
other here: from the early second
millenium BC through the Bronze Age
and Iron Age on into the late Dark
Ages with a Viking settlement and
ending with a 13th-century farmhouse
and a 16th-century manorhouse.

Some of the site has been eroded by
the sea, but an extraordinary amount
remains to be seen, including houses
similar to those at Skara Brae (see Day
Out 868), a Pictish broch (see Day Out
831) and circular 'wheel houses' from
the second and third centuries AD.
Open at standard DoE hours.
□ 22 miles (35km) S of Lerwick on
Mainland, clearly signposted off A970
at grid ref HU 398096 (OS map 4).
Map ref 21B2.

865. MAES HOWE, ORKNEY
Prehistoric site

Rarely can the works of prehistoric
man be classed as 'architecture' but
Maes Howe is an exception: an
enormous green mound, 24ft (7.3m)
high and 115ft (35m) in diameter,
containing a long passage leading to a
central chamber 15ft (4.6m) high. The
quality of the workmanship is remarkable. The largest stones weigh
four tons (4000 kilos) but the great
slabs are so accurately levelled and
plumbed and so skilfully laid – without
mortar – that a knife cannot be inserted
between them. Maes Howe was built
more than 4000 years ago and may
once have contained great riches – if
you can believe the inscriptions left by
Viking raiders in the 12th century.
Even bare of ornament, however, the
tomb remains a treasure in itself.

Nearby are further notable works of
prehistoric man: the Standing Stones
of Stenness; the henge and stone circle
of the Ring of Brodgar; and the
chambered cairn of the Onston Burial
Chamber. Maes Howe itself is open
during standard DoE hours. If locked,
apply for key at nearby farmhouse.
□ Maes Howe is five miles (8km) E of
Stromness on Mainland, Orkney, just
off A965 at grid ref HY 318128 (OS
map 6). The Stones of Stenness are at
grid ref HY 306126; Ring of Brodgar at
HY 294134; and Onston Burial
Chamber is at HY 283117. Map ref
21A1.

866. MARWICK HEAD, ORKNEY
Seabird cliffs

Between May and July these sandstone
cliffs are alive with the cries of
thousands of seabirds. On these
beautiful, flower-covered heights you
can find a comfortable spot from which
to observe closely the razorbills,
guillemots, gulls and kittiwakes. There
is access along the shore and on the
clifftop from the south. Open at all
times. Tel: RSPB Reserves Dept.,
Sandy 80551.
□ On Mainland. Access from path N
from Marwick Bay (W from B9056).
Map ref 21A1.

867. MOUSA BROCH, SHETLAND
Iron Age site

Not the most accessible of locations but
this is the best preserved example of the
Iron Age brochs in Scotland (see Day
Out 831). It still stands over 40ft (12m)
high and is open to visitors standard
DoE hours. Visitors will have experienced something of a 'day out'
before reaching the broch: it is on an
island off Sandwick. Boats can be hired
at Sandwick on Sat and Sun mornings
throughout year (weather permitting)
and on afternoons, May to Sept.
□ Sandwick is seven miles (11km) S of
Lerwick off A970. Map ref 21B2.

868. SKARA BRAE, ORKNEY
Prehistoric site

An Atlantic storm in the 19th century

Scotland

uncovered the stone huts of this Neolithic settlement which had been buried by sand dunes for almost 3000 years. The sandstorm which had destroyed Skara Brae must have been almost as dramatic as the gales and rain that uncovered it. In the rooms of the village's seven houses the cupboards, 'dressers' and beds recall life in Neolithic times and suggest that the site was hurriedly abandoned. The fact that the houses were built of local stone – whereas most lowland Neolithic settlements were of wood and mud – also contributed to Skara Brae's survival. The village is open standard DoE hours.

☐ Seven miles (11km) N of Stromness, along signposted footpath for 700 yards (640m) off B9056. Grid ref HY 231188; OS map 6. Map ref 21A1.

869. STROMNESS, ORKNEY
Orcadian harbour

One of the two main towns of Mainland, largest of the Orkney Islands. Although it has no one building which can compare with Kirkwall's Cathedral, the narrow winding streets of Stromness exert great charm. The life of Stromness revolves around its harbour overlooking Hoy Sound and beyond it, Scapa Flow. Stromness has been used as a harbour since Viking days and is the main port for Orkney. Orkney Natural History Museum in Stromness opens

Wed and Thur mornings.

☐ 18 miles (29km) W of Kirkwall on A964. OS map 6. Map ref 21A1.

Strathclyde

The most densely populated region since it covers the Glasgow conurbation, but still containing attractive countryside – the coast and sea lochs from the Clyde to Oban, and islands such as Arran and Mull. Other attractions include Fingal's Cave and the Burns Country of Ayrshire. Strathclyde Regional Council: Glasgow 221 6136/7.

870. AILSA CRAIG
Island gannetry

This granite island, two miles (3.2km) in circumference, is the home of a large seabird colony with a considerable gannetry. These magnificent seabirds breed at only 16 sites around Britain. Also razorbill, guillemot, kittiwake, puffin. Several local skippers run summer trips to the island (weather and tide permitting) from Girvan harbour. Tel: Girvan Tourist Information, Girvan 2056.

☐ 10 miles (16km) offshore W of Girvan. Map ref 19C1.

871–2. ARGYLL FOREST PARK
Forest drives/walks

Covers 100 sq miles (259 sq km) of rugged West Highlands broken by sea lochs. Over 165 miles (265km) of forest roads are open to the public on foot. Facilities include:
871. Benmore Forest. Picnic places: Finart Bay, sandy beach on Loch Long at forest edge. Off A880 one mile (1.6km) N of Ardentinny; Rubha Garbh on wooded shore of Loch Eck. Off A815 11 miles (17.7km) N of Dunoon. Black Gates to Puck's Glen or Gairletter walk: a path up the gorge to Puck's Glen doubles back to start or to car park; main route continues over Creag Mhor 1500ft (457m) to Gairletter with a view of Loch Long and Firth of Clyde. Starts off A815 six miles (9.6km) north of Dunoon. Ardentinny

to Carrick Castle walk: forest road and open hill giving views of Loch Goil and Loch Long, starts from Finart Bay picnic place.

☐ Map ref 18C2.

872. Glenbranter Forest. Dornoch Bay picnic place on shore of Loch Eck off A815 12 miles (19.3km) north of Dunoon. Two waymarked hill walks of about eight miles (12.8km) start from Starchurmore and Coire Ealt to Lettermay on Loch Goil. Routes start off A815 17 and 13 miles (27.3 and 20.9km) north of Dunoon.

☐ Map ref 18C2.

---

873. BONAWE
Industrial archaeology

Despite the existence of granite quarries the mountainous shores of Loch Etive around Bonawe seem remote from an industrial development. Yet here for a time in the 18th century was Scotland's only source of natively-produced iron. Using the abundant local timber for making charcoal, Richard Ford built a furnace and forge to smelt iron brought in by sea from his native Furness. The quality of the product (and the low wages paid to Scottish workers) enabled the works to continue in use until 1873, in spite of increased competition from coke-fired smelting introduced in better-sited lowland areas. After many years of decay the Bonawe works, including the furnace, storage sheds and workmen's cottages, have been restored by the Scottish Office as a memorial to the first industrial settlement in Argyllshire.

☐ Nine miles (14km) E of Oban on B845 off A85. OS map 49. Map ref 18C1.

---

874. CRARAE WOODLAND GARDEN
Woodland garden

Crarae Lodge, seat of the Campbells of Succoth, is beautifully set on the northern shore of Loch Fyne. The extensive garden rambles up a small glen, noted for fine conifers and ornamental shrubs, including a won-

derful display of azaleas and rhododendrons in spring. Open daily, Mar to Oct. Tel: Furnace 286.

☐ One mile (1.6km) NE from Minard on A83. Map ref 18C2.

---

875. CRINAN CANAL
Scenic waterway

The canal is only nine miles (14km) long but it saves the long boat trip round the often stormy Mull of Kintyre. When constructed at the end of the 18th century it was scarcely envisaged that the principal users of the canal would eventually be yachtsmen taking a short cut to the Western Isles. There are 15 locks, including the sea locks, and the passage takes about five hours. Nearby, on the northern shores of Crinan Loch, is Duntroon Castle, a 13th-century Campbell stronghold. At Crinan, on the Sound of Jura, you look out through the Dorus Mor – the Great Door – between Garbh Reisa and Craignish Point, the sea gateway to the Hebrides.

☐ The canal runs from Ardrishaig on Loch Fyne at E end to Crinan on the Sound of Jura at W end. Map ref 18C2.

---

876. CULZEAN
Castle and country park

Culzean Castle (NTS) is a magnificent mock-Gothic stronghold begun by Robert Adam in 1777 around an older castle of the Kennedys. The castle is open daily, Apr to Sept.

The spacious grounds of Culzean are the site of Scotland's first country park, established in 1969. Attractions include a walled garden, swan pond, camellia house and orangery, deer park, beach and cliff walks with panoramic views of Bute, Arran, Ailsa Craig and Kintyre. The red sandstone farm buildings designed by Robert Adam now contain an Interpretation Centre with exhibition, shop and Ranger/Naturalist service. Grounds always open; Exhibition Centre open Mar to Oct.

☐ Near Maybole, on A719, 12 miles (19km) S of Ayr. Map ref 19C1.

Scotland

877. DRUMADOON BAY, ISLE OF ARRAN
Semi-precious stones

In an island of geological treasures, the intrusive igneous sill at Drumadoon Point, near Blackwaterfoot on the A841 on the western side of the island, is a major highlight. Here columnar cliffs mark the intruded layer of hard quartz porphyry which was forced in molten form between horizontal, bedded sandstones, some 60 million years ago. Occasional pebbles of amethyst, topaz, or agate may be found on the beaches.

Two miles (3km) north is the King's Cave and its legendary associations with Robert the Bruce. South of Machrie 1½ miles (2.4km) east of A841, are the Standing Stones of Machrie Moor (AM). For a magnificent walk into the mountainous granite heart of northern Arran, follow lonely Glen Forsa from Dougrie, north of Machrie Bay. The steep-sided, U-shaped glacial trough, though not as spectacular as the more famous Glen Rosa, is wilder and more open and takes you into an imposing amphitheatre of high peaks. Care should be taken among these summits, where much of the terrain is for experienced mountain walkers only.
□ On W coast of Isle of Arran off A841. Map ref 19C1.

878. INVERARAY
Castle/planned town

Most visitors come to see the castle – home of the Dukes of Argyll and hereditary seat of the chiefs of the Clan Campbell since the 15th century. But the attractive white-walled town of Inveraray itself is interesting as a fine example of a new or estate town. The original village was burnt down in 1644 and built in its present form as a Royal Burgh during the second half of the 18th century when the castle was also rebuilt. The castle is usually open to visitors daily, Apr to Oct, but is closed on Fri, Apr to June. Tel: Inveraray 2203.
□ Inveraray stands on the N shore of Loch Fyne mid-way between Glasgow and Oban. Map ref 18C1.

879. ISLE OF IONA
Place of pilgrimage

This tiny island was the most important centre of Christianity in northern Britain. Only three miles (5km) long and 1½ miles (2.4km) wide it is a grey spine of rock separated from Mull by the translucent green waters of the Sound of Iona. It was to Iona that St Columba came from Ireland in AD 563 to bring Christianity to Scotland, and a 13th-century abbey now stands on the site where Columba founded his monastery. Iona quickly became a place of pilgrimage and a burial ground of chiefs and kings. Both Duncan and his alleged murderer, Macbeth, are among the 48 Scottish kings buried at St Oran's Cemetery on the island.
□ Iona lies off the SW coast of Mull and is reached by two ferries. A car ferry runs between Oban and Craignure on Mull. A passenger ferry runs from Fionnphort to Iona. Also day trips in summer from Oban which pass Fingal's Cave on Staffa and stop at Iona. Map ref 18A1.

880. ISLAY
Hebridean isle/bird-watching

The most southerly of the Inner Hebrides. The island is 25 miles (40km) long by 20 miles (32km) wide with a great variety of landscapes – woods, peat bogs, moors, lochs, rivers, dunes, cliffs and beaches. Some of the beaches are magnificent – Laggan Bay has six miles (9.6km) of sand but there are also tiny sandy creeks dotted around the coast such as Kilchiaran Bay west of Port Charlotte. The variety of habitats allied to its position has made it a haven for birds – and bird-watchers. The island is the world's principal wintering resort of barnacle geese but 96 other species were spotted in just two days during one recent winter. Good spots to see birds are on Lochs Gruinart and Indaac and off the cliffs of the Mull of Oa in the south of Islay. Other attractions of the island include its many whisky distilleries.
□ Port Ellen and Port Askaig are the

ports of access to Islay from the Mull of Kintyre. Map ref 18B2.

881. JURA
Hebridean island

The Paps of Jura, three conical quartzite peaks all over 2400ft (731m) high, dominate this ruggedly beautiful island. Jura means 'Deer Island', and there are 20 times more red deer than people on this, one of the most sparsely populated islands of the Inner Hebrides. There is only one road, the A846, which runs from Feolin Ferry up the east coast to Ardulussa. Raised beaches, formed towards the end of the Ice Age, can be seen on the deserted west coast, while to the north, the notorious Corrievreckan Whirlpool can be seen – and heard – seething and rumbling in the narrow strait between Jura and Scarba. This dangerous tide-race is at its fiercest during the spring tides of early autumn.

☐ Jura can be reached by ferry from Kennacraig on A83 south of Tarbert to Port Askaig on Islay, where another ferry crosses the narrow Sound of Islay to Feolin. Map ref 18B2.

882. KILBARCHAN
Weaver's cottage

Weaving was the original cottage industry. Only with the coming of water and steam power did production of cotton and woollen goods begin to move to the new factories from their old cottage base. Here, a 1723 weaver's cottage has been preserved as a museum of the old days complete with the last two hand looms used in a village that once had nearly 400 such looms.

☐ 10 miles (16km) W of Glasgow off A737 or A761. Map ref 18D2.

883. KILDALTON, ISLE OF ISLAY
Celtic crosses

Two of the finest sculptured Celtic crosses in Scotland are located in an isolated churchyard at the south-eastern tip of Islay. It is a wonderfully peaceful setting reached by a drive along a narrow unclassified road from Ardbeg. Shortly north of the Kildalton churchyard the road peters out altogether but it is worth continuing in this direction for splendid views over the Sound of Jura.

☐ 7½ miles (12km) NE of Port Ellen at grid ref NR 458509; OS map 60. Map ref 18B2.

884. KILMARTIN
Prehistoric remains

One of the few areas of Scotland to rival Orkney or the other northern isles of Scotland in the richness of prehistoric remains. The valley which widens westward to the shore of Loch Crinan has several impressive monuments from Neolithic and Bronze Age times. Outstanding are Temple Wood stone circle (Bronze Age cemetery) and the dramatic hillock of Dunadd – the centre of the 6th-century kingdom of Dalriada. A carved boar and footprint mark the crowning place of ancient kings. Kilmartin church also contains a fine collection of medieval crosses.

☐ Kilmartin is eight miles (13m) N of Lochgilphead on A816 with the monuments mentioned above shown on OS map 55. Map ref 18C2.

885. KYLES OF BUTE
Scenic seaway

The Kyles of Bute are the beautiful narrow channels separating the Isle of Bute from the Cowal peninsula. It is a seaway much loved by those Scots who grew up with the tradition of going down the Clyde on the old paddle-steamers of yesteryear. Ferries ply between Wemyss Bay on the Scottish mainland and Rothesay, Bute's chief resort and steamer port, and ferries from Colintraive cross the Kyles themselves. In summer, excursions through the Kyles are a popular attraction.

☐ Map ref 18C2.

886. LEADHILLS
Ancient village

As its name suggests this area on the

Scotland

northern edge of the Lowther Hills has had a long history of mining, probably going back to Roman times and for not only lead but silver and possibly gold as well. The present scattered village is typical of mining communities, even though lead mining ceased a century ago. It lies at a height of 1350ft (416m) – only neighbouring Wanlockhead at 1380ft (425m) is higher in Scotland. Clearly it was only the prospect of a rich find which encouraged miners and their families to endure such a hostile environment. However this setting has become an asset: the village is now a ski resort.

□ 25 miles (40km) S of Lanark on B797 off A74. OS map 72. Map ref 17A1.

887. LOCHWINNOCH RESERVE
Wildfowl reserve

This shallow loch and the surrounding marsh provide a perfect wildfowl habitat as well as some interesting marshland and woodland plants. There are birds to see here in most seasons. In summer, good numbers of breeding duck, black-headed gull and great crested grebe (rare in this part of Scotland). In autumn many waders, and excellent winter wildfowl. Nature Centre. Limited opening. Tel: RSPB Reserves Dept., Sandy 80551.

□ Lochwinnoch, 12 miles (19km) SW of Paisley. Map ref 18D2.

888. MULL OF KINTYRE
Remote peninsula

The lonely lighthouse at South Point on this long and narrow peninsula can be reached by a steep and twisting narrow road from the Bridge at Carskey to the west of Southend off B842. The lighthouse is open to the public, Tel: Campbeltown 83234. To reach the southernmost point on the rocky coastal cliffs entails several miles' walk across wild moorland with fine views to the island of Sanda, and further off, the coastline of Co Antrim. To the east are beautiful sandy bays on either flank of the rocky headland of Keil Point. Here is the traditional first landfall on Scottish soil of St Columba, en route from Ireland to Iona. From Tayinloan on the west coast of Kintyre, a passenger ferry will take you to the tiny island of Gigha, where you can visit the sub-tropical gardens of Achamore House.

□ Take A83 to Campbeltown, then B842. Map ref 19B1.

889. NEW LANARK
Historic village

This cotton-milling village was built on the wooded slopes to the south of Lanark to exploit the potential of water power. It is popularly associated with the social reforms of Robert Owen, but was created in 1784 by Owen's father-in-law David Dale in conjunction with Richard Arkwright of Cromford (see Day Out 579). Dale himself was an enlightened employer, taking on many dispossessed crofters and housing them in cottages which he built to remarkably high standards for that time. The original mill building survives as do many of the houses, which are slowly being restored to a condition suitable for their place in British industrial history.

□ One mile (1.6km) SW of Lanark off A72. Map ref 17A1.

890. OBAN
Hebridean springboard

Life here revolves around the harbour which serves as the mainland port for many ferry services to islands of the Inner and Outer Hebrides. In the summer there are also regular day excursion trips by steamers to places such as Iona and Staffa. A few small sailing boats can be hired in Oban by those with experience. The striking Colosseum look-alike monument above the town is McCaig's Tower, built in 1890 to provide work for the unemployed

Oban is also a good base for a car drive exploring the sea lochs of Scotland which are among the impressive results of the Ice Age in the British Isles. The main characteristics of sea and fresh water lochs are their

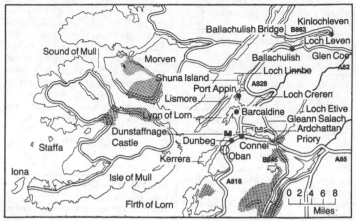

Oban: a 110 miles (176km) round trip drive from here takes in mountains, forests, beaches and sea lochs

depth and length.

To get the best out of a drive in this area you need not only a good map (as you do anywhere) but sometimes patience since the most dramatic roads can be narrow with passing places and plagued by caravans. The rewards are astonishing. A round trip from Oban via Connel, Gleann Soloch, Barcaldine, Ballachulish, Port Appin, Ballachulish Bridge, Kinlochleven and back to Oban again involves around 110 miles (176km) past 3500ft (1080m) mountains, forests, beaches and three sea lochs – Etive, Creran and Leven.

Particular points of interest along the way include Dunstaffnage Castle (off the A85 at Dunbeg); the NTS gardens at Ardchattan Priory; Port Appin peninsula with a sailing school and ferry to the island of Lismore (good for seabirds); several forest trails signposted by the Forestry Commission; Lettershuna for horse-riding or boat trips to the tiny island of Shuna; wildlife from buzzards to seals.

The OS Tourist map, 'Ben Nevis and Glencoe', one inch to the mile (1:63,360) covers the entire area of the car drive suggested above and for this it is the best value. The tourist office at Oban, Tel: Oban 3122 or 3551, is the best source of information about the area, including ferry services.

☐ Map ref 18C1.

891. SEIL ISLAND
Atlantic bridge

The only Hebridean island linked by a bridge to the Scottish mainland. This hump-backed stone bridge at Clachan, designed by Thomas Telford in 1792, is amusingly described as the 'Bridge over the Atlantic'. Follow the road, fringed with montbretia, as far as the tiny port of Easdale, on the west of the island. This former slate quarrying village and its brightly painted cottages stand below a prominent hill which gives excellent views of Mull, Jura and the smaller isles of the Firth of Lorn. A good centre for sea-angling and boat trips, with a car ferry to Luing from the south of the island on B8003. The beautiful garden of An Cala at Easdale with cherry trees, azaleas, roses, water and rock gardens is open Apr to Sept, Thur afternoons only.
☐ On B844 from Kilninver, 15 miles SW of Oban. Map ref 18B1.

Tayside

A region famed for fine rivers, noble trees, spectacular hills, old country houses and rich farming. Perth is a beautiful old town on the River Tay (Scotland's longest river). Pitlochry (theatre) is an old established resort. Dunkeld has a historic cathedral. Blair

Scotland

Castle is the seat of the Dukes of Atholl who still maintain a private army.

892. BEN LAWERS VISITOR CENTRE
Arctic-alpine wild flowers

The lime-rich slopes of lofty Ben Lawers, 3984ft (1196m), are renowned as a last refuge for rare arctic-alpine flora. The NTS has established a Visitor Centre here, which tells the story of the Ben, from the Ice Age to the present day. Nature trails start from the adjoining car park, and there are guided tours with ranger/naturalists during the holiday season (open daily, May to Sept). Please do not pick or uproot any plants.
☐ Off A827 midway between Aberdeen and Crianlarich. Minor road turns off near W end of Loch Tay to Visitor Centre near Loch na Lairige. Map ref 18D1.

893. DRUMMOND CASTLE GARDENS
Castle and gardens

A 13 acre (5.3 hectares) parterre laid out in the form of an elaborately decorated St Andrew's Cross on the floor of a valley below the steep escarpment off which stand the dwelling-house and the keep of an old castle. In the middle is a multiple sundial, with about 50 separate dials, bearing the date 1632. Open regularly, Apr to Oct. Tel: Muthill 321.
☐ Three miles (5km) S of Crieff on A822. Map ref 16A1.

894. DUNKELD
Market town

The charm of this small town is partly its setting in the wooded valley of the Tay. But it also stems from excellent buildings representing several periods of history. The cathedral dates back to the 9th century but although the parish church is formed by the restored 14th-century choir it is largely in ruins. However, the pattern of streets still reflects the town plan laid down in the Middle Ages.

The 'little houses' of the town (in Cathedral Street and High Street, for instance) were built in the years of the late 17th and early 18th centuries when Dunkeld was awarded burgh status for merchants to trade between Lowland ports and Highland markets. One further building of note is the bridge built by Telford in 1809 across the Tay. Pony-trekking, angling, nature and forest trails are all available in the locality.
☐ 15 miles (24km) NW of Perth on A9. Map ref 16A1.

895. EDZELL CASTLE AND GARDENS
Early 17th-century castle garden

A small parterre completely enclosed by walls and the ruins of an old castle. The walls are elaborately carved and further ornamented with niches arranged in a chequer pattern, and intended to be filled with plants. This unique and beautiful Renaissance garden was completed in 1604. Open all year. Tel: Edzell 631.
☐ Six miles (9.6km) N of Brechin off B966. Map ref 21B4.

896. GLAMIS
Castle/rural museum

The original 14th-century Glamis Castle was rebuilt in the 17th century in the romantic, conical-turreted style of a French château. It is reputedly haunted, and has strong royal connections, having been the childhood home of Queen Elizabeth the Queen Mother and the birthplace in 1930 of Princess Margaret. The castle is open afternoons only, May to Sept. Glamis itself is a picturesque village on the edge of the Vale of Strathmore with the Sidlaw Hills in the background. Some old cottages in the village have been restored to house the Angus Folk Museum. The museum contains agricultural exhibits from the largely self-supporting community of Angus over the past 200 years.
☐ Four miles (6.4km) S of Kirriemuir at junction of A94 and A928. Map ref 21B4.

897. LOCH LEVEN NATURE CENTRE
Lochside wildlife

This lochside reserve consists of 298 acres (120 hectares) of shoreland, farmland, birch-wood and heather. Visitors are asked to keep to the nature trail and picnic area. The nature centre is a converted farm building which has exhibition, sales and observation facilities. There is a wide range of birds to be seen including terns and many wading birds. In winter there may be as many as 70 different species, with spectacular flocks of geese, swans and duck. No dogs allowed. Open most days (except Fri). Tel: Warden, Kinross 2355.

□ Eight miles (15km) SW of Kinross on shores of Loch Leven (on B9097). Map ref 16B2.

898. MONTROSE
Tidal basin

With its gable-ended houses and narrow winding closes, Montrose is an old town full of character and seafaring atmosphere. Indeed, the town is almost surrounded by water, standing on the mouth of the River Esk with the huge tidal lagoon of Montrose Basin at its back. The harbour provides a haven for yachtsmen and a back-up service for North Sea oil exploration, and the basin itself is a favourite haunt for birds, especially wintering geese.

□ Map ref 21B4.

899. PITLOCHRY FISH PASS
Salmon-watching

From May to mid-November, visitors can watch salmon going through the 'fish pass' on their way upstream to their spawning grounds. Windows set in an underground chamber provide a good viewing point. There is also a permanent exhibition with aquaria, working models of fish passes and an audio-visual display. The Linn of Tummel nature trail guides you up-river to the Linn. This was known as the Falls of Tummel before the water level was raised by the Pitlochry Dam to form Faskally Reservoir. A trail booklet is available.

□ The Dam is at S end of Loch Faskally, signposted on A9. Map ref 21A4.

900. ROAD TO THE ISLES
Scenic drive

Though famed in song this well known Scottish road, past Loch Tummel and Loch Rannoch, now goes no further than the railway station on Rannoch Moor. The NTS has a visitor centre at Killiecrankie, open Easter to mid-Oct, in the wooded gorge where the Jacobites routed the English troops in 1686. Four miles (6.4km) from here on B8019 is the Loch Tummel Visitor Centre at Queen's View (Forestry Commission), open daily. Queen's View is where Queen Victoria enthused about the view over Loch Tummel to stately Schiehallion's brooding summit, 3547ft (1064m). The road continues to Tummel bridge and the thick birch and pine woods fringing the shores of Loch Rannoch to the lonely peat bogs of Rannoch Moor.

□ B8019 from Pass of Killiecrankie then B846. Map ref 21A4.

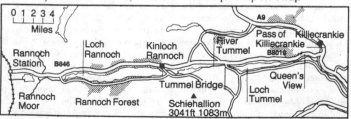

Road to the Isles: a delightful scenic drive past the shores of Loch Tummel and Loch Rannoch

Northern Ireland

901. ANTRIM COAST AND GLENS
Area of Outstanding Natural Beauty

The 68 mile (110km) stretch of coastline between Larne and Portrush is one of the most beautiful in the British Isles and is of exceptional interest to geologists. Its scenic highlights include Rathlin Island, the 37,000 basalt columns of the Giant's Causeway, the Carrick-a-Rede rope bridge near Ballycastle, the lovely White Park Bay owned by the NT and the spectacular limestone cliffs and caverns of the White Rocks near Portrush (see individual entries). The Antrim Coast Road is one of the most scenic corniche routes in Europe, though there is always the temptation to turn inland and explore the famous Glens of Antrim, nine green fingers thrusting deep into the lonely moorlands of the Antrim Mountains, all of which are included within this glorious AONB. Glenariff, most famous of the Antrim Glens; (see Day Out 911), with its gorges and waterfalls, Ossian's Cave, the Stone Age 'axe factory' on Tievebulliagh Mountain and the 'Vanishing Lake' of Loughareema, near Cushendun are other places of interest. Area 280 sq miles (725 sq km).
□ Map ref 22D1.

902. LAGAN VALLEY
Area of Outstanding Natural Beauty

Small area beside the River Lagan between South Belfast and Lisburn. You can follow the river for seven miles (12km) on a gentle towpath walk from Molly Ward Locks, on the Stranmillis Embankment, to Shaw's Bridge and Minnowburn Park, passing locks, rapids, woods and marshes. Area 8 sq miles (21 sq km).
□ Co Down. Map ref 22D2.

903. LECALE COAST
Area of Outstanding Natural Beauty

The Lecale Peninsula, between Newcastle and the narrows of Strangford Lough, is renowned for its immense sandy beaches. At Tyrella Strand on Dundrum Bay you can actually drive along the $3\frac{1}{2}$ mile (6km) beach. At the centre of this dune-scaped coast is the little port of Ardglass, renowned for its prawns. Now no more than a pleasant fishing village, it was a far more important settlement in the early days of the Anglo-Norman colonisation of Ireland. This is apparent in the existence of no fewer than seven castles or fortified tower houses. One of the castles is now a small museum. Fine walks go south to St John's Point, and north to Guns Island (accessible at low tide), where seals sometimes gather. Area 12 sq miles (31 sq km).

□ Co Down. Map ref 22D2.

904. MOUNTAINS OF MOURNE
Area of Outstanding Natural Beauty

A celebrated landscape of rounded, swelling summits – 15 of them rising above 2000ft (610m) within a 25 mile (40km) circle. The innermost heart of the Mournes is a roadless wilderness of heather, lakes and tumbling streams. The area also includes Rostrevor, Castlewellan and Tollymore Forest Parks, all open to the public, and the Down coast between Newcastle and Warrenpoint. Annalong, with its boats, stone quays, cottages and mountain backdrop, is one of the most picturesque of fishing harbours. Area 140 sq miles (362 sq km).

□ Co Down. Map ref 22D2.

905. NORTH DERRY
Area of Outstanding Natural Beauty

A vast, empty triangle of dunes and low-lying farmland thrusting out towards Donegal across the neck of Lough Foyle. Facing the Atlantic breakers is Magilligan Strand which is considered to be the longest beach in Ireland, seven miles (11km) of shell-strewn sands, with excellent bass fishing. The loughside mudflats attract large numbers of duck, wild geese and wading birds. Inland to the east rises the spectacular rocky escarpment of Binevenagh Mountain 1260ft (384m). Area 50 sq miles (130 sq km).

□ Co Londonderry. Map ref 22D1.

906. SPERRIN MOUNTAINS
Area of Outstanding Natural Beauty

This sparsely populated mountain range stretches for about 40 miles (64km) from west to east and is bounded by the towns of Omagh, Strabane, Cookstown, Dungannon and Magherafelt. The highest point, Sawel, is only 2240ft (684m), but the countryside is hauntingly beautiful, rich in prehistoric standing stones, and threaded by salmon rivers and trout streams such as the Mourne, Ballinderry and Moyola. Area 390 sq miles (1010 sq km).

□ Co Londonderry and Co Tyrone. Map ref 22C1.

907. STRANGFORD LOUGH
Area of Outstanding Natural Beauty

Sheltered by the long arm of the Ards Peninsula, this great sea lough is almost land-locked, being connected to the Irish Sea by the turbulent tidal narrows at Portaferry. Through this half mile (800m) gap 400 million tons of water pass twice daily with the changing tides. The fierce current here gives the lough its name for Strangford is Norse for 'violent inlet'. With its enormous flocks of wild duck, waders and wintering geese, its 70 islands and basking seals, the lough and its shores are of immense interest to naturalists. The A20 runs close to the water in many places giving good opportunities for bird-watching. There is also good sea-angling – skate and tope are the main attractions – and sailing. Mahee Island, reached from the shore by a causeway, has the ruins of Nendrum Monastery (see Day Out 920).

The area has all the classic features of a glaciated lowland and the 49 mile (79km) circuit round the lough from Newtownards takes in many of them, especially drumlins, the low, whale-backed hills of boulder clay deposited by the ice sheets. The sinuous coastline of the lough has been produced by the drowning of numbers of these by the sea. Many of the drumlin islands are linked to the mainland by causeways. One of the best viewpoints in the area is Scrabo Hill, which lies just south of Newtownards. Area 72 sq miles (187 sq km).

□ Strangford Lough lies 10 miles (16km) SE of Belfast. It is circuited by A20, A21, A22 and A25. Map ref 22D2.

Northern Ireland

Antrim forms the north-east corner of Ireland. Much of it is an irregular upland plateau dropping sharply to the sea on the north and east. Lough Neagh, the Bann Valley and the Glens of Antrim are major landscape features. Belfast is situated where the River Lagan enters Belfast Lough. Tourist office, Tel: Antrim 4131.

908. BALLINTOY
Sands, cliffs and downs

From the coast road at Ballintoy there is a view to the west which seems alien to Ireland. The patches of downland sloping seawards to dazzling white chalk cliffs, the beautiful curve of the strand and the sand dunes of White Park Bay, suggest south-east England rather than Ireland. This beautiful stretch of coast is owned by the NT. A rich area for naturalists and geologists with faults, landslips, raised beaches and fossils. The cliff path looks across the bay to Sheep Island, breeding ground for many seabirds. The bay is noted for its birds of prey including buzzard, kestrel and peregrine. A one mile (1.6km) nature trail shows the flora of sand and chalk as well as geological features. The ready supply of flints in the chalk helped support a relatively large prehistoric population and numerous remains have been found here. The nearby hamlet of Portbraddan, nestling in the cliffs, has the smallest church in Ireland. The ruin of Dunseverick Castle is perched on the edge of a cliff. The castle marks the northern end of the oldest road in Ireland, used by Celts to make the crossing to Scotland. A precipitous road leads to the small harbour of Ballintoy. To the east of the village is the extraordinary Carrick-a-Rede rope bridge which spans a wide chasm between the mainland and a steep rocky island. The bridge, used in summer by local fishermen, swings some 80ft (24m) above the sea. About two miles (3.2km) along the coast at Kinbane Head is Kinbane Castle, a beautifully sited ruin on a long white headland. There are good views of cliff and coast and a car park and picnic site nearby.

☐ Ballintoy is on B15 off A2, White Park Bay runs along A2 to W of Ballintoy. Map ref 22D1.

Some common Irish place-names and their English meanings

Modern form	Meaning
Ard	Height
Bal	Place or town
Curragh	Marsh or plain
Dun	Castle or fort
Ennis	Island or water meadow
Kel	Church
Lis	Enclosure
Lough	Lake
Seari	Old
Tipper	Well

---

909. CUSHENDUN
Scenic and architectural variety

This attractive village on the North Antrim coast has two claims to fame: one geological, the other architectural. The 10 mile (16km) drive along the narrow road from Fair Head past Murlough Bay and Torr Head to Cushendun takes the traveller through a remarkable variety of landscapes in a short distance. The rocky, treeless plateau of Fair Head changes into a narrow belt of open chalk downland which drops to the wooded slopes of Murlough Bay. The coastal slopes here are formed from a landslip of chalk and basalt. Then, at Cushendun, there are sea caves cut in Old Red Sandstone conglomerate. Here Scotland's Highland Border Fault (with the Southern Upland Fault it encloses Scotland's Midland Valley) can be traced across the sea south-westwards into Northern Ireland as it comes onshore at

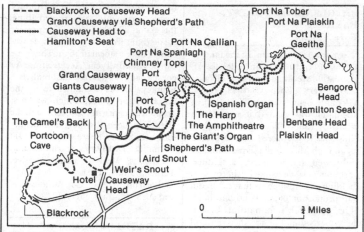

The Causeway Coast of Co Antrim, showing the three main walks and the places of interest you can see from them. Day Out 910

Cushendun. The architectural interest springs from the fact that the village was largely built by Welsh architect Clough Williams-Ellis who created Portmeirion in North Wales (see Day Out 318).

□ 12 miles (19km) E of Ballycastle off A2. Map ref 22D1.

910. GIANT'S CAUSEWAY
Strange rock formation

This promontory of symmetrical basalt columns ranks among the world's leading scenic land forms. It is cut into three bays running from Port Ganny to Port Noffer. Although formed by the slow cooling of volcanic lava, legend has it that the causeway was built by the Irish giant Finn MacCool trying to reach his Scottish enemy. Similar, less grand structures are found on Scotland's Isle of Staffa at Fingal's Cave. The rock formations have been given fanciful names: the Giant's Organ at Port Noffer rises to about 40ft (12m). There are also the Giant's Grandmother and the Wishing Chair. Three main walks are: Blackrock to Causeway Head, 1½ miles (2.4km), taking in Portcoon Cave; the Grand Causeway along Shepherd's Path, 2 miles (3.2km), which allows you to examine the causeway at close quart-

ers; and the 5 mile (8km) circular walk from Causeway Head to Hamilton's Seat. The North Antrim Cliff Path continues to Dunseverick Castle, 4½ miles (7.2km) past Bengore Head, the highest point on the Causeway. The main walks in the area of the Causeway are indicated on the map above.

□ B146 from Portrush or Bushmills, off A2, to Causeway Head car park. Map ref 22D1.

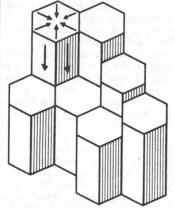

Honeycomb columns of solid basalt, formed by slow-cooling volcanic lava, created the Giant's Causeway.
Arrows show rock contracting into an hexagonal pattern

Northern Ireland

911. GLENARIFF FOREST PARK
Forest glens

The park is situated amidst the famous Glens of Antrim and includes forest, recreation areas and several small lakes and rivers. Early settlers found Glenariff heavily forested and when the land was cleared it revealed a marshy valley floor while upper hillslopes were covered with scree and peat. Only the middle slopes could be cultivated and a system of 'ladder' farming was developed where each holding ran upslope so that all had a fair proportion of good and bad land. The beautiful semi-natural broad-leaved woodland beside the Glenariff river and its waterfalls is managed solely for conservation and is a nature reserve and area of scientific interest. One of the first manufacturing industries in Ireland may have started with Neolithic man's axe factory at Tieve-bulliagh, just north of Glenariff.
□ Off A43 Ballymena to Waterfoot road. Map ref 22D1.

912. PORTRUSH
Headlands and sea caves

On a long peninsula jutting into the Atlantic, Portrush is famous for its golf courses and sea fishing from the rocks. Walks to the tip of the headland, Ramore Head, give fine views of the Donegal mountains, Rathlin Island and the Mull of Kintyre. There is a nature reserve by Lansdowne Green where the rocks contain the spiral patterns of fossil ammonites. Boat trips are available to the nearby Skerries and the Giant's Causeway. White Rocks, three miles (4.8km) from Portrush, at the eastern end of East Strand, can also be seen by boat. These chalk cliffs are riddled with caves. Non-sailors can reach Cathedral Cave by a steep path from the road or walk from Portrush. Two huge rock columns support the roof of the cave which runs 200ft (6om) into the cliff. Other curious formations include the Priest Hole; the Giant's Head, which looks like a face staring out to sea; the Lion's Paw and the Wishing Arch. Nearby is Dunluce Castle, a romantic ruin, poised above the sea on a craggy rock. The present castle dates from around 1300. It was ruined after a storm in 1639. The castle can be visited all year. Access is from A2 coast road. At nearby Bushmills is a whiskey distillery, claimed to be the oldest in the world, which was first granted a licence in 1608, although the Irish had been distilling unofficially long before that! There are tours of Old Bushmills Distillery, mornings and afternoons, Mon to Thur inclusive. Tel: Bushmills 31521.
□ Portrush is N of Coleraine on A2 and A29. Map ref 22D1.

913. RATHLIN ISLAND
Nature reserve and cliffs

The island is L-shaped, about six miles (10km) long and one mile (1.6km) across. Almost completely treeless, its cliffs present an unusual combination of colour and rocks, the black and white of basalt and chalk. They are rich in caves. Some have magnificent interiors, their walls and pillars of white limestone resembling a cathedral. Most can only be entered by boat. In the Stone Age the island had an axe 'factory' at Brockley. Axe heads of porcellanite, a fine grained bluish rock, identified as Rathlin-made, have been found in many parts of the British Isles. The cliffs which form almost the entire 16 mile (25.7km) coastline are the breeding place of huge numbers of seabirds – an estimated 20,000 guillemot alone. West Lighthouse is one of the best spots to see them. The islanders depend on fishing (particularly for lobster) and cattle and sheep for their livelihoods. There are two shops, a school, post office and a guesthouse. Further information about boat services and accomodation, Tel: Tourist Office, Ballycastle 62024 (May–Sept), 62225 (year round).
□ Situated in the Waters O'Moyle, eight miles (12.8km) from the mainland resort of Ballycastle. Boat service in fine weather from Ballycastle Pier. Crossing takes about 50 mins. Map ref 22D1.

914. SHANE'S CASTLE
Nature reserve

The Shane's Castle Reserve, on Lough Neagh, the largest freshwater lake in the British Isles, is managed by the RSPB. There is a nature trail and an interesting range of habitats with deer, red squirrels, badgers and foxes in the woods, and flowers, ferns, mosses and liverworts by the streams. There are also large numbers of birds and wildfowl and in winter many seaducks. Two public hides. The information centre at the castle is open Sun, June to Sept; Wed, Sat, Sun in July and Aug and every day from 12 July for two weeks. Tel: Antrim 66776.
☐ Off A6 to NW of Antrim on edge of Lough Neagh. Map ref 22D1.

Co Armagh

This is a county of gentle hills and has been the setting of many events in the epic history of Ireland. The city of Armagh, once the seat of the Ulster kings, has long been an important ecclesiastical centre. Tourist office, Tel: Armagh 524052.

915. OXFORD ISLAND
Nature trail

Oxford Island Nature Reserve is on the south-east corner of Lough Neagh, the largest freshwater lake in Britain. It is now a peninsula rather than an island due to the lowering of the water level in the lough. There are sheltered bays which attract large numbers of wildfowl, especially in winter; reedbeds which provide a haven for one of the largest colonies of great crested grebe; wet meadows, where in summer you may be lucky enough to hear the rare corncrake; and areas of young woodland. The Nature Centre houses an exhibition about the wildlife of the reserve and its conservation. The centre is open daily all year but at weekends by special arrangement. Tel: Lurgan 22205. The nature trail itself is nearly two miles (3km) long (there is a short cut) and includes an observation hide.

☐ Craigavon. Entrance on Kinnago Embankment Road adjacent to Lurgan exit from M1. Map ref 22D2.

Co Down

In the south are the Mountains of Mourne with Slieve Donard rising from the sea. Slieve Croob tops another range of hills in the centre of the county and in the east the Ards peninsula forms a barrier between the sea and land-locked, island-dotted Strangford Lough. Tourist office, Tel: Belfast 46609.

916. CASTLEWELLAN FOREST PARK
Mountain viewpoint

The park lies in the northern foothills of the Mountains of Mourne. Highest point in the forest is Slievenaslat, 901ft (275m), from which there are fine views of the surrounding countryside. The main features of the park are the castle, a 100 acre (40 hectares) lake stocked with brown and rainbow trout, five other small lakes and the arboretum. The latter was originally planted in the 1870s and has one of the most interesting collections of trees and shrubs in the British Isles. Activities include pony-trekking and fishing.
☐ Just N of A25 at Castlewellan. Map ref 22D2.

917. DROMORE
Motte-and-bailey castle

Dromore is sited where the main road linking Lisburn with Newry crosses the Lagan Valley. As part of the Anglo-Norman conquest many motte-and-bailey castles were built in the 12th century and Dromore can boast a fine survival, perhaps the best preserved in Ulster. It was built on a defensive site above an entrenched bend of the River Lagan. The medieval town which grew up under its protection remained small until the 18th century when the linen industry brought urban expansion.
☐ Eight miles (13km) SW of Lisburn just off A1 which now by-passes the town. Map ref 22D2.

Northern Ireland

918. MOUNT STEWART
Garden fantasy

A very large garden landscaped in the 18th century and largely replanted and redesigned in the 20th century by the Marchioness of Londonderry. She filled Italian terraces with permanent plants, made a Spanish garden, a fantastic topiary garden and commissioned, from a local craftsman, strange and amusing statues and ornaments. There are many rare and beautiful plants. The garden is on the eastern shore of Strangford Lough. Open daily from Apr to Sept, except Fri. Tel: Greyabbey 387.
☐ On A20 S of Newtownards. Map ref 22D2.

919. MURLOUGH NATURE RESERVE
National nature reserve

Northern Ireland's first nature reserve was established in 1967. Seven hundred acres (282 hectares) of sand dunes, based on a series of raised beaches, extend for about three miles north-east of the Royal County Down Golf Course. The oldest dunes, inland from the sea, date back at least 5000 years. The area has a wealth of wildlife including badgers and foxes. There is also evidence of early settlement, for example the Megalithic grave at Sliddery Ford. The Norman castle at Dundrum is a good viewpoint for the Mourne Mountains and coastal scenery. An interpretative centre is open daily, June to Sept, and at weekends rest of year. Tel: Dundrum 311 or 467.
☐ Entrance at car park just past Twelve Arches Bridge on A2 between Dundrum and Newcastle. Map ref 22D2.

920. NENDRUM
Early monastery

An old monastic site whose location on Mahee Island in Strangford Lough could not save it from destruction in the 10th century. Tradition has it that Nendrum was founded by St Mochoi in

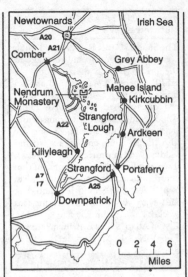

Strangford Lough and Nendrum: this is the place the Norseman called the 'violent inlet'. It has the ruins of Nendrum Monastery on one of its islands. Days Out 907, 920

the 5th century, but the earliest firm archaeological evidence comes from 200 years later. Excavations have revealed a remarkably complete plan of an early monastic settlement containing several circular houses, a church, graveyard and a round tower (now reduced to a stump) enclosed within three walls. The impressive monastic remains, which can be visited at any time, were important in establishing the secular as well as the religious role of monasteries in 'Dark Age' Ireland.
☐ 12 miles (19km) SE of Belfast off A22 to road bridge onto Mahee Island. Map ref 22D2.

921. ROWALLANE GARDENS
Rare trees and shrubs

Rare trees, shrubs and herbaceous plants in 50 acres (20 hectares) divided into a series of gardens. The rhododendrons, azaleas, magnolias and cherries are outstanding. Open throughout the year daily. Tel: Saintfield 510721.

☐ 11 miles (17.7km) SE of Belfast, one mile (1.6km) S of Saintfield on A7. Map ref 22D2.

922. SLIEVE DONARD
The easiest way up Northern Ireland's highest mountain

Slieve Donard, 2796ft (852m) where the Mountains of Mourne rise over the rest of Ulster before they come down to the sea, is a popular mountain with walkers. From the top you can see over a score of other peaks. It is also the easiest of the higher mountains of the British Isles to walk. From sea cliffs at its base to wild valleys viewed from the summit, the mountain has great beauty. The ascent takes 2½ hours, climbing through woods, past deep green pools, gorse-fringed cascades, blocks of granite and rough brown heather. The path is well trodden. It starts from Donard car park at the south end of Newcastle. Following the right-hand bank of the Glen River to the first bridge, it crosses this and continues along the left bank. When the path is almost ready to leave the forest, another bridge leads back to the right bank again. A fence is climbed over a stile, and a rough track taken up the right hand side of the burn – to

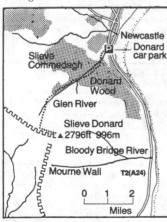

Slieve Donard: this map shows hill walkers the easiest route to the summit of Northern Ireland's highest mountain

where it eventually fords the stream and climbs uphill. At the col between Slieve Commedagh and Slieve Donard you are now at the Mourne Wall, the boundary of the water catchment. Wide enough to be walked upon, it leads eastwards to the summit cairn.
☐ Newcastle is 31 miles (50km) S of Belfast on T2 (A24). Map ref 22D2.

923. ULSTER FOLK MUSEUM AND TRANSPORT MUSEUM
Buildings of old Ulster

The open-air section of the museum consists of old reconstructed buildings from all over Ulster. There are water-powered flax and spade mills, a weaver's house and a number of other farm dwellings. There are demonstrations of horse-ploughing and harvesting with original farm machinery. Open daily all year, Sun afternoon only. Tel: Holywood 5411.
☐ Cultra Manor, Holywood. On A2 Belfast to Bangor road, about seven miles (11km) from centre of Belfast. Map ref 22D2.

Co Fermanagh

The county's outstanding feature is the river Erne and island-strewn Upper and Lower Lough Erne. Enniskillen, the chief town, stands between the two lakes. Elsewhere the county is hilly. The Marble Arch area is noted for its limestone scenery. Tourist office, Tel: Enniskillen 4361.

924. CASTLE COOLE
Neo-classical house

For admirers of neo-classical architecture this is a house of rare, if cold, perfection, surviving scarcely altered since it was built and finished in 1789–c1820, for the 1st and 2nd Earls of Belmore. James Wyatt modified slightly earlier plans by the Irish architect Richard Johnston and designed all the interiors. Among the many fine rooms is a great circular saloon. The furniture made for the house remains *in situ*, including the splendid contents of the saloon and the

Northern Ireland

state bed, with its elaborate Regency draperies. The castle is owned by the NT and is open afternoons daily (except Fri) Apr to Sept. Tel: Saintfield 510721.

☐ 1½ miles (2.4km) SE of Enniskillen off A4. Map ref 22C2.

925. LOUGH ERNE
Fishing and sailing

The Erne waterways are less well known for boating than the famous Shannon, but they are just as beautiful and interesting. They offer 300 sq miles (777 sq km) of navigable water and 135 miles (217km) of cruising through canalised and natural river, open and island-studded sheltered loughs. Take your own boat on a trailer, or go to almost any boatyard and they will hire out dinghies for a day or longer. The waters of the Erne are regarded as some of the best for coarse fishing in the British Isles. Roach, bream, pike, perch and eels are abundant. Brown trout is the main quarry for game fishermen. The waters are the most developed fishing area in Northern Ireland with many parking places, paths and fishing stands specially provided for anglers.

☐ Lower Lough Erne is NW of Enniskillen, Upper Lough Erne to the SE. Map ref 22C2.

Lough Erne: here miles of open water and river offer all the delights of cruising and fishing

926. MARBLE ARCH
Limestone arch and
disappearing rivers

This name relates to a remarkable land form, a natural arch of white carboniferous limestone spanning the Cladagh River where it emerges from its one mile (1.6km) long underground journey through the mountainside. At various points this subterranean water-course can be viewed down deep vertical shafts such as Cradle Hole, 100ft (30m) deep, where the limestone has collapsed. On the limestone plateau above the Cladagh Gorge several rivers disappear underground as they pass from gritstone on to permeable limestone. Cat's Hole is one of the most interesting of these 'swallow' holes.

☐ Take T53 (A32) out of Enniskillen then minor road W to Wheathill. Alternatively take N16 (A4) to Blacklion and take minor road E to Wheathill. Map ref 22C2.

Co Londonderry

Here the scenery is of hill, glen and river. To the south are the Sperrin Mountains, to the north the Atlantic coasts are fringed with surf-washed beaches. Derry, overlooking a broad tidal curve of the River Foyle, is the chief town. Tourist office, Tel: Londonderry 65151.

927. DOWNHILL CASTLE
Rural mansion

For those who like something out of the ordinary. The 'Earl-Bishop' Frederick Augustus Hervey, Earl of Bristol and Bishop of Derry, travelled Europe collecting statues and pictures and built a series of eccentric houses to contain them. Downhill was built up above the sea in the late 18th century, but was gutted by fire in 1851. The bleak shell of the great house remains and, at the edge of a windswept landscape which was once the park, an exquisite circular temple, the Mussenden Temple, survives untouched, on a dizzy site at the edge of the cliffs. Inside,

262

a fine room contains contemporary furniture. The temple is open afternoons daily (except Fri) Apr to Sept.
□ Four miles (6.4km) W of Coleraine off A2. Map ref 22D1.

928. MAGILLIGAN STRAND
Shellbanks and beach

This seven mile (11km) stretch of beach runs from Downhill (see the entry above) to Magilligan Point at the mouth of Lough Foyle. The point is an enormous flat triangle of alluvium and blown sand which juts northwards, almost closing the entrance to the lough. The best views of this remarkable terrain are from the basalt cliffs of Binevenagh. A massive Martello tower stands on the point. The strand is the haunt of conchologists, who say there are over 120 different kinds of shells to be found on this enormous beach.
□ A2 to Downhill. Map ref 22D1.

929. ROE VALLEY
Country park

The park consists of a three mile (4.8km) stretch of river banks and woodland. There are car parks, picnic sites, walks and an information centre. Activities include canoeing, rock climbing, trout and salmon fishing (permit required). Since the Ice Age the river has cut through the rocks at Carrick, Dogleap and O'Cahan's Rock, to form deep gorges.
□ Off B192 between Dungiven and Limavady. Map ref 22D1.

Co Tyrone

Tyrone is an inland county with mountains, glens, moorlands and plains. Low-lying land borders Lough Neagh in the east. The rest is hilly, rising to the heights of the Sperrins on the Derry border. Tourist office, Tel: Omagh 45321.

930. DAVAGH FOREST PARK
Forest drive

The park is situated on the north facing slope of Mount Beleevnamore 12 miles (19km) west of Cookstown. Its main feature is a six mile (9.6km) tarmac scenic drive through mixed conifer forest. From the summit of Mount Beleevnamore there are views to every part of the province. There are also sheltered picnic places, trails and a visitor centre.
□ Access via by-road off A505 Cookstown to Omagh road. Map ref 22C1.

Republic of Ireland

Co Carlow

The second smallest county in Ireland is green and wooded with streams and soft hills. Through it flows the River Barrow, one of Ireland's most scenic rivers. Carlow town, the county capital, was once an Anglo-Norman stronghold. Tourist office, Tel: Waterford 75788.

931. BARROW VALLEY
Scenic river

In the green and wooded country of the Barrow River valley there are a number of attractive villages which can be visited by boat or by car. Muine Bheag (Bagnelstown) is a pleasant place on the river and in Myshall village, a few miles to the east, is one of the gems of the Church of Ireland, the Adelaide Memorial Church of Christ the Redeemer, modelled on Salisbury Cathedral. Borris is a picturesque town at the foot of the Blackstairs Mountains and at Leighlinbridge, seven miles (11.2km) south of Carlow town, the ruins of Black Castle built in 1181 stand by the river. Nearby is Dinn Righ, Hill of the Kings, ancient seat of the Kings of Leinster. All that remains is a large mound. From New Ross to Saint Mullins there is some of the loveliest river scenery in Ireland.

□ The best of the valley lies between Carlow and New Ross. Map ref 23C1.

Co Clare

This is the natural hinterland of Shannon Airport. Clare is rich in antiquities churches, castles and over 2000 stone or earthen forts. The coast has sandy beaches, mighty cliffs and coves and, in the north, the limestone wilderness of the Burren. Ennis is the county capital. Tourist office, Tel: Ennis 21366.

932. THE BURREN
Limestone scenery

The finest example of 'Karstic' limestone scenery in the British Isles. The term 'karst' comes from Yugoslavia, where waterless limestone terrain is common, and here in western Ireland, fringed by the Atlantic and boggy lowlands, the waterless plateau of the Burren is an unusual phenomenon. It has all the classic land forms of such scenery, including disappearing streams around the slopes of Slieve Elva; completely enclosed depressions, termed 'poljes' (e.g. Carran Depression); broad limestone 'pavements'; bare mountain summits such as Slieve Carran; and numerous periodically flooded depressions or 'Turloughs'.

Drive across this limestone desert from Lisdoonvarna eastwards through Caherconnel and Carran to appreciate its treelessness, although botanists will be delighted with its great wealth of rare lime-loving flora. The area was thickly populated in prehistoric times and some 700 stone forts and dolmens still stand. The new Display Centre at Kilfenora helps visitors understand the unique features of this fascinating area. Open daily in the summer and by special request – for school parties and so on – in winter. Tel: Kilfenora 30.
□ Kilfenora is on the L53 road between Lisdoonvarna and Killinaboy. The L51 from Ballyvaghan to Leamaneagh Castle cuts across the area. Map ref 23B1.

933. MILTOWN MALBAY
Town of painted houses

This small town a little more than one mile (1.6km) from the sea is unusual in that it was planned when town planning as such was unheard of.

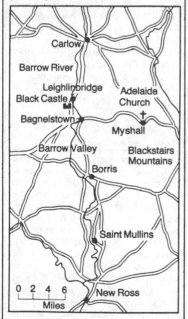

Carlow
Barrow River
Leighlinbridge
Black Castle
Adelaide Church
Bagnelstown
Myshall
Barrow Valley
Blackstairs Mountains
Borris
Saint Mullins
0 2 4 6
Miles
New Ross

Barrow Valley: some of the finest river scenery in Ireland. Day Out 931

Originally all its streets were to have been of equal length and, though this is not so today, it is still easy enough to see the original concept. It is an attractive place with many excellent examples of traditional Irish colour-washed houses. Spanish Point, two miles (3.2km) to the west, has a sandy beach.
□ Ten miles (16km) SW of Ennistymon on N67/T69. Map ref 23A1.

934. CLIFFS OF MOHER
Spectacular cliffs

Regarded by many as the finest stretch of coastal cliff scenery in the British Isles. Driving northwards on the N67 from Liscannor, the road ascends gently over a featureless grassy plateau with no hint of the dramatic coastline ahead. A signposted path brings you abruptly to the brink of the 600ft (183m) vertical cliffs which run for five miles (8km) along this ironbound Atlantic coastline. Layer upon layer of horizontal flagstones, shales and sandstones rise to a thick layer of yellow sandstone which forms an excellent viewing platform near the cliff-top. Climb to O'Brien's Tower, or wander along these breezy cliffs with marvellous views out to the fabled Aran Isles in Galway Bay. The cliffs are the homes of thousands of seabirds – guillemot, razorbill, puffin, kittiwake, gulls, fulmar, chough and peregrine.
□ Three miles (4.8km) NW of Liscannor on N67 (L54). Map ref 23A1.

Co Cork

Cork has mountains, lakes, river valleys, a rugged coastline with rocky peninsulas jutting far into the Atlantic. In the north and east, tracts of undulating limestone country are interrupted by ridges of sandstone with picturesque river valleys between. Tourist office, Tel: Cork 23251.

935. ANNES GROVE
Riverside garden

Beautifully set out on slopes overlooking River Awbeg. Includes a formal walled garden, an extensive woodland garden with a notable collection of rhododendrons, and exotic plants naturalised along riverside walks. Open mid-Apr to Sept, Sun to Wed afternoons.

□ One mile (1.6km) N of Castletownroche on main Fermoy to Mallow road N72/T30. Map ref 23B2.

---

936. BALTIMORE
Sailing centre

This is where yachtsmen sailing Irish waters reckon the Atlantic starts: at nearby and aptly-named Roaringwater Bay where the relatively sheltered southern coast becomes the exposed western coast. It offers a choice of sailing according to boat, experience and preference. Boats ranging from Mirror dinghies to a Drascombe Lugger can be hired by the day from the local sailing school. Motor boats from Baltimore run to Sherkin and Clear Islands. Sherkin Island has numerous coves and the ruins of a Franciscan Abbey and ancient castle.

□ Seven miles (11km) SW of Skibbereen on L59. Map ref 23A2.

---

937. GARINISH ISLAND
Italian gardens

When it was purchased in the early years of this century, the intention was to build an Italian style mansion on this tiny islet, with a garden to match. The architect was to be Harold Peto. Unhappily, the house was never begun, but the garden was. It is now stocked with a wide range of plants, many of which are too tender to grow outdoors in most parts of the British Isles.

□ Ferry from Glengariff Pier, Mar to Oct. Map ref 23A2.

---

938. GLENGARRIF
Village of the rugged glen

A splendid centre from which to explore the magnificent scenery of Bantry Bay and the Caha Mountains. Long drives can be taken westwards to Castletownbere and then back via the opposite coast of this mountainous peninsula. A shorter drive is over the spectacular Healy Pass, from Adrigole to Lauragh, set like a jewel in the surrounding mountains. Equally enjoyable is a stroll along the wooded coastline of the deeply indented Glengarrif Harbour with its compelling view of the neighbouring Sugarloaf Mountain. The harbour is dotted with many islets.

□ Take N71/T65 to Glengarrif then L61 along the N coast of Bantry Bay. Map ref 23A2.

---

939. KILLEAGH
Limestone valley

The N25 (T12) road runs along a wide limestone valley hemmed in by sandstone ridges to the north and south. Killeagh stands on the Dissour River, once noted for its bleaching properties. The delightful wood of Glenbower stretches up into the hills above the village, a rare example of Irish indigenous forest. The Dissour flows through the trees, partly in a cleft known as Glaunbour, or 'deafening valley'. North-east of Carrigtwohill are natural limestone caves with dripstone formations and at Midleton a stream disappears underground. The road goes on to Youghal, a popular seaside resort with a five mile (8km) beach.

□ On the N25 (T12) from Cork to Youghal road. Map ref 23B2.

---

940. MIZEN HEAD
Ireland's Land's End

Generally regarded as the Land's End of Ireland because it is the most southwesterly point of the Irish mainland. The sandstones and shales of the cliffs exhibit every shade of red and pink and they have been carved by the waves into stacks, walls, buttresses and ledges. Nearby is Barley Cove (between Mizen Head and Brow Head) one of the few extensive sandy beaches along this indented southern coastline. Excellent cliff scenery can be seen anywhere along network of roads and paths which criss-cross the peninsula, but especially between Brow Head and Streek Head to the south, although the scenery is slightly marred by the abandoned copper mines. These once produced most of the world's copper prior to the discovery of the African deposits. Out in the Atlantic the flashing light of the Fastnet Rock can be seen, five miles (8km) beyond the bird sanctuary of Clear Island.

☐ Acces via L56 south of Bantry or L57 from Ballydehob. Map ref 23A2.

941. OLD HEAD OF KINSALE
Peninsula viewpoint

This bony finger of slates and grits projects some three miles (4.8km) out into the Celtic Sea off Co Cork. The vertical rocks have been etched by waves into cliffs and bays and erosion has almost succeeded in breaching the narrow peninsula at East and West Holeopen Bays. Drive or walk out to the lighthouse for a splendid viewpoint, but eerie in fog as the fog-horn booms. (It was off the Old Head of Kinsale that the *Lusitania* was sunk.) A few miles north is the fascinating drowned river valley (or ria) of the Bandon River meandering past the picturesque town of Kinsale, with several fine 18th-century houses, into the attractive harbour. The monolithic English forts which guard the harbour entrance are worth a visit. Kinsale is a centre for shark fishing. Its inner and outer harbours provide miles of scenic water for the day sailor. Dinghies can be hired locally. So can boats for trips along the coast or up the Bandon River.

☐ Take L42 out of Kinsale to Ballinaspittle, via Western Bridge, and minor road past Old Head. Map ref 23B2.

Co Donegal

The north of the county has some of the most spectacular coastal scenery in Ireland and coastal routes such as the 100 mile (161km) circuit of the Inishowen Peninsula are outstanding. Bundoran, a popular seaside resort, and Ballyshannon are gateway towns from the south. Behind the coast are hills, moors, glens and lakes and a wealth of archaeological remains. Letterkenny is the chief town. Tourist office, Tel: Sligo 5336.

942. ARDS
Forest park

Superb situation on the wild, remote and deeply indented North Atlantic coastline between Bloody Foreland and Malin Head, with the Donegal Highlands at its back, notably Muckish, 2197ft (670m), and the gaunt pyramidal summit of Errigal, 2466ft (752m). In the 1200 acre (485.6 hectares) park itself there are forest walks and spots for picnics.

☐ On Sheephaven Bay two miles (3.2km) N of Creeslough on T72. Map ref 22C1.

943. HORN HEAD
Wild headland

A wild peninsula with a spectacular 600ft (183m) cliff. The view from the crest of this awesome cliff is one of boundless Atlantic Ocean, broken only by numerous islands and headlands, and inland of magnificent mountains, especially Muckish and Errigal. To the west of Horn Head is Templebreaga Arch and a blowhole called MacSwiney's Gun, a long cavern in which the sea booms in stormy weather. From the village of Dunfanaghy you can walk around Little Horn to get a magnificent view of the cliffs of the larger peninsula. About one mile (1.6km) east of Port-na-Blagh is Marble Hill, a secluded and beautiful spot with a splendid beach.

☐ Take N56 to Dunfanaghy then minor road. Map ref 22C1.

944. MALIN HEAD
Beaches of the geological past

The northernmost point of the Irish mainland, known to millions as a stormy sea area in the shipping forecast. Follow the L79 west along the edge of Trawbreaga Bay and then past the sand dunes of Soldier's Hill and on through the village of Ballyhillin. Here

Republic of Ireland

the ancient striped, hedgeless fields of the village run seawards until they are truncated by the abandoned sea cliff of a post-glacial raised beach. Malin Head has probably the best collection of raised shorelines in Ireland. Three all at different levels – can be seen and Ballyhillin is perched on the crest of the highest of them. They were formed at the end of the Ice Age and after, when the land, relieved of the weight of the ice, was uplifted. The watch tower on the headland has splendid views of the rock-bound coast. On clear days the Scottish Hebrides can be seen. To the north is the tiny island of Inishtrahull, its lighthouse perched on Ireland's oldest rock formation – the Lewisian gneiss. To the east is the cliff-girt coast of Inishowen and the large Stackarnddan sea stack.

☐ Four miles (6.4km) N of Carndonagh. Take the L79 out of Malin. Map ref 22C1.

945. POISONED GLEN
Strange valley

This curiously named glen in the heart of Donegal's highest mountains received its reputation from a poisonous plant, the Irish Spurge, which formerly grew on its marshy floor. Its U-shaped profile points clearly to its glacial overdeepening and its smoothly polished bare granite walls glitter in the sunlight and rain alike. From this mysterious cleft, it is easy to drive a short distance east on the L82 before striking westwards on foot to the summit of north-west Ireland's highest peak, Errigal (2466ft, 752m), a stately cone of white quartzite with great encircling skirts of shimmering screes and a jagged summit ridge. The reward for a steep ascent is a magnificent view of Donegal's renowned coastline.

☐ Take L82 from Meenacung to Dunlewy. The Glen runs SE of the village. Map ref 22C1.

946. SLIEVE LEAGUE
Cliff and viewpoint

Beyond the little fishing village of Teelin is a mountain track leading over Carrigan Head to the secluded Lough O'Mulligan and the cliffs of Bunglass. Here the view has to be seen to be believed: a magnificent range of cliffs ending in Slieve League, towering 1972ft (601m) above the sea. More adventurous walkers can continue along One Man Pass, a narrow ledge with a drop to the sea on one side and to a lonely lake on the other. Having traversed this precarious pathway you are nearly at the summit of Slieve League where there are exceptional views and the remains of a hermitage. Boats can be hired at Teelin for those who wish to see the cliffs from the sea. It may be advisable to find a local guide to show you the cliff walks.

☐ Teelin is 7½ miles (12km) W of Killybegs off T72A. Map ref 22B1.

The county is dominated by the capital, a place of spacious streets and fine buildings, beautifully situated on a crescent-shaped bay which sweeps from the Hill of Howth to Dalkey. To the north of the city are pleasant beach resorts, to the south Dun Laoghaire and Killiney Bay. Tourist office, Tel: Dun Laoghaire 806984 (May to Sept); 807048 (Oct to Apr); for Dublin City 747733.

947. HOWTH
View of Dublin

The peninsula was once an island which is now tied to the mainland by a tombolo of sand built by wave action. There are footpaths around the headland (as well as a road) offering fine views across the sea to the mountains south of Dublin. Howth harbour, on the northern side, is a noted yachting centre and picturesque fishing village. One mile (1.6km) offshore is the tiny island of Ireland's Eye, a favourite spot for picnics. Rowing and motor boats can be hired at the harbour. Howth Castle was a medieval building much reconstructed in the 18th century when formal gardens (now open to the public year round) were laid out around it. They are famous for their rhododendrons and contain a massive dolmen known as Aideen's Grave.

☐ Howth Head forms the northern arm of Dublin Bay and is reached by L86 road. Map ref 23D1.

Co Galway

Galway stretches from Connemara to the banks of the Shannon. It is Ireland's second largest county and its capital, Galway City, stands at the mouth of the Corrib River, a settlement with nearly 1000 years of history behind it. Offshore, across the mouth of Galway Bay, are the Aran Islands. Tourist office, Tel: Galway 63081.

948. ARAN ISLANDS
Historic islands

Three islands strung across the waters of Galway Bay. Boat trips to the islands from Galway City are popular, although they only call at Inishmore and Inishmaan. People and goods destined for Inisheer are ferried to land by *curragh*. The fortress of Dun Aengus (see next entry) is the greatest single attraction of Inishmore but there are the remains of other forts from Iron Age to medieval times and of early Christian churches on all three islands. Inisheer has the large fort of Creggankeel and tiny Kilgobnet Church, for instance; Inishmaan has Dun Conor fort and some Bronze Age tombs; and Inishmore has Dun Onaght and Dun Oghil forts as well as Dun Aengus and the early churches of Temple MacDuagh and Templenaneeve near Kilmurvey. Kilronan on Inishmore is the largest settlement on the islands. The cottages are neat, the fields laid out between limestone walls and the land itself is in places the results of a remarkable man-made process. Farmers spread sand, seaweed and manure, with any clay or mulch that can be found, on the natural bare limestone surface to create soil. The result is surprisingly fertile land producing good crops.

☐ Inishmore is 30 miles (48km) SW of Galway. There are regular boat services from Doolin, Co Clare, from Galway City and by motorboat from Rossaveal on the Connemara coast. There is also a daily air service from Arnmore, four miles (6.4km) from Galway City, from May to Sept and less frequently in winter, depending on weather and demand. Map ref 23A1.

949. DUN AENGUS
Prehistoric hill-fort

This stone-built hill-fort has been described as 'one of the most magnificent prehistoric monuments in western Europe'. It stands spectacularly on the edge of a sheer 300ft (92m) cliff on Inishmore (see previous entry), the most westerly of the three Aran islands that form an isolated natural breakwater in the wide mouth of Galway Bay. Dun Aengus – the prefix 'Dun' is Gaelic for fort or castle covers 11 acres (4.5 hectares) and consists of three 'concentric' enclosures, defended by stout walls of dry masonry. There is argument as to whether or not its inner enclosure was once circular and has been halved by the collapse of the cliff; or whether it was built with this configuration to take advantage of the excellent defensive rampart provided by the cliff itself. Visitors can walk round the site at any time.

☐ ½ mile (800m) S of Kilmurvey on Inishmore, Aran Islands. See previous entry for boat and air service. Map ref 23A1.

950. PORTUMNA
Forest park

Portumna, where the Shannon enters Lough Derg at its northern end, is a popular angling centre. Within the 1000 acre (404.7 hectares) forest park there are walks and nature trails, wildfowl ponds and stands for viewing wildlife, which includes red and fallow deer. Nature trail leaflets are available from a dispenser at the information centre.

☐ Entrance one mile (1.6km) from Portumna on Ennis road. Map ref 23B1.

Republic of Ireland

951. ROUNDSTONE
Coast road and corals

This coastal resort, beautifully situated on the west side of Roundstone Bay, is a favourite of artists and botanists. On the Ballyconneely road about two miles (3.2km) from Roundstone, at the foot of Errisbeg Mountain, are the beaches of Dog's Bay and Gurteen Bay which sit back to back, either side of a shell-sand spit, joining a granite island to the mainland. This is made from the microscopic shells of tiny creatures which formerly lived in deep water offshore. Both bays have sparkling white shellsand and numerous shells. Errisbeg, which rises to 987ft (301m) north of the town, gives fine views of the coast, low-lying bogs and the Twelve Bens, or Pins, in the distance. Its ascent is easy. Unusual and rare plants grow on the slopes of Errisbeg, including *Erica Mediterranea*. The coast road beyond Dog's Bay runs along the shores of Ballyconneely Bay to Mannin Bay. Here the so-called 'coral' beach is not an animal product like true coral but is of vegetable origin, derived from a calcareous seaweed, *Lithothamnion*, which thrives on the sea-floor beneath the clear waters of western Connemara.
☐ Minor road L102 S, off T71 Maam Cross to Clifden road. Map ref 22A2.

952. YEATS COUNTRY
Literary landscape

William Butler Yeats (1865–1939), Ireland's greatest poet, is not associated with any one particular area in the way that Hardy is with Dorset. Nonetheless he drew powerful inspiration for his work from the Irish countryside. The landscape of Ireland, particularly that of the west, is a constant thread through his writings. There are two areas in particular which are now regarded as 'Yeats country'.

Sligo. As a child Yeats stayed here with his maternal grandparents, as a poet he returned to write about places such as Lough Gill and Drumcliff. And it is at Drumcliff that he is buried, with a gravestone bearing his own epitaph:
  'Cast a cold eye
  on life, on death,
  Horseman, pass by!'

Gort, Co Galway. In this pleasant small Irish town Yeats stayed, along with other Irish writers, at Coole Park, the home of Lady Gregory. There they fostered a mutual enthusiasm for Irish literature which encouraged writers such as Yeats and Sean O'Casey and led to the founding of Dublin's Abbey Theatre in 1904. Little now remains of Coole Park other than a huge beech tree carved with the initials of Lady Gregory, Yeats and other literary figures. Close to Gort is Ballylee Castle, sometimes known as Ballylee Tower after the book of poems, *The Tower*, which Yeats wrote while living there in the 1920s. The building had been built in the 16th century and cost Yeats just £35 when he bought it in 1917. After being allowed to decay in the years after his death, the castle has now been renovated and is open to visitors during summer months as a Yeats museum.
☐ Drumcliff is five miles (8km) N of Sligo and Lough Gill is immediately SE of the town. Gort is 18 miles (29km) N of Ennis, Ballylee Castle is five miles (8km) NE of Gort. Map ref 7C3, 23B1.

Co Kerry

South Kerry has some of the finest and best known scenery in Ireland – the Lakes of Killarney, Carrantuohill, the Ring of Kerry and, offshore, the rocky Skelligs. North Kerry is less dramatic, a pleasant undulating lowland stretching away to the Shannon estuary. Tourist office, Tel: Tralee 21288.

953. CARRANTUOHILL
The easiest way up Ireland's highest mountain

This walk is the easiest way up the Republic of Ireland's highest mountain: the 3414ft (1040m) Carrantuohill. The highest point of the MacGillycuddy Reeks, this mountain is every bit as serious as Snowdon, Scafell Pike or Ben Nevis – if not more so. Rescue facilities are not as assured as in North

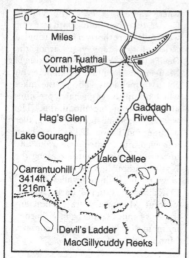

Carrantuohill: this map shows hill walkers the easiest route to the summit of Ireland's highest mountain

Wales; the massif is near enough to the Atlantic to mean frequent cloud cover at short notice; and this is a region of Old Red Sandstone with its characteristic sharp ridges and sheer corries, much of it little explored. The popular approach is from the north via Hag's Glen and the Devil's Ladder. More than any other mountain climb featured in this book, some hill-walking experience helps here. There is another route to the top from Black Valley to the south, but it has not the character of the one described. Nor has it the testpiece of the 'Ladder' which if it intimidates you means you should not be on the mountain in the first place. For the summit ridge is 'big country'.

From the Dunloe to Glencuttane road an access road passes Corran Tuathail Youth Hostel. A short distance away a footbridge crosses the Gaddagh River. Follow this to a 'green road' which pierces the glen to the twin lakes of Callee and Gouragh, where the scenery is tremendous. The Devil's Ladder is the gash running to the col south-west of the lakes, and after passing between these keep Cur-

rantuohill on your right during the approach. Climb the left hand side of the stream while ascending the Ladder up grass, clay and rocks. From the saddle the summit cross (and windmill which powers the bulbs which illuminate it) beckons. Make for it following the cairns in a north-westerly direction after your ascent of seven miles (11km), which will take five or six hours.

☐ 12 miles (19km) SW of Killarney. Map ref 23A2.

954. CUMMERAGH VALLEY
Corries and lakes

A rarely travelled back road gives you an opportunity to see some of Ireland's finest glacial corries and their accompanying lakes. Along this road you will see a magnificent mountain panorama unfolding to the right. The large lakes of Namona, Cloonaughlin and Derriana are held in by enormous crescent-shaped glacial moraines, with that around Lough Derriana being particularly impressive. Its southernmost arm is so massive that it has dammed up a tiny marginal lake, Lough Nellinane high up between its outer slope and the rocky hillside. The work of ice – scouring, plucking and polishing – is to be seen around these large corries, carved in the massive red and purple layers of Old Red Sandstone.

☐ Near Waterville. Leave main N70/T66 at Waterville and take minor road to Dromod. Map ref 23A2.

955. DERREEN
Woodland garden

Notable for its collection of New Zealand tree ferns this garden on the southern shore of the Kenmore River was established over 110 years ago. The setting is magnificent with many fine trees and shrubs. Open from Apr to Sept on Sun, Tues and Thur afternoons. Tel: Lauragh 3.

☐ On L62 SW of Kenmore, ½ mile (800m) from Lauragh village on a small peninsula in Kilmackillogue Harbour. Map ref 23A2.

Republic of Ireland

956. GALLARUS ORATORY
Drystone chapel

This Dark Age chapel is the most perfectly preserved early Christian building of its kind in the British Isles. The walls, between 3 to 4ft (1m) thick, were built of dry stone, almost entirely without mortar, in a technique similar to that deployed in the Bronze Age construction of the burial chamber at Newgrange (Day Out 978). Its high ridged roof looks like an upturned boat. The chapel is approached through lanes lined with lush fuchsia hedges.

☐ Five miles (8km) NW of Dingle and two miles (3.2km) S of Kilmalkedar on L98 and L101 via Neale. Map ref 23A1.

957. LAKES OF KILLARNEY
Scenic splendour

This magnificent 11,000 acre (4,451 hectares) park embraces most of the lake district and its better known attractions. A short, comprehensive drive can start at Muckross Abbey, founded in 1448, recently renovated and now open to the public, then to Muckross House which houses the Kerry Folklife Museum (open daily except Mon in winter). The next stop is Torc Waterfall, 60ft (18m) high and surrounded by trees. At Torc Bridge,

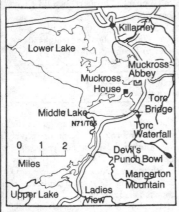

Lakes of Killarney: their scenic splendour is one of the highlights of western Ireland

where there is a Park Information Centre, take the winding path up to the waterfall where the river falls through a series of sandstone crags from the Devil's Punch Bowl high on the side of Mangerton Mountain. From here you get a tremendous view of the lakes which occupy large glacial depressions at the foot of the mountains. The wooded limestone shores of the smaller Middle and Lower Lakes have been dissolved into strange formations and mysterious caves. Continue along the N71 to Ladies View for one of the best views of the Killarney valley.

☐ Killarney National Park (Bourne Vincent Memorial Park): Main entrance 2½ miles (4km) from Killarney on main N71/T65 road to Kenmare. Map ref 23A2.

958. MACGILLYCUDDY'S REEKS
Dramatic mountain pass

The seven mile (11.3km) mountain track through the awesome valley known as the Gap of Dunloe starts from Kate Kearney's cottage, originally a coaching inn where illegal 'poteen' was sold. The track takes you between MacGillycuddy's Reeks, with Carrantuohill (3414ft, 1040m) the highest mountain in Ireland among the peaks, and Tomies and the Purple Mountain. This great U-shaped gash, 1500ft (457m) in depth, was the work, not of a local mountain glacier, but of a huge ice-sheet centred over Kenmare. You can walk through the Gap, or make the journey by pony and trap, or on horseback past a string of dark mysterious tarns. Details of jaunting car and boat trips from Tourist Information Office at Killarney. Tel: Killarney 31633.

☐ Minor road off T67 at Beaufort leads to the Gap. Map ref 23A2.

959. PORTMAGEE
Seabirds and sea views

Three miles (4.8km) south of the village is Coomanaspig Pass, 1100ft (335m), one of the highest and most spectacular viewpoints in Ireland accessible by car. Continue to St Finan's Bay (sandy beach, fuchsia lanes), then walk north along rugged coast for grandstand view of Puffin Island. Here can be seen not only puffin, but Ireland's largest colony of Manx shearwaters (10,000 pairs), together with fulmar, storm petrel, chough and raven. Also glorious views of distant Skellig Rocks, Blasket Islands and Dingle Peninsula.

☐ Eight miles (12.8km) SW of Cahirciveen. Map ref 23A2.

960. ROSS CASTLE
Launch place for the lakes

The castle, now a ruin, is sited on a peninsula which extends into Lough Leane, the lower of the Killarney lakes. Owners can launch their own boats with prior permission. Tel: Killarney 32252. Innisfallen Island is near the northern end of Lough Leane and about one mile (1.6km) offshore from Ross Castle. Evergreens flourish all over the island and holly is particularly luxuriant. The ruins of Innisfallen Abbey (AD 600) are near the island's landing stage. Boats and boatmen can be hired at Ross Castle.

☐ 1½ miles (2.4km) from Killarney town centre off Killarney to Kenmore road. Map ref 23A2.

961. SKELLIG ISLANDS
Ancient island monastery

The Skelligs are three rocky islands that rise from the Atlantic like peaks of drowned mountains. It would be hard to imagine a more remote position for these jagged pinnacles of grit and shale: seven to eight miles (11 to 13km) out in the ocean off Ireland's south-west coast. Great Skellig rises to 700ft (213m) and provides the bleak setting for the best preserved ancient monastery site in Europe, reached from the landing jetty by a stone stairway which is still intact after 1000 years. This Dark Age monastery site, spread over a number of levels, contains beehive-shaped huts, oratories, cemeteries, stone crosses, holy wells and the church of St Michael. It has survived partly

because of its isolation, and because unlike some other early monasteries (e.g. Nendrum, see Day Out 920) it was built of stone. On the western side of the island small terraced walls nurse patches of earth used as gardens or small fields. Little Skellig, the second largest gannetry in the North Atlantic, has over 20,000 pairs of gannets. The nearest mainland viewing point for the Skelligs is Bolus Head, a pleasant day's walk from Waterville. In summer boats to Great Skellig operate from Valentia Island and other places on the Kerry coast. The trip takes 1½ to 2 hours each way. The tour of the island lasts about three hours. Passengers should take warm and waterproof clothing. The trip is not advised unless you are a good sailor.

☐ Seven to eight miles (11 to 13km) W of Bolus Head. Map ref 23A2.

962. SLEA HEAD
Cliff coast drive

The most westerly point of the Irish mainland overlooking the drowned valley of Dingle Bay. The coast road winds precariously along the cliffs to Slea Head and on to Ballyferriter. From the head you can see the Blasket Islands. Centuries ago this headland was cut off from the rest of the peninsula by a defence system. The area is full of prehistoric and early Christian remains, the most notable being at Fahan where there is a concentration of bee-hive huts, known as clochans, as well as souterrains and standing stones. At nearby Dunquin, with its spectacular harbour built into the cliff, the film *Ryan's Daughter* was made.

☐ Follow minor road from Dingle along coast. Map ref 23A2.

963. VALENTIA ISLAND
Scenic island

This rocky island offers magnificent seascapes, tropical vegetation, and breathtaking cliffs. It is an excellent centre for sea fishing and diving. There are fine views from Geokaun Mountain (880ft, 268m), which lies to the north of the island, overlooking Knightstown, the 'capital' of Valentia. These include Glenlean, with its huge rhododendron banks and fuchsia glades, Valentia Harbour, Dingle Bay and the Blasket Islands. Boat trips can be arranged from Knightstown harbour to Beginish and Church Islands and the Skelligs. Bay Head, 792ft (241.4m), on the southern tip of the island also has superb views.

□ Minor road off N70 (Ring of Kerry Road) at Portmagee where a bridge spans the narrow channel to the island. Map ref 23A2.

Co Kildare

This, the flattest of the Irish counties, is the centre of the horse country with the Curragh races and the bloodstock sales at Kill. The north, beyond Naas, is bog country, while the south has the Curragh plain and the outer foothills of the Wicklows. Tourist office, Tel: Kildare 97636.

964. CASTLETOWN HOUSE
Georgian style mansion

A huge early 18th-century house built for Thomas Conolly, a self-made Speaker of the Irish House of Commons, it was part designed by the Florentine architect Galilei during a brief Irish visit, part by the Irish architect Edward Lovett Pearce. What has been described as the 'magnificent monotony' of the central block is like a Baroque town palace transposed to Ireland, and to either side colonnades curve to wings in the Palladian manner. Inside, the most memorable features are the cool white Rococo plasterwork of the great staircase, and the long gallery elaborately re-decorated in the Pompeian style in the 1780s. The vista north of the house terminates in the extraordinary Conolly's Folly (open to those of the public who can find their way to it). Super-imposed arches, like a fragment of a Roman aqueduct, pile up to a huge crowning obelisk, with hallucinatory effect. It is now the headquarters of the Irish Georgian Society which has restored the building and furnished it with Irish furniture and paintings of the period. A music festival is held at the house, normally in June. It is open daily except Tues from Apr to Sept; in winter only during afternoons on Sun.

□ Just north of Celbridge 12 miles (19km) W of Dublin off L2. Map ref 23C1.

965. TULLY
Japanese gardens

The gardens are in the grounds of the National Stud. They were laid out by Lord Wavertree's Japanese gardener, Eida, from 1906 to 1910. Perfect miniature gardens, they symbolise the life of man through all its stages, from the cradle to the grave. The gardens have some of the oldest bonsai in Europe. Open daily Easter to Oct, and Sun afternoons. Tel: Kildare 21251.

□ One mile (1.6km) SE of Kildare. Map ref 23C1.

Co Kilkenny

Kilkenny has two of Ireland's most beautiful waterways, the Nore and the Barrow. These and the hills of Booley and Slievedaragh give the area quiet beauty. With its narrow streets and arched passages Kilkenny city has an old world atmosphere. Tourist office, Tel: Kilkenny 21755.

966. KILKENNY
County town

The town of Kilkenny was essentially the creation of the Anglo-Normans who regarded towns as centres of civilisation, commerce and political power. This political role caused many towns to be attacked or deserted when Norman influence began to wane. But Kilkenny was lucky. Not only does the castle survive (although partly re-constructed) but so, too, do probably more late medieval buildings than can be found in any other Irish town. Evidence of its continuing importance and prosperity as a market and administrative centre can be seen in the way that 18th-century buildings were incorporated in the old medieval walled city. Fragments of the walls survive in the old town. So does the typical Norman rectangular street pattern.

☐ 30 miles (48km) N of Waterford. Map ref 23C1.

Co Laois

Portlaoise is the capital of the county, an historic place which was settled by the English in the 16th century. The remains of their castles can be seen everywhere. The Rock of Dunamase and its ruined fortress, the Timahow Round Tower and Abbeyleix are among the attractions. Tourist office, Tel: Mullingar 8761.

967. ABBEYLEIX
Woodland gardens

Beautiful woodland gardens with a fine collection of plants, trees, shrubs and magnolias. Monk's Bridge over the River Nore, dating from the 13th century, is still in use. Lily pond. The garden, but not the house, is open to the public, Easter to Sept afternoons only. Tel: Abbeyleix 31227.

☐ 60 miles (96.5km) from Dublin on N8/T16 to Cork. Map ref 23C1.

Co Leitrim

Leitrim stretches for over 50 miles (80.5km) from Longford to the sea at Tullaghan where it has a coast of just a couple of miles. Lough Allen virtually divides the county in two. Carrick-on-Shannon, the county town, is on one of the ancient crossing places of the river. Tourist office, Tel: Sligo 5336.

968 LOUGH ALLEN
Lake of the Shannon

Seven miles (11.2km) long and three miles (4.8km) wide this is one of three great lakes of the River Shannon. A 30 mile (48.2km) circuit of the lake can be made from Drumshanbo on its southern shore to Dowra, through Drumkeerin and back to Drumshanbo. On the island of Inishmagrath, near the northern end of the

lake, are the ruins of a church said to have been built by St Beoy. The lough is noted for big pike. Boats can be hired in Drumshanbo.

☐ Drumshanbo is N of Carrick-on-Shannon. Map ref 22C2.

Co Limerick

The Shannon is the county's northern boundary and on its other three sides it is bounded by a semi-circle of mountains and hills. Limerick city has grown from a settlement founded by the Danes. To the south-east of it is Adare, reputedly the most picturesque village in Ireland. Tourist office, Tel: Limerick 47522.

969. ADARE
Thatched village

Adare is one of the most picturesque villages in Ireland and its thatched cottages and wide main streets give it a marked English character. Most Irish villages seem to have developed haphazardly, and only those built by landlords close to the gates of their estates – or 'demesnes' – appear to have any preconceived plan. Adare is such a village. Although its long history of settlement is evident in the remains of a 13th-century castle, an abbey and two friaries, the village as it now stands owes most of its finest buildings to the efforts of the Dunraven family in the early 19th century. At time of going to press, the manor house and grounds were being offered for sale and it is not known whether they will be open to the public in future years.

☐ 10 miles (16km) SW of Limerick on N21/T28. Map ref 23B1.

970. CUSH
Ancient farming

A complex of ancient fields and enclosures on the western slopes of Slievereagh. Six enclosures or 'raths' averaging 65ft (20m) in diameter are joined together in a settlement where 70 rotary querns, glass beads and an abundance of iron slag have been found. Around the raths is a field

Republic of Ireland

system, marked out by earth banks and ditches, of the same late Iron Age/early Christian period.

☐ Seven miles (11km) SE of Kilmallock off L28 at Kilfinnane. Map ref 23B2.

Co Louth

The smallest county in Ireland has two areas of exceptional beauty: the Cooley Peninsula where wild, heather-covered mountains rise from the sea and in the south part of the Boyne Valley. The village of Louth, south west of Dundalk, once important, gave its name to the county. Tourist office, Tel: Dublin 806984 (May to Sept); 807048 (Oct to Apr).

971. MELLIFONT
Cistercian abbey

The abbey ruins are those of the first Cistercian house – and therefore of classical European form rather than in the Celtic tradition – to be founded in Ireland. The monastery was founded in 1142 and the church consecrated in 1157. Mellifont can be the starting point for an attractive 10 mile (16km) walk to and from the burial chamber of Newgrange (see Day Out 978). Leave Mellifont and head via Obelisk Bridge for the somewhat overgrown Navan-Drogheda canal towpath to Slane. Three miles (5km) further east lies Newgrange and the other burial

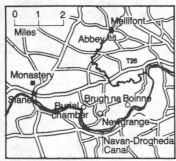

Mellifont: the ruins of the abbey make the starting point for a walk to the prehistoric cemetery of Newgrange. Days Out 971, 978

mounds of Brugh na Boinne. Return to Mellifont via the road north from T26.

☐ Four miles (6.4km) NW of Drogheda off T25. Map ref 22D2.

972. MONASTERBOICE
Monastic settlement

A monastic settlement possibly dating back as far as the end of the 5th century and founded by St Buithe. The remains are comprehensive: two churches, a round tower, two early grave slabs, a sun-dial and three fine sculptured crosses. The most important of these is the 10th-century Cross of Muireadach, named after an abbot who died in 922. It stands 17ft 8in (5.4m) high and almost every inch of its surface is ornamented with sculptured panels depicting scenes from the Gospels. The remains of the Round Tower are 110ft (33.5m) high and at one time it must have been the tallest of its kind in the country. Tall and slender, these towers had a doorway about 10ft (3m) from the ground and ran to five or more storeys with windows on each floor, and four or more windows on top under a conical roof. They are thought to have been bell towers to call monks to prayer but it is also believed that they were used as places of refuge in times of danger. Once the last person was safely in, the ladder to the entrance door was drawn up behind him. The latest examples date from the 12th century. The key to this tower can be obtained from the house at the gate.

☐ Five miles (8km) N of Drogheda on N1/T1. Map ref 22D2.

Co Mayo

County Mayo stretches from Lough Corrib and Killary Harbour in the south to Erris and Killala Bay in the north. It lies at the heart of Ireland's 'Western World'. Castlebar is the county capital. Tourist office, Tel: Westport 269.

973. ACHILL ISLAND
Ireland's largest island

This island joined to the mainland by a

bridge is the largest off the Irish coast. It is a unique combination of golden sands, moors, mountains and towering cliffs. The sea cliffs of Croaghaun Mountain (2193ft, 668m) on its western tip are the highest cliffs in northwest Europe, with a sheer drop of almost 2000ft (609.5m). This remote spot can be reached from Dooagh village via Lough Acorrymore. An easier walk is from Dooagh to Keem Bay where harmless basking sharks can sometimes be seen. The golden beach at Keel curves away to the Minaun cliffs where the famous Cathedral Rocks have been fretted by the waves into the pillars and arches of a great Gothic cathedral. Dugort, on the northern coast, is the place to start a climb up Slievemore Mountain, 2204ft (612m). Alternatively you can walk the seven miles (11.3km) around its base. On the eastern side is the deserted village of Slievemore, abandoned in the Great Famine. Boats from Dugort visit the seal caves under Slievemore. Also boat trips from Achill Sound around the coast and to various islands.
□ N59 to Achill Sound then 10 miles (16km) west to Dooagh. Map ref 22A2.

974. CLARE ISLAND
Island in the bay

Set at the mouth of the island-studded Clew Bay, this island steeped in legends and history offers only one hotel and a welcome from its tiny population of about 160 people. The southern coast is almost entirely bounded by cliffs up to 100ft (30m) high. Knockmore Mountain on the west side drops dramatically from 1550ft (472m) to sea level, terminating in sheer cliffs up to 300ft (91m) high which run about three miles along the coast. It is worth walking around Grainne Ui Mhaille's castle although it is not generally open to visitors. It stands above the little harbour on the east coast, the home of the ferocious Grace O'Malley, Sea Queen of the West, in the 16th century.
□ Clew Bay. Boat trips from Roonagh Point daily, four miles (6.4km) S of Louisburgh on T39 and L100. Map ref 22A2.

975. CONG
Canal that lost its water

This historic village stands on the narrow neck of land between Lough Corrib and Lough Mask. Its dry canal is a melancholy monument to man's folly – and a vivid reminder that limestone is a permeable rock through which water soaks freely. In the mid-19th century in an attempt to link the two loughs millions of tons of carboniferous limestone were dug out by hand. The task took five years. But today the canal wharf, bridges and locks stand unused, just as they have been since they were built. For the day the canal was opened the water flowed in for only a short distance. Then it disappeared underground. There is a four mile (6.4km) walk along this canal-that-never-was. There are over forty caves around the village and among the most accessible are Kelly's Cave and Captain Webb's Hole, $\frac{1}{2}$ mile (800m) east on the L101; Pigeon Hole, $\frac{1}{2}$ mile (800m) north of Cong Sawmill on the L101. Here there is a car park and forest walk as well as a cave with an underground river running through it. The ruined Augustinian Abbey, near Ashford Castle, lies to the north of the village. The latter, now a hotel, was the residence of the Guinness family. A forest walk, with a viewing tower, runs through the abbey grounds. Cong is also a trout fisherman's dream. Boats can be hired for fishing in the loughs or to visit the many beautiful islands.
□ Six miles (10km) S of Ballinrobe on the L98 and L101 roads, via Neale. Map ref 22B2.

976. KILLARY HARBOUR
The finest fjord in Ireland

If you want to see Ireland's answer to a Norwegian fjord then Killary Harbour in the beautiful west of Ireland will not be disappointing. Take the road from Westport beneath the frowning crags of Devil's Mother (2131ft, 649m) to the idyllic oasis of trees and flower gardens to be found at the isolated village of Leenane or Leenaun, where the full sweep of the burrowing Atlantic waters can be viewed. Alternatively take the L100 from Louisburgh southwards as it wends past wild Doo Lough cradled in a gash in the south Mayo mountains. Towering peaks rise on all sides and it is difficult to believe that the enclosed waters of Killary are indeed tidal. The shores of the fjord can be followed on foot out to the open sea, but if you want hidden beaches near the fjord mouth then follow the minor road round the northern flanks of the majestic Mweelrea (2668ft, 813m) which leaves the L100 at Cregganbaun and creeps round to the spectacular Atlantic coast at Killary Lodge.

□ Take N59/T71 S out of Westport. Map ref 22A2.

977. TOURMAKEADY
Lake fishing centre

The Irish-speaking village of Tourmakeady is an excellent centre for brown trout fishing and touring. It has a beautiful situation at the foot of the Partry Mountains (highest peak Benwee, 2239ft, 682m) and on the western shores of Lough Mask. Adjacent to the village there are forest walks, a waterfall and nature trail.

□ Take minor road out of Westport through Partry Mountains or skirt the northern shores of Lough Mask from Ballinrobe, approx 11 miles (17.6km). Map ref 22B2.

Co Meath

From Tara, in the heart of the county, the high kings of Ireland once ruled. The countryside is rich in such reminders of the past and a visit to the Boyne Valley is like a course in Irish history from prehistoric tumuli to Norman castles. Tourist office, Tel: Dublin 806984 (May to Sept); 807048 (Oct to Apr).

978. NEWGRANGE
Prehistoric cemetery

This is the name given to the most famous of a series of Neolithic passage graves in a 'prehistoric cemetery' set on a ridge above the River Boyne. It is a great mound or cairn, 42ft (12.8m) high and composed of hundreds of thousands of water-worn river pebbles. Twelve huge standing stones surround the cairn and, inside, a 62ft (19m) long passage leads to a central chamber which has intricate rock carvings displaying the whole repertory of megalithic art. There are two other mounds nearby at Knowth and Dowth. The whole site is known as Brugh na Boinne, or the Boyne Valley Cemetery. Newgrange is open to visitors daily May to Sept, closed Mon the rest of the year.

□ Six miles (9.6km) SW of Drogheda off L21. Map ref 22D2.

979. TARA
Capital of the Irish kings

The hill of Tara, although little more than 500ft (154m), dominates the area and is one of the most famous Irish historical sites. It is the traditional seat of the kings of Tara and the centre of a pagan cult in the Iron Age. The many earthworks and man-made mounds on the hill have been given romantic names (e.g. Fort of the Kings, Royal Seat, King's Chair etc) for which there is no proof of accuracy. Most of these monuments belong to the Celtic Iron Age, but the burial mound known as 'The Mound of the Hostages' has been dated to 2000 BC by radio-carbon techniques. The site can be visited at any time.

□ Seven miles (11km) E of Trim off N3/T35. Map ref 23C1.

Co Offaly

Offaly lies near the very centre of Ireland. To the west flows the Shannon and near its banks is the old monastic city of Clonmacnois. Tullamore is the principal town and lies in the north of the county. Tourist office, Tel: Mullingar 8761.

980. CLONMACNOIS
Monastic settlement

One of central Ireland's most characteristic land forms is the esker, a long sinuous ridge of sand and gravel which snakes across the lowland bogs. Formed when glacial melt-streams honeycombed the former ice-sheets, eskers represent the sediments deposited in the sub-glacial ice-tunnels. These sediments were left behind when the ice-sheets disappeared. In the earliest historic times the eskers provided dry routeways through the peat bogs and the ancient Pilgrim's Road runs westwards along an esker to the historic monastic and cathedral ruins of Clonmacnois in a lonely and beautiful setting on the east bank of the Shannon. It was founded in the 6th century by St Ciaran and became famous as a centre of scholarship and craftsmanship as well as religion. But it suffered so severely under Viking raiders and later the English that it was abandoned in the 16th century. Yet its importance can be gauged by the variety of the remains. Here, in varying stages of disrepair, are one cathedral, seven churches, two round towers, three crosses and the largest collection in Ireland of early gravestones.

☐ 15 miles (24km) S of Athlone off N62/T32 at Ballynahowen. Map ref 23C1.

Co Roscommon

Roscommon stretches from the Arigna Mountains in the north to low-lying Lough Ree in the south with the majestic Shannon flowing along the county's eastern boundary. The Lough Key Forest Park near Boyle has a fine lakeside setting. Tourist Office, Tel: Mullingar 8761.

981. LOUGH KEY
Forest park

Facilities in this 685 acre (350 hectares) park include a camping area and caravan park with shop and restaurant at the lakeside. A popular place for boating, cruising, fishing and swimming it also contains a bog garden, deer compound, forest walks and nature trail (booklet available on site). Tel: Cootehall 7 for details of cruising. For boats, enquire at shop.

☐ Two miles (3.2km) E of Boyle, seven miles (11.2km) NW of Carrick-on-Shannon on T3. Map ref 22B2.

Co Sligo

When William Butler Yeats wrote about 'The Land of Heart's Desire' he had the beauty of the Sligo countryside in mind. Mountains, seas and lakes combine to make a poet's landscape. Sligo town lies in a valley between two mountains. Tourist office, Tel: Sligo 5336.

982. CARROWKEEL
5000 year old village

A Neolithic settlement and cemetery in a fantastic landscape of limestone platforms and precipices in the Bricklieve Mountains. The village consists of a cluster of nearly 50 stone rings on a bare rocky platform 800ft (243m) above sea level. Such a collection of Neolithic dwellings, 4000 to 5000 years old, is unrivalled in the British Isles.

☐ 15 miles (24km) S of Sligo. Follow routes T3 and L11 to Ballymote. Proceed along L11 towards Boyle, branching off for Carrowkeel at the Traveller's Rest. Map ref 22B2.

Co Tipperary

In the north Ireland's largest inland county is a land of plains, lakes – it has Lough Derg, largest of the Shannon lakes and river valleys. The south has high mountains and wide fertile valleys. Tourist offices, Tel: North Tipperary, Nenagh 31610; South Tipperary, Cashel 61333.

983. CAHIR
Castle and colourful houses

This small old-world town, straddling the River Suir at the eastern end of the Galtee Mountains, provides excellent examples of traditional Irish painting of houses and cottages. The colours used are often unlikely combinations of pinks, dark green and browns – almost 'fairground-style' – but surprisingly

Republic of Ireland

effective for all that. Each household mixes its own paints and chooses the colours to blend with those already adopted by their neighbours. A genuine survival of an Irish tradition. Cahir Castle with its massive keep, high enclosing walls and spacious courtyard is the focal point of the town. It is open daily June to Sept and is floodlit all year.

☐ 12 miles (19km) SE of Tipperary on N24/T13. Map ref 23B2.

984. GLEN OF AHERLOW
Secluded glen

This fertile glen is spread between the Galtee mountains and the Slievenamuck hills to the north. Formerly an important pass between the plains of Tipperary and Limerick, it has been the scene of many ancient battles and the retreat of dispossessed and outlawed Irishmen who took refuge in the numerous caves on the Aherlow side of the Galtees. At the head of the glen near the village of Galbally, almost on the Co Limerick border, are the ruins of the Franciscan Moor Abbey. On the northern slopes of the glen, on the Slievenamuck hills, is a 16ft (5m) statue of Christ which was put there in 1950. A walk along the ridge is a rewarding way of exploring the glen.
☐ Access on minor roads to the W of the N24/T13 Cahir to Tipperary road. Map ref 23B1.

985. KNOCKMEALDOWN'S VEE ROAD
Scenic drive

The remarkably engineered Vee Road, named from its hairpin bends on the northern slopes of the Knockmealdown Mountains (2609ft, 795m) is one of the most scenic drives in southern Ireland. From Clogheen the road climbs the forested mountainside until it breaks out on to open moorland. There are superb views northwards over the narrow limestone vale of Mitchelstown to the imposing Old Red Sandstone and Silurian massif of Galtymore (3016ft, 919m), one of Ireland's highest mountains. Behind

you the conical outliers of Sugarloaf Hill overlook the narrow mountain pass of the Gap where a tiny lake, Bay Lough, occupies a glacial corrie, now overflowing with wild rhododendrons. South of the pass the road descends gently to the Blackwater river valley where, just 10 miles (16km) from the sea at Dungarvan, this mighty river makes its anomalous southward turn at Cappoquin. Instead of following an easy limestone corridor to the sea, the river turns back to flow in wooded gorges through successive sandstone ridges *en route* to its estuary at Youghal.
☐ Tipperary/Cork border. Take the L34S from Clogheen. Map ref 23B2.

986. ROCK OF CASHEL
Acropolis of Ireland

In the seemingly endless plains of central Ireland, the Rock of Cashel comes as something of a surprise: one of the most historic and visually exciting places in the British Isles. This small upfold of carboniferous limestone rising 300ft (92m) above the plain was utilised in pre-Christian times by the early Irish as a citadel for their Munster kings' palace. The splendid grouping of grey limestone buildings dominated by the ruined cathedral and round tower has enormous aesthetic appeal and has drawn comparisons with Athens' Acropolis, notwithstanding their very different architectural character. In the 12th century it became entirely ecclesiastical, but even before then it had some religious significance. St Patrick visited it about AD 450 and some kings were also bishops. One of the last of the latter was Cormac MacCarthy who was responsible for Cormac's Chapel, the most complete and largest of the Irish Romanesque buildings. This was consecrated in 1134 and now stands amid the ruins of the great cathedral erected on the rock in the 13th century. The two acre (0.8 hectare) site on top of the rock also has a 92ft (28m) Round Tower from the 11th century in a good state of preservation. The rock and its ruins are floodlit in summer. From the rock itself there are splendid views over the surrounding lowlands, which are known as the Golden Vale. Here is some of the richest farmland in Ireland. Cashel is the market town for the area. The rock is open from June to Aug daily. Closed on Mon in winter.

□ Eight miles (13km) E of Tipperary on N74/T36. Map ref 23B1.

Co Waterford

The north is mountainous with the Comeragh and Knockmealdown ranges the most prominent. Between them and the coast there are gentler landscapes with castles, cathedrals, river valleys and well kept plantations. The coast has fine beaches and sheltered coves. Tourist office, Tel: Waterford 75788.

987. ARDMORE
Best of the Round Towers

A coastal monastic site with perhaps the finest example of the 100 or so Round Towers which survive in Ireland. These tapering stone cylinders date from the period of the Norse raids between the 10th and 12th centuries. Sometimes reaching as high as 106ft (32.3m), as at Kildare (see Day Out 972), they were watch towers, places of refuge and stores for monastic treasures. The 12th-century cathedral at Ardmore is among the most impressive of early Christian buildings in Ireland. The site can be visited any time.

□ Five miles (8km) E of Youghal off T12/N25. Map ref 23B2.

988. CARRICK CASTLE
Elizabethan mansion

For Ireland, an almost unique survival: a gabled Elizabethan manor house, built in about 1600 by the 10th Earl of Ormonde, chief of the great Anglo-Irish clan of the Butlers. The original late medieval castle survives as a ruin, attached to the house. Inside there is a long gallery and the remains of fine plasterwork. The whole is like a transplant from the Cotswolds, and acquires an exotic and unlikely quality in its Irish landscape setting, at the edge of the picturesque little town of Carrick-on-Suir. The house is open on request. There are no guided tours.

□ 15 miles (24km) NW of Waterford off A24. Map ref 23C2.

Co Westmeath

Westmeath is an inland county pleasantly endowed with low hills. In the north-east they command good views over lake-dotted landscapes. Mullingar is the county capital. Tourist office, Tel: Mullingar 8650.

989. FORE ABBEY
Benedictine priory

Snugly situated in a valley hemmed in by jagged limestone cliffs is a 9th-century church and the remains of a medieval walled town, including a fine gateway. Here, too, are the only authenticated remains of a Benedictine priory in Ireland so that the richness and variety of remains, allied to their setting, make this one of the most attractive sites in this part of the country. Keys are available at the Post Office in Fore village.

□ 15 miles W of Kells (also known as Ceanannas) on L142. Map ref 22C2.

Co Wexford

A countryside of low hills, river valleys, lush pastures, well kept thatched cottages and sandy beaches. To the north it is bounded by the Wicklow Hills, to the west by the River Barrow and Blackstairs Mountains. Wexford is the chief town. Tourist office, Tel: Wexford 23111.

990. MOUNT LEINSTER
Mountain viewpoint

There is a road to the summit of this high mountain in the Blackstairs Mountains, on the borders of Carlow and Wexford, but it was built to service the giant TV transmitter which stands on the 2610ft (795m) summit, and is extremely steep. Visitors are recommended to leave their cars at the lay-by

Republic of Ireland

at the gate to the summit road and finish the climb on foot. The Blackstairs Mountains are an isolated group so the summit is a magnificent viewpoint, not only over the surrounding lowlands, but north to the high Wicklow Mountains. From Bunclody the road strikes westward up the beautiful forested valley of the Clody River before emerging on the high, windswept granite moorlands. It then snakes up the ridge to the summit, with breathtaking views of the Barrow and Slaney valleys, to the west and east respectively.

☐ The mountain is on the border between Wexford and Carlow counties. Access via a minor road off the N80/T16 just NW of Bunclody. Map ref 23C1.

991. SALTEE ISLANDS
Bird islands

These islands are Ireland's most famous bird sanctuary with a population of over three million birds during late spring and early summer. There are two islands, Lesser and Great Saltee, the latter being of greater interest. It has one of the three gannet colonies in Ireland, and is the only one off the south-east coast.

☐ The Saltees lie off Kilmore Quay from where there are boat trips to the islands in summer. Map ref 23C2.

Co Wicklow

County Wicklow, just south of Dublin, is called the 'Garden of Ireland'. Its coast is mostly low and sandy while the granite mountains of central Wicklow are cut by deep glens and wooded valleys. Here is some of the finest scenery in the east of Ireland. Wicklow, the county town, overlooks a wide crescent-shaped bay. Tourist office, Tel: Dublin 806984 (May to Sept); 807048 (Oct to Apr).

992. AVONDALE
Forest park

Pleasant walks, nature trails and picnic place in the beautiful valley of Avonmore. Avondale House (home of Charles Stewart Parnell) is open afternoons Fri to Mon, May to Sept.
☐ Just S of Rathdrum. Map ref 23D1.

993. GLENDALOUGH
Wild beauty and rich history

The most picturesque of all the Irish monastic sites. It lies at the head of a secluded valley containing two lakes and is surrounded by the Wicklow Mountains. Dark Age and Medieval remains abound. The oldest church, although much restored, is Templenaskellig which is at the foot of a sheer cliff and can only be reached by boat. The trip, giving wonderful views of Glendalough Valley, takes 15 minutes. Other churches in varying stages of ruin on the old monastic site on the valley floor include the 10th-century cathedral and the tiny 11th-century St Kevin's Church, named after the saint said to have founded the monastery here in the 7th century. The imposing Round Tower, 110ft (33.5m) high, is still almost perfect after 1000 years. The valley site is scenically attractive with many footpaths leading through the wooded slopes around the lakes. Glenmalure offers a magnificent drive up-valley for about nine miles (14.5km) to Baravore. This, once a thriving centre of lead mining, is one of the most beautiful of the Wicklow glens.

☐ Three miles (5km) W of Laragh off L107. Map ref 23D1.

994. GLEN OF IMAAL
Amphitheatre in the hills

The Glen of Imaal is a vast natural amphitheatre nearly five miles (8km) long and three miles (4.8km) wide. It is surrounded by hills which, on three sides, rise to over 1000ft (305m). The River Slaney, which flows into the sea at Wexford, rises on Lugnaquilla, which stands at 3039ft (926m) to the east of the glen. Baltinglass, on the River Slaney to the south, is overlooked by Baltinglass Hill, crowned with the remains of a Bronze Age burial mound and hill-fort. There is a ruined Cistercian Abbey in the town.
□ Minor road via Donard off the N81/T42 Hollywood to Baltinglass road. Map ref 23C1.

995. MOUNT USHER GARDENS
Riverside garden

Many rare trees and shrubs planted in a natural setting in this privately owned garden by the Vartry River where it tumbles down over an impressive series of small weirs. At time of going to press, these gardens had changed hands and the new owners had not yet decided whether they would continue to open to the public.
□ Three miles (4.8km) N of Wicklow at Ashford. Map ref 23D1.

996. POWERSCOURT DEMESNE
Waterfall and gardens

In the Deer Park of Powerscourt is one of the highest single-leap waterfalls in the British Isles. Its setting is magnificent, nestling in a hollow of the Wicklow Mountains. The Dargle River pours down into a sylvan glen over a 400ft (122m) cliff before entering a deep pool surrounded by fallen boulders. A fascinating spot for a picnic, with time to explore the very contrasting landscape gardens of Powerscourt itself, one of the finest formal gardens in Europe, with large terraces descending to a circular lake and, to one side, a Japanese garden. In all, a magnificent example of an aristocratic garden laid out with taste and imagination. The view from the terraces across the woodlands to Sugar Loaf Mountain on the skyline is memorable. The mansion itself burned down several years ago. The gardens open from Easter to Oct daily. The waterfall is open all year. Tel: Dublin 863546.
□ SW of Enniskerry, off the T43A. Map ref 23D1.

997. ROUNDWOOD
Rivers and waterfalls

Reputed to be the highest village in Ireland at 780ft (237m) above sea level. The scenery and fishing for brown trout are the two main attractions. There are boats for hire to fish in the reservoir. A short distance west of the village are the beautiful Loughs, Dan and Tay. Devil's Glen, about five miles (8km) south-east of Roundwood off the minor road to Ashford, is a deep chasm with craggy sides which nurses the Vartry River after it has fallen almost 100ft (30m) into the Devil's Punch Bowl. The thickly forested ravine of the Devil's Glen is an excellent example of a glacial meltwater channel which was cut by the torrents flowing from the snow-capped summits of the Wicklows. Restrained by the edges of the lowland ice sheets the waters cut spectacular rocky gorges in the margins of the Vartry Plateau as they tried to escape southwards. A nature trail and walks have been constructed, leaflet available on site.
□ 12 miles (19km) S of Enniskerry on main T81 road. Map ref 23D1.

998. RUSSBOROUGH
Palladian mansion

The most sensational surviving example of the Anglo-Irish aristocracy's favoured method of keeping up with their much richer English counterparts in the 18th century. A comparatively small house built c 1740 for the Earl of Miltown, made to seem three times its size by stringing out wings, walls, stables, arches and obelisks to either side. The result is a sensationally

beautiful stage set, looking over to the Wicklow Mountains. Inside, room after room is decorated with fine Rococo plasterwork, and the great Beit collection of pictures, furniture, porcelain and bronzes, of international repute. The house is open on Sun afternoons and Bank Holidays from Easter to Oct and also on Wed June to Sept and Sat in July and Aug, afternoons only. Tel: Naas 65239.
□ 2½ miles (4km) S of Blessington off N81/T42. Map ref 23C1.

999. VALE OF AVOCA
Bright waters meet

Two miles north of Avoca village is the Meeting of the Waters in this beautiful valley. Here the Rivers Avonmore and Avonbeg join to form the Avoca River, a place made famous by Thomas Moore's poem of the same name. Near the confluence is the tree, or what is left of it, beneath which the poet spent many hours resting. The Vale of Avoca is especially pretty in late spring when wild cherry is in blossom. This district is rich in mineral deposits, particularly copper, lead, zinc and sulphur. At nearby Woodenbridge the goldsmiths of ancient Ireland obtained much of their gold from Croghan Kinsella, to the south-west of the village. In 1796 the finding of a nugget started a minor gold rush. To the north of Avoca is Avondale Forest Park (see Day Out 992).
□ Seven miles (11.3km) NW of Arklow, on T7. Map ref 23D1.

1000. WICKLOW
Sailing and sands

This county town overlooking a wide crescent-shaped bay was, like many ports and towns on Ireland's eastern coast, based on a Viking settlement. Its harbour is not the prettiest in Ireland, but it provides good safe day-sailing and there are one-day dinghy sailing courses in the town. Wicklow Head, two miles (3.2km) to the south is a fine viewpoint. Brittas Bay, six miles (9.6km), south of the town has a three mile (4.8km) stretch of beach.
□ 30 miles (48km) S of Dublin on N11/T7. Map ref 23D1.

ACKNOWLEDGMENTS

The names of our major contributors have been listed at the front of this book, but they by no means cover all the individuals and organisations to whom we are indebted. Among individuals who provided ideas or raw material for Days Out were Hunter Davies, the Cumbrian author and former editor of *The Sunday Times Magazine*; Andrew Gilg, lecturer in geography, University of Exeter; John Prizeman; and John Watney.

We would also like to acknowledge the help of a number of contributors or consultants who were primarily concerned with the non-Days Out elements of *The Sunday Times Book of the Countryside*: Suzanne Hodgart and Graham Rose of *The Sunday Times* and Professor T.W. Freeman, Emeritus Professor of Geography, University of Manchester. The words of John Fowles, quoted in the Introduction to this book, came from the Foreword which he wrote for *The Sunday Times Book of the Countryside*. Additional research for this book was provided by Jeremy Bruce-Watt, Norine Riches and Stephanie Thompson. The secretarial help of Annette Smith was also invaluable.

Many specialist organisations helped us both compile this book and check its accuracy. If any errors have survived a stringent series of checks and double-checks, then the responsibility lies with the books' editors rather than the following organisations whose help we now gratefully and gladly acknowledge: the Nature Conservancy Council; the Countryside Commission; the Royal Society for the Protection of Birds; the Council for the Protection of Rural England; the National Trust (and also the National Trust for Scotland); the Department of the Environment; all the national park authorities; the Forestry Commission nationally and its many regional offshoots; the British Tourist Authority; the national tourist boards of England, Wales, Scotland, Northern Ireland and the Republic of Ireland; the regional tourist boards within England and Wales; local authorities which administer country parks; and, of course, the owners and staff of the many privately-run institutions which feature in this book. Many individuals within these organisations bore the brunt of our enquiries and we hope they will understand that lack of space inhibits a more personal acknowledgment.

We are particularly grateful to Anthony Cheetham, managing director of Macdonald Futura, whose idea it was to give these 1000 Days Out a life of their own separate from the parent book. And we gladly record our thanks to our agent, Richard Simon, for his constructive cheerfulness in sometimes strained times. Finally, we must acknowledge our debt to *The Sunday Times*, whose then editor, Harold Evans, encouraged us to undertake the original book. We hope all those who have helped in its creation will find something within it as rewarding as we have found the continued discovery of our own astonishing countryside.

TOURIST INFORMATION

National Tourist Boards

English Tourist Board, 4 Grosvenor Gardens, London SW1.

Irish Tourist Board, Baggot Street Bridge, Dublin 2.

Isle of Man Tourist Board, 13 Victoria Street, Douglas, Isle of Man.

Northern Ireland Tourist Board, River House, 48 High Street, Belfast.

Scottish Tourist Board, 23 Ravelston Terrace, Edinburgh EH4 3EU.

Wales Tourist Board, Brunel House, 2 Fitzalan Road, Cardiff.

English Regional Tourist Boards

Cumbria Tourist Board, Ellerthwaite, Windermere, Cumbria.

Northumbria Tourist Board, 9 Osborne Terrace, Jesmond, Newcastle upon Tyne.

North-West Tourist Board, The Last Drop Village, Bromley Cross, Bolton, Lancashire.

Yorkshire and Humberside Tourist Board, 312 Tadcaster Road, York, North Yorkshire YO2 2HF.

Heart of England Tourist Board, PO Box 15, Worcester, Worcestershire.

East Midlands Tourist Board, Bailgate, Lincoln, Lincolnshire.

Thames and Chilterns Tourist Board, PO Box 10, Abingdon, Oxfordshire.

East Anglia Tourist Board, 14 Museum Street, Ipswich, Suffolk.

London Tourist Board, 26 Grosvenor Gardens, London SW1.

West Country Tourist Board, Trinity Court, 37 Southernhay East, Exeter, Devon.

Southern Tourist Board, Old Town Hall, Leigh Road, Eastleigh, Hampshire.

Isle of Wight Tourist Board, 21 High Street, Newport, Isle of Wight.

South-East England Tourist Board, Cheviot House, 4–6 Monson Road, Tunbridge Wells, Kent.

Welsh Regional Tourist Boards

North Wales Tourism Council, Civic Centre, Colwyn Bay, Clwyd.

Mid Wales Tourism Council, Owain Glyndwr Centre, Machynlleth, Powys.

South Wales Tourism Council, Darkgate, Carmarthen, Dyfed.

Scottish Regional Tourist Boards

Borders Regional Council, Tourism Division, Regional Headquarters, Newtown St Boswells.

Central Regional Council, Tourism Department, Viewforth, Stirling.

Dumfries and Galloway Tourist Association, Douglas House, Newton Stewart.

Fife Tourist Authority, Fife House, North Street, Glenrothes.

Grampian Regional Council, The Leisure, Recreation and Tourism Department, Woodhill House, Ashgrove Road West, Aberdeen AB9 2LU.

Highlands and Islands Development Board, PO Box 7, Bridge House, Bank Street, Inverness.

Lothian Regional Council, Department of Recreation and Leisure, 40 Torphichen Street, Edinburgh.

Strathclyde Regional Council, Department of Leisure and Recreation, McIver House, Carogan Street, Glasgow.

Tayside Regional Council, Department of Recreation and Tourism, Tayside House, 26–28 Crichton Street, Dundee.

Regional Tourist Boards for Republic of Ireland

Athlone, 17 Church Street.

Cashel, Town Hall.

Cork, Tourist House, Grand Parade.

Dublin, 14 Upper O'Connell Street and 51 Dawson Street.

Dun Laoghaire, 1 Clarinda Park North.

Ennis, Bank Place.

Galway, Aras Failte, Eyre Square.

Kilkenny, The Parade.

Killarney, Town Hall.

Letterkenny, Derry Road.

Limerick, 62 O'Connell Street.

Mullingar, Dublin Road.

Nenagh, Kickham Street.

Skibbereen, 14/15 Main Street.

Sligo, Stephen Street.

Tralee, 32 The Mall.

Waterford, 41 The Quay.

Westport, The Mall.

Wexford, Crescent Quay.

AN INVITATION
Tell Us About Your Own Favourite Day Out

Readers of this book are invited to nominate their own favourite day out for possible inclusion in a new edition.

The only requirements are that

- your suggested day out is not already featured in this book
- you have personally undertaken your nominated day out within the last 12 months
- you are in no way connected directly or indirectly with any of the facilities or attractions you describe.

Your report should be as specific as possible. The entries in this book will serve as helpful models in writing it. Do not bother about giving your day out a number. You should make sure that the details you give on the report form are absolutely accurate and cover such essential information as the title of the day out, a descriptive sub-title indicating the kind of day out it is, and a precise location for it. Please provide any other information which will help make this an enjoyable day out. For example, outstanding points of interest, facilities for the public and, where applicable, opening times and telephone numbers for further information. You can, of course, make more than one nomination.

Readers' reports should be sent to: The Editors, *1000 Days Out*, Freepost, Macdonald Futura Publishers Ltd, Paulton House, 8 Shepherdess Walk, London, N1 7LW.

INDEX

All references are to the Day Out number; those in bold refer to the main entries.

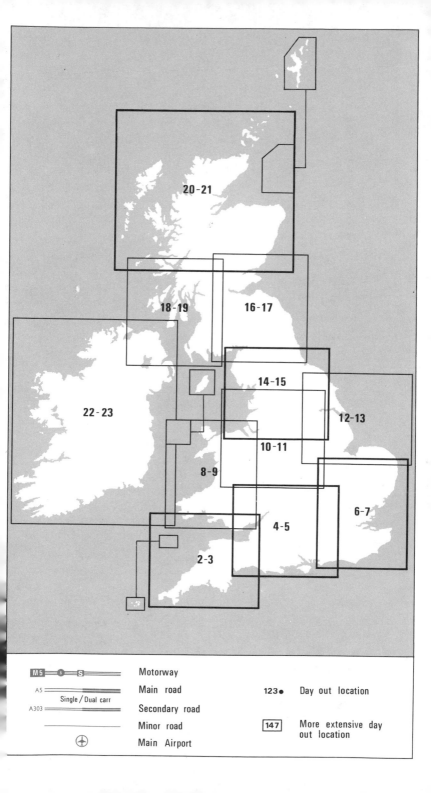

M5━━━**6**━━━**S**	Motorway	
A5 ═══════	Main road	**123●** Day out location
Single / Dual carr		
A303 ━━━━━	Secondary road	
────────	Minor road	**147** More extensive day out location
⊕	Main Airport	

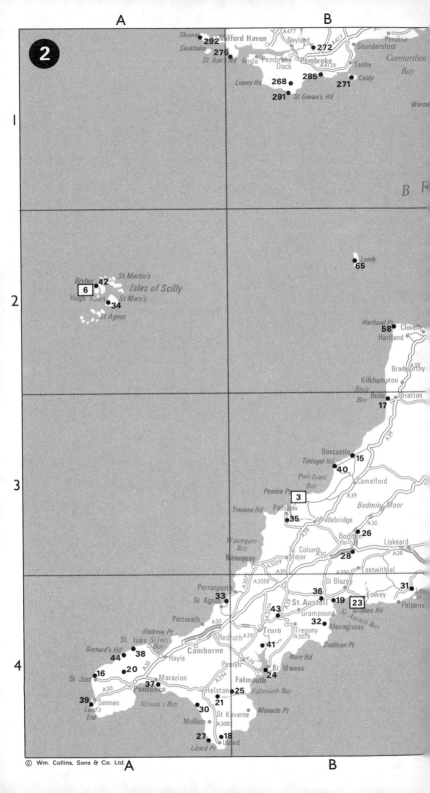

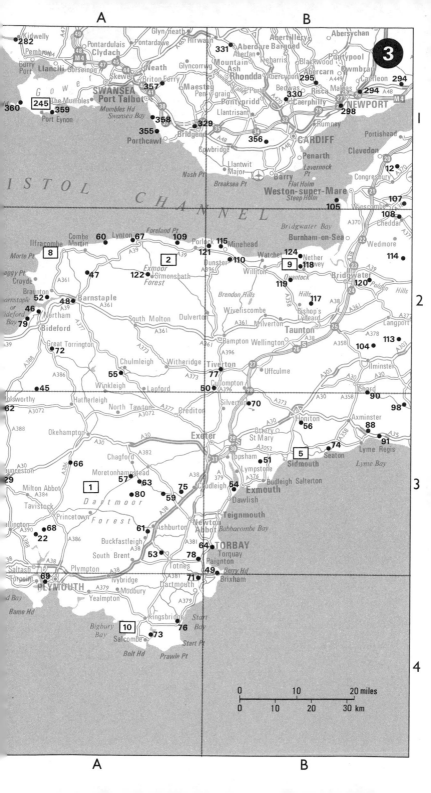

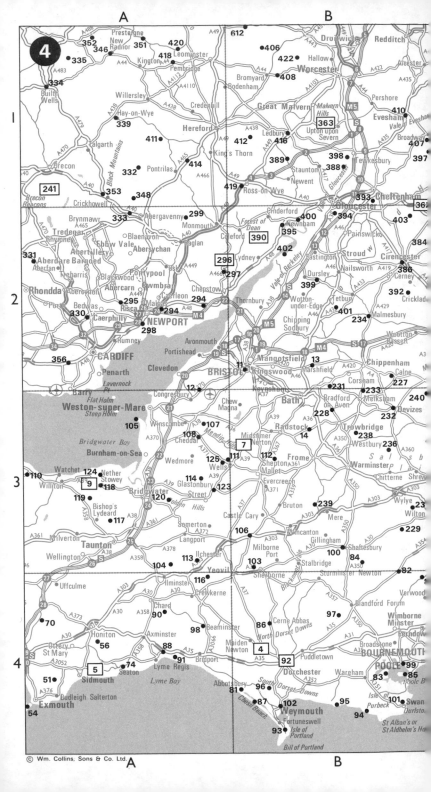

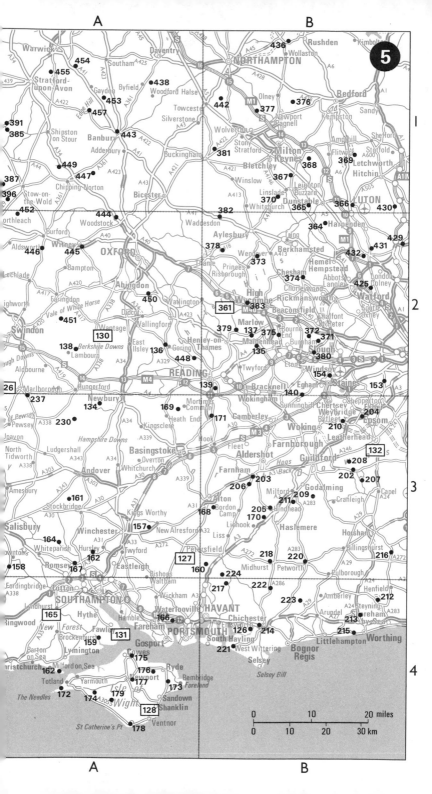

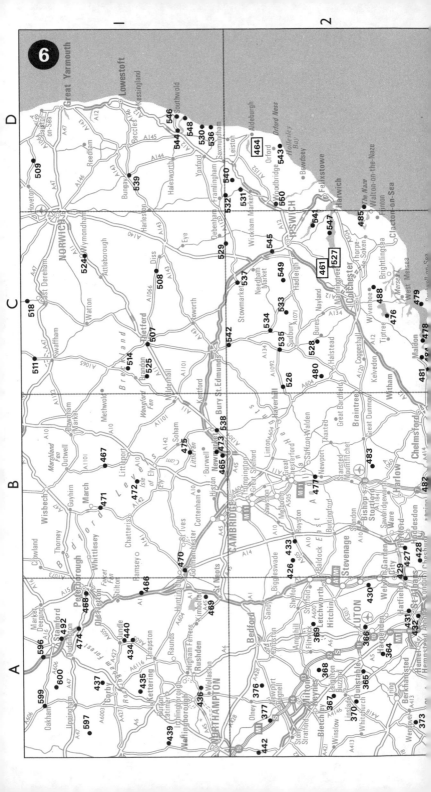

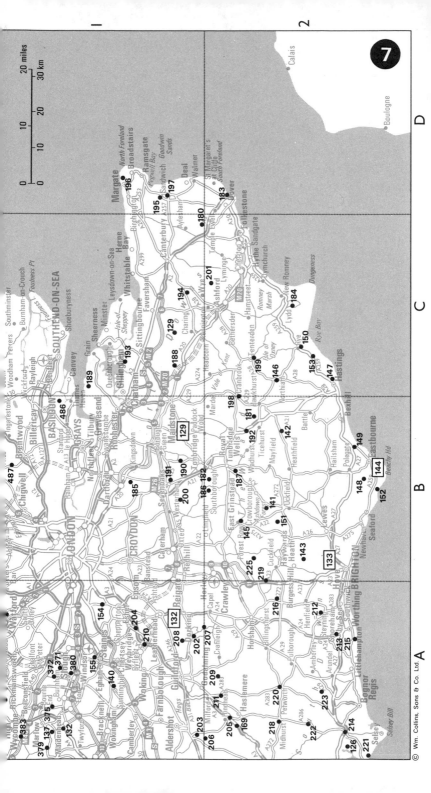

7

20 miles
30 km

0   10   20
0   10   20

© Wm. Collins, Sons & Co. Ltd.

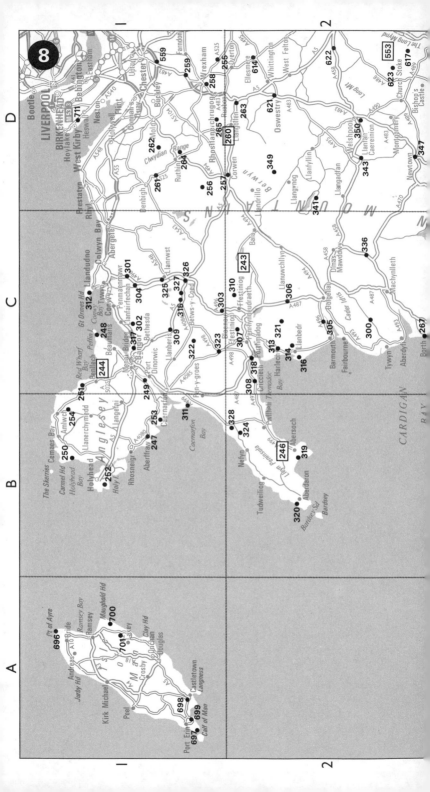

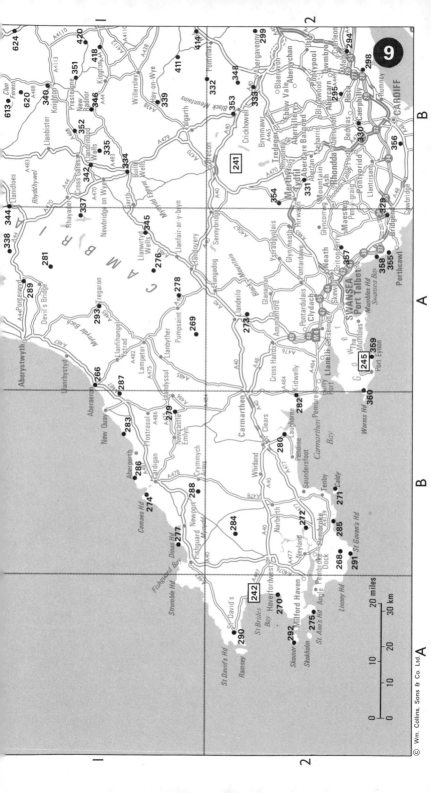

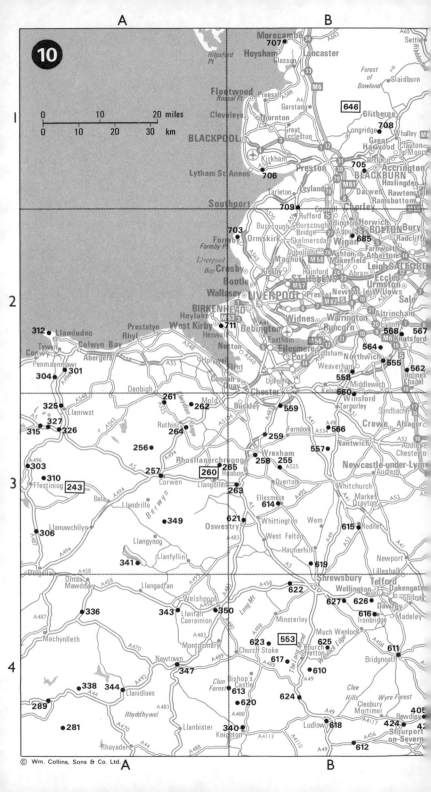

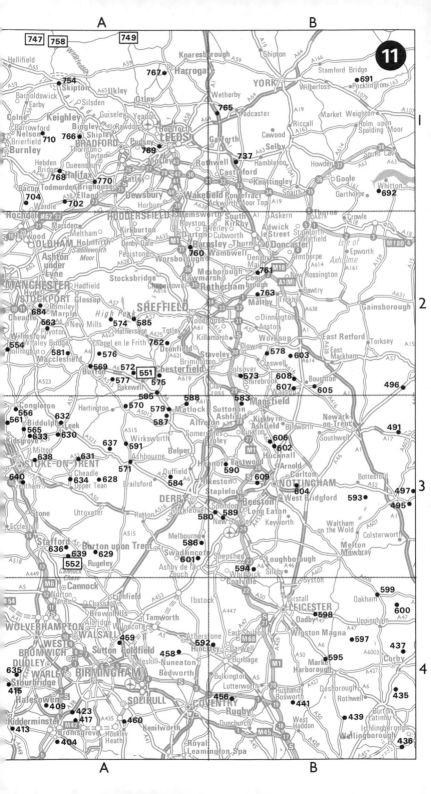

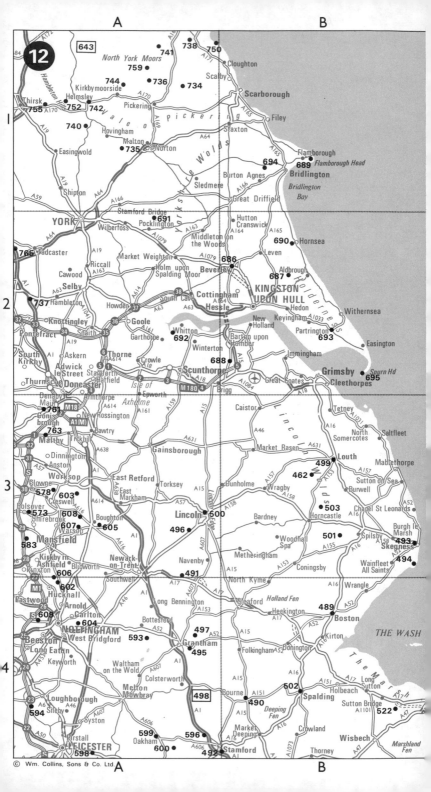

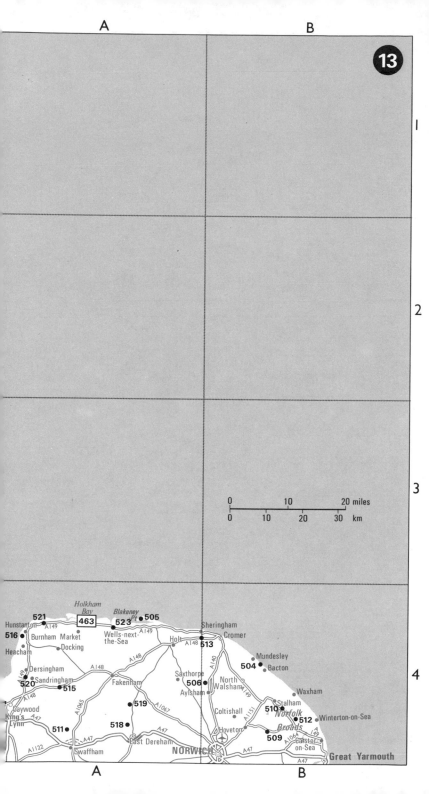

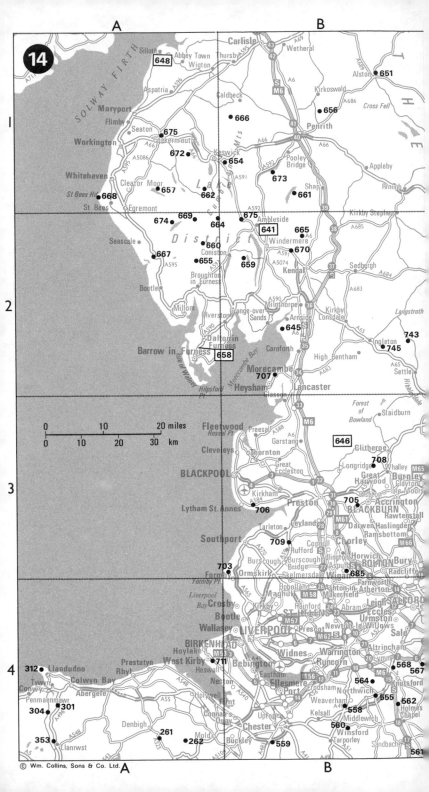

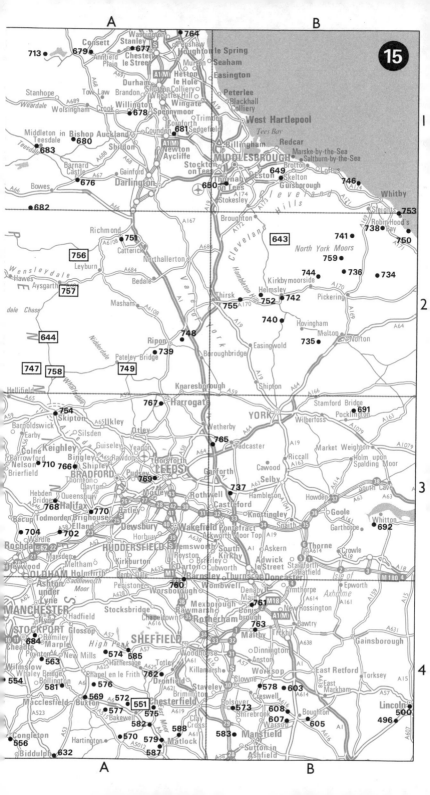

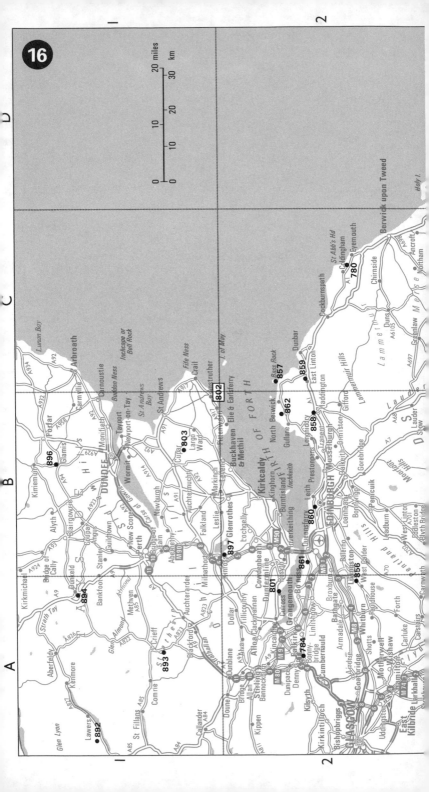

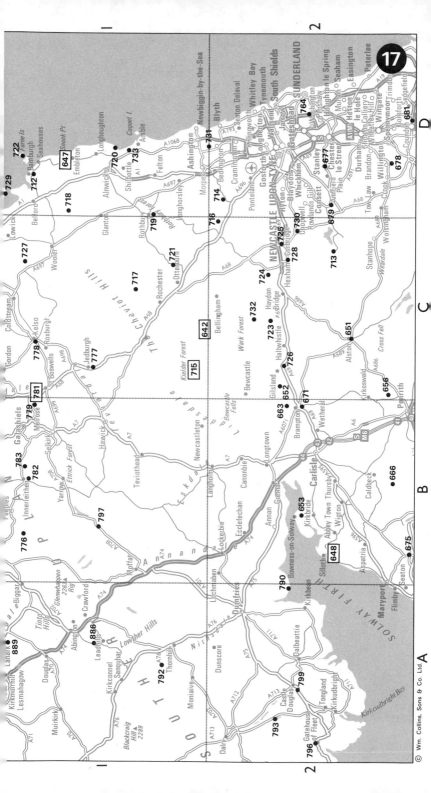

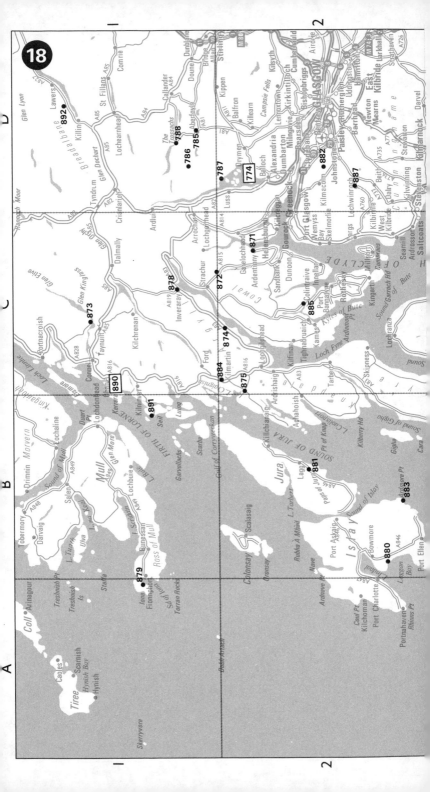

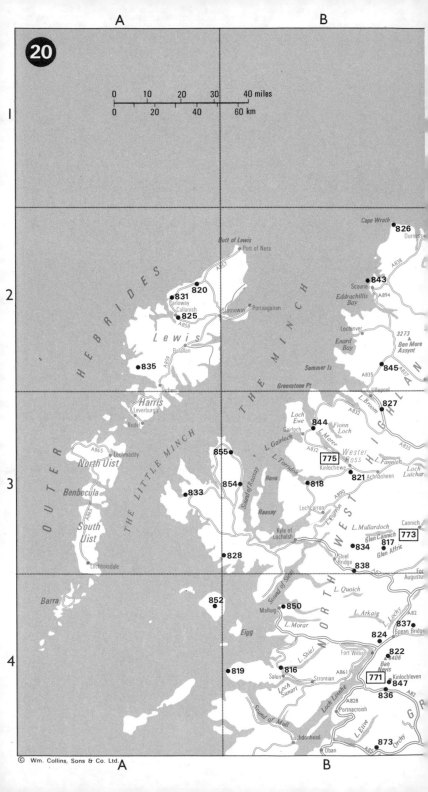

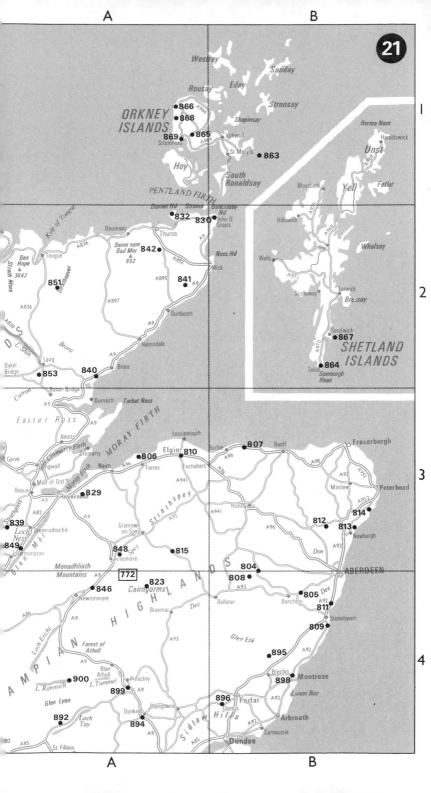

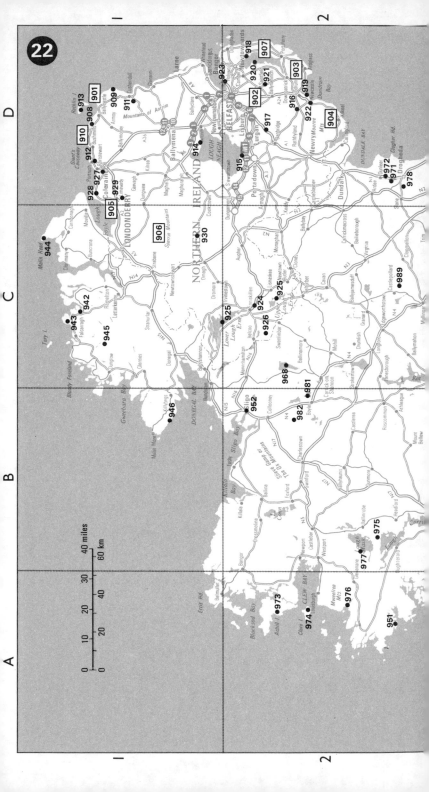